PHYSIOLOGICAL ASPECTS OF
DRYLAND FARMING

MESSAGE

I feel great pleasure in introducing this book on Physiological Aspects of Dryland Farming edited by Dr. U. S. Gupta of this University. This is the first compilation of its kind in the world literature where the physiological principles underlying Dryland Farming have been discussed by reputed specialists in different aspects of this field, working in different parts of the world. This brings out a clear concept of the subject. The treatment is authoritative and international in scope, providing basic information to Plant Breeders and Agronomists, engaged in increasing crop production. I am confident, this will enthuse a lot of interest in young scientists to take up farming in dry regions as a challenge. I consider this publication, most timely, when millions of people are at the verge of starvation.

N. N. KASHYAP
Vice-Chancellor
Haryana Agricultural University
Hissar, India

PHYSIOLOGICAL ASPECTS OF DRYLAND FARMING

Edited by
U. S. GUPTA
HARYANA AGRICULTURAL UNIVERSITY
HISSAR

LAND MARK STUDIES
ALLANHELD, OSMUN ·
UNIVERSE BOOKS

ALLANHELD, OSMUN & CO. PUBLISHERS, INC.
19 Brunswick Road, Montclair, N.J. 07042

Published in the United States of America in 1976
by Allanheld, Osmun & Co., and by Universe Books
381 Park Avenue South, New York, N.Y. 10016
Distribution: Universe Books

LC 76-42138   ISBN 0-87663-811-6

Printed in India

PREFACE

Since the dawn of civilization, man started cultivating plants and in doing so he was faced with several problems. These problems were and are still scientifically studied and published in scientific journals. The literature is not only large but also diffuse, with isolated pieces of information scattered among a variety of journals. As a result, the accumulated knowledge has been difficult to grasp by the students, teachers, researchers, and farmers.

In a wide belt across parts of South Asia, India, Africa, the Middle East, and in other areas from northern Argentina and north-east Brazil to Mexico, food production for millions of people in the semiarid tropics is limited primarily by the erratic nature of the rains. Some of the countries of major concern within the seasonally dry and semiarid tropics include: Senegal, Mali, Guinea (North), Upper Volta, Niger, Ivory Coast (North), Chad, Liberia (North), Central African Republic, Ghana (North), Nigeria (North), Sudan, Ethiopia, Kenya, Uganda, Somalia, Tanzania, Pakistan and India. Other countries in southern Africa, Central and South America, and an important area of Australia also fall within this ecological zone. The semiarid tracts are not only large but also agriculturally important. In India, such tracts cover 84 districts, spreading over 47 million hectares which is more than one-third of India's net sown area. They constitute 60 per cent of the total area under cotton, 74 under groundnut, 73 under chick pea, 83 under sorghum, 81 under pearl millet, 66 under Ragi (*Eleusine coracana*), 40 under barley, 30 under wheat, 47 under pegion pea and 36 under oil seeds. But their out turn constitutes about a fifth of the total food grain production in the country.

The need for a scientific approach towards farming in rainfed dryland areas was felt with the increasing realization that the occurrence of drought is more or less inevitable. The only way to beat the drought is to join hands with it. Instead of waiting and hoping for adequate rain, the modern concept is to make the cropping strategy so flexible that it can be suitably changed even at short notice to suit the pattern of rainfall available. Short duration varieties, the concept of ratooning, high yielding fodder crops and water harvesting techniques, all make this basic strategy feasible. New agronomic practices like balanced nutrient management, tillage and weeding are strongly recommended. In dry regions, crop production is not a simple question of introducing new varieties and supplying adequate fertilizers. In dryland agriculture each season is a particular season, and therefore cropping practices must considerably be geared to the dictates of that particular season.

The factors on which yield depends must be identified, often in the face of the differing interpretations of the data and no proper understanding of causal relationships. The gigantic variability of these factors must be determined, and for this the breeder needs suitable information. The break-through leading to a new order of yield in crop production in dry regions will most likely come from a long term team effort of breeders and physiologists where both are involved directly in the experiments, evaluation and decision making, at every step of the process.

For a better understanding of the physiological problems of crops under dry regions, with a view to increasing production by assisting agronomists and plant breeders, this book was planned. Care has been taken to discuss the prevailing conditions in such regions which affect crop production, such as low humidity, high wind velocity, loss of moisture both from the plant and the soil, high light intensity and temperature which affect the photosynthate balance. Such plant characters like drought resistance, root patterns, and photorespiration are also important considerations. All these aspects have been reviewed by specialists in their field and arranged in a manner to develop a clear concept of the Science of Crop Physiology under Dryland Agriculture.

This book is authoritative, well-documented, and international in scope. It represents the distillate of experience and knowledge of a group of authors of demonstrated competence from universities and government laboratories in England, Israel, America, Canada, New Zealand and Japan. I would like to express my deep personal appreciation to each of the authors for his contribution and patience during the production phases. I would further express my grateful thanks to Dr. J. S. Kanwar, Associate Director, International Crops Research Institute for the Semi-Arid Tropics, Hyderabad, India, for kindly writing the Foreword of this book.

January 1975

U. S. Gupta

LIST OF CONTRIBUTORS

Numbers in parenthesis indicate the pages on which the author's contribution begins

1. ARNON, I., Settlement Study Centre, Rehovot, Israel (3).

2. DAVENPORT, D. C., Department of Water Science and Engineering, University of California, Davis, California, U. S. A. (315).

3. GOLDSWORTHY, A., Imperial College of Science & Technology, London (329).

4. HAGAN, R. M., Department of Water Science and Engineering, University of California, Davis, California, U. S. A. (315).

5. HURD, E. A., Research Station, Research Branch, Agriculture Canada, Swift Current, Saskatchewan, Canada (167).

6. IWATA, F., Tohoku National Agricultural Research Station, Japan (351).

7. LARSON, K. L., Department of Agronomy, University of Missouri, U. S. A. (147).

8. O'LEARY, J. W., University of Arizona, Arizona, U. S. A. (261).

9. SPRATT, E. D., Research Station, Research Branch, Agriculture Canada, Brandon, Manitoba, Canada (167).

10. STURROCK, J. W., Crop Research Division, Department of Scientific and Industrial Research, Lincoln, New Zealand (283).

11. UNGER, P. W., USDA South Western Great Plains Research Centre, Bushland, Texas, U. S. A. (237).

CONTENTS

Foreword v
Preface vii
List of Contributors ix

1. PHYSIOLOGICAL PRINCIPLES OF DRYLAND CROP PRODUCTION
   —*I. Arnon* .. 3

   Introduction 3
       The basic problems of rain-fed crop production in dry regions 3
       Water use efficiency 5
   Climatic factors and their effect on yield (Y) and evapo-
   transpiration (ET) 8
       Atmospheric moisture 8
           Rain, Dew, Fog
       Solar radiation 12
           Light
       Temperature 15
           Effects of temperature on crop production, Frosts
       Winds 18
       Microclimate 19
           Microclimate at plant level, Soil microclimate
   Interrelationships between yield (Y) and moisture supply (ET) .. 21
       Crop response to moisture supply 21
           Soil factors, Plant factors, Climatic factors
       Effect of yield levels on consumptive use of water .. 25
       Physiological effects of water stress 26
           Turgor, Photosynthesis, Respiration, Anatomical changes, Metabolic
           reactions, Hormone relations, Protoplasmic dehydration, Root
           development, Growth, Reproduction and grain development,
           Crop yield
       Sequential effects of water deficits on plants 35
       Effects of renewed moisture supply after stress periods .. 35
       Drought hardening 36
           Presowing hardening of plants to drought
   Crop productivity (Y) in dryland farming 39
       The physiology of yield 39
           Maximum dry matter production, Assimilating area, Biological and
           economic yields, The components of economic yield
       Crop improvement for efficient water use 47
           Atmospheric drought, Soil drought, Plant adaptations to growth in
           dry regions, Heat resistance

Basic breeding objectives for rain-fed crop production under semiarid conditions 57

Specific breeding objectives for rain-fed crop production under semiarid conditions 61
The genetic approach, The physiological approach

Additional breeding objectives 65
Phenology, The ratio of economic to biological yield, Improving the components of yield

Management practices for increasing yields 68
Fertilizer use, Planting dates, Plant population and distribution patterns, Interrelationships between plant density and factors affecting production, Adjusting planting patterns to limited moisture supply

The moisture regime in dryland crop production 96

Evapotranspiration (ET) 96
Actual and potential evapotranspiration, Relationship between Actual ET and PET

Improving the water supply available to the crop .. 99
Increasing water storage in the root-zone, Management practices for improving the moisture regime, Reducing losses due to evapotranspiration

References 124

2. DROUGHT INJURY AND RESISTANCE OF CROP PLANTS
—*K. L. Larson* 147

Introduction 147
Role of water 147
Plant response to drought 148
Environmental stresses 149
Mechanism of stress injury and resistance 150
Drought and physiological processes 151
Drought stress and grain yield 156
Antitranspirants 157
Drought hardening 159
Effective drought control 159
References 162

3. ROOT PATTERNS IN CROPS AS RELATED TO WATER AND NUTRIENT UPTAKE—*E. A. Hurd* and *E. D. Spratt* 167

Introduction 167
Water movement 168
Energy and water movement 168
Soil to plant water movement 169

Plant to air water movement   173
Plant modelling   175
Nutrient uptake by roots   177
  Source and availability of nutrients   177
  Absorption mechanisms   179
  Mineral nutrition of roots   180
  Effects of limited soil moisture on root growth and nutrient
    uptake   183
  Effects of physical factors and root environment on root
    growth and nutrient uptake   185
Root patterns and drought resistance   186
  Physiology and function of root systems   186
  Methods of studying roots   194
  Canadian cultivars and parental material   203
  Semidwarfs   205
  Breeding for improved rooting systems   207
Cultural practices affecting root growth   213
  Crop rotations   213
  Effect of fertilizers on root growth   214
  Effect of tillage practices on root growth   215
References   217

4. ROLE OF MULCHES IN DRYLAND AGRICULTURE—*P. W. Unger*   ..   237

Introduction   237
  Reasons for using mulches   237
  Definitions   238
  Previous reviews   238
Effects of mulches on some soil properties and conditions   ..   239
  Soil water   239
  Soil temperature   242
  Soil structure   243
  Soil salinity   245
Effects of mulches on erosion   246
Effects of mulches on plants   247
Conclusions   251
References   252

5. THE EFFECT OF HUMIDITY ON CROP PRODUCTION—*J. W. O'Leary*   261

Introduction   261
Survey of plant responses to humidity   262
Humidity and transpiration   264

Transpiration and leaf growth 266
Humidity and stomata 268
Absorption of atmospheric moisture by leaves 269
Humidity and salinity 271
High humidity effects 271
Humidity and water use efficiency 274
Conclusions and suggestions 274
References 275

6. WIND EFFECTS AND THEIR AMELIORATION IN CROP PRODUCTION
—*J. W. Sturrock* 283

Introduction 283
Air flow and the nature of the shelter-belt 285
Shelter microclimate 288
The nature of crop responses 291
    Water relations 291
    Temperature 300
Mechanical damage 300
Crop yields 300
Crop quality 303
Diseases and pests 303
Crop pollination 304
Planning shelter 304
Management 305
Other wind control measures 306
References 309

7. ROLE OF ANTITRANSPIRANTS IN ARID AGRICULTURE
—*D. C. Davenport* and *R. M. Hagan* 315

Introduction 315
Effects of antitranspirants 316
Role of antitranspirants 318
    Water conservation 318
        Watershed and riparian vegetation, Water quality, Field and horticultural crops
    Increasing plant water potential to improve growth .. 320
        Transplanting, Annual field crops, Perennial crops
Conclusions 323
References 323

8. PHOTORESPIRATION IN RELATION TO CROP YIELD
—*A. Goldsworthy* 329

FOREWORD

The future of humanity lies in the arid and the semiarid lands, as the humid and more favourable rainfall areas have been extensively and intensively cultivated and heavily populated by the human beings. It is also recognised that even if all the available financial resources are mobilised to develop irrigation for the arid and semiarid areas, still largest percentage of land in these areas will remain unirrigated and practice dry farming. Thus there is a well recognised and urgent need for development of dry farming technology for increasing agricultural production in these areas of low rainfall and its erratic distribution.

The establishment of international research institutes like the International Crops Research Institute for the Semi-Arid Tropics (ICRISAT) at Hyderabad, and the projection of another International Research Center for Agriculture in the Dry Areas (ICARDA) at Beirut are proofs of the urgency and importance which the world community attaches to dry farming research.

The whole philosophy of dryland farming revolves around the principle that water is a limiting factor in these areas and one needs to maximise the efficiency of the natural rain water for agricultural production. The physiological aspects of dryland farming are of great significance for successful agriculture under these conditions. I am glad that Dr. U. S. Gupta could persuade a number of leading scientists to write on the different aspects of plant physiology relative to dry farming situations.

The topics discussed are very important and the contributors combine deep knowledge of the subject and experience of dry farming research to physiological aspects of crop production, drought, photorespiration and crop maturity. Besides it has good reviews on root patterns of crops, mulches for soil moisture conservation, use of antitranspirants, humidity and the wind effect on crop production.

The authors have reviewed the existing knowledge on these aspects. The topics are important for understanding the problems of crop production by plant physiologists and agronomists. The arrangement of topics and their interrelationship may not be ideal, but these are the aspects which have a direct bearing on the problems of crop production in dryland agriculture. I think the information contained in this book will be useful to all interested in research, extension and development of agriculture under dry farming conditions.

January 1975   J. S. KANWAR

Introduction 329
The measurement of photorespiration 330
Differences between photorespiration and true respiration .. 331
   The effect of oxygen concentration 331
   The requirement for the photosytnhetic apparatus .. 331
   The nature of the substrate 332
   Energy relationships 332
The metabolism of photorespiration 332
   Evidence for glycollate as the substrate for photorespiration .. 332
   The biosynthesis of glycollate 333
   The further metabolism of glycollate 335
      Metabolism of glycollate by the peroxisomes, Metabolism of glycine
      by the mitochondria, The conversion of serine to carbohydrate
   The energetics of photorespiration 338
The inhibition of photorespiration and the increase in yield .. 339
   Increasing productivity at low oxygen concentrations .. 339
   Increasing productivity at high CO_2 concentrations .. 339
   Increasing productivity with chemical inhibitors .. 340
   C_4 plants—Nature's answer to the problem 341
   References 345

9. HEAT UNIT CONCEPT OF CROP MATURITY—*F. Iwata* .. 351

Introduction 351
Remainder index 352
Exponential index 357
Physiological index 357
Hydrothermal index 359
Photothermal units 360
Interrelationship of various heat units 363
Some environmental factors fluctuating consistency of heat units 364
Some climatic factors affecting heat unit systems under dryland
   conditions 365
Conclusions 366
References 367

Author Index 371
Subject Index 385

Physiological Aspects of
Dryland Farming

Prof. Isaac Arnon

Born in Belgium in 1909. Studied at the State Faculty of Agricultural Sciences in Gembloux (Belgium); Diploma of Ingenieur Agronome (equivalent to M.Sc.) in 1929; Ph.D. from the Hebrew University, Jerusalem in 1957. Immigrated to Palestine in 1932. After the establishment of the State of Israel, was appointed Head of the Agronomy Department of the Volcani Institute, and Professor of Agronomy at the Faculty of Agriculture, Hebrew University.

During the period under review was involved in research on all aspects of crop production in the dry region, both rainfed and under irrigation, in particular the breeding and agronomy of wheat, barley and sorghum; the agronomy of industrial crops, such as cotton and sugar beets; forage production and pasture utilization.

In 1958, was appointed Director of the Volcani Institute of Agricultural Research, and commenced a study of the organization and administration of agricultural research with particular emphasis on developing countries. This led to the publication of a book on this subject, published first in English and subsequently translated into Spanish by the Inter-American Institute of Agricultural Sciences, and to an appointment as Chairman of a F. A. O. panel on research organization. In recent years has become more and more interested in the problems of translating research findings into agricultural practice and in the planning and implementation of agricultural development in the less developed countries. Has been appointed Director of Research of the Settlement Study Centre in Rehovot and has served as Consultant to the Food and Agricultural Organization of the U. N. and Senior Consultant to the United Nations Development Fund. In this capacity has been a member of a number of missions to developing countries with which the most recent was to the Agricultural University of Tamil Nadu, India. In 1971, received the Award for Agriculture of the State of Israel and in 1972 was elected member of the French Academy of Agriculture.

Has written over 100 papers and bulletins on the various research topics in which he has been involved. Most recent publications include: *The Organization and Administration of Agricultural Research*; *Crop Production in Dry Regions*: Vol. I—Background and Principles, Vol. II—Systematic Treatment of Principal Crops; *Mineral Nutrition of Maize*; *The Planning and Programming of Agricultural Research*.

1. PHYSIOLOGICAL PRINCIPLES OF DRYLAND CROP PRODUCTION

ISAAC ARNON
Settlement Study Centre
Rehovot

Introduction

THE BASIC PROBLEMS OF RAIN-FED CROP PRODUCTION IN DRY REGIONS

Regular arable crop production, depending on rainfall only, is not possible in the truly dry regions but is practised in the so-called semiarid regions. The minimum rainfall for producing a crop in the dry regions is estimated as 250-350 mm in winter rainfall areas, and 500 mm in summer rainfall areas (Koéppe & Long, 1958) though local factors and rainfall distribution may cause deviations from these figures. A semiarid climate is, however, not necessarily always intermediate between dry and humid, but is generally a mixed climate, in which a completely dry season alternates with a fairly humid season. A further characteristic of the semiarid regions is that the drier the climate, the greater the variability of the rainfall, so that years of scant rainfall may alternate with seasons of above-average rainfall, and the dividing lines between arid, semiarid and humid may shift from year to year (Fig. 1.1).

Therefore, the basic characteristic of crop production in the semi-

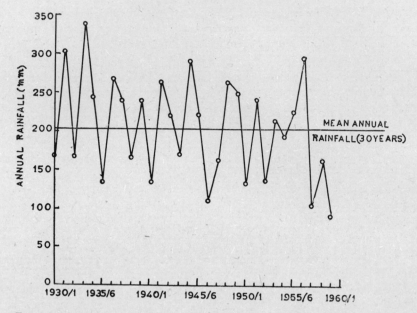

FIG. 1.1.   Seasonal variability of rainfall in a dry region (Bersheeba, Israel).

arid region is that, even in a given location, it is carried out under a wide spectrum of soil moisture regimes, ranging from seasons with below-average conditions, under which it may be difficult to avoid complete crop failures,

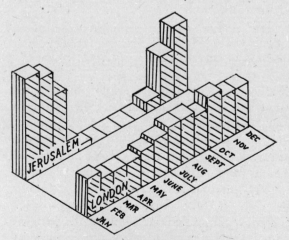

FIG. 1.2.   Typical seasonal patterns of rainfall distribution in semiarid (Jerusalem) and humid (London) climates with approximately the same annual precipitation rates (averaging 600 & 620 mm, respectively).

to seasons with a moisture supply that may be almost or as favourable as that usually obtained in a temperate and fairly humid climate (Fig. 1.2).

At first sight, therefore, the choice of crops and varieties, as well as the production methods to be adopted must be directed towards two diametrically opposite tendencies:

1. Grow and manage crops that can be profitable under the near-arid conditions of the rainfall deficient years, during which drought resistance

or tolerance and low water use are the main requirements, and

2. Grow and manage crops that are capable of making the most efficient use of the favourable environmental conditions provided during the good rainfall years.

It must further be pointed out, that even during favourable seasons, soil moisture in at least part of the root zone will usually fluctuate in a range between soil saturation and permanent wilting point. Therefore, more or less severe water stress may be experienced at any stage of development.

As there is no possibility of knowing in advance the kind of rainfall season and the distribution of rainfall that are to be expected, the crops and varieties to be grown and the management practices used must, therefore, be adapted to the wide range of possible conditions, from near-arid to highly favourable.

In the final analysis, the aim will have to be to choose crops, varieties and management practices *for the efficient use of water*—under conditions of a limited moisture supply during the years of below-average rainfall, and of a favourable moisture regime such as is provided during good rainfall years.

WATER USE EFFICIENCY

Water use efficiency (WUE) is the yield of marketable crop produced per unit of water used in evapotranspiration. Therefore, $WUE = \dfrac{Y}{ET}$, where Y = yield of marketable crop and ET = evapotranspiration or "seasonal water use".

If yield were completely independent of ET, any factor which caused an increase of yield, or a decrease of ET, would have a favourable effect on WUE. If yield were proportional to ET, water use efficiency would be constant. Actually, the numerator and denominator of the formula, are not independent of each other. Both Y and ET can be influenced, either independently or differentially, by crop management and environment. The numerator Y is also greatly dependent on moisture regime, in particular in dryland farming: the more water available to the crop, the higher the yields will generally be. The greater water supply will, however, also increase the denominator ET.

The two terms: "Evapotranspiration" (ET) and "Water Use" (WU) are generally considered to be identical. This may be true quantitatively, but actually these two alternative terms highlight the dilemma presented by this formula.

The term "Evapotranspiration" implies a loss of water, which should be reduced to the lowest possible level in order to increase WUE. The term "Water Use" implies the beneficial utilization of water for producing a commercial crop. From the purely mathematical point of view—increasing the denominator will decrease WUE; however, from the physiological point of view, it is essential to increase ET (up to a certain level) in order to achieve an increase in the numerator Y—our basic objective.

The practical conclusion to be drawn from the above is that every effort should be made to increase the amounts of water available to the crop for production, and reduce to the minimum the losses of water due to evaporation and transpiration. At first sight, these two objectives may appear to be at cross-purposes—but in practice the contradiction is more apparent than real: fortunately, the effect on yields of an increase in ET will almost always be greater than the actual increase in ET involved, so that the WUE is generally improved by an improved water supply, even though the latter signifies an increase of the denominator of the formula.

Because the effects of climate on both yield and evapotranspiration are so intricately interwoven, we shall, for the sake of convenience, consider its effect on both numerator and denominator together. We shall then review separately the other factors that mainly affect the numerator Y, and then those mainly affecting the denominator ET. The complex of factors involved in water use efficiency and the interrelationships between them are shown schematically in Fig. 1.3.

The numerator Y depends on environmental factors—in particular moisture supply, the kind of crop grown, and is, of course, amenable to factors that increase yield; first and foremost being crop improvement for efficient water use, and concurrently management practices such as fertilizer use, planting dates, plant populations, etc.

The denominator ET depends on atmospheric conditions, on the amount of stored soil water available at the time of sowing and on osmotic components of the soil water; on effective rainfall during the growing season; on the ability of the plant to take up water and the control it exerts over water uptake (root system) and water loss (transpiration); and to a small degree, on the actual yield obtained (Y).

Increased water storage in the root zone can be achieved by control of runoff, improved infiltration and by water harvesting methods. Crop management practices such as tillage and rotation are also very effective in this respect and can incidently also improve yields.

Reducing water losses due to evaporation from the soil can result from mulching and from chemical treatment of the soil, water losses due to transpiration can be reduced by plant treatments aimed at directly decreasing transpiration and indirectly by management practices such as weed control, planting density and patterns.

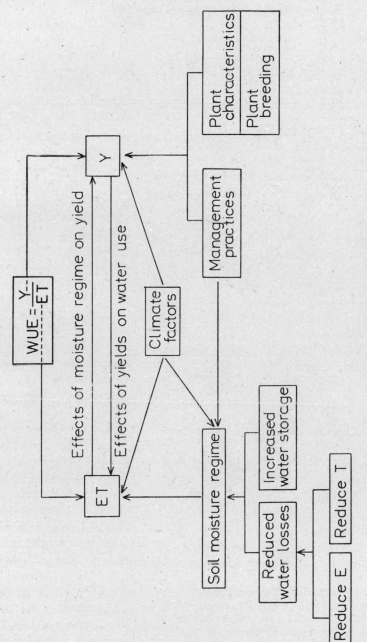

Fig. 1.3.   Factors involved in water use efficiency (WUE) and their interrelationships: Y—yield; ET—evapotranspiration or water use.

Climatic Factors and Their Effect on Yield (Y) and Evapotranspiration (ET)

ATMOSPHERIC MOISTURE

Rain

The distinctive trait of the arid lands is, of course, insufficient precipitation. Where precipitation is sufficient for the production of rain-fed crops, the so-called semiarid areas—these are generally *seasonally* dry areas—receiving practically all their precipitation during one season of the year, while the rest of the year is more or less dry. The following cycle of water supply and water use usually occurs in regions with alternating wet and dry seasons (Thornthwaite, 1956):(a) a period during which precipitation is in excess of water requirement and water accumulates in the soil and in reservoirs, and (b) a dry period, during which a water deficiency occurs, as stored water is used for evapotranspiration and actual evapotranspiration falls below potential evapotranspiration (Fig. 1.4).

Excluding the monsoonal deserts of Asia, as a general rule the semiarid fringe bordering on the temperate deserts gets

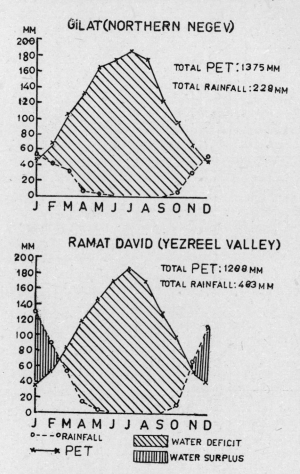

FIG. 1.4. Comparison of seasonal precipitation and potential evapotranspiration: annual march of rainfall and potential evapotranspiration (PET) through the year at two contrasting regions of Israel (PET was calculated according to Penman's formula).

winter precipitation, while the similar fringe bordering on tropical deserts gets summer rainfall (Bagnold, 1954). The season of the year at which precipitation occurs has a considerable bearing on rainfall efficiency and on the amount of runoff. It has already been pointed out that cool-season rainfall is more efficient than that which is concentrated during the warm season, when evapotranspiration is at its maximum. Depending on the season, precipitation may occur mainly as rain or as snow. If the ground is frozen, infiltration will be low or nil. If the vegetation is in full leaf, a larger proportion of the rainfall than otherwise will be intercepted and lost by evaporation before reaching the soil. If most of the vegetation is dormant, the soil will become saturated sooner than when the vegetation is active, thereby also increasing runoff.

Dependability of rainfall

Variability of rainfall is the greatest hazard to crop production in the semiarid regions. In above-average rainfall seasons, cultivators may be tempted to plough and sow large areas on the drier fringe of a semiarid region; then in the following below-average seasons, which are usually accompanied by higher-than-average temperatures, disastrous crop failures may result.

In a study covering a period of 68 years, from 1878 to 1946, on the effect of rainfall variability on the prosperity of agriculture in eastern Montana, the following picture emerged (Lommasson, 1947):

Table 1.1. Rainfall variability in eastern Montana

Distribution of rainfall over a period of 68 years			No. of years	Percentage of total No. of years
Abundant rainfall (double the average)	..	..	3	4.4
Average or above-average rainfall	..	..	31	45.5
Dry years, below average	..	..	24	35.3
'Killer' years, with extreme droughts	..	..	10	14.8

The probability of obtaining a bumper crop in this 'wheat region' is not more than one year out of twenty-three while complete crop failures, as a result of drought, can be expected in one year out of seven.

Frequency of rainfall and its intensity

A further characteristic of rainfall in the arid regions is that rain frequently comes in a few heavy showers of short duration, which engender considerable runoff. It is not uncommon for 50 per cent of the annual precipitation to occur on 10-15 per cent of the rainy days (White, 1966).

In connection with conditions under which light rainfalls only wet the soil surface and usually evaporate without having any appreciable effect, the concept of *effective rainfall* has been proposed; this is the minimum amount of rainfall, occurring on a single occasion, that ensures at least some water storage under favourable soil conditions.   To be reasonably safe from evaporation, the rain must penetrate to a depth of at least 10-12 cm (Staple, 1964).   The amount needed for this has been estimated as 15-20 mm for a single rainfall.   The annual effective rainfall commonly amounts to about one-third of the total rainfall (Bagnold, 1954).

Relation between rainfall and yield

Notwithstanding the major influence of rainfall on yield levels, yields are not always directly proportional to the amount of precipitation. Generally, yield levels are determined by the amount of precipitation above the basic minimum required to enable the crop to achieve maturity.   If, for instance, under given circumstances 250 mm is the necessary minimum precipitation for a grain crop, 225 mm or a reduction of only 25 mm may result in complete crop failure.   Conversely, 50 mm above the minimum requirement may double the yields.   In experiments with rain-fed groundnuts in a low rainfall area of India, WUE was found to equal 1.71 kg of pods per mm of rain when actual ET was limited by low rainfall to 67.6 mm during the growing period from the 36th to 91st day.   This compares with 4.32 kg of pods per mm, when ET during the same period was 243 mm (Bhan & Misra, 1970b).

It is accordingly important in dryland farming to have even a relatively small amount of water stored in the soil, prior to sowing the crop.   This is the main justification for maintaining a period of fallow—even if this method is generally wasteful of land and of water.   The response to additional rainfall will also depend on soil fertility.

Rainfall may also be in excess of the optimum and thereby cause reduced yields.   This may sound paradoxical in relation to semiarid climates. However, it will be remembered that the total rainfall in a semiarid region may equal that characterizing a humid climate and yet be concentrated in a very short period.   When this rainfall is concentrated in 4-5 months of the year, there may easily be periods when the rate of precipitation exceeds the capacity of the soil to absorb the rainfall.   As a result, considerable runoff occurs from the waterlogged soil, plant nutrients are leached out of the root zone, and crops are adversely affected by anaerobic conditions —especially if the excess precipitation occurs during the cool season.

The distribution of the rainfall and the coincidence or otherwise of a plentiful supply of soil moisture at periods of maximum crop requirement, also have a bearing on yield levels.   A period of drought at the time of earing of cereals will have a more adverse effect on yields than if it occurs earlier or later in the growing period.   Excess moisture after sowing may reduce germination; heavy rainfall during earing may cause lodging and impair pollination.

Dew

The formation of dew occurs mainly at night because it depends on radiational cooling of leaf and soil surfaces until they reach dew-point temperatures. The total amount of dewfall is unlikely to exceed 1 mm nightly (Slatyer, 1967).

Effects of dew on plant growth

Dew absorption has been found to vary widely with plant species; it is largely dependent on the intensity and duration of dewfall as well as on the soil moisture regime, being higher under dryland conditions than under irrigation (Waisel, 1958). Dew can only provide a very small proportion of the water requirements of a normally transpiring plant, but may be of some importance to plants under water stress. Occurring as it does at night, it may accelerate the restoration of leaf turgor, and in the morning can delay the onset of renewed stress (Slatyer, 1967). In dry regions, dew may, therefore, be beneficial to plant growth and make a positive contribution to the water balance of the plant. However, Monteith (1963) estimates that these benefits are probably of little significance as in cloudless summer weather, in an arid climate, the ratio of potential condensation to evaporation is approximately 1 : 4. Moreover, the severest stress for plants that are inadequately supplied with water occurs during the hottest hours of the day, long after the dew has completely evaporated.

Fog

When a warm, saturated air mass rapidly replaces a cool, dry air mass over a cool surface, fog or mist results. During overcast nights, this may cause the deposition of relatively large amounts of water on plants and on the soil surface (Long, 1958). Fog is of very frequent occurrence along rather narrow coastal regions which border on oceans with cold currents that run parallel to the coast. It affects plant growth through the high air-humidity, through wetting of the aerial parts of plants, and through humidification of the surface of the soil (Emberger & Lemée, 1962). There are no accurate measurements of the amount of moisture supplied by fog to the hydric balance of plants, but both type and density of vegetation appear in places to be influenced by the frequency of fog occurrence.

Frequent fogs or mists, by reducing evapotranspiration, may considerably increase the effective humidity of a region without this being reflected in the various formulae devised for defining aridity (Troll, 1958).

Relative humidity

The desiccating effect of the atmosphere is the main factor influencing the water needs of the plant. The plant is a water conducting system between the soil and the atmosphere. The overall free energy difference of the water moving into, through, and out of the plants is from 0.1 to 15 atm in the soil, and about 1000 atm in the atmosphere, when relative humidity of the air is 47 per cent (Richards & Wadleigh, 1952).

Relative humidity has a considerable effect on evapotranspiration, and hence on the water requirements of crops. At constant temperature, changes in atmospheric humidity affect transpiration by modifying the vapour pressure gradient from leaf to air (Kramer, 1969). In the dry regions relative humidity tends to be low, a mere 12-30 per cent being common around mid-day (Trewartha, 1954). The low humidity combined with the high temperatures increases the difficulties of maintaining an adequate supply of water to the plants.

The effect of relative humidity, through its influence on transpiration, is important as a determinant of WUE. High relative humidity tends to counteract low soil moisture, and low relative humidity tends to exaggerate soil moisture deficiencies (Tranquillini, 1963).

The lower the relative humidity is, the greater will be ET, and the lower WUE. Moderately low air humidity is favourable for seed-set in many crops, provided soil moisture supply is adequate. For example, seed-set of wheat was higher at 60% relative humidity than at 80%, when water availability in the soil was not limiting (Campbell *et al.*, 1969). When relative humidity is high, pollen may not be dispersed from the anthers (Kaufmann, 1972).

Dry regions are generally favoured for seed production. However, excessively low air humidity may have an adverse effect on fertilization, by causing excessive dehydration of pollen or stigma. (Also see the chapter on "Effect of humidity on crop production" by Prof. J. W. O'Leary in this volume.)

SOLAR RADIATION

The arid regions are characterized by predominantly clear skies during both day and night, permitting a large amount of solar energy to reach the earth. Solar energy provides two essential needs of plants: (a) light required for photosynthesis and for many other functions of the plant, including seed germination, leaf expansion, growth of stem and shoot, flowering, fruiting and even dormancy (Stoughton, 1955); and (b) thermal conditions required for the normal physiological functions of the plant. However, radiation also increases evapotranspiration. Transpiration rates increase almost in proportion to the intensity of solar radiation, while in many crops, the rate of photosynthesis increases less rapidly.

Light

The three characteristics of light which affect plant growth and development are duration, intensity and quality (wavelength).

Duration or length of day

The duration of light is of major importance to the growth and development of plants. The effect of photoperiodism—the relative length of daily light and dark periods—on the vegetative and reproductive stages of development is well-known. Actually, the duration of the night or of complete darkness is more important than the length of daylight. Most typical tropical crops are short-day plants (requiring long nights for flowering), while those of the higher latitudes are generally long-day plants. Some plants have different photoperiodic requirements for different developmental stages: wheat, for example, is day-neutral for floral initiation, but long-day for fruiting. Control of the time of flowering is extremely important for the adaptability of a crop to a given environment (Calder, 1966).

Light intensity

While the formative processes under the influence of photoperiodism are usually influenced by very low light intensities for optimal photosynthesis high light intensities are essential (Wassinck, 1954). The large amount of sunshine is a great potential asset of the semiarid regions for agriculture, and may reach 75-90 per cent of the possible sunshine. Even during the winter months in the semiarid areas, with winter rainfall, sunshine is plentiful. The hot and the mild semiarid regions of the world are better endowed with long hours of bright sunshine, combined with moderately high temperatures, than are many other parts of the world.

As moisture supply is frequently limiting in rain-fed crop production, the high potentials of these regions cannot always be realized. However, in relatively good rainfall seasons, very high yields can be achieved, if appropriate measures are taken.

Minimum light requirements

It has generally been found that at low light intensities, for the individual leaf, there is a linear relation between light intensities and rate of photosynthesis. Theoretically, photosynthesis is possible at any light intensity, however low; practically, respiration dominates when light intensity is too low. Net assimilation will be zero at a light intensity of 500 foot candles, and a minimum of 500 to 1000 foot candles is required for effective rates of photosynthesis, at which the photosynthetic gas exchange is greater than the respiratory gas exchange (Blackman & Black, 1959).

Light saturation

With increasing light intensity, photosynthesis of the single leaf obeys the law of diminishing returns. Extremely high light intensities even have an inhibitory effect on photosynthesis—a phenomenon called solarization (Wang, 1963). In most crop plants, light saturation for single leaves is reached at a light intensity of 0.2 cal/cm²/minute, which is typical of the light intensity on an overcast day with the sun at its zenith. On a clear day light intensity may be four times as great (Wit, 1967), so that a large proportion of the light is far in excess of what fully exposed leaves can utilize. For this reason, it was previously assumed that light could not generally become limiting for crop production.

However, in the field, light is not spread evenly over the photosynthetic surface but commonly passed by reflection and transmission through several layers of leaves, its intensity falling off exponentially with the path-length through absorbing layers. The fully exposed leaves in the canopy may absorb several times the amount of light needed for saturation, thereby absorbing a large proportion of the available light energy without increasing photosynthesis. The intensity of the light falling on the leaves in the lower layers depends on the initial light intensity, on the ratio between direct and diffuse light, or the number and size of the leaves, their angle of incidence, and distribution, and on the transmission and reflection of the leaves (Verhagen *et al.*, 1963). At ground-level, the final light intensity is usually below compensation point, i.e. that light intensity at which the gas exchange resulting from photosynthesis is equal to that resulting from respiration (Bonner, 1962).

Very high light intensities are, therefore, rarely capable of saturating the whole canopy in the field, and the photosynthetic rate of the foliage as a whole continues to increase up to very high light intensities, as more and more leaves in the shaded parts of the canopy reach light saturation.

On a worldwide basis, photosynthetic efficiency is less than 1 per cent, generally as a result of deficiencies in nutrition, limited moisture supply, inadequate crop production methods, etc.

Much of the difference between actual yields in the field, and the calculated potential yield based on maximum possible conversion of light energy by the photosynthetic process (estimated at 77 g of dry matter per square metre per day (Loomis & Williams, 1963), appears to be due to light saturation of the upper part of the canopy only, while the lower leaves may be contributing very little on clear days, and possibly show a negative net assimilation on cloudy or rainy days. Therefore, as long as light saturation of the canopy as a whole does not occur, any increase in light intensity will increase productivity, provided other factors are not limiting. Even in environments with very high peak intensities, productivity was found to show a linear relationship with the logarithm of relative light intensity (Loomis *et al.*, 1967). For example, the growth-rate of Subterranean Clover was found to be determined solely by the amount of light-energy received, and to be independent of temperature. However, this is only a part of the picture. A leaf subjected to such radiation heat-loads must be able to dissipate rapidly the greater part of the absorbed energy, or its temperature could rise to as much as 100 °C over air temperature within less than a minute (Idso *et al.*, 1966). This dissipation of heat occurs in three ways: by thermal radiation from the leaf, by removal of heat via convection currents and by transpiration.

Solar radiation can, therefore, affect plant productivity in two different ways simultaneously: directly by its intensity, and indirectly by its effect on leaf temperature.

On a relatively cool day, the rate of photosynthesis follows the incidence of solar radiation closely, for both shaded and unshaded leaves. By contrast, on a warm day, the sunlit leaf undergoes a mid-day slump at which it stops photosynthesizing, resuming the process only just before sunset. The shaded leaf, on the other hand, shows only a slight reduction in its rate of photosynthesis during the mid-day period, but keeps on photosynthesizing throughout the day, so that its total daily photosynthesis is three times as great as that of the sunlit leaf—in sharp contrast to what occurs on a cool day (Idso *et al.*, 1966). The mid-day slump is only partially due to an internal water deficit, the major reason being the effects of the energy environment on leaf temperatures.

Visible light, which has no direct effect on evaporation, affects the rate of transpiration by influencing stomatal aperture (Kramer, 1969). Cloudy weather, especially during the cool season causes decreased stomatal opening in most species that are native to sunny habitats (Wilson, 1948).

Light quality

Many factors, such as the amount and kind of cloud cover, fog, air pollution, and the colour of the foliage interrupting light, influence the quality of the incident light. Radiation up to 0.25 micron (ultraviolet spectrum) is harmful to most plants; from 0.30 to 0.55 micron it has a photoperiodic effect; from 0.40 to 0.69 micron it is most effective in photosynthesis. Above 0.74 micron (the infrared spectrum), 'light' has practically no effect on photosynthesis; its main effect is thermal, and respiration is encouraged (Wang, 1963).

TEMPERATURE

Temperatures in the hot arid climates are the highest in the world (Critchfield, 1966). The generally clear skies facilitate maximum radiation in day, and rapid loss of heat in night—resulting in high diurnal ranges of temperature, which may reach 30 to 40 °C in the hot deserts during the summer.

The annual ranges of temperature are less marked in hot deserts than in many other regions, but are far greater than in the humid tropics. Daily average ranges during the hottest months in the hot desert area are 27-35 °C, with daily maxima of 37-43 °C. The coolest months in these areas average around 10 °C, with occasional night frosts. Temperatures in the semiarid hot climate are generally similar to those of the more arid regions (Critchfield, 1966).

Effects of Temperature on Crop Production

Plants can grow only within certain limits of temperature. For each species and variety there are not only optimal temperature limits, but also optimal temperatures for different growth-stages and functions, as well as lower and upper lethal limits.

We have seen that light has an overriding effect on the rate of photosynthesis. However, it is involved in only one aspect of the photosynthetic process, namely, as a source of energy for the conversion of carbon dioxide and water to carbohydrates. There are certain biochemical processes preceding and following the reduction of carbon dioxide, which are affected mainly by temperature (Gaastra, 1963). As long as light is limiting, temperature has little effect on the rate of photosynthesis. However, when light is not limiting, as is generally the case in dry regions, the biochemical processes associated with photosynthesis become the limiting factor, so that the effect of favourable temperatures on the rate of photosynthesis is increased.

In general, high temperatures accelerate growth processes. Rarely are high temperature *per se* the direct cause of death of plants, provided the water supply is adequate. However, beyond a certain limit, which depends on the crop, the stage of development, and the physiological process involved, high temperatures may have detrimental effects on crop production. The photosynthetic process appears to become heat-inactivated at excessively high temperatures which, however, do not inhibit respiration, so that apparent photosynthesis declines rapidly under these conditions (Moss et al., 1961) (Fig. 1.5).

Retardation of growth and difficulties in fertilization, even in heat-loving crops such as maize and sorghum, occur at temperatures that are often well below the lethal limit. The harmful effects of excessive temperatures are usually aggravated by lack of available moisture. Hot dry winds will further increase the damage. The yield of grain sorghum is adversely affected by heat waves occurring at flowering (Skerman, 1956). The damage can be the result of high temperature, water stress or both factors. It was found that there was a loss of pollen viability due to dryness, not heat, which was, however, insufficient to reduce the number of grains set. The reduction of grain set recorded was found to be entirely due to heat, and not dryness. The degree of damage caused by high temperature depends on the phenological stage of the plant at the time of heat wave, yield being most affected at, or soon after, the boot stage (Pasternak & Wilson, 1969).

In the Great Plains of U.S.A., it was found that high summer temperatures may even override the effects of summer rainfall on the yields of crops. Thus variability in yields of spring wheat was clearly associated with variability in average maximum temperatures in June, and variability in maize yields was most closely associated with variability in average maximum temperatures in July (Moldenhauer & Westin, 1959). At-

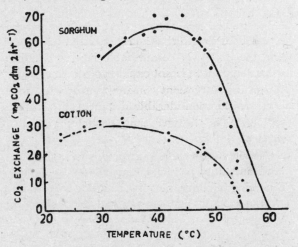

Fig. 1.5. Effect of temperature on net photosynthesis of sorghum and cotton leaves (Slatyer, 1967, after El-Sharkawy & Hesketh, 1965) (by courtesy of the J. Aust. Inst. agric. Sci.).

mospheric temperature affects evaporation through its influence on leaf temperature and hence on leaf water vapour pressure (Kramer, 1969). With increasing temperatures, evapotranspiration increases. Hence, a moisture supply that is adequate in a cooler climate may be deficient in a warmer region—a situation which may be aggravated by hot winds.

Frosts

The clear skies at night permit considerable radiation from the earth in arid regions. The rapid cooling of the land at night causes an inversion of temperature, the air near the cool soil becomes heavy and does not rise, so that night temperatures at soil level are typically low in the desert and may reach freezing point, even after a relatively hot day. Cold air will tend to flow into low places, so that localized pockets of frost may occur in an area which is generally frost-free. In the middle-latitude dry zones, the incidence of killing frosts determines the length of the growing season, which is practically limited to the time-interval between the last killing frost of spring and the first killing of autumn. The shorter this period is, the earlier maturing will be the varieties that can be grown and the lower their potential yielding ability.

In warm regions, occasional and exceptional frosts may do considerable damage because the crops grown in such regions are usually very susceptible to low temperatures.

WINDS

The dry regions are characterized by frequent and strong winds, which are due partly to considerable convection during the day. The usually sparse vegetation is not capable of slowing down air movement, so that dust storms are a frequent concomitant of wind movement. Much of the dust is carried for considerable distances to form loose deposits in neighbouring regions. The heavier sand particles carried by the wind scour the soil surface.

Winds also affect growth mechanically and physiologically. The sand and dust particles carried out by wind may damage plant tissues. Emerging seedlings may be completely covered or, alternatively, the roots of young plants may be exposed by strong winds. Winds may also cause considerable losses by inducing lodging, the breaking of stalks and the shedding of grain.

The physiological effect of winds consists mainly in increasing transpiration as well as evaporation from the soil. Winds increase transpiration by removing the moist air surrounding the leaves; they decrease transpiration by cooling the leaves. The former effect will be most marked at low levels of radiation and the latter at high levels (Knoerr, 1966). Hot dry winds may also adversely affect photosynthesis, and hence productivity, by causing closure of the stomata even when soil moisture is adequate (Crafts et al., 1949).

The arid regions are under the influence of winds which originate either over the sea or over deserts. In summer, the desert regions become heated to high temperatures; the heated air rises, causing an indraught of winds from neighbouring regions. If these winds pass over an ocean, they become moisture-laden. These are the monsoon winds, such as those that invade the Sahara from the south-west during the northern summer.

During the winter, the opposite effect occurs: the desert areas are cooler than the adjacent tropical areas and the winds blow from the deserts towards the tropical areas. These winds are relatively cool and dry at the beginning of the growing season, but become progressively hotter and drier as the spring advances. They are called Harmattan in most of tropical West Africa north of the Equator, Khamsin in the Near East, and Loo in India. The total number of days in spring during which these dry, hot winds blow may be relatively small, but their effect on the crops and their yields may be considerable. Overnight temperatures may soar from 25 to 46 °C, and the relative humidity may drop to 5-10 per cent.

If the cereal crops are earing when a Khamsin strikes, the ears may be actually 'blasted', turning white, without any seed formation following. When the Khamsin occurs at a later stage, seeds may shrivel and mature ahead of time.

The hot dry winds may also occasionally have beneficial effects. The main reason for the low incidence of the very dangerous Yellow Rust of Wheat (*Puccinia glumarum*) in the Far East, is the susceptibility of the pathogen to the high temperatures that occur when the sirocco winds blow. In the rare years when no Khamsins occur in the spring season, this Rust may cause devastating reductions in yield (Arnon, 1972).

Moderate winds have a beneficial effect on photosynthesis by continuously replacing the carbon dioxide absorbed by the leaf surfaces. The favourable effect of wind on photosynthesis is most marked at the lower leaf-layers; increasing wind strength permits ever deeper leaf-layers to approach the maximum rate of photosynthesis possible under the amounts of radiation received (Lemon, 1963). (Also see the chapter on "Wind effects and their amelioration in crop production" by Dr. J. W. Sturrock in this volume.)

MICROCLIMATE

Microclimatology deals with the pertinent factors of the environment in the zone lying between the highest level reached by the plants and the lowest depth to which air penetrates into the soil (Albe & Fournier, 1958).

Microclimate at Plant Level

The microclimate just above a crop and under its canopy (ecoclimate) is influenced by the particular type of crop, and may be strikingly different from the climate of the surrounding environment. Even emerging seedlings will alter the climate near the soil surface, by reducing air movement and by shading the ground. As the plants grow, the extremes in temperatures of the soil surface are reduced; even so, the range of temperatures at the soil surface may be double that of the temperatures recorded in the standard meteorological screen.

The ecoclimate may be more humid and cooler than the atmosphere above the crop, which circumstances may create favourable conditions for the spread of certain diseases. Leaf temperatures in sunlight may be higher than the air temperature in day and lower than the air temperature in night. The intensity and quality of light change as the rays pass through the plant canopy.

Soil Microclimate

The climate in the soil may be strikingly different from that of the atmosphere above it. Only part of the radiation that reaches the soil surface is absorbed, the amount reflected depending on certain characteristics of the soil's surface. The percentage of the incoming radiation that is reflected is called the 'albedo', which varies according to plant cover, soil type, and moisture content, etc., as shown by the figures in Table 1. 2.

Table 1.2.   Albedo of different soil surfaces (Thornthwaite, 1958)

Surface				Albedo (Percentage of incoming radiation)
Wet sand	..	..	..	9
Dryland	..	..	..	18
Grass cover, green crops	..	..	..	15–30
Forest	..	..	..	15–18

As a result of differences in albedo, different thermal regimes will exist on different types of soil surface layers and the air above them—even when the amounts of incoming radiation are identical. For example, a mulch on the surface of the soil absorbs most of the incoming radiation; the soil remains cool, while the surface of the mulch itself and the overlying air become very hot during the daytime and cool rapidly during the night hours.

Wet soils absorb more radiant energy than dry soils. Most of the energy is used for the evaporation of the soil water; the remaining radiant energy will warm deeper soil layers. By contrast, the surface of dry soils, and the air layer above them, will be at higher temperatures than is the case with moist soil.

At field capacity nearly 80-85% of the incoming energy is used for evapotranspiration; as soil moisture depletes, this proportion decreases. In arid regions, as a result of the low moisture content of the soil and the sparse vegetation, actual evapotranspiration is low and most of the incoming radiation serves to heat the soil and the air above it. When the surface of a moist soil is covered by vegetation, the amount of evapotranspiration is determined mainly by the amount of incoming radiation and is otherwise affected by differences in albedo between different plant covers. However, as the soil dries, the ability of different types of vegetation to use soil moisture will make itself felt, and thereby affect actual evapotranspiration.

In dry regions, diurnal temperature fluctuations in the seed-bed zone frequently reach, and even exceed an amplitude of about 20 °C on bright dry days and about 10 °C during cloudy and rainy periods (Tadmor et al.,

1964). The temperature of the top layer of the soil is usually higher than that of the overlying atmosphere, while daily fluctuations in temperature decrease with increasing depth in the soil. At a depth of 50 cm, daily variations of temperature in the soil practically cease (Migahid, 1962). At a depth of 1-3 m, temperatures are fairly stable throughout the year.

As a result of the heating of the soil surface, which may be considerable in arid climates, a steep temperature gradient occurs, which may cause a considerable movement of water through the soil. There is also a continuous exchange of air between soil and atmosphere. When water penetrates into the soil, air is expelled; as the soil dries, fresh air is drawn into the soil. The air in the soil is usually moisture saturated, excepting under conditions of extreme dryness.

Soil temperature has considerable influence on plant growth and on the soil microorganisms. Warm (20-30 °C), moist soils are a favourable medium for most of the cultivated crops that are grown in arid regions. However, as the soils dry, temperature tends to rise. High soil temperatures can severely limit root growth, and may eventually rise to a level at which roots are injured and even killed (Kramer, 1969). The reduction in growth is attributed to water stress caused by reduced absorption of water at high temperatures (Brouwer, 1964).

Interrelationships between Yield (Y) and Moisture Supply (ET)

CROP RESPONSE TO MOISTURE SUPPLY

Soil Factors

For many years, the important question of crop response to various levels of soil moisture has been debated by research workers; one view holds that soil moisture is equally available to plants over the whole range from Field Capacity* (FC) to Permanent Wilting Point** (WP), while the opposing view contends that plant growth is adversely affected as soon as the

---

* Field Capacity (also called Capillary Capacity) is the water content of the soil, to 3 days after a thorough wetting of the soil by rain or irrigation after drainage of gravitational water has become very slow and water content is relatively stable. It is not a true equilibrium value, but movement of water is too slow that for practical purposes it can be considered as the upper limit of soil water storage for plant growth.

** Permanent Wilting Point (or Percentage) is the water content of the soil at which plants remain permanently wilted, unless water is added to the soil. Soil water potential at wilting has a mean value of about −15 bars [a unit of pressure in the metric system, equal to 106 dynes per cm² (slightly less than the English unit of one atmosphere.)] This should be considered as an approximation which holds true for most crop plants.

soil moisture stress is increased beyond a certain level, long before the WP is reached. It is now widely agreed that soil moisture becomes progressively more limiting to plants as soil moisture stress increases.

The work required to withdraw water from the soil increases gradually as soil moisture is progressively depleted—until near WP, when, in certain soil types, it increases steeply.

For most crop plants, which are generally mesophyllic in nature, the considerable amount of work required to remove water from the soil, as it is gradually depleted, will definitely affect growth and development and, therefore, crop yields. For these crops, maximum yields are generally dependent on maintaining the soil moisture between the limits of FC and some critical range of soil moisture that is higher than the WP. This critical range will depend on the type of crop and its stage of development, on the nature of the the marketable produce, on soil characteristics, and on the environmental conditions under which the crop is grown.

The sensitivity of plants to increasing soil moisture stress increases under conditions of high temperature, low relative humidity, high wind velocity, and increased light intensities—all conditions which increase the transpiration rate considerably. Therefore, on a hot dry day, the rate of transpiration is so much in excess of water uptake that plants will wilt at a soil moisture content at which on a cooler or more humid day they would not have shown any sign of stress. For each day, there is therefore a stress-point, which is the moisture content of the soil that is required to keep plants from being subjected to moisture stress under the prevailing atmospheric conditions. Days on which a moisture content is reached that is lower than the stress point are called 'stress days'. In maize, there is a linear relation between dry matter production and the number of stress days (Shaw & Burrows, 1966), showing that the relative water availability fluctuates according to weather conditions as well as to the soil moisture content.

Thus, an inadequate supply of soil moisture has an adverse effect on plant growth and productivity; the same is true of excess moisture in the soil. Both conditions are therefore conducive to low WUE. There is, therefore, no basis for the assumption that plants grown under dryland conditions will generally be more efficient in water use than the same crop grown under irrigation, or that water stress improves WUE. For each crop and combination of environmental conditions there is a narrow range of soil moisture levels at which WUE will be higher than with a lesser or greater supply of water.

Plant Factors

Crops differ in their capacity to absorb water, to transpire water and to react to moisture stress. These differences in crops become more and more evident as the difficulties of maintaining an adequate water balance increase. The physiological processes of the plant are primarily a function of the water status of the plant and only indirectly affected by soil and atmospheric water stress (Kramer, 1969).   Therefore, a certain level of soil water stress will not necessarily be accompanied by an equivalent degree of plant water stress.

The water status of plant tissues depends on:

(a) resistance to flow of water in the soil, which varies with water content;

(b) resistance to flow from the stomata into the atmosphere, which varies with atmospheric conditions; and

(c) resistance to flow within the roots and other tissues of the plant, which depends on physiological factors and is by no means constant. Hence, it is usually impossible to predict the internal water status of a plant from conditions in the soil alone or the atmosphere alone, and it is possible for a plant to wilt with abundant water in the soil and to remain turgid when the soil is relatively dry (Gardner, 1964).

The principal plant factors which affect the availability of water are rooting characteristics and the ability to withstand an adverse water balance.

Rooting characteristics

Both root proliferation and depth of penetration are important characteristics. Roots may have an enormous surface area in intimate contact with soil particles.

When a major portion of the plant's root system is subject to water stress at the WP, permanent injury to the plant may result; the degree of injury and the rate of recovery will depend mainly on the length of time that elapses before water is added to the soil, and on the proportion of the root system that is in soil with a moisture content above the WP. When the plant has an extensive and efficient root system, penetrating a deep, well-structured soil, it can, under favourable climatic conditions, maintain an optimum supply of moisture to its aerial parts until part of the root zone reaches WP, without growth being markedly affected.

This combination of circumstances is the exception rather than the rule, especially in arid climates. Young plants, with an underdeveloped rooting system, will be adversely affected at a level of soil moisture at which full-grown perennial plants, such as most grasses, remain unaffected. The latter have a wide and deep root system which penetrates the soil to a considerable depth. Therefore, when part of the root zone is already at WP, other parts will continue to supply water from soil that is still moist. As water movement in an unsaturated soil is extremely slow, a continuous supply of water to the plant will depend largely on the growth of the roots towards the water.   A crop whose root system develops rapidly will be able to explore the soil for moisture and will therefore be at an advantage over crops whose root systems grow slowly.   The latter will suffer as soon as the water supply in the soil which is in intimate contact with their roots gets exhausted.   Root elongation decreases as soil becomes water deficient (Gingrich & Russell, 1956), so that not only does it become progressively more difficult for the roots to extract water, but their ability to seek it is also affected adversely.

Deep penetration by their roots provides many crops with a continued supply of soil moisture, even when the upper layers, which usually dry out between rains or irrigation, have already reached WP.   However, there are great differences between different crops, and even between different varieties of the same crop, in the characteristics of their rooting systems (see Table 1.3).

Table 1.3.   Characteristics of rooting systems of three crops (Dittmer, 1938)

Crop			Root surface area (in²) per in³ of soil	Number of root hairs per in³ of soil
Oats	..	..	15	150,000
Rye	..	..	30	300,000
Kentucky Bluegrass	..	..	65	1,000,000

In the examples presented in Table 1.3 Kentucky Bluegrass should be the most efficient, and oats the least efficient, in extracting moisture from the soil.

Plant growth may be retarded by the drying out of the upper soil layers, even when there is ample moisture available in lower layers of the root zone, in cases in which some essential element is concentrated in the dried out layer and therefore becomes unavailable to the plants.   There are indications that certain plants are capable of depleting water from the soil to much drier levels than the WP, to an ultimate extent that is equivalent to several hundred atmospheres of stress (Slatyer, 1958).   Wheat plants with a well-developed root system were found to be capable of absorbing water at tensions greater than 26 atm (Haise *et al.*, 1955).   The moisture absorbed at levels below WP is not effective in maintaining vegetative growth but affects yield and quality of the grain (Kozlowski, 1964).   Therefore, in considering the amount of water available to native plants in arid soils, the WP is of little significance as the lower limit of soil moisture.   The lowest limit of availability will depend on the species involved and on the prevailing conditions.

A further possibility raised by Slatyer (1958) is that moisture may even be absorbed by plants from an unsaturated atmosphere, as long as there is a favourable diffusion-pressure deficit gradient. This is of special significance in semiarid and arid regions, where high humidity levels and dewfall are frequent at night may be considered of importance for survival, if not for growth. (Also see the chapter on "Root patterns in crops as related to water and nutrient uptake" by Dr. E. A. Hurd and Dr. E. D. Spratt in this volume.)

Ability to withstand an adverse water balance

This aspect will be treated in detail on p. 47 under the head "Plant adaptations to growth in dry regions."

Climatic Factors

The important climatic factors affecting the plant's response to moisture regime are temperature, relative humidity, light intensity and wind velocity. All these factors influence the water needs of the plant, as has already been described. There is a relatively complex interaction between the plant, climate and soil factors which determines the plant's reaction to a given moisture regime. All climatic factors conducive to high rates of evapotranspiration will accelerate the adverse effect of soil moisture stress and *vice versa*. Therefore, plants may be under severe water stress under conditions of high temperature, and/or low relative humidity, even when soil moisture is not limiting; conversely, a fairly high soil moisture tension may have no adverse effect on the crop when environmental conditions are not conducive to high transpiration rates.

The discrepancy between water supply to the roots and loss of water by transpiration may be aggravated by the considerable resistance to movement of water through the roots. On the other hand, the parenchyma tissue acts as a buffer losing water when transpiration exceeds absorption and gaining water when the reverse occurs (Kramer, 1969).

Effect of Yield Levels on Consumptive Use of Water

As ET is largely regulated by the evaporative demand of the aerial environment, increases in yield due to inherent productivity or management practices have relatively little influence on ET, *when soil moisture is not limiting and once the crop stand attains complete soil cover.*

However, conditions under which soil moisture is not limiting are not exactly characteristic of the semiarid conditions with which we are concerned. An increase in yield obtained under these conditions usually results in increased ET; however, very wide differences in yield may result in only relatively small differences in ET.

The possibility of increasing yields significantly under conditions of water deficiency without an appreciable increase in the use of water may be due to a number of reasons.

Certain practices, such as fertilizer use, which enable the crop to develop a more extensive root system, and to extract water from deeper depths and possibly higher tensions than an unirrigated crop, may increase ET significantly. In this and similar cases, the increase in yield is due both to the direct effect of the fertilizer, and to its indirect effect in increasing the amount of water that becomes available to the crop.

Another possible way in which the relationship between yield and ET may be influenced under conditions of water deficiency, is by changes in the rate of water use at different periods of growth (Black, 1968). For example, crested wheatgrass grown under desert conditions in Oregon, when fertilized—made more rapid growth early in the season, exhausted the water supply more rapidly, matured earlier and produced higher yields of dry matter than did the unfertilized grass (Sneva *et al.*, 1958). In this case, the higher yield was achieved without a change in the total seasonal ET.

PHYSIOLOGICAL EFFECTS OF WATER STRESS

Water deficit occurs in the plant whenever transpiration exceeds water absorption: this may be due to the excessive water loss, reduced absorption or both. According to the degree of internal water deficit and its duration, one can distinguish between incipient, temporary and permanent wilting (Kramer, 1959). A small loss in turgor, causing incipient wilting, is an almost daily occurrence in warm, dry weather, even when the soil is moist. This does not produce visible symptoms of wilting. A more severe loss of turgor, causing leaf drooping and subsequently spreading through the plant, will reduce growth. If plants regain their turgidity when the water supply is re-balanced, this is termed 'temporary wilting'. A longer period of dehydration causes 'permanent wilting', from which plants are no longer able to recover—even in a saturated atmosphere.

Moisture stress does not affect all aspects of plant growth and development equally: some processes are highly susceptible to increasing moisture stress, while others are far less affected (Shaw & Laing, 1968). The final yield of the crop will be the integrated result of these effects of stress on growth, photosynthesis, respiration, on metabolic processes, reproduction, etc. These various effects will therefore be discussed separately.

Turgor

With the onset of dry conditions, a progressive and continuous decline in turgor of the plants is observed. At first, the lag in absorption behind transpiration results in loss in turgor which appears to be due to a rapid rise in transpiration due to the increase in atmospheric dryness with the onset of the dry period. As atmospheric conditions become more static, the continued decline in turgor may be attributed primarily to the influence of soil moisture stress, in limiting absorption (Slatyer, 1958).

In Australia, the response of three crops: grain sorghum, cotton and groundnut to moisture stress was studied. Of the three crops, sorghum, with the best developed root system, also appeared to possess the most effective internal control over transpiration. This was reflected in generally higher turgor levels in sorghum than in the other crops, and a slower rate of decrease in turgor with the onset of dry weather. Cotton appeared to be the least well-equipped of the three crops to withstand moisture stress, and reacted with a rapid decrease in turgor. The differential resistance to turgor loss was reflected in growth rate reductions in cotton, which occurred as soon as soil moisture stress appeared, while in sorghum these did not appear until severe soil moisture stress was evident. The groundnut responses were intermediate of the two other crops (Slatyer, 1958).

Photosynthesis

Photosynthetic activity is related to three main groups of processes, all of which are affected by moisture stress:

(a) the supply of CO_2 to the photosynthetic sites;
(b) the photochemical process associated with the utilization of light energy; and
(c) dark chemical processes associated with the chemical reduction of CO_2.

As soil moisture stress increases, photosynthesis drops to the compensation point (Pallas et al., 1962). Water stress can affect photosynthesis directly, by affecting various biochemical processes involved in photosynthesis, and indirectly, by reducing the intake of CO_2 through stomata as a result of their closure in response to water stress. The translocation of assimilates can also be affected by water stress, and the resulting assimilate saturation in the leaves may limit photosynthesis (Hartt, 1967).

In studies on the effect of water stress on photosynthesis in wheat, it was found that from the onset of wilting, there was a progressive decline in the rate of photosynthesis (Wardlaw, 1967) (Fig. 1.6).

In maize, apparent photosynthesis was reduced by 40-50%, when soil moisture tension reached 1 atm, and signs of wilting were barely visible. Recovery of photosynthetic efficiency always occurred immediately on reduction of the moisture stress (Baker & Musgrave, 1964). Soil water stress and atmospheric water deficit act additively in reducing the rate of photosynthesis (Baker & Musgrave, 1964).

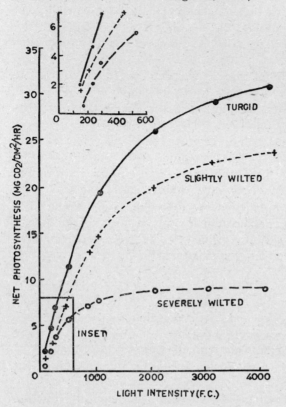

FIG. 1.6. Photosynthesis in response to light intensity of turgid and wilted leaves (Wardlaw, 1967) (by courtesy of the Aust. J. biol. Sci.).

An adverse water regime also reduces leaf area and hastens leaf senescence, thereby decreasing the productivity of the crop to a greater extent than the depressive effect resulting from a reduced net assimilation rate (Fisher & Hagan, 1965). For example, water stress that reduced the net assimilation rate by only 50 per cent was sufficient to cause complete cessation of leaf growth, indicating that leaf area is more affected by water stress than is the case for net assimilation rate (Ashton, 1956).

Respiration

Respiration generally responds to loss of turgor in the inverse direction of photosynthesis: respiration rate first increases, but, as the deficit becomes more severe, it decreases (Evenari, 1962). For example, in studies with wheat plants, CO_2 output was found to increase in the early stages of drought before there was any measurable effect on the water content of the shoots. More severe drought lowered water content and respiration (Kaul, 1965).

Anatomical Changes

Periodical water stress leads to many anatomical changes: these include decrease in the size of cells and of intercellular spaces, thicker cell wall, and greater development of the mechanical tissues (May & Milthorpe, 1962). However, the number of stomata per unit of leaf surface tends to increase (loc. cit.).

Metabolic Reactions

The proportion of water in the plant is far higher than in the soil, and very small fluctuations, within very narrow limits, can interfere with active metabolism (Slatyer, 1967). Almost all metabolic reactions are affected by plant water deficits. Severe water deficits generally cause an overall decrease in enzymatic activity. These effects are however selective: as the cytoplasm is dehydrated, activity of some enzymes involved in synthesis is reduced before that of others, while levels of others increase as a result of water deficit. For example, in maize, an increase in water stress causes nitrate reductase activity to decline at a much greater rate than peroxidase activity (Todd, 1972). Levels of enzymes involving hydrolysis or degradation usually either remain the same or increase, but they do not decrease until fairly severe desiccation has taken place. Hydrolytic reactions therefore increase: starch is hydrolysed into sugars, and proteins into amino acids. It has been found in cotton that, as a result of water stress, the sugar content of the leaf increases and starch content decreases. By contrast, in the stems, the concentration of both sugar and starch increases—indicating that the reduced water supply not only affects photosynthesis, but also that the ability of the plant to utilize the products of photosynthesis is still more impaired (Eaton & Ergle, 1952). Similar results were obtained with wheat, in which the percentage of soluble carbohydrates in the leaves of plants under moisture stress increased steadily, reaching a level from three to four times as high as that in unstressed plants —after which death followed (Petinov, 1961).

The conversion of starch to sugars, and their accumulation, increases osmotic pressure. This causes a reduction in the permeability of the plant cell, so that internal resistance to water flow increases, thereby lessening water loss (Shields, 1958).

Water deficits impair the nucleic acid system as a result of increased R-Nase activity; the degradation of RNA proceeds more rapidly than its synthesis, and this, in turn, affects enzyme production and growth (May & Milthorpe, 1962). West (1962) studied the effect of water stress on growth of and metabolic processes in young maize seedlings. Protein and nucleotide contents were reduced, while RNA accumulated in the seedlings. The reduced growth of the stressed seedlings was attributed to an alteration in the nucleotide composition of the RNA. Water stress also results in a changed base content of RNA.

Protein synthesis is intimately connected with the activities of the nucleic acid system, and is therefore very much affected by drought (Kessler, 1961). These adverse effects are more marked in drought susceptible varieties than in drought resistant varieties (Charles & Todd, 1968). Substantial accumulation of certain amino acids, especially proline, occurs concomitantly with water stress in many plants (Todd, 1972). This accumulation probably relates to decreased protein synthesis. In controlled environment experiments, it was found that barley plants, when subjected to water deficit, showed considerable accumulation of free proline in their leaves, and there were marked differences in this respect between varieties (Singh et al., 1972). It has been suggested that the accumulation of proline may be a protective agent; the application of proline helped wheat plants to recover from drought (Tyankova, 1967).

Certain plant species, of which *Atriplex* sp. is an outstanding example, are capable of maintaining a high protein content even when grown under severe moisture stress. This implies that these plants can maintain the organization and functioning of protoplasts despite severe internal water deficits, though perforce at a low level of activity (Gates, 1968). For example, *A. vesicaria*, of vital importance to the sheep industry of Australia, was able to maintain levels of approximately 20% protein, throughout the year, though exposed to severe water stress (Gates & Muirhead, 1967). It should however be noted that most agricultural and pastoral plants do not have such proportion (Gates, 1968).

Hormone Relations

Water stress exerts a profound effect on hormonal distribution in plants, particularly on the contents of cytokinins and abscisic acid (ABA). As a consequence of water deficit, cytokinin activity is reduced whereas ABA is increased (Livne & Vaadia, 1972). The enhanced aging in shoots of stressed plants may be due to a reduced supply of cytokinins from the roots (Itai & Vaadia, 1965). Abscisic acid appears to be involved in the regulation of physiological responses of plants under moisture stress (Mizrahi et al., 1970). A several fold increase in ABA was observed after two hours in wilted leaves of wheat seedlings (Wright, 1969).

Protoplasmic Dehydration

There are great differences between plant species in their ability to endure desiccation, in relation to both the duration and the degree of dehydration. The more water the plant can hold in its tissues under stress conditions, the greater will be the ability of the protoplasm to withstand permanent injury during drought. The 'bound water'* prevents the

---

* Bound water: Due to the presence of hydrophilic colloids, a fraction of the water in the tissues is so tightly held, that the energy of the water molecules is apparently reduced to such a low level that other properties are also changed. This fraction is called 'bound water' (Currier, 1967).

protein molecules of active sites from coagulating (Vaadia & Waisel, 1967). As tissue becomes desiccated, protoplasm becomes increasingly dense and its viscosity gradually increases; when dehydration is severe, complete gelation of the protoplasm occurs and finally it may become rigid to the point of brittleness (Levitt, 1956).

Root Development

Root development is affected by soil water potential in a number of ways, among which we should note the following:

1. The growth-rate of roots decreases with increasing water stress; however, growth of the roots is less affected by water shortage than is that of the aerial parts, so that the overall shoot : root ratio is increased (Peters & Runkles, 1967).

Drought was found to reduce the weight of roots produced in groundnuts (Bhan & Misra, 1970a) and in wheat (Kmoch *et al.*, 1957), without appreciably reducing their number. The roots were finer and more fibrous under the dry than under more favourable moisture conditions. Roots subjected to moisture stress tend to become suberized up to their tips and thereby lose part of their absorbing capacity (Kramer, 1969). A marked reduction in growth of flax roots was observed when soil water potential was reduced to 7 bars, but some growth was still found to occur in soil drier than −20 bars. Root growth in each soil layer appeared to be independent of the moisture content in other soil layers or in the shoot (Newman, 1966). Plants of *Phalaris tuberosa* were found to survive when the water potential in the upper metre of the soil was below −15 bars, because some of the roots penetrated to deeper horizons which contain readily available water (McWilliam & Kramer, 1968).

2. Roots grow towards water in the soil, provided the distance from the water is small (Hunter & Kelley, 1946).

3. When rains are light and frequent, only a small fraction of the potential root zone is wetted, root penetration will be restricted to a shallow layer and the crop will be particularly sensitive to drought periods at a later stage.

Growth

Growth is suspended during moisture stress and resumed upon its elimination. The extent of the damage caused to the plants depends on their physiological age, the degree of water stress, and the species concerned (Gates, 1968). Generally, the organ growing most rapidly at the time of stress is the one most affected (Aspinall *et al.*, 1964).

The effect of water stress on the growth of embryo and seedlings was studied in wheat (Milthorpe, 1950). Three distinctly different degrees of susceptibility, related to seedling age at the time of drying, was found. Seedlings were completely resistant from the dormant embryo stage until the coleoptiles were 3 to 4 mm long. At later stages, however, growth was permanently impaired by small water losses (Fig. 1.7). Susceptibility to drought increased markedly after rapid expansion of the first leaf began; however, the capacity to recover from severe drought was not entirely lost, as long as some root primordia remained in a meristematic condition. If functional roots became active in water uptake, leaf primordia were able to resume growth.

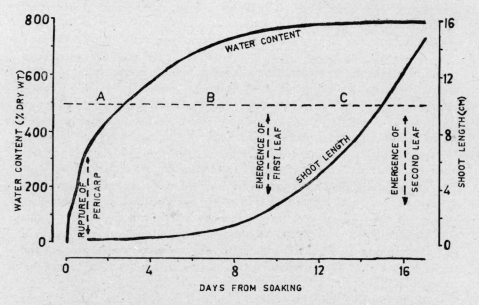

Fig. 1.7. Approximate duration of three phases of drought resistance (A, B & C) in relation to shoot length and water content of developing wheat seedlings. Drought stress was imposed by drying over sulphuric acid solutions for varying times (Gates, 1968, based on data of Milthorpe, 1950).

Growth is reduced by a decrease in relative turgidity to below 90 per cent (May & Milthorpe, 1962). The relations between turgor and growth are, however, not fully understood (Kramer, 1959). Water deficits cause dehydration of the protoplasm, associated with loss of turgor. The expansion of cells and cell division are reduced, resulting in a decrease in the growth of stems, leaves and fruits.

The final effect on growth will depend on the frequency and the duration of the periods of water stress.

Reproduction and Grain Development

The reproductive cycle can be divided into three stages (Kaufmann, 1972): (a) *flowering*, beginning with the initiation of flowers and culminating in fruit set. Moisture regime during this phase largely determines the number of fruits which will be produced; (b) the period of *fruit enlargement*, during which considerable amounts of nutrient reserves are transported into the fruit. The weight of the individual fruit will be mainly affected by moisture supply during this phase. Severe moisture stress during this period will usually result in small or shrivelled grains; and (c) *ripening*, which involves dehydration and certain biochemical processes. Moisture regime during this stage has very little effect on yield components, but may affect the length of the ripening period.

Moisture stress during the vegetative phase may stimulate the reproductive phase in some plants (Richards & Wadleigh, 1952). Aerial or storage parts of the plant may be adversely affected by a certain low level of soil moisture, while the economic yield may remain unaffected. For example, cotton was found to show marked difference in growth at different levels of moisture supply that had no significant effect on the yield of cotton seed (Adams *et al.*, 1942).

For many crop plants, moisture stress at the flowering period is critical. Aspinall *et al.* (1964) studying the effect of moisture stress at varying stages of plant development, found that all stages were affected, but the most sensitive stage was between the completion of spikelet formation and anthesis. Even a short period of water stress at anthesis will markedly reduce the number of flowers that set seed (May & Milthorpe, 1962). The critical period in cereals begins with the appearance of pollen mother cells (pollen viability appears to be particularly susceptible) and ends after pollination (Henckel, 1964). This is especially marked in crops with determinate flowering, in which the period of pollination through seed-set is relatively short. Grain yields of maize were found to be reduced by 25 per cent when soil moisture was depleted to WP for two days during the tasselling period, and by 50 per cent when the period of stress was increased up to six to eight days (Robins & Domingo, 1953). Yield was reduced because grains were formed on only a part of the ear.

When the linseed variety Punjab, was subjected to water shortage at the time of appearance of the inflorescence, seed yield was depressed to 65% of the control, but the 100 seed weight was scarcely affected. The oil content of the seed was also slightly reduced, and oil yield at maturity was reduced by nearly 40% (Tiver & Williams, 1943).

The effects of stress during grain maturation are far less marked, than during flowering. Wardlaw (1967) found in wheat, that the development of the grain, which constituted the main "sink" for the flag assimilates, was initially unaffected by a water deficit that caused wilting of the leaves and reduced photosynthetic rates. The reduced photosynthetic activity of the leaves and ear were compensated for by an increased translocation of assimilates to the grain from the lower parts of the plant.

In cotton, a plant with indeterminate flowering, water stress during the period of early flowering caused shedding of new flower buds, but had no effect on current flowering or on boll retention. A similar stress during peak flowering caused flower bud shedding and also reduced boll retention, while a late stress reduced current flowering and almost completely prevented boll retention (Grimes *et al.*, 1970).

Crop Yield

The effect of water stress on yield will depend largely on what proportion of the total dry matter produced is considered as useful material to be harvested (Fisher & Hagan, 1965). When the yield consists of most or all of the aerial part of the crop (forage crops, tobacco, etc.), the effects of stress on yield are much the same as those on total growth. When the yield consists of storage organs other than seeds or fruits (stock beets, potatoes, etc.), it will generally be as sensitive to moisture stress as in the plant's total growth. When the yield consists of the seeds or fruits, the situation is very different, and it has been shown for a number of crops that the dry matter stored in the seeds or grain is mainly the result of photosynthesis that occurs after flowering (Thorne, 1966). The effect of water stress will, therefore, depend on the stage of growth at which it occurs. At an early stage, the number of primordia formed may be reduced; on the other hand, the drastic effect of stress at the time of flowering has already been indicated. In general,

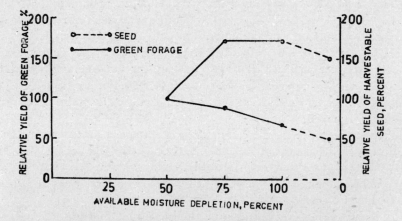

Fig. 1.8. Response of seed yield and vegetative dry-weight of Ladino clover to soil moisture potential (from Hagan, 1957) (by courtesy of California Agric.).

water stress, except at the most critical time, will have less effect on the yield of grain than on the plant's total growth (Fig. 1.8).

When the yield is a chemical constituent (sugar, pharmaceuticals, fibres, etc.), the economically valuable part of the crop is only a small fraction of the total dry matter produced, and moderate stress that affects growth may have no or even a beneficial effect on yield. The assumption being that wilting favours the decomposition of starch and proteins which may favour the formation of certain chemical constituents. Cool and humid growing conditions have been found to reduce the alkaloid content of many plants (Mothes & Romeike, 1958).

SEQUENTIAL EFFECTS OF WATER DEFICITS ON PLANTS

Slatyer (1967) has described the sequence of effects on plants of water deficits as they become progressively more severe: a plant that has an adequate water and nutrient supply, and normal transpiration, will have accelerated breakdown of RNA and possibly DNA (without any cessation of RNA synthesis). Metabolism will, at first, be impaired only during the daily periods of maximum water deficit; but these periods will become progressively longer. Stomatal closure during these periods will lead to reduced transpiration and also CO_2 absorption; photosynthesis is reduced and leaf temperatures are increased. Increased respiration will further reduce apparent photosynthesis.

As the moisture stress in the soil approaches the WP, turgor pressure in the plants approaches zero. Cell enlargement virtually ceases, and the rate of cell division is markedly reduced (causing a slowdown in the expansion of leaf area and growth rates). The stomata remain closed for most of the day and transpiration is limited to cuticular transpiration. Leaf temperature increases markedly. Most metabolic processes, including respiration, slow down apparent photosynthesis and production of dry matter becoming practically nil.

The disruption of normal cell metabolism is accompanied by the breakdown of proteins and carbohydrates, causing an increase in the concentration of sugars; leaf phosphorus and nitrogen migrate from older leaves to the stem. Finally, as protoplasmic dehydration continues, individual cells and tissues die. Root hairs die and the roots suberize. In some cases the tops of plants die before the roots, in others the opposite occurs.

EFFECTS OF RENEWED MOISTURE SUPPLY AFTER STRESS PERIODS

While cases of crop desiccation and hence complete loss are not rare in arid and even semiarid regions, what generally happens is that the crops suffer periods of stress of varying duration and severity, terminated each time by a renewed supply of moisture. It is consequently important to understand crop reactions to a renewed water supply after periods of stress of various degrees of severity and duration and at different stages of growth.

Recovery of photosynthetic efficiency occurs immediately on reduction of moisture stress (Baker & Musgrave, 1964). The initial decrease in the rate of photosynthesis as a result of water deficit may even be followed by an increase to a point exceeding the original level (Eckardt, 1953). This phenomenon is not well-understood (Evenari, 1962). Rapid drying has a more adverse effect on the rate of photosynthesis than does slow drying (Stocker, 1960).

The ability of stomata to recover after moisture stress may be impaired, so that the plant is unable to reestablish its normal functions even after regaining turgescence. There are, apparently, differences between various crops in the ability of their stomata to recover from the effects of water stress, and this may be a factor in their apparent drought resistance. Presumably, this is one of the reasons for the greater ability of sorghum to recover from the effects of drought as compared to maize (Glover, 1959).

If the moisture supply is renewed only shortly before death would have occurred, metabolic processes do not immediately return to normal (Denmead & Shaw, 1960). The death of the root hairs and the suberization of the roots delay recovery—because of the reduced capacity for water uptake (Slatyer, 1967). The adverse effects of water stress are less severe at some stages of growth than at others. At certain stages, there may be irreversible damage which will affect the final yield while at other stages, a renewed water supply may stimulate growth to such an extent that the plant may 'catch up'.

Sorghum is characterized by an unusual ability to interrupt growth under moisture stress for extended periods and resume growth as soon as favourable conditions again occur. When sorghum plants were subjected to wilting prior to floral initiation, growth in height virtually ceased; upon rewatering, growth resumed and showed little influence of the previous drought. Flower emergence was delayed for approximately the same time as the duration of drought and the seed-set per head was not affected (Whiteman & Wilson, 1965).

Drought Hardening

Drought resistance of many plants can be increased by subjecting them for several days to moderate dehydration, to low temperatures, or to treatment with growth retarding substances. Plants that recover from a period of drought are also usually less affected by a renewed period of water stress (May & Milthorpe, 1962). When hardened plants are subjected to drought, their protoplasm shows a lower viscosity and higher permeability to water than that of similar but non-hardened plants. Thus the adapted protoplasm does not become rigid and brittle as soon as that of unadapted plants, and is better able to hold water against dehydrating forces (Levitt, 1956). Higher rates of photosynthesis, lower rates of respiration, and a higher root/shoot ratio, also characterize hardened plants (May & Milthorpe, 1962). Todd and Webster (1965) also found that four varieties of wheat were able to carry on photosynthesis at a higher rate when the plants were previously subjected to a single drought period. Drought hardened plants are also better able to survive exposure to heat than are unhardened plants (Levitt, 1956).

Presowing Hardening of Plants to Drought

Very young seeds, which are still in the milky stage, and have attained only one-eighth of the volume of the mature seed, can be completely air-dried without losing their vitality (Hubac, 1962). The excised embryo can be dried to a moisture content of 5 per cent, and will resume normal development and germinate if remoistened and placed on a suitable substrate. As germination proceeds, the sprouting embryo rapidly loses its ability to withstand desiccation without loss of viability. The critical period occurs at the time of emergence of the radicle (or first seminal root). It is the radicle that dies first under dehydration, but, before it reaches this point through desiccation the seed or embryo can be submitted to a number of alternate hydrations and desiccations without harm. Indeed, a succession of alternate hydrations and desiccations of the seeds was found to increase the resistance of the seedlings to desiccation. As long as dehydration and desiccation have only a purely physical effect on the colloids of the embryo, its vitality is not affected. By contrast, biological dehydration, involving death of the radicle, is irreversible.

Based on these findings, a method for increasing drought resistance of plants by treatment before sowing was proposed and developed by Russian researchers (Genkel & Henckel, 1961). The method consists in repeated cycles of soaking the seeds in water or other dilute solutions, such as 0.25% $CaCl_2$, and drying.

In field experiments in Queensland, it was found that presowing drought hardening (soaking the seed, then drying) reduced the rate at which critical levels of leaf relative water content (RWC) declined and critical levels are reached during periods of severe internal moisture stress. These differences of RWC were reflected in a greater retardation of growth of the plants from untreated seeds, which could have caused a loss in apical dominance of the main stem and may explain the increased number of regrowth tillers formed on plants from untreated seeds (Aspinall et al., 1964). The consequently increased inter-tiller competition, under conditions of limited moisture supply, may be partially responsible for reduced grain set and hence occasionally lower yields (Woodruff, 1969). However, grain increases due to the hardening varied from 0 to 20% in different experiments. The variation in yield response is ascribed to the phenological stage at which RWC differences occurred, and to the transient effect of the RWC differences (loc. cit.).

Husain et al. (1968) found that presowing hardening increased the size of the grains by 15% in treated plants that were stressed at a late stage, but this was partially counteracted by the lower number of treated plants surviving to maturity in these treatments, so that there was no statistically significant effect on yield in these trials.

In Yugoslavia, pre-treated seeds of maize gave an average yield increase of 526 kg/ha; the pre-treatment decreased transpiration rate at tasseling (Pencic et al., 1966). In Israel, hardening pre-treatment of seed increased the resistance of leaves of sorghum to water loss, but had no effect on yield under conditions of severe drought (Jacoby & Oppenheimer, 1962).

Other methods of presowing "hardening" of seeds have also been investigated; solutions containing various inorganic salts, organic acids, mannitol, CCC, auxins, extracts from different plant tissues, etc. were used. Seed treatment with 0.09% solution of succinic acid, for 3 hours before sowing, was found to improve germination, promote plant growth and increase crop survival (Manohar & Mathur, 1966).

Presoaking of seeds of wheat in 3% solutions of NaCl and Na_2SO_4 gave quite considerable increases in yield in trials carried out in western Rajasthan (Yields of 1620 and 2326 kg per ha, respectively, as compared to 376 and 733 kg/ha for the untreated controls—Puntamkar et al., 1971). Field experiments in Azerbaidzan, under moderately saline conditions, with seeds soaked in a 0.2% $MgSO_4$ solution before sowing, resulted in the following yield increases: of seed cotton : 29.8%, of wheat : 15.3%, and of maize : 6.2% (Azizbekova, 1962).

In India, presowing exposure of seeds to gamma radiation (3000r) was found to induce drought tolerance in barley plants. Growth was improved and an active metabolism was maintained in plants, even under conditions causing wilting (Garg et al., 1972). Many other successful attempts to induce drought resistance by various presowing hardening treatments of seeds are reported in the literature (Commonwealth Agricultural Bureaux, 1971).

However, the favourable results from drought hardening obtained by certain authors were not confirmed by experiments carried out in the United States (Waisel, 1962), in Israel (Evenari, 1962; Jacoby & Oppenheimer, 1962); in Argentina (Jarvis & Jarvis, 1964) and in Australia (Philpotts, 1972).

The extremely variable results obtained from experiments on presowing drought hardening of wheat can be ascribed to (a) differences in the techniques of drought hardening used, (b) differences in the degree, duration of the drought, and the phenological stage at which it occurred (Woodruff, 1969), and (c) differences in varietal response (Salim & Todd, 1968).

For example, Evenari (1962) applied cyclic drought treatments from emergence onwards. If the premise on which the technique is based, namely that the resistance of plants to water stress is increased by a previous history of exposure to stress (Levitt, 1956) is correct, the cyclic treatments could not have been effective (Woodruff, 1969). It is quite possible that yield advantages due to the treatments would be apparent when the drought was not too severe, and be obliterated by extreme moisture stress. Differences in response can also be expected in accordance to the phenological stage at which the stress occurred, and the stress duration. Salim & Todd (1968) found that different varieties of the same species reacted differently to seed presowing treatments, both in character and degree of response, and therefore assumed that this may be one of the reasons of the contradictory reports.

Crop Productivity (Y) in Dryland Farming

THE PHYSIOLOGY OF YIELD

Maximum Dry Matter Production

The first prerequisite for high yields is a high production of total dry matter per unit area. Carbon compounds account for 80-90 per cent of the total dry matter produced by plants. Photosynthesis is the basic process for the building of organic substances by the plant, whereby sunlight provides the energy required for reducing carbon dioxide, with sugar as the end-product of the process. This sugar serves as 'building material' for all the other organic components of the plant. The amounts of dry matter produced will therefore depend on the effectiveness of photosynthesis of the crop and, furthermore, on plants whose vital activities are functioning efficiently.

The effectiveness of photosynthesis is dependent on: (1) a large and efficient assimilating area, (2) an adequate supply of solar energy and carbon dioxide, and (3) favourable environmental conditions. The total products of photosynthesis throughout the lifetime of the crop growing in given circumstances will depend on the size of the assimilating area, the efficiency with which it functions, and the length of the period during which it is active. Differences in productivity between cultivars will therefore depend to a large extent on inheritable characteristics of the structure and function of the organs involved in photosynthesis (Stoy, 1963).

A proportion of the organic substances produced by photosynthesis will be needed for the vital processes of the plant, and consumed—by respiration—by the plant itself. The respiration intensity depends on hereditary characteristics and on growing conditions. The total yield of dry matter will therefore be the total amount of dry matter produced, less the photosynthates used in respiration.

Finally, the manner in which the net dry matter produced is distributed among the different parts of the plant will determine the magnitude of the economic yield.

Assimilating Area

The leaves of a plant are normally its main organs of photosynthesis, and the total area of leaves per unit area of land surface, called leaf area index (LAI), has therefore been proposed by Watson (1947) as the best measure of the capacity of a crop for producing dry matter; this he called its productive capital.*

Variation in total leaf area (LA) of a plant may result from changes in leaf number or in leaf size. The number of leaves present at any particular time equals the total number of leaves produced minus the number of leaves that have been lost by abscission. Leaf number depends on the number of growing points, the length of time during which leaves are produced, the rate of leaf production during this period, and the length of life of the leaves. Leaf size is determined by the number and size of the cells of which the leaf is built, and is influenced by light, moisture regime, and the supply of nutrients.

Growth curve of leaf area index—optimum LAI

After germination, LAI increases very slowly at first, over a fairly long period; then follows a period of rapid expansion (Fig. 1.9). As LAI increases, light absorption and the rate of dry matter production increases, until the foliage becomes sufficiently dense to cause mutual shading. Then less light penetrates to the lower leaves, whose photosynthetic activity is therefore reduced. As shaded leaves respire about as actively as leaves receiving full sunlight, their contribution to the total assimilation pool of the crop becomes less or often negative. There is therefore an optimum LAI for maximum dry matter production, which is reached when the lowest leaves receive just sufficient light for photosynthesis to balance respiration—e.g. when the lower leaves are at the compensation point, and the canopy

---

* It would appear logical to include also the area of other green parts, such as leaf-sheaths and the ears of cereals. In these, the assimilating area of the ears provides about half the assimilates used in grain formation (Asana & Mani, 1949).

as a whole has reached maximum net assimilation. Below optimum LAI, light energy is not being fully intercepted; above optimum LAI, the leaf area is not being utilized at maximum efficiency.

Differences in optimum LAI depend on the light intensity (being higher under high light intensity) and on the manner in which light is intercepted by the crop canopy. This latter factor varies with crop species, and even between varieties of the same species. The light received by a crop with a large optimal LAI is spread over more leaf surface than is the case with a crop having a low value for optimal LAI; this results in a lower intensity of illumination for most leaves, at which photosynthetic efficiency is

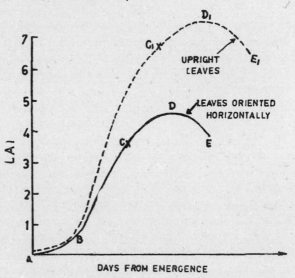

FIG. 1.9. Schematic presentation of growth-curve of leaf area index (LAI):
AB—period after emergence (LAIs increase slowly); BC & BC$_1$—period of rapid growth (steep increase in LAIs); C & C$_1$—optimum LAI, when lower leaves are at compensation point; D & D$_1$—maximum leaf area.

higher than with more intense illumination (Watson, 1967). For crops with horizontally oriented leaves, such as sesame, optimum LAI may be between 3 and 4. For crops with upright leaves, such as cereals, optimum LAI may be as high as 6 to 9 (Fig. 1.9). When LAI increases beyond the optimum, the lower leaves lose carbohydrates and will eventually die—usually long before the leaf canopy as a whole reaches the compensation point (Donald, 1961).

The rate of loss of the lower leaves increases as LAI increases, until a point is reached at which it equals the rate of production of new leaves; at this point LAI has become static, and leaf area is at its maximum. At this stage dry matter production is still increasing, though usually at a somewhat slower rate than at 'optimum LAI'. When LAI exceeds its optimum, many of the leaves of the lower levels will actually be 'parasitic' even under conditions of full light intensity. At the same time the formation of new top leaves is stimulated, as is stem elongation; in many crops this is conducive to excessive vegetative development at the expense, for example, of grain formation (Nichiporovic, 1966).

Effect of canopy structure on light interception

The proportion of incident light that is intercepted by the canopy does not depend on LAI alone, but also on the so-called 'architecture of the plant community' (Loomis *et al.*, 1967; Baker *et al.*, 1974). In a crop, the leaves are not isolated but are arranged in a canopy. The way they are arranged will affect the proportion of incident light that is intercepted by the crop canopy as a whole. The extinction coefficient (K) is a measure of the light intercepting efficiency of the leaf area (Wilson, 1969). Leaf characters of importance in this respect are: leaf angle, leaf area, continuity of leaf layers and randomness of dispersion of leaves (Donald, 1961).

Interrelationship between LAI and K

Under conditions of limited moisture supply which can support only a relatively low plant population per unit area, the LAI optimum is low and a high K is therefore advantageous in maximizing interception. By contrast, when moisture is not limiting, a low K becomes beneficial because it enables optimum LAI to be high. Under these conditions, photosynthetic efficiency of light utilization is optimal: at high LAI, a lower K ensures that the total light available is dispersed over a greater area of leaves, but the light is proportionally weaker. Photosynthetic efficiency of light utilization being greatest in weak light, this is a manifest advantage in improving dry matter production.

All these characters influencing K are controlled genetically, and could serve as a basis for breeding with the aim of increasing the optimum level of LAI. It has been stated that the high productivity of modern varieties of sugar beet, as compared with the ancestral wild beet, is due to a different disposition of the leaves. Instead of the rosette of the ancestral type, the upright leaves of the cultivated varieties enable a more efficient use of light (Watson, 1967). This aspect will be further considered in the discussion on breeding for high yielding potential in semiarid conditions (p. 61).

Biological and Economic Yields

We have discussed the ability of the plant to produce a high yield of carbohydrates. In certain crops, such as those produced for forage, the total dry matter production or biomass has economic significance; however, this is not the case with most cultivated crops. Generally, only a part of the crop is important to the farmer, the rest being either of inferior value (such as in the case of straw of cereals), or a nuisance to be disposed of (as in the case of stalks of cotton). It is the part of the biomass that is converted into the economic product, that has been called the 'economic yield' (Nichiporovic, 1960). The relationship of the economic yield to the total, or 'biological yield', is expressed as the 'coefficient of effectiveness' or 'harvest index'

(K), according to the equation:

$$Y_{biol} \times K = Y_{econ}.$$

A balance between the productive parts of the plant and the reserves which form the economic yield is essential. Experience has shown that a considerable increase in the yield of the economic product is usually dependent on an increase in the total dry matter produced. However, this is not an absolute relationship; indeed, in extreme cases, the opposite may be true. In cereals, high plant populations, which produce the greatest biomass (and are therefore the most efficient in utilizing radiant energy) may produce little or no grain because of excessive competition between the plants for light or for moisture.

In many cereals, most of the dry matter in the grain is produced by photosynthesis after the ears emerge. Grain yield therefore depends to a large extent on the photosynthetic activity of the parts of the plant that are still green after anthesis. In wheat, barley, and similar cereals, the photosynthetic activity of the ear, which is situated at the top of the stalk, makes a considerable contribution to grain formation (Rawson & Bremner, 1974). Practically all the dry matter of the grain is produced by the part of the shoot above the flag-leaf node; of this dry matter the ear contributes about 50 per cent in wheat (Asana & Mani, 1949) and up to 70 per cent in barley (Frey-Wyssling & Buttrose, 1959). Asana et al. (1958) have shown that the importance of photosynthesis in the head was greatest in dry environments which favoured the early senescence of the flag leaf. However, the size and longevity of these organs, as well as the number and potential size of the grains, are determined during the vegetative phase. The importance of the influence of the vegetative phase is demonstrated by the effect of yellow rust of wheat, which, when attacks the early leaves of wheat, causes a considerable decrease in the yields of total dry matter and of grain (Bunting & Drennan, 1966).

From the foregoing, it can be assumed that, provided LA before anthesis is adequate so as to allow the full genetic expression of kernel number and size, grain yield per plant in cereals should be proportional to the photosynthetic area above the flag-leaf node, assuming there are no marked differences in NAR between varieties. This hypothesis was tested on 120 varieties of wheat under green-house conditions by Simpson (1968), who found high, positive correlation coefficients between grain weight and the components of photosynthetic area above the flag-leaf node, both on per tiller and per plant bases. However, the author stresses that these findings, obtained under green-house conditions, require confirmation under field conditions.

The possibility has been raised that an increase in size of the storage organs (the economic yield) results from a stimulation in the productivity of photosynthesis or from a greater transfer of photosynthates from other organs of the plant to the storage organs and that, therefore, an increase in K is possible without a corresponding increase in Y_{biol} (Stoy, 1963). The latter possibility is illustrated by the following example:

Table 1.4. Ear/Shoot ratios of two varieties of barley
(Thorne, 1962)

Stage/Variety			Plumage-Archer	Kenia
Emergence	..	..	13.8	12
Anthesis	..	..	22.5	20
Maturity	..	..	128.0	150

The relative ear/shoot ratios of the two varieties of barley changed completely between emergence and maturity. As the absolute dry matter production values of the two varieties were similar, the assumption is justified that there exists a mechanism whereby the growing kernels are able to withdraw varying amounts of photosynthates from other parts of the plant. It is not known whether this is an active or a passive process, but it appears from the work of Mothes (1956) that certain substances, such as kinetin and benzimidazole, have a profound influence on the movement of nitrogen to different parts of the plant. There might therefore be an activating principle, produced by the rapidly growing parts of the plant, in amounts that are genetically controlled, which affects the above-mentioned process.

It is important that after the harvestable part has been initiated, all dry matter in excess of what is required for the maintenance of an efficient photosynthetic structure should be diverted to the economic part of the plant. In addition, the maximum possible of dry matter should be translocated from the non-harvestable parts of the plant to the economic product during the later stages of maturation.

The Components of Economic Yield

Attempts have been made to achieve better understanding of the economic yield of many crops, so as to provide criteria for management and breeding purposes, by breaking down yield into yield components.

A familiar formula for grain yield of cereals is:
$$Y = a \times b \times c \times d$$
in which $Y =$ grain yield per unit area,

$\quad$ a = number of plants per unit area,

$\quad$ b = number of fertile tillers per plant,

$\quad$ c = number of grains per ear, and

$\quad$ d = weight of the individual grain.

At first sight, an increase in one of the components on the right hand side of the equation should lead to an increase in yield. To understand why this is not necessarily so, requires an understanding of the influence of various components on yield, and the effect of crop management on each of them.

Tillering

The first genetically controlled component of yield is the number of ears or of fertile tillers per plant. The number of ears per unit area is a function of planting density, tillering and tiller survival; it is influenced by genotype and is amenable to agronomic practices. Grains per ear and weight per grain are functions of physiological processes of growth and development. The optimum number of ears per unit area is, of course, closely dependent on the soil moisture regime during the growing period of the crop. Most cereals have a considerable capacity to increase the number of tillers per plant, when sufficient space is available to the individual plant. An optimum number of ears per unit area can therefore be achieved in two different ways: by a low plant density compensated by an increased number of fertile tillers per plant, or by a high plant density which will keep the number of tillers per plant low. At first glance, the former approach appears to be the more rational: savings in seed can be achieved by it, and the plant will autoregulate the number of ears per unit area according to whether environmental conditions are favourable or not. In practice, however, this approach has a number of drawbacks. Thus a sparse stand is more susceptible than a dense one to weed infestation, and unfavourable conditions may reduce plant population below the point at which increased tillering can compensate for missing plants. The principal limitation, however, is that the tiller is not an independent unit: it is considerably influenced by other tillers produced on the same plant. There is therefore a great difference in principle, in whether the number of ears per unit area is derived from a large number of plants with a few fertile tillers each or from relatively few plants with abundant tillers. The following considerations seem most pertinent in this connection:

(a) The ear-bearing capacity of an individual tiller depends on the number of tillers per plant. A negative correlation is known to exist between tiller production and tiller survival, indicating the existence of a regulatory mechanism which keeps the rate of ear production per plant down on a determined level (Frankel, 1935). It has been shown that only tillers formed before a certain period in the life of a plant will produce ears (loc. cit.). Therefore, on the same plant, tillers appearing at a relatively late date will have less chance of producing ears. The final number of ears per unit area can therefore be achieved by increasing either tillering or the proportion of those tillers that survive and produce ears. There appears to be better justification to produce fewer tillers and increase the survival rate than *vice versa*.

In India, in field trials with 13 cultivars of rain-fed wheat, it was found that the main shoots contributed the major proportion of the crop production and that ears of tillers contributed very little to grain yield (Asana *et al.*, 1968).

(b) The primary tiller usually produces the largest ear, each successive ear-bearing tiller producing ears of decreasing size. The second and third ears are generally nearer in size to the first ear than are the subsequent ones to be formed. The tendency in recent years has therefore been to breed for varieties with sparse tillering capacity but higher ear-producing tiller survival, and to adjust plant density so as to decrease dependency on tillering as a means of achieving optimum density. However, retaining a limited ability to tiller (2-3 tillers per plant) enables auto-adjustment of the plant according to environmental conditions and compensation for missing plants, without adversely affecting the ultimate yield. It has also been shown that one-ear plants may produce smaller ears than two-ear plants—mainly because the former are frequently weak or diseased (Frankel, 1935).

(c) Finally, it has been found that tillering is undesirable in dry areas because favourable conditions during tillering may establish many tillers that use up moisture rapidly and cause the plant to suffer from moisture stress later in the season. Thrifty plants with few tillers tend to yield more in dry years (Hurd, 1971).

Number of grains per ear and weight of the individual grain

Increased carbohydrate production will contribute to increased yields only when the total storage capacity of the plant is adequate, in other words, an adequate 'sink' is required, that is capable of receiving the carbohydrates in excess of the metabolic needs of the cereal plants. It has been shown in non-cereals that there is a feedback effect, in the sense that the size of the 'sink' affects the production and the movement of carbohydrates in the plant. It is therefore possible that in cereals also, too few grains, or unsatisfactory grain development, may restrict the photosynthesis of the shoot (Thorne, 1966). Consequently, the number of grains per ear, is important (Rawson & Bremner, 1974). As the maximum yield that can be achieved under given environmental conditions has a ceiling that cannot be surpassed, an increase in the number of seeds must be accompanied by a decrease in the weight of the individual grain, and *vice versa*.

Generally speaking, factors acting early in the season mainly influence the grain number, while the size of grain is affected by the factors acting after anthesis. The significance of these facts for plant breeding will be discussed later.

Crop Improvement for Efficient Water Use

Little systematic work for the specific objective of breeding crop varieties for drought resistance has been carried out. Drought resistance is the result of many, frequently independent, morphological and physiological characters, whose interaction has not yet been sufficiently elucidated. Most physiological components of resistance are polygenic, and general analysis of the heredity of this complex has not yet been achieved.

Drought itself is not a uniform concept; the relation of the plant is different to atmospheric drought and to soil moisture deficiency, and will also depend on the stage of development at which drought occurs.

Atmospheric Drought

This is caused by low air humidity, frequently accompanied by hot dry winds. It may occur even under conditions of relatively high soil-moisture (Aamodt & Johnston, 1936). For example, hot dry winds occurring at the time of earing of wheat may completely kill the young ears, irrespective of the amount of water available in the soil. Actually, plants that have grown continuously under favourable soil moisture conditions, are the most susceptible to atmospheric drought. (Also see the chapters on "Effect of humidity on crop production" and "Effect of wind and their amelioration" in this volume.)

Soil Drought

This occurs when soil moisture supply lags behind evapotranspiration: it is usually gradual and progressive. Plants can therefore adjust, at least partially, to the increased moisture stress.

Plant Adaptations to Growth in Dry Regions

Levitt (1972) distinguishes between two basic ways in which plants can grow and survive in dry habitat: (a) escaping drought, and (b) actual drought resistance.

Escaping Drought

Evading the period of drought is the simplest means of adaptation of plants to dry conditions. Many desert plants, the so-called ephemerals germinate at the beginning of the rainy season and have an extremely short growing period, which is confined to the rainy period. Between germination and seed maturity, as few as five (Polunin, 1960) to six (Kassas, 1966) weeks may suffice. These plants have no mechanism for overcoming moisture stress and are therefore not drought resistant.

The presence of germination inhibitors in such seeds serves as an 'internal rainguage', which permits germination only after an amount of precipitation has fallen that will be sufficient to remove the inhibitor (Went, 1952).

Early maturity

In cultivated crops, the ability of a cultivar to achieve maturity before the soil dries out is the main adaptation to growth in a dry region. However, only very few crops have such a short growing season, that they can be considered similar to the 'ephemerals' in escaping drought. One example is of certain varieties of millets that can produce mature seeds within 60 days from germination. Even the earliest maturing varieties of most crops have longer growing periods and will usually experience one or more periods of moisture stress during their lifetime. While their "earliness" reduces the number and the time of incidence of the moisture stress periods in relation to the phenology of the plants, and is therefore an important characteristic; it does not ensure their escaping drought completely as do the real ephemerals. They therefore need, and usually have, actual drought resistance attributes.

Drought Resistance

Plants that cannot escape periods of drought can adapt to these conditions essentially in two ways:

(*a*) *Avoiding stress*

Stress avoidance is the ability to maintain a favourable water balance and turgidity even when exposed to drought conditions, thereby avoiding stress and its consequences. Stress avoidance is mainly due to morphological-anatomical characteristics, which themselves are the consequence of the physiological processes induced by drought (Levitt, 1972). These xeromorphic characteristics are quantitative and may vary according to the environmental conditions.

A favourable water balance under drought conditions can be achieved either by: (i) conserving water, by restricting transpiration before or as soon as stress is experienced (the so-called water savers); or, (ii) accelerating water uptake sufficiently, so as to replenish the lost water (water spenders).

The mechanisms for conserving water—(1) *Stomatal mechanisms:* Stomata of different species vary widely in their normal behaviour and range from staying open continuously to remaining closed continuously. Many cereals open their stomata only during a short time in the early morning and remain closed during the rest of the day. There are however differences in this respect between varieties of the same crop, as shown by the following examples: in two varieties of oats, the one more resistant to

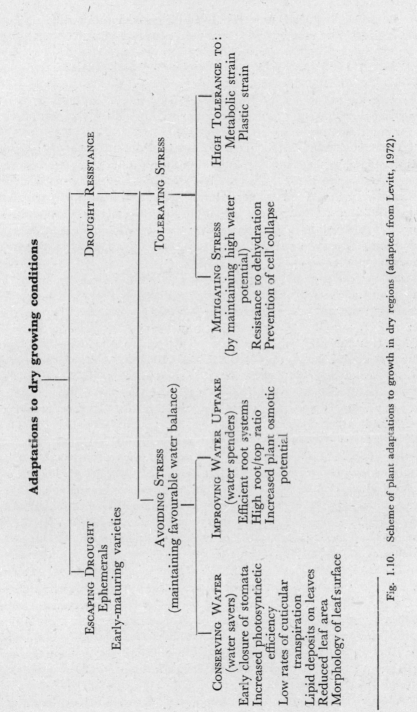

Fig. 1.10. Scheme of plant adaptations to growth in dry regions (adapted from Levitt, 1972).

drought opened its stomata more rapidly in the early morning when moisture stress is at its minimum and photosynthesis can proceed with the least loss of water (Stocker, 1960). An interesting observation made in the course of trials on the effects of soil moisture regime on different wheat varieties, was that the stomata of a semidwarf variety remained open throughout the day, while those of the tall variety were open for only a few morning hours, remaining closed thereafter even under favourable conditions of soil moisture and transpiration (Shimshi & Ephrat, 1970).

The relative transpiration (T/E) of a drought sensitive variety of ground-nuts was found to be generally greater than that of a more drought resistant variety (Gautreau, 1970). These differences were however apparent only in water-stressed plants, indicating that the mechanism of stomatal regulation of water loss is not operative above a certain threshold level of water content. However, mechanisms of conserving water based on the closure of stomata will inevitably lead to reduced photosynthesis and may lead to "drought induced starvation injury" (Levitt, 1972).

(2) *Increased photosynthetic efficiency:* One possibility for overcoming the limitations on photosynthesis imposed by stomatal closure as a means for increasing resistance to loss of water by transpiration would be a higher rate of CO_2 assimilation for a given stomatal opening (Hatch & Slack, 1970). A number of important crop plants (maize, sugarcane, sorghum, proso, foxtail and finger millets) (Hatch *et al.*, 1967) as well as certain forage species, Bermuda grass (*Cynodon dactylon*), Sudan grass, Bahia grass (*Paspalum notatum*), Rhodes grass, (*Chloris gayana*) (Murata & Iyama, 1963) and certain *Atriplex* spp., fix most of the CO_2 into the C_4 of malic and aspartic acids; the so-called C_4-dicarboxylic acid (C_4) pathway. They have a primary carboxylating enzyme which has both a high potential activity and a high affinity for CO_2. With such an enzyme, high rates of fixation of CO_2 can be maintained with much lower internal concentrations of CO_2 and with relatively restricted stomatal opening (Loomis *et al.*, 1971). The species using the C_4 pathway have a high rate of CO_2 assimilation for a given stomatal opening, higher temperature and light optima for photosynthesis (El-Sharkawy *et al.*, 1968), and higher light saturated rates of apparent photosynthesis (El-Sharkawy & Hesketh, 1965).

There appears to exist a threshold value for the concentration of CO_2 in the air, below which no assimilation takes place. Most plants in a closed system will reduce the CO_2 concentration in the air to a minimum value between 50 and 100 ppm. For these plants, not more than two-third of the CO_2 in the atmosphere is available for photosynthesis. There are however striking differences in this respect between species; both maize and sugarcane are capable of reducing the concentration of CO_2 to less than 10 ppm (Moss, 1962).

A close relationship has been established between the photosynthetic pathway used by most cultivated crops, the so-called Calvin cycle, and a light dependent release of CO_2, called photorespiration,which does not occur in plants with the C_4 cycle (Jackson & Volk, 1970). Photorespiration contributes to the lower rates of apparent photosynthesis of the Calvin cycle species (Downton & Tregunna, 1968). It has been found that when photorespiration is inhibited by special treatments, the net photosynthesis of these species has been enhanced by as much as 50% (Downes & Hesketh, 1968). Moreover, the photosynthates are translocated very rapidly from leaves of the C_4 species (Moss & Rasmussen, 1969), thereby preventing the slowdown of photosynthesis resulting from the accumulation of assimilates in the leaves. For these reasons, the C_4 species have higher growth potentials and more efficient use of water as compared with plants that use the Calvin cycle under the same moisture regime. (Also see the chapter on "Photorespiration in relation to crop yield" by Dr. A. Goldsworthy in this volume.)

Another photosynthetic process which reduces water loss without a concomitant reduction in photosynthesis is found in a number of succulent plants, which keep their stomata closed during most of the day. These plants have the so-called Crassulacean acid metabolism (CAM) which enables them to fix large amounts of CO_2 as organic acids at night and convert it into carbohydrate during the day. As the primary assimilation of CO_2 occurs at night, the lower temperatures prevailing limit the amount of water transpired for a given stomatal opening. The pineapple, for example, which has the CAM type of photosynthesis, produces about the same amount of dry matter per year as sugarcane, but often uses only 10 to 20% as much water (Ekern, 1965). With the exception of the pineapple and certain *Agave* spp. grown for fibre and paper pulp, CAM plants have not been exploited agriculturally (Loomis *et al.*, 1971).

Plants having the C_4-dicarboxylic acid pathway belong to a taxa whose predominant natural distribution is in areas having intense solar radiation, and hot daytime temperatures—mainly in the drier parts of these areas, in particular those with a regular severe drought for a part of the year (Loomis *et al.*, 1971). Similarly, CAM plants are probably all nonhalophytic succulents and generally adapted to arid environments (loc. cit.). Because of anatomical adaptations of C_4 species and their frequent exposure to drought in their natural habitats, it has been suggested that these species are less sensitive to periods of desiccation than species not possessing this pathway (Laetsch, 1968).

There is no doubt that the C_4 photosynthetic pathway is extremely efficient; sugarcane and maize are among the most highly productive crops when grown under favourable conditions of moisture regime, nutrient supply etc. The biochemical, physiological and structural features shared by the C_4 species are apparently adaptations to high light intensity, by increased resistance to photosynthetic photo-saturation (Laetsch, 1968).

Whether the C_4 pathway can be considered as a mechanism for drought resistance appears however to be much more doubtful. If we compare two crops with the same C_4 mechanism, such as maize and sorghum, the considerable differences in actual drought resistance exhibited by the two indicate that the resistance is due to factors other than the actual photosynthetic process. Many types of millets, another group of C_4 crops, are able to produce reasonable yields with a limited amount of rainfall because of their extremely short growing periods; their ability to survive drought under conditions of severe moisture stress, even for short periods, is far lower than that of a typical C_3 crop such as barley. This view is confirmed by Boyer (1970) who studied rates of net photosynthesis in maize (a C_4 plant) and soybean (a Calvin-cycle plant). Rates of photosynthesis in maize were inhibited whenever leaf water potentials dropped below -3.5 bars, while photosynthesis of soybean remained unaffected by desiccation until leaf water potentials were below -11 bars. Soybeans were also less subject to death of tissue during severe drought than was maize. On the basis of these findings, soybeans appeared better able to withstand drought than maize. However, the photosynthetic rate of maize was higher than that of soybean over most of the desiccation range. It appears therefore that the main characteristic of C_4 and CAM crops is their high water use efficiency and not drought resistance *per se*.

(3) *Low rates of cuticular transpiration:* The typical example is the cactus.

(4) *Decreasing transpiration* by a deposit of lipids on the surface of the leaves on exposure to moderate drought. This has been shown to occur in soybeans (Levitt, 1972).

(5) *Reduced leaf area:* The principal means of reducing water loss of xeromorphic plants is their ability to reduce their transpiring surface. Apart from the common means of keeping the aerial parts small, perhaps the simplest form of this reduction of the transpiring surface is the rolling or curling of leaves at times of water stress, a characteristic phenomenon exhibited by many grasses. The rolling of leaves has been shown to reduce transpiration by almost 55 per cent in semiarid conditions, and by 75 per cent in desert xerophytes (Stalfelt, 1956).

(6) *Leaf surface:* Various morphological characteristics of leaves help to reduce the transpiration rate and may affect survival of plants under drought conditions: leaves with thick cuticle, a waxy surface and with the presence of spines, etc., are common and effective. In certain species, drought stimulates the production of epidermal hairs (Shields, 1958). The mere presence of pubescence on the leaves is no longer considered as an advantage in reducing transpiration (Kramer, 1959), unless it be through increasing their albedo.

(7) *Stomatal frequency and location:* A smaller number of stomata can

retard the development of water deficits. In certain species, the stomata are located in depressions or cavities in the leaves, which is a feature that can further reduce transpiration by limiting the impingement of air currents.

(8) *Effect of awns:* Awned varieties of wheat predominate in the drier and warmer regions, and have been found to yield better than awnless ones, especially under drought conditions, though there are exceptions (Grundbacher, 1963). Awns have chloroplasts and stomata and so can photosynthesize; it has been found that the contribution of the awns to the total dry weight of the kernels was 12% of that by the entire plant (McDonough & Gauch, 1959).

Accelerating water uptake—(1) *Efficient root systems:* The root systems of drought resistant plants are characterized by a wide variety of apparent adaptations. These are responses to such predominant soil conditions as the duration of soil dryness and the depth that is normally wetted, the presence and nature of soil constituents and the degree of soil salinity. Plants become adapted to dry conditions mainly by developing an extensive root system, rather than by structural modifications of the roots (Shields, 1958). The concept "extensive root system" also includes, in addition to growth in depth and lateral growth, the density of roots per unit volume of soil and the number of secondary hair roots (Oppenheimer, 1960).

There are considerable differences between cultivated plants in the extent, depth, and efficiency, of their root system. Sorghum has nearly twice as many small branch roots per unit length of main roots as has maize and it is assumed that this is one of the main reasons for its greater drought resistance. Another adaptation of some xerophytes is their speedy response to a rewetting of the soil by the rapid formation of secondary rootlets ('rain roots') which may appear only two to three hours after a fall of rain (Evenari, 1962). An important characteristic of certain cultivated plants is their ability to respond quickly to fluctuations in moisture content by having roots that grow rapidly towards sources of available moisture. It has been shown experimentally that drought resistance of varieties of spring wheat is related to the rapidity of growth of the primary roots (Aamodt & Johnston, 1936).

Plants are also known to differ with respect to the ability of their root systems to penetrate relatively dry soils. Oats, wheat and barley show little penetration of the soil, at or below wilting point, while two range grasses— Side-oats grama (*Bouteloua curtipendula*) and Love-grass (*Eragrostis eragrostis*) penetrated the soil quite extensively (Salim *et al.*, 1965).

(2) *High root-to-top ratio (R/T):* A high root-to-top ratio is a very effective means of adaptation of plants to dry conditions (Killian & Lemée, 1956), as under such conditions the growth rate of the roots considerably exceeds that of the shoots. The transpiring surface is thereby reduced, while the root system of the individual plant obtains its water from a large volume of soil. Simonis (1952) has shown that an increased root : top ratio may

actually result in a greater amount of total dry weight of plants grown under
dry conditions as compared to similar ones grown with full moisture.

(3) *Differences in osmotic potential of the plants:* Levitt (1958) has
calculated that a difference of 0.5% in the soil moisture content that induces
permanent wilting, could supply a plant with enough water to keep it alive
for 6 days; this could mean, in certain cases the difference between survival
and death.

(4) *Conversion of water spenders to water savers:* Because of their increased
water absorption, water spenders are characterized by very high rates of
transpiration. However, as soon as the absorption rate becomes insufficient
to keep up with water loss, the water spenders generally develop some of the
characteristics of the water savers (Levitt, 1972).

(*b*) *Drought tolerance*

When the plant is actually submitted to low water potentials it can show
drought tolerance by either mitigating the actual stresses induced by the
moisture deficiencies, or by showing a high degree of tolerance to these stresses.

Mitigating stress: Adaptations to drought based on mitigating the effects
of stress permit the plants to maintain a high internal water potential in
spite of drought conditions. They therefore are able to maintain cell turgor
and growth, avoid secondary drought induced stress, as well as direct or
indirect metabolic injury due to dehydration (Levitt, 1972).

(1) *Resistance to dehydration:* The simplest method of avoiding drought
induced damage is by resisting dehydration—preferably to the extent of
maintaining turgor, and at least by avoiding cell collapse after loss of turgor
(Levitt, 1972).

Together with the morphological adaptation already mentioned, a
higher internal osmotic pressure obtained by accumulating sufficient
solutes helps to prevent dangerous internal desiccation, and apparently
makes the plasma itself more drought enduring (Vaadia & Waisel, 1967).
The cells can retain their turgor and therefore can continue to grow when
exposed to drought stress.

When plants are grown in their natural environments, their osmotic
potentials tend to be characteristic for each ecological group: most crop
plants have values of 10-20 atm, xerophytic plants commonly have values
of 30-40 atm, halophytes may reach values of 100 or more atm.

(2) *Prevention of leaf collapse:* In many instances the principal effect
of leaf adaptation to dry conditions, such as thick cell walls, is to prevent
wilting or collapse of the leaf, rather than to ensure reduced water loss
(Kramer, 1959). Indeed the palisade type of mesophyll actually favours
higher transpiration (Shields, 1958). This explains why xeromorphic
types of leaves frequently transpire more, when amply supplied with water,
than mesomorphic types (Shields, 1958; Kramer, 1959), and thus make

possible an efficient use of water during the short periods of wet conditions which are typical for dry environments. As soon as the soil moisture-level again becomes critical, the stomata close and the morphological adaptations to reduced water supply mentioned above, become operative.

Tolerating stress—(1) *Resistance to metabolic strain:* The greater the elastic dehydration strain*, the greater the danger of a resulting plastic metabolic strain. When dehydration occurs, there are mechanisms for tolerating an accompanying plastic metabolic strain.

(i) *Starvation:* The greater the dehydration a plant can tolerate and still keep its stomata open the lower will be its dehydration compensation point**. This kind of drought tolerance will be due to the specific ability of the guard cells to remain turgid even when the leaf cells are wilted, and is possibly due to an increase in the solutes of the guard cells (Levitt, 1972). However, crop plants generally possess only a very modest degree of starvation avoidance, and in all probability an ability to maintain stomata open at a greater degree of dehydration would do more harm than good. Not only injury due to a higher transpiration rate would be more likely, but photosynthesis would still slow down and stop, notwithstanding continued CO_2 uptake, because of the slowdown of translocation of the assimilates (loc. cit.).

Plants that drastically reduce their metabolic activity below their hydration compensation point will have low carbohydrate needs and therefore a greater tolerance to low net assimilation rates than do plants that are without this mechanism. This may be one reason for the high drought resistance of succulents (loc. cit.).

(ii) *Protein loss:* The *avoidance of protein loss* under drought conditions is the net result of two processes: a decreased rate of protein breakdown or an increased rate of synthesis. Young leaves are more resistant to drought than older leaves and this is ascribed to their greater protein content (Mothes, 1956). In drought resistant plants, the net loss of RNA is prevented and the plant is able to continue to synthesize proteins (Chen *et al.*, 1968). In tests with varieties of winter wheat, for example, water stress caused a greater decrease in RNA content in a nonresistant variety than in the resistant variety (Stutte & Todd, 1967).

Protein breakdown may result in an accumulation of products to a toxic level. A mechanism for decreasing the toxicity would then increase *tolerance to protein loss.* This might be an explanation for the accumulation of proline that appears to be associated with drought tolerance (Levitt, 1972).

(2) *Avoidance or tolerance of direct drought-induced plastic strain:* Some

---

* Cell dehydration is elastic and completely reversible up to a point, beyond which it is plastic, irreversible and therefore injurious (Levitt, 1972).

** This is the water potential at which rates of photosynthetic CO_2 absorption and respiratory CO_2 evolution are equal, so that net photosynthesis equals zero.

higher plants may show little restriction of transpiration during drought and can become air dry without suffering permanent injury. Grama grass, for example, may lose 98.3% of its free water without injury (Oppenheimer, 1960). Exposure to a sublethal stress may cause an increase in resistance so that the plant is able to survive an otherwise lethal stress. This has led to the developing of methods for increasing hardiness of crop plants.

There are great differences between different plant organs in their ability to withstand desiccation. Seeds that are filled with good reserves but have no vacuole can survive very long dry periods, often of many years. Buds of higher plants also have no vacuole, and are very resistant to desiccation. Certain plants survive a degree of desiccation that causes the death of their leaves, as the buds on the stems remain alive and resume growth when the drought ends.

In many species of perennial plants, the above-ground parts die off at the onset of the hot dry season and the underground parts, such as rhizomes, bulbs, corms, and tubers, remain alive but dormant (Vegis, 1963).

Heat Resistance

In arid lands, dryness and high temperatures are generally associated with each other. Because of the high net radiation and the little water that is available for evapotranspiration, resistance to heat by the plant plays a very large role (Emberger & Lemée, 1962). Growth of plants ceases at below-lethal temperatures; the longer the plants are exposed to high temperatures, the longer it takes them to recommence growth (Levitt, 1972). The resistance of plants to heat is accordingly just as relevant to their adaptation to arid conditions as their resistance to drought. When the plant has an ample supply of water, its metabolism may be adversely affected by excessively high air or soil surface temperatures, that may eventually cause the death of the more susceptible species.

The simplest kind of metabolic injury due to heat is starvation, because of the higher optimum temperature for respiration than for photosynthesis. The temperature at which respiration and photosynthesis are equally rapid is called the *temperature compensation point* (Levitt, 1972). When plant temperatures rise above the compensation point the reserves are depleted, and if the temperature stress continued, ultimately death due to starvation will result. Injury may also be due to the production of toxic substances: injury to seedlings of Bajra (*Pennisetum typhoides*) as a result of exposure to 48 °C for 12-24 hours has been attributed to the appreciable quantities of ammonia-N formed in the plants (Lahiri & Singh, 1969).

It is assumed that at certain temperatures, specific essential enzymatic reactions are completely inhibited. This limits or prevents the elaboration of certain metabolic products that are essential to the growth of plants. If, for each plant, it were possible to ascertain what specific metabolic step is affected by high temperatures, it might be possible, by an appropriate intervention, to improve plant productivity under high temperatures (Kurtz, 1958).

Heat may cause the breakdown of proteins. This was shown to be the case in 3-week old plants of Bajra growing under favourable soil moisture conditions, when exposed to 48 °C for durations up to 24 hours (Lahiri & Singh, 1969). Heat stress during seed maturation may affect germinability, either negatively or favourably, depending on the stage of maturation at which the stress occurred: germination of freshly harvested barley seed was reduced by heat stress 7-10 days after awn emergence, and was increased by the same degree of stress 3 weeks after awn emergence (Khan & Laude, 1969).

According to Soviet workers (Petinov & Molotkovsky, 1962), the protective mechanism of heat resistant plant is based on the regulation of the respiration process. Under the influence of excessive heat, protein formation is seriously affected, leading to excessive formation and accumulation of HN_3, which is toxic to plant tissues. Heat resistant plants react by the accelerated production of organic acids during the respiratory process; these organic acids bind HN_3 in the form of salts, thereby minimizing the effects of heat. The researchers found that foliar zinc sprays increased the heat resistance of plants, because zinc activates certain enzymes and stimulates oxidation reactions in vegetative cells.

BASIC BREEDING OBJECTIVES FOR RAIN-FED CROP PRODUCTION UNDER SEMIARID CONDITIONS

Drought resistance can be defined in a number of ways, particularly in terms of the ability of plants to (1) survive under drought conditions, (2) endure drought without injury, and (3) be efficient in their use of water.

Survival under drought conditions

Typically xerophytic plants have frequently adapted themselves to arid conditions by developing survival mechanisms, of which the most prominent is usually a reduced transpiring surface resulting in dwarfed plants with very limited total leaf surface. Survival is therefore achieved at the expense of productivity. However, the farmer is not concerned with the survival of the species and varieties he grows; in case of crop failure he can always buy a new supply of seeds from a commercial source, he is concerned rather with the productivity of his crops. Many of the typical xerophytic characteristics are therefore not, a priori, necessarily desirable in cultivars to be grown under conditions of limited water supply.

Kaul (1969) assessed the drought resistance under field conditions in Saskatchewan (Canada) of wheat varieties and found consistently significant differences between some varieties and their water potential and osmotic pressure values. However, no consistent positive or negative relationship between water status and yield could be demonstrated. Conversely, varieties, that did not differ in water potential or osmotic pressure values, showed striking differences in productivity: the author postulates that under conditions of restricted water supply, a delicate balance needs to be maintained between water flow in the plant and water stress. Presumably, wheat varieties, when grown under semiarid conditions, differ in their ability to balance water flow and water stress optimally, either because they close their stomata at too low stress levels, or maintain too high transpiration rates, thus inducing too high stress levels.

In general, no satisfactory physiological, anatomical, or morphological characteristics have yet been defined which could serve as reliable criteria in selecting for drought resistance.

Nevertheless, many attempts have been made to use xerophytic characters as indices of drought resistance for breeding purposes, the osmotic pressure of germinating seeds (Buchinger, 1930), viscosity (Schmidt et al., 1940), resistance to artificial atmospheric drought and heat in drought chambers (Aamodt & Johnston, 1936), etc. Most of these tests have given inconsistent correlations with yields under drought. This inconsistency is, according to Asana (1957), probably due to the fact that desiccation tests assess only the capacity of tissues to endure dehydration but they do not indicate the relation of yield to dehydration of tissues. These tests could therefore serve at best for screening strains that are more or less capable of enduring drought, but without any direct relation to their productive ability.

Ability to endure drought without injury

A more modern school of thought believes that the only true criterion of drought resistance is the ability to endure drought without injury. In this sense, drought resistance is defined as "the ability of plants to adapt to the effect of drought and to grow, develop, and produce normally under drought conditions, because of a number of properties acquired in the process of evolution under the influence of environmental conditions and natural selection" (Henckel, 1964).

The 'ratio of the yield under dry conditions to the yield under optimal conditions of water supply' is considered as a valuable criterion of this concept of drought resistance (Levitt, 1951). However, two examples will suffice to show that this criterion of drought resistance can be misleading in practice.

Harrington (1935), in varietal trials with wheat in semiarid Saskatchewan, found that the variety Marquis gave more constant yields over a period of ten years and was less affected by drought than the variety Reliance. According to the above criterion, Marquis could be considered the less drought susceptible variety of the two (Ashton, 1948). Yet during five of the seasons, which had a favourable moisture supply, Reliance out-yielded Marquis by an average of 645 kg/ha; during dry seasons, the difference in favour of Reliance was reduced to an average of 41 kg/ha. The advantage for the whole period was clearly with Reliance; indeed this variety which is apparently more susceptible to drought, but which has a higher yielding potential, produced for the ten-year period 3430 kg/ha more than Marquis (Harrington, 1935). Even in drought years, the yield of Reliance was not lower than that of Marquis.

In trials with three varieties of barley submitted to moisture stress at various stages of growth, the variety that was most tolerant to stress gave the lowest yields and did not use water more efficiently than the other varieties (Wells & Dubetz, 1966).

In these examples, if the farmer has chosen the 'more drought resistant variety', he would have been the loser. A further point that has to be consi-dered is the great variability in rainfall from season to season that character-izes all dry regions—indeed, the greater the aridity is, the greater will be this variability.

A farmer will in all probability be better off if he grows varieties that have the yielding potential to give good returns in the good seasons, even if they are relatively disappointing in drought years. In general, the varieties with typical xeromorphic characters will also give poor yields in drought seasons, without being able to make up for this deficiency in seasons with favourable moisture conditions.

Of course, there exist adaptations to an inadequate or fluctuating mois-ture supply which *do not* affect productivity adversely and these, of course, can and should serve as important characters, mainly for the selection of suitable parents in breeding programmes. These aspects will be later treated in more detail.

Adapted varieties or varieties with wide adaptation

One of the traditional tenets of plant breeding is the importance of 'adapting varieties to the specific conditions of each region'. As a result, enormous efforts have been expended the world over in breeding varieties that are adapted to narrow ecological niches. This approach is, however, basically unsound—at least so far as arid regions are concerned. A variety with very specific adaptations is limited in its ability to adjust to changing conditions. But arid climates are characterized by their great variability— variability within a region and variability from one season to another.

It appears almost self-evident that the objective of the breeder, at least for dry regions, should therefore be to obtain varieties with the maximum ability to adjust to a wide range of ecological conditions.

In uniform varietal trials carried out in 18 localities in the Near East under the auspices of the International Wheat Programme, the variety Pitic 62 bred in Mexico, yielded close to 2275 kg/ha—about 650 kg/ha more than the average of the 25 varieties tested, and 1300 kg/ha more than the average national yields in that area.   Three varieties: Pitic 62, Penjamo 62, and Nainari 60, gave the highest yeilds in 14 out of the 18 locations. Pitic 62 gave the highest yield in 9 locations (Stakman *et al.*, 1967).   The trials were located between 35 °S and 17 °N latitude and at elevations from about 170 m below sea-level to 1700 m above sea-level.   Soil fertility ranged from low to high; temperature, length of day, and incidence of pests and diseases, varied considerably; at some locations the wheat was rain-fed and at others it was irrigated.   Obviously, the three outstanding varieties, and in particular Pitic 62, had a very wide adaptability.

An important characteristic of varieties with wide adaptation is their stability.   In contrast to most varieties with specific disease resistance, which commonly breaks down after ten to fifteen years of commercial production because new strains of the disease organism have evolved, a variety such as Florence × Aurore wheat, that is outstandingly successful in all the North African and Middle Eastern countries, has maintained its superiority unimpaired for over thirty years.

Fortunately, in most of the important crops, one or more varieties that perform extremely well over a wide area have 'happened' in the course of breeding work in different parts of the world.   Examples are varieties such as Florence × Aurore wheat, and more recently some of the Mexican semi-dwarf wheats, and Rs 610 hybrid sorghum, that are very successful over wide areas in semiarid lands.   Of course, the term 'universal' is a misnomer; but it is accepted for denoting varieties with a very wide range of adaptability.

An example of the fallacy of the requirement to breed varieties with very specific adaptation is the early introduction and breeding work on wheat which was carried out in Palestine by the present author (Arnon, 1961).   By tradition, almost every district in Palestine grew a standard local variety of wheat.   These 'land' varieties were remarkably uniform in their respective types, probably as a result of mass selection and adaptation over a very long period.   In view of this centuries-old tradition, it was originally thought that the breeding programme should aim at creating improved varieties adapted to the specific conditions prevailing in various districts.   In consequence, a large number of selections and crosses were made among native varieties, and a comprehensive introduction programme was initiated.   However, after a few years, it became apparent that the views on which this programme was based were not well-founded.

In the course of the first six years of work on this crop in Palestine, 51 experiments were carried out at 11 locations, from Dan in the north to Negba in the south, each location being typical of a certain district.   The annual rainfall recorded during these trials ranged from 300 to 940 mm;

the varieties sown experienced drought, waterlogging and dry hot winds, the so-called 'khamsins'. The experimental sites were located at altitudes varying from 100 m below to 500 m above sea-level, and the soil types on which the experiments were carried out ranged from loose to heavy soil. These trials were therefore representative of most conditions that were likely to be encountered in the country by wheat, and the generalizations drawn from the data could be considered well-founded.

The surprise result of these trials was to find that it was not the local, 'adapted' varieties that gave the best overall results, but that one or two varieties were outstanding in almost all trials, notwithstanding the great range of environmental conditions encountered.

In the light of this work, the objectives of the breeding programme were revised. The development of special varieties for specific local conditions at district level was abandoned as an objective, and efforts were directed towards the development of varieties with as wide adaptation as possible. This approach was justified subsequently by the results obtained from introduction and breeding programmes with such other field crops as barley, maize, sorghum, cotton and sugar-beets. In all these crops it was found that breeding designed to adapt varieties to suit each of the numerous ecological niches in the country was a waste of effort; practically in every case it was found that the outstanding varieties were those which excelled in most districts and most seasons. In fact, outstanding varieties of all the crops mentioned showed not only countrywide adaptation but also regional adaptation, and proved successful in most countries in the Mediterranean region. Apparently these outstanding varieties combine high yielding ability with a great degree of adaptability.

The basic genetic reasons for the superiority of varieties with a wide range of adaptability are not known. These varieties appear to be equipped with physiological and/or structural buffers that enable them to adjust to changes in environment (Grafius, 1956).

SPECIFIC BREEDING OBJECTIVES FOR RAIN-FED CROP PRODUCTION UNDER SEMIARID CONDITIONS

From the foregoing it is clear that the emphasis in selecting or breeding varieties for growing in semiarid regions, in which moisture deficiencies occur in some seasons, or during part of the growing period, should be on achieving a high efficiency of water use, as expressed in the ratio of yield produced per unit of water.

High yielding potential

Basically, this will first and foremost be a question of selecting for high yielding potential under the semiarid conditions, under which they are to be grown. An enormous effort has been expended on this objective; it is, however, doubtful whether much of this effort was specifically directed toward high productivity *per se*. Varieties have been selected that are disease resistant, early maturing, or possessed other important characters influencing yield. Efforts have also been made to isolate the most productive individuals from within big populations, but without direct knowledge of the genetic and physiological factors responsible. Impressive results have been achieved by these methods, but further major breakthroughs will require new approaches and a more basic understanding of the factors involved.

The ultimate yield of a crop is determined by the interaction of its genetic characteristics with the environment in which it is grown and the management practices to which it is subjected. In the warm, dry regions, the combination of favourable temperatures and the large amount of sunshine make possible very high levels of crop production, if moisture supply is adequate and crop management efficient.

When growth is not limited by light, temperature, water, or nutrients, the remaining limiting factor will be the genetic characteristics of the plant, which should enable it to make full and efficient use of the available growth factors. Breeding for high yields can follow either of the two pathways: eliminating characters that limit productivity or cause it to fluctuate from season to season, or combining characters that increase the potential productivity of the plant. The two pathways are not in conflict with each other—on the contrary, they are mutually complementary. Examples of the first approach are breeding for drought resistance and for resistance to diseases and pests.

In the following paragraphs, we are concerned with breeding aimed directly at high yielding ability.

The Genetic Approach

We have seen that breeding for drought resistance, with the objective of ensuring maximum returns to the farmer, in the present state of our knowledge, can only be based on yielding ability under a fairly wide range of varying moisture regimes, both during a given season, and between seasons.

There are, however no genes for yield *per se*, and therefore there can be no heretability of yield. There are genes determining only the components of yield (Grafius, 1959). According to Asana (1957), varietal differences in yield can be accounted for on the basis of such characters as branch number, flower number, fruit number and its size.

A very large number of genes are involved, making the genetic analysis of the sum total of effects of yield components, as a basis for scientific breeding, extremely complicated. It is also always very difficult to distinguish between the effects of the various genotypes, as these are frequently masked or modified by the environment.

The planned maximum accumulation of genes for productivity into a single genotype, capable of transmitting this complex intact to its progenies, is not feasible at the present stage of our knowledge. This does not, however, preclude using "yielding ability" as the basic criteria for breeding for drought resistance, as suggested by Hurd (1971). The method he proposes is "designed to accumulate plus genes that are plus in a semiarid climate". Hurd stresses the need for careful selection of parents well-adapted to dry growing conditions and with different genotypic backgrounds, large segregating populations and early generation yield tests.

The key to his approach is that the selection for desirable combination can only be done by "selecting for yield under stress". Hurd insists that "in breeding for drought resistance it is more important to breed for maximum yield in the most adverse year rather than the highest yield in a good year". The fallacy of this approach has already been pointed out (pp. 58-59), and it is the author's opinion that the criterion that will give the farmer the highest overall return is 'breeding for maximum average yield over a number of seasons, good and bad'.

Heterosis: The great success of commercial hybrids in increasing the productivity of maize and, hence, the efficiency of water use by this crop, is well-known (Wittwer, 1974). One of the most important developments in plant breeding of recent times has been the extension of the use of heterosis (hybrid vigour) to many other crops, by the use of male sterility characteristics. In Texas, the best hybrid sorghum, in dryland tests, yielded on an average 39.5 per cent more than the best-adapted open-pollinated strain; under irrigation, the yield advantage of the hybrid was 27 per cent (King & Collier, 1961).

In Israel, the best sorghum hybrids out-yielded the best-adapted open-pollinated variety on an average by 20 to 28 per cent under dryland conditions, by 67 per cent with supplemental irrigation, and by 103 per cent with full irrigation. Their advantages were, therefore, considerable under conditions of both limited moisture supply and optimal soil moisture. Their ability to utilize the additional moisture—mainly for grain production was far greater than that of the best self-pollinated varieties (Arnon & Blum, 1964).

The Physiological Approach

One of the principal tools of the plant breeder has always been the choice of appropriate parents for crossing programmes, in which the objective is to breed new genotypes, combining the favourable characters of the parents. A serious limitation of this method has been the lack of knowledge of the physiological processes on which crop productivity depends making the choice of the parents a haphazard process. In recent years, great efforts have been made to clarify the physiological basis of yield and to draw practical conclusions that would be applicable to defining breeding objectives. These aspects have been discussed by Rawson and Bremner (1974) in "Crop Physiology" edited by the present editor.

An understanding of plant characters which are related to efficient utilization of light could serve as a guideline for defining model plants for breeding work. For example, in barley varietal trials it was found that the three highest yielding varieties had narrow upright leaves which permitted light to penetrate deep into the leaf canopy, while the three low yielding varieties had wide, drooping leaves. Approximately 300 lines of wheat, oats, and barley, were evaluated visually on the basis of the angle of incidence and width of the leaves. With few exceptions, it was possible to select the high yielding varieties on this basis alone (Tanner & Gardner, 1965) (Fig. 1.11).

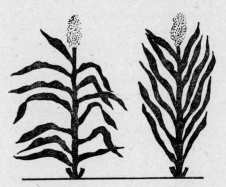

FIG. 1.11. Contrasting plant types: *Left*—plant with drooping leaves (see width); *Right*—plant with same number of relatively erect leaves.

It should also be possible to develop new varieties which have higher specific net assimilation rates, even when submitted for certain periods to water stress. Photorespiration does not appear to be essential for productivity of crop plants; elimination or reduction of photorespiration in plants having the Calvin cycle could result in sustained higher rates of photosynthesis (Loomis *et al.*, 1971). (Also see the chapter on "Photorespiration in relation to crop yield" by Dr. A. Goldsworthy in this volume.)

There is also considerable opportunity for selection for variation in light-saturated net photosynthesis. The latter exhibits more variation and correlates better with yield than light-limited net photosynthesis (Loomis *et al.*, 1971). Work along these lines has already been initiated in a number of crops (loc. cit.). Large intervarietal differences of 10 to 200% of net photosynthesis, at light saturation, has been observed in maize (Heichel & Musgrave, 1969).

The ability of the stomata in certain crops to resume normal functioning rapidly after a period of water stress has already been mentioned. The drought resistance of sorghum and certain varieties of maize and groundnuts is attributed, at least partly, to the ability of the stomata to resume their normal functioning rapidly after a period of waters tress (May & Milthorpe, 1962).

Differences in the depth, extent and efficiency of the rooting system, may enable plants to withdraw the maximum possible amount of water from a limited supply in the soil. Pelissier, which is reported to be the most drought resistant cultivar of wheat grown in western Canada, has a very extensive root system, and only a very small proportion is in the surface 0-10 cm. By the time the upper soil layer has dried out, Pelissier has been found to have established an extensive root system deep in the soil and was thus less affected by drought than were other varieties (Hurd, 1971).

Bagga *et al.* (1970) attributed the consistently higher yields of two varieties in wheat varietal trials under dryland conditions in India, to their deeper root growth and therefore better moisture exploitation from deeper soil zones.

ADDITIONAL BREEDING OBJECTIVES

A number of additional breeding objectives can be useful in improving yielding ability under conditions of limited water supply, and thereby improving the yield/water ratio.

Phenology

In most crops, the adverse effects of drought vary in intensity according to the stage of growth. It is therefore important that the critical stage of development of the crop, when it is most susceptible to drought, should not coincide with the period when drought usually occurs. In cereals, for example, adverse moisture conditions during the period of earing, pollination, and seed formation, have disastrous effects on grain yield. Adjusting the growth rhythm of the crop to fit the precipitation pattern that is normal for the region is, therefore, an important breeding objective. Varieties with the desirable phenological characters can be selected or bred. Usually, though not always, this will entail breeding for early maturity, as the rainy season is commonly short in the dry regions.

For example, in trials in Australia, earliness in plant maturity appeared to be by far the most important characteristic of drought tolerant varieties. The highest yields of grain were obtained from wheat varieties which produced ears early in the growing season, because these varieties avoided the late season drought. The water use was also less for these varieties (Derera *et al.*, 1969). Chinoy (1960) found that the greater susceptibility of late flowering varieties to drought during their shooting and flowering stages was not due to any hereditary differences in their drought resistance. The increase in susceptibility of progressively later flowering varieties was the result of progressively higher temperatures prevailing at the flowering and the concomitant more rapid drying of the soil at this critical stage.

However, there is generally an inverse relationship between early maturity and yielding potential, so that care must be taken not to shorten the growing period more than is absolutely essential. For example, in a recent study of a number of wheat varieties in India, it was found that varieties whose earing occurred 60 to 100 days after emergence gave, on the whole, better yields than earlier varieties of 60 to 70 days duration (Bagga *et al.*, 1970). The advantage of the later varieties was attributed to their ability to exploit moisture from deeper soil zones. There are even cases, as in certain regions of the Soviet Union, in which late maturity is an advantage, as dry periods occur relatively early in the growing season (Fuchs & Rosenstiel, 1958).

The Ratio of Economic to Biological Yield

There exist two different, though not necessarily antagonistic, pathways that can be followed in breeding for high yields. These are:
(a) increasing the total production of dry matter (Y_{biol}), which has already been dealt with, and
(b) increasing the proportion of the total dry matter produced that is accumulated in the parts of the plant which are of economic importance (Y_{econ}), e.g. by increasing the coefficient of effectiveness (K) (see pp. 42-43).

Plant breeding efforts aimed at increasing the coefficient of effectiveness (K) have shown that it is definitely possible to increase the ratio of economic yield to biological yield. The most striking success achieved in this respect in recent years is probably the development of the semidwarf wheat varieties, which characteristically have short straw, fewer leaves, and a very large ear. This is illustrated by a few examples. In a trial carried out in Israel, comparing the standard wheat variety, Florence × Aurore, with a semidwarf variety which produced the same biological yield, the following results were obtained (Ephrat *et al.*, 1964):

Table 1.5.　Biological and economic yields of two wheat varieties (kg/ha)

				Y_{biol}	K	Y_{econ}
Florence × Aurore	..	..	..	9500	0.43	4130
N 67 (dwarf variety)	..	..	..	9350	0.65	6220

In fertilizer experiments on clay loam soils in Pantnagar (India), during three years, comparing the effects of N-fertilizers on tall and semidwarf wheats, it was found that in the best treatments, the yields of the dwarf wheats were double than those of ten tall wheats, whereas straw yields were almost equal for both types (Sharma *et al.*, 1970).

The main advantage of dryland wheats, in a semiarid region of Australia, was found to reside in their ability to produce larger ears, a higher proportion of ear weight at anthesis, to set more grain and to have a higher ratio of grain weight to post-anthesis leaf area than was the case for the conventional wheat types. There was little difference between the varieties in their total dry matter production at anthesis (Syme, 1969).

Another example is that of the recently introduced sorghum hybrids. Thus in trials with sorghum in Israel, the grain weight of outstanding hybrids equalled that of the vegetative material, while in the best open-pollinated variety—Martin—grain production constituted only one-third of the total above-ground production of the plant (Arnon & Blum, 1964).

When the biological yield is limited by external conditions, this does not always imply that the economic yield will be reduced, as surplus carbohydrate may move to the grain (Thorne, 1966). There may also be conditions in which an increase in K, accompanied by an overall decrease in potential biological yield, may be desirable—e.g., under conditions of drought, a crop with less vegetative growth than others will be less affected by drought. Thus, cereal types with very short straw and large ears may be more efficient under relatively arid conditions than types having the opposite characteristics.

Improving the Components of Yield

When we consider that the economic yield of grain in cereals, for example, is largely dependent on the number of ear-bearing tillers per plant, number of grains per ear and the weight of the individual grain, it is easy to understand that in the past, a considerable amount of attention has been paid by plant breeders to these factors in the hope that yields could be increased by combining in a single genotype, a combination of components such as increased tillering capacity, large ears, heavier grain, etc.

Tillering capacity

An important agronomic practice, enabling adaptation to limited soil moisture supply, is the adjustment of plant population to the expected moisture regime. This is practically impossible to achieve with crop varieties that have a too strong tendency to tiller. Tillering may be profuse in the early stages of growth, when soil moisture is still adequate, producing an excessive vegetative cover and a number of ears which cannot be brought to maturity because of the early depletion of the limited moisture supply. Breeding for limited tillering can therefore be very useful, in crops such as wheat, barley, sorghum, etc., for growing under dry conditions.

Number of grains per ear and grain size

In breeding wheat for drought resistance, it was found that when soil moisture was adequate, the yield component which had the greatest effect was number of ears per unit area; under conditions of moisture stress the grain number per ear and, occasionally, average grain weight, have as much effect as the number of ears. Asana (1962) therefore suggested grain-number per ear and 100-kernel weight as criteria for selecting varieties for dryland production.

Attempts to obtain high yielding varieties by combining high tillering capacity, large ears, and large kernels, into a single genotype, have generally not been successful. Experience has shown that an inverse correlation exists among the yield components, and that the highest yielding cereal varieties are not those with extremely large heads or heavy kernels, but usually those in which these components attain only average size.

From the lack of achievements in breeding work resulting from the use of yield components as criteria for selection of desirable prototypes, it should not be assumed that no worthwhile significance can be attached to the traditional yield components. It is true that yields cannot be increased beyond an upper limit by manipulating individual yield components; but much can be done to approach this limit by breeding for yield components that are well-balanced and adjusted to the environmental conditions in which the crop is to be grown.

MANAGEMENT PRACTICES FOR INCREASING YIELDS

It can be stated as a general rule that all factors which increase plant production do so without markedly increasing the amount of evapo-transpiration, and will, therefore, improve water use efficiency. Hence, we can conclude that good crop management is a precondition for the most efficient use of water by the crops.

Fertilizer Use

The general physiological effects of plant nutrients, with the exception of nutrition × moisture supply interactions, are not specific to rain-fed crops grown in dry regions and, therefore, do not need to be treated here. In arid agriculture, the basic problem in plant nutrition is that of adjusting fertilizer applications to the moisture regime under which the plants are expected to grow. Even under conditions of limited moisture, nutrient deficiencies will reduce WUE and, therefore, a moderate amount of suitable fertilizers, adjusted to the soil moisture level, may increase WUE. If, however, the fertilizers increase water use excessively in the early stages of growth, so that severe water stress occurs at the critical stages, the opposite effect will result.

Basically, the problem is one of nutrient soil moisture interactions. At one end of the spectrum, under conditions of sparse rainfall, is the need to limit fertilizer application to rates which will not promote more growth than the available soil moisture can sustain until harvest—or in other words, to prevent upsetting the very delicate and critical balance between vegetative and reproductive growth under conditions of limited moisture. At the other end of the spectrum, when rainfall is favourable, the farmer's aim is to ensure a level of nutrient supply that will enable the plant to make full and efficient use of the favourable moisture conditions which it enjoys.

The dynamics of response to fertilizers in dry regions

In the non-irrigated soils of the arid regions, the weathering of the soil and the leaching of soluble salts are minimal. Nitrate content of the soil depends mainly on the amount of plant cover present. As this is usually very sparse, the decomposition of organic debris cannot provide large amounts of available nitrogen.

Most arid and semiarid soils originally have large reserves of potassium and these are generally adequate for rain-fed cropping. By contrast, the soil phosphorus reserves have generally been considerably depleted by cropping and the amounts of available phosphorus are usually inadequate for satisfactory yields.

The nutrient status of these soils, and hence the response of crops to fertilizers, does not remain static. Changes occur—either in the direction of continued depletion or of a build-up of soil fertility—according to the cropping system and the management practices adopted. Both these factors are dependent, in turn, on the moisture regime under which the crops are grown.

In the semiarid areas, in which rainfall can suffice for arable crop production, land which has previously laid undisturbed under scrub or other vegetation usually has sufficient natural fertility to produce cereal or forage crops for a more or less prolonged period without the addition of fertilizers. Eventually, however, yields begin to decline.

It is suggested that after a build-up of phosphorus reserves has been achieved during the early growth period, relatively small applications of superphosphate to each cereal crop at sowing time are sufficient. These supply an easily available source of phosphorus when the root system of the plants is still small, thereby stimulating the crop at an early stage and securing good establishment and better root penetration. The graph in Fig. 1.12 illustrates dramatically the residual value of phosphorus applied in previous years, showing that it is possible to build-up reserves that provide adequate P independently of current application. Experience in Israel shows that, once the initial severe phosphorus deficiency has been overcome, a single application of phosphorus to the leguminous crop in a three course rotation (legume-wheat-sorghum) is sufficient to supply all the needs of the cereal crops in the rotation. Nitrogenous fertilization continues to be effective on rain-grown cereals, even under conditions of improved fertility. The optimum time of application of nitrogen varies, as it is dependent on rainfall distribution.

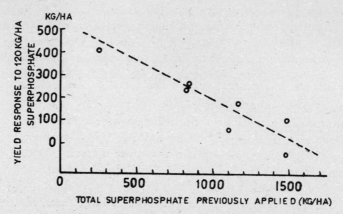

Fig. 1.12. Effect of prior applications of superphosphate on the response by wheat to a current application of phosphorus in western Australia (after Donald, 1954).

Micronutrient deficiencies are frequent in the alkaline and calcareous soils which are prevalent in many of the dry regions, and in which the availability of certain elements, such as boron, iron and manganese, is relatively low (Jewitt, 1966). In India, appreciable increases in yields have been obtained by applications of magnesium, zinc, molybdenum and iron in crops like sorghum and bajra (*Pennisetum typhoides*) (Misra, 1964a).

Soil moisture and response to fertilizers

Soil moisture affects the efficiency of fertilizer use mainly in two ways: by improving the uptake of nutrients and by increasing dry matter production. When considering the effect of soil moisture level on the uptake of nutrients by plants, indirect effects of soil moisture must also be allowed for—such as the effects on the physiological activities of the plant, on soil aeration, and on the osmotic pressure of the soil solution (Brown *et al.*, 1960). The effects of soil moisture on the availability and uptake of macro- and micronutrients have been discussed by Dr. E. A. Hurd and Dr. E. D. Spratt in this volume.

Effect of fertilization on ET and soil water depletion

Under dry, subhumid conditions, it was found that applications of N-fertilizer which substantially increased yields of winter wheat, also increased total water use (Brown, 1972) and daily water use. The depletion of stored soil moisture was also accelerated, as shown in Table 1.6.

Without N, soil water extraction was largely limited to the upper 91 cm; while with N, wheat plants extracted water to double this depth. N increased water use efficiency (WUE) by an average of 56% (Brown, 1972). By contrast, in spring wheat, depth of extraction of soil water is generally limited to a depth of about 120 cm, presumably because of the shorter growing period involved, as compared to winter wheat.

Table 1.6. Effect of N-fertilization on ET and soil water depletion
(Brown, 1972)

N rate (kg/ha)	Yield (kg/ha)	ET (mm)	Extraction of stored soil water (mm)	Amount of stored water remaining at maturity (mm)	WUE
0	1,610	221	61	180	71
67	3,090	272	112	132	114
268	3,630	315	155	96	115

In field experiments with spring-sown dwarf wheat varieties in the Northern Plains, U.S.A., it was found that N-fertilization increased total seasonal ET by 14-28%, according to season. The applied N had little effect on the depth of water extraction; the increased water uptake due to N-fertilization came from the same rooting depths as for non-fertilized wheat. Each year, most of the increase in water use caused by applied N occurred during the tillering to heading stage, and coincided with the period of peak vegetative growth. Total dry matter production by N-fertilized wheat from jointing to heading was two to three times as great as with no N application. However, the greater depletion of soil water reserves by the N-fertilized wheat between tillering and heading, caused a reduction in ET from heading to harvest, in seasons in which water use after tillering was appreciably greater than precipitation, and the soil water reserves were inadequate to meet the excess water requirement. When this was the case, applied N did not increase grain yields. When available moisture was sufficient to maintain ET by the N-fertilized crop between heading and harvest, yields were markedly increased by fertilization (Bond et al., 1971).

Brag (1972) has clearly shown that the transpiration rate of two species, wheat and peas, is affected by potassium both species showing the same pattern of reaction. Low potassium concentrations in the nutrient solution during a long growth period produce plants with a high transpiration rate. Short-term experiments, investigating the effects on transpiration rate of K concentration in the nutrient solution, showed that transpiration rate could be regulated by varied K concentrations. Adding KCl to K deficient wheat plants, resulted in a decrease in the transpiration rate of up to 50 per cent within two hours. This effect was ascribed to changes in stomatal aperture.

In peas, plants with high amounts of K had the lowest transpiration rates, and stomatal aperture was found to be correlated with K concentration in the leaves.   It is still not clear whether the decrease in transpiration rate is due to a slower water uptake produced by changes in the osmotic potential of the nutrient solution, to changes in the permeability of the root membranes, or to some other influences on the stomata by the ions (Brag, 1972).

Relationships between rainfall and fertilizer practice

Where rainfall is too limited for arable cropping, the land is generally used to support a very extensive pastoral economy.   Even in developed countries such as Australia, fertilizers are not commonly used under these conditions.

A special problem arises on the fringe of the semiarid regions in which rainfall is normally low and droughts are frequent.   In these regions the effects of fertilizers under varied conditions of precipitation have not been studied as intensively as in the humid regions; many of the fertilizer experiments that have been carried out in semiarid regions are not sufficiently reliable for predicting crop response to fertilizers.   The results of the fertilizer trials are erratic, and often fail to correlate with chemical soil tests. Therefore, no clear-cut answer has yet been formulated to the question of whether and when fertilizer application is justified under conditions of low moisture supply.

The following example gives an indication of the difficulties with which farmers and researchers are faced in deciding on fertilizer policy under these conditions.   In one season, yields of wheat were increased significantly by fertilizer application in Oklahoma in seven locations out of eight; in the following season, which was much drier, a yield increase with fertilizer application was obtained in only one location out of these eight (Eck & Stewart, 1954).

Basically, there are profitable responses to P on P-deficient soils, *even* when yields are very low because of lack of moisture, but this is *not* the case with N (Russell, 1967) (Fig. 1.13).

Long-term weather records may be helpful for calculating the *probability* of a good or a dry season, so that the farmer may know what are the 'odds' of fertilizer applications being profitable.   Less guess-work is involved when the crop is not dependent exclusively on precipitation that falls during the growing season.   In research carried out in Kansas on sorghum, for example, it was found that the greater the depth of soil moisture occurring at seeding time, the greater was the effect of nitrogen on yields (Orazem & Herring, 1958).   The depth of soil moisture at seeding time can be determined without difficulty, and this information will, therefore, reduce the amount of uncertainty involved in deciding on whether to apply fertilizers, and if this decision is in the affirmative, at what rates.

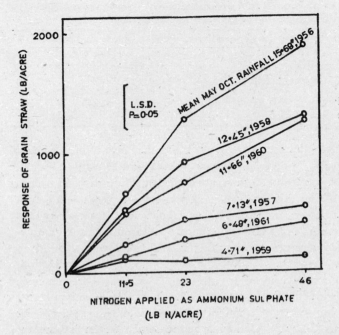

FIG. 1.13. Mean yearly response of wheat (grain +straw) to fertilizers in relation to precipitation (mean of four locations during the seasons 1956-61) (Russell, 1967) (by courtesy of Aust. J. exp. Agric. & An. Husb.).

Under the distinctive climatic pattern of the dry regions, with their relatively limited and erratic rainfall and long drought periods, certain patterns of fertilizer use have been evolved. Farmers have frequently been disappointed, under conditions of limited moisture supply, by crop response to fertilizers; in certain cases their use was actually detrimental to yields. Under such conditions, an extremely cautious use of fertilizers should be made; even progressive farmers usually employ limited rates of application. However, when judiciously applied, fertilizers make possible increased utilization of the limited moisture available to plants.

Minimum precipitation required

When soil moisture is definitely inadequate, crops may fail to respond to fertilizers, or the response may be too small to be economic. The minimum amount of rainfall needed to ensure a fairly satisfactory yield level of grain crops which, in turn, makes possible an economic return on the fertilizers applied, depends on many factors, such as the efficiency of the rainfall, moisture reserves in the soil, preceding crop history, temperature, evaporation, etc. An empirical and somewhat arbitrary figure is 300 mm of rainfall in a winter rainfall region, combined with soil moisture reserves from fallow or else a moisture conserving crop, and about 500 mm in a summer rainfall area.

Table 1.7.   **Relation of rainfall and crop sequence to response of winter grain to nitrogen fertilization (Martin & Mikkelsen, 1960)**

| | Per cent of tests responding to nitrogen with seasonal rainfall of | | |
	250 mm	250-300 mm	300 mm
Annual barley	20	46	96
Fallow barley	30	35	56
Fallow wheat	31	50	56
Average	*27*	*44*	*67*

The results presented in Table 1.7 show clearly the effect of both rainfall and fallow on the crops' response to fertilizers in a winter rainfall region. With less than 250 mm of rainfall, moisture is the only limiting factor, and less than one-third of the tests showed a response to nitrogen—and even then fertilization was not profitable. When rainfall was in excess of 300 mm, grain yields were almost increased under continuous cropping; however, when the crops were grown after fallow, which allowed a build-up of available nitrogen, not more than half the tests responded to fertilization, notwithstanding ample soil moisture.

In experiments with rain-fed groundnuts in a low rainfall area of India, WUE was slightly improved by moderate amounts of nitrogen (20 kg N/ha) and phosphorus (30 kg P/ha), during two seasons. In the first season, the rainfall was only 186.8 mm (plus 75.1 mm stored water in 1 m depth of soil) and the second season 357.3 mm (plus 67.2 mm of stored water) (Bhan & Misra, 1970b).

In Mysore State (India), hybrid sorghum growing under conditions of summer rainfall during the growing period of 508-590 mm, responded well to N applications. The best results were obtained with a dose of 67 kg N/ha, applied in two equal rates, at sowing and one month later. The average yields for two years were 2906 kg/ha without fertilizers and 5110 kg/ha with the optimum N treatment (Lingegowda *et al.*, 1971). In a 2-year field trial at Agra (India), it was found that applying half the amount of fertilizers as a top-dressing to the soil and half sprayed on the foliage gave higher yields and a higher protein content of the grain of wheat than when the full amount was top-dressed (Sharma *et al.*, 1966).

Timing and balanced fertilizer application

Fertilizers, especially nitrogen, may stimulate early growth and thereby exhaust the soil moisture supply before the period of maximum water requirement of the crop, as shown in the following example: applications of N and P on sowing to rain-fed groundnuts in India, increased root growth, improved the root/shoot ratio, gave higher ET values and increased total dry matter production but caused a considerable decrease in yields of pods. The rapid increase in root development and leaf area apparently caused depletion of the limited soil moisture supply early in the growing period (Bhan & Misra, 1970a).

Occasionally, early stimulation of crop growth may enable a more rapid and deeper penetration of the roots into the subsoil, so that the fertilized crop is able to draw more effectively on the subsoil reserve of water that has accumulated during the previous period of fallow; or possibly the stimulation may favour a more active root system with greater water extraction ability (Smith, 1954). Phosphorus has been found to improve yields of wheat under conditions of relatively low rainfall, provided the drought is not too severe, by improving early growth and vigour, favouring increased root development, and advancing the maturity of the crop (Norum, 1963).

In India, it was found that applications of N and P to groundnuts grown under conditions of limited moisture increased root length, root number, root weight and nodule weight when compared with unfertilized plants. Separate applications of N and P were less effective. When soil moisture was deficient, the plants fertilized with P, however, showed a greater ability to take up available moisture than those fertilized with N (Bhan & Misra, 1970a).

Except in cases in which drought is so severe as to prevent normal absorption of nutrients, P is usually beneficial in improving drought resistance. For example, in a year of extreme drought, on a phosphate deficient red-brown soil, yields of wheat were extremely low, and yet response to phosphoric fertilizers, in relative terms, was very striking, as is shown in Table 1.8.

Table 1.8. Effect of phosphorus application on yield of wheat grown under drought conditions (Piper & Vries, 1964)

Treatments				Yield (kg/ha)	Percentage of control
Control	..	..	..	81	100
12.4 kg P_2O_5/ha	..	..	..	236	289
24.8 kg P_2O_5/ha	..	..	..	466	574

Nitrogen can also be effective under conditions of limited moisture. In Nebraska, wheat fertilized with nitrogen was found to remove 25-50 mm more water from the 2 m soil profile than did the non-fertilized wheat. The additional soil moisture was removed at tensions greater than 15 atmospheres, presumably as a result of the increased root growth stimulated by the nitrogen (Ramig & Rhoades, 1963).

Generally speaking, a balanced nutrient supply is beneficial even under conditions of limited rainfall, as it actually enables the crop to make more efficient use of the limited soil moisture available. By applying only a phosphoric fertilizer at the time of sowing (or to the preceding crop) and withholding the nitrogenous fertilizer until the cereal crop, by its appearance, shows the need for a stimulant, excessive initial growth can be avoided. This was found to be the case in Nebraska, where water use efficiency in rain-fed grain crops was increased by an average of 29 per cent, when nitrogen application was delayed so as to coincide with the period of maximum requirement. Excessive vegetative development of the young crop was thereby avoided, and maximum efficiency in water utilization resulted (Olson *et al.*, 1964a). When nitrogenous fertilizers are applied in this way, they can actually advance crop maturity by as much as 10-14 days and unfavourable crop reactions occur, when excessive and unbalanced nitrogenous fertilizer is applied.

In trials in India, N application in sorghum markedly advanced the time of earing resulting in earlier maturity. The earlier emergence of the ears was ascribed to a more rapid development of the leaves, resulting in an earlier optimum LAI, with parallel acceleration of photosynthesis, enabling an earlier initiation of the reproductive phase (Shrivastava & Singh, 1970). However, when the rainfall is insufficient to ensure a satisfactory crop, the additional yield resulting from the fertilizer may be too small to be economically justified.

The use of fertilizers on forage crops is less critical than on grain crops under dry conditions. Their growing period is shorter, and any stimulation of growth improves yields—irrespective of when the stimulation occurs. Many of the forage crops are legumes, to which only phosphoric fertilizers need be applied. As has already been pointed out, except in cases in which drought is so severe as to prevent normal absorption of the nutrients, phosphorus is usually beneficial in improving drought resistance.

In soils which are deficient in potassium, which are the exception in semiarid regions, it was found that large responses to fertilizer potassium are obtained when rainfall is low. The responses to fertilizer decreased as rainfall increased, presumably because of increased availability of native soil K (Paauw, 1958).

Crops grown on stored soil moisture

In regions where a summer drought alternates with a winter rainfall season, it is possible to grow summer crops whose entire moisture supply is provided by water stored in the soil during the rainy season. Typical crops which give fairly good yields under these conditions are sorghums, cotton, sesame and cucurbits.

Under these conditions, crops do not usually respond to fertilizers that are applied to them directly. Although early growth may be somewhat stimulated by such application, under the conditions of limited moisture supply, this is no advantage. The lack of sustained response is probably due to the fact that the fertilizers are applied in the top-soil. By the time the plants have reached a stage of development when nutrient requirements are maximal, this soil layer has completely dried up, and the nutrients contained in it are virtually ineffective. This view is supported by the fact that crops grown on stored soil moisture give very poor yields on low fertility soils, but react favourably to a fertility build-up resulting from fertilizing preceding crops.

The situation is different when a crop that is dependent on stored water also receives a limited amount of rainfall, as in summer rainfall areas. The results of 66 trials on wheat, grown in North Dakota on non-fallow land, show that the response to fertilizers increased with increasing amounts of stored water and of rainfall occurring during the growing season. On the basis of these results, fertilizer recommendations are being made by regions, according to the probability of rainfall during the growing season, and for each region they are related to the amount of stored moisture at the time of sowing (Weiser, 1960). For example, in Nebraska, it is recommended to apply 25 kg N/ha for every 75 mm available water in 2 m soil profile (Tisdale & Nelson, 1966).

Trends: The general tendency, even in advanced agriculture, to be extremely cautious in fertilizer use has already been mentioned. In the dry regions of developed countries, the general trend is for a more and more widespread use of fertilizers, even where it was formerly taken for granted that fertilizer use was detrimental (Viets, 1967). This is due, in part, to nutrient deficiencies becoming more acute, as the original native fertility of the soil is gradually depleted through continuous cropping.

However, the main factor in promoting this trend: efforts to improve moisture storage and reduce moisture losses by crop rotation, improved tillage practices and chemical weed control, result in a more favourable moisture regime which increases crop responses to fertilizers.

Planting Dates

In arid and semiarid regions, the choice of an appropriate planting date may have a considerable effect on water use efficiency (in relation to economic yield) by ensuring that the pattern of growth of the crop is adjusted to the pattern of precipitation or to available soil moisture.

Adapting sowing dates to precipitation patterns

It has already been pointed out that a semiarid climate is usually a mixed climate, in which a completely dry season alternates with a fairly moist season. The humid season of the semiarid regions can be subdivided into three principal periods (Cochemé & Franquin, 1967) (Fig. 1.14).

(a) *The pre-humid period,* during which, precipitation is markedly inferior to potential evapotranspiration. This period begins with the first rain

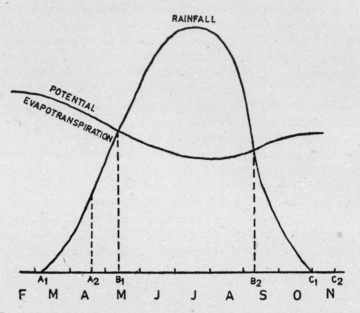

Fig. 1.14. Subdivisions of the cropping season in a semiarid climate: A_1—beginning of rainy season; A_2—beginning of transition period (precipitation = half of PET); B_1—end of transition period, beginning of humid period; B_2—end of humid period; C_1—end of rainy season; C_2—exhaustion of moisture reserves in the soil (from Cochemé & Franquin, 1967) (by courtesy of Food & Agric. Org., United Nations).

(point A_1 in the figure) and ends when precipitation equals potential evapotranspiration (point B_1). This period is normally the time for sowing in dry soil if it precedes the first effective rainfall, or in a moist soil if unusually early rains occur. Sowing in dry soil of course involves the risk that the rainfall, while sufficing to cause germination, may fail to provide sufficient moisture for emergence and continued growth. Only crops that can effectively withstand a number of periods of desiccation between the beginning of germination and full emergence—such as wheat and barley, can be sown under these conditions. The risk involved in sowing in dry soil is considered to be justified by the possibility of increased yields, due to the likelihood of a longer growing season and more effective use of precipitation early in the season.

Where the risk of sowing in dry soil is too great, or in regions in which the soil is too dry and hard for tillage with primitive equipments, the prehumid period is mostly devoted to the preparation of a seed-bed if appropriate equipment is available. The tillage operations in this case become easier as one approaches point B_1; but once this point is passed, they become increasingly difficult and even impossible in heavy soils as the soils become too wet for effective tillage.

At point A_2 on the graph, precipitation equals one-third to one-half of potential evapotranspiration (depending on albedo). This is the normal mean evaporation rate of a bare soil (or one with a sparse vegetative cover) which is only occasionally moistened by rainfall. In principle, this is the time when germination and emergence become possible, and from this period onwards real evapotranspiration will increase exponentially, together with leaf area, until the crop shades the soil entirely. Ideally, this should coincide with point B_1 on the graph.

(b) *The humid period,* during which, total precipitation is in excess of potential evapotranspiration and, therefore, potential and real evapotranspiration are equal. The 'humid' period does not coincide with the rainy season: it begins later and ends earlier. During the humid period, the excess of precipitation over real evapotranspiration, provided it is not lost as runoff, is stored in the soil. If precipitation is sufficient, the entire root zone is saturated to field capacity, and excellent moisture conditions for crop production and especially for crop maturation during the third (c) period will prevail. Excess precipitation will either cause runoff or drain beyond the root zone, or both.

The relative positions of B_2 on the graph, and the dates of flowering (or earing for cereals), have a considerable impact on potential yield levels. The longer the humid period, and the later it ends, the greater will be the prospects for the maturation under favourable conditions of a larger number of fruits per unit area. However, the greater the coincidence of flowering period and peak-moisture supply, the greater will be the danger of epidemic diseases.

(c) *The post-humid period,* in which, total precipitation is inferior to potential evapotranspiration; at the end of the rainy period, real evapotranspiration continues until the reserves of water in the soil formed during the humid period are exhausted.

Crop production may also be possible during the completely dry period, provided the land remains fallow during the humid season, and precipitation has been sufficient to fill the soil reservoir to the depth of the root zone. Adapted crops can then be sown during the dry season, and even produce high yields without receiving a drop of rainwater throughout their growing period.

The date of sowing may affect yields, and water use efficiency. In trials with hybrid sorghum, grown entirely on stored soil moisture, Blum (1972) found that early planting, under conditions of limited moisture supply, increased grain yield as the result of a more favourable seasonal water use distribution. During the period prior to heading, early planted sorghum used roughly half the amount of water compared to late-sown sorghum. Thus more water was left for the critical period from heading to seed formation. The total amount of water used up to heading was the same for early and for late plantings.

Plant Population and Distribution Patterns

The number of plants required per unit area to achieve the highest yields will depend on the nature of the crop and on its environment. This number cannot be too small, or not all the production potential will be fully utilized; nor can it be too large, or excessive plant competition will reduce the overall efficiency of the crop, in particular because of excessive moisture stress.

Maximum exploitation of the factors needed for growth is achieved only when the plant population exercises maximum pressure on all the production factors (Donald, 1963). As a result, the individual plants are under relatively severe stress because of inter-plant competition. In Subterranean clover, for example, the total dry matter produced per plant at a wide spacing (6 plants/m²) was 34 g, while at the density which produced maximum yields (1500 plants/m²) the individual plant produced only 0.6 g, or less than 2 per cent of the former amount (Donald, 1954). Thus we come to the somewhat paradoxical conclusion that maximum yields are obtained from plant populations which do not allow the individual plants to achieve their maximum potential.

Economic yield

Many studies have shown that the relationship of yield of seed or fruit (economic yield) to density is different from that of total dry matter production (biological yield). In the latter, total production rises with increasing density to a maximum, which then remains practically constant (Donald, 1963). At this density, any increase in total dry matter yield per unit area due to an additional number of plants, is offset by an equal loss due to the decrease in weight per plant.

The relationship of seed production to population density is different. As plant density increases, the yield of seed increases to a maximum, which remains constant within a certain range, and then declines more or less steeply as population pressure increases still further—even when moisture and nutrients are not limiting (Holliday, 1960). With maize, for example, the decline in yields is fairly steep when the optimum density is exceeded, while with cotton—a crop in which individual plants have a far greater ability to adjust to population density—the graph depicting yield of cotton seed exhibits a fairly wide plateau of optimum densities (Fig. 1.15).

Donald (1963) points out that the two curves of seed yield and biological yield are interdependent, and that peak seed yields occur approximately at the same density at which the biological yield starts levelling off. He, therefore, suggests that 'the minimum density giving the ceiling biological yield may also be the density giving the maximum seed yield.'

In the young plant, most of the net assimilates are used for the production of additional leaves. With the appearance of the inflorescence, competition for assimilates between the leaves and the inflorescence takes place. Then, when seed formation starts, most of the assimilates move to the grain. Thus there exists an internal competition within the individual plant in its vegetative and reproductive organs. This internal competition becomes more severe as competition between plants increases,

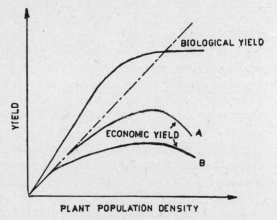

FIG. 1.15. Generalized curves showing effect of plant population on biological and economic yields:
A—maize (grain); B—cotton (seed cotton).

e.g., with increasing plant population pressures. As plant density is increased, changes may occur in the allocation of assimilates to different parts of the plant, as a result of which a greater proportion of the plants (or of the reproductive parts of an individual plant) may become barren. Grain production then shows a decline in yield, whereas the total dry matter production may remain constant (Harper, 1961).

As a result of differential effect of competition on biological and economic yield, the amount of stover required to produce a kilogram of grain in maize decreases with increasing plant density up to a certain level; further increase in density beyond this level then results in a lower grain/stover ratio (Dungan *et al.*, 1958).

Components of yield

As planting density increases, most components of yield of the individual plant are reduced. An interesting feature is that among the several highly plastic components of plant yield, the weight of the individual seed is only rarely influenced by changes in plant density. Harper (1961) considers this to be an internal or physiological homeostasis with respect to the organ that is essential for reproduction and dispersal. However, there may be very considerable differences in the manner in which different crops react to plant density in other connections.

Crops with indeterminate growth systems, such as *Vicia faba,* 'in which the flowering apices do not arise directly from the major vegetative apices', respond to density mainly by changes in the number of parts formed. On the other hand, crops with determinate growth, such as sunflowers, respond mainly by changes in the size of the parts.

Crops in which a determinate phase follows an indeterminate phase (after vernalization and photoperiodic response), such as winter wheat, may respond by changes in the number of parts during the indeterminate phase, and by changes in the size of parts during the determinate phase (Harper, 1961).

In wheat, it has been shown that when moisture supply is adequate, ear number (i.e., plant population density) had the most marked effect on grain yield—whereas under water stress the grain number per ear, and occasionally the 100-grain weight, had the same effect as ear number (Asana & Singh, 1967). This explains why, when soil moisture was limiting, reduced seeding rates were found to increase yields of spring wheat in Saskatchewan, provided weeds, insects and diseases were efficiently controlled. Low seeding rates (22 & 45 kg/ha), on an 8-year average, gave significantly higher yields than did the higher seeding rates (67 & 101 kg/ha). Low seeding rates produced longer heads, heavier kernels and in some cases, taller plants. The number of mature kernels per unit area did not differ significantly for the different rates tested (Pelton, 1969).

Interrelationships between Plant Density and Factors Affecting Production

Moisture supply

It is well-known that the optimum density for a crop has to be lower than normal under conditions of a limited water supply.

Nutrients

All available evidences indicate that, at highest levels of nutrient supply, more plants per unit area are required to exploit fully the higher soil fertility potential and thereby to produce maximum yields, than is the case at lower levels of supply. Conversely, as plant density increases up to a certain limit, the crop will continue to respond to higher levels of added nutrients.

At low levels of nutrient supply, dense populations may have specific adverse effects on crop plants. In spacing experiments with rye grass (*Lolium rigidum*) in Australia, it was found that when the nitrogen supply was limited, the nitrogen content of the grass fell from 1.8 per cent for widely spaced plants to 1 per cent for extremely crowded plants (Donald, 1954). In addition, the total nitrogen taken up by the sward was less with crowded plants than with more widely spaced plants. Donald (1963) suggests that the plants submitted to *excessively* severe competition have a poorer root system and are less efficient in the uptake of nutrients from the soil than the less stressed plants.

Light

Water regime and nutrient supply to the crop can be regulated to enable the maximum number of plants to achieve their full yielding potential; however, increasing the number of plants per unit area will reduce the amount of light available to the individual plants, due to greater shading.

There is a basic difference in competition between plants for light and for other factors needed for growth. Moisture, nutrients, and CO_2 are withdrawn by the plants from a common pool. In plant populations of a single crop, assuming that differences in competitive ability between individuals of a similar genotype are not very great, the plants will share equally in the supply, until it is exhausted. By contrast, there is no pool of light that becomes exhausted as a result of withdrawal by the plant community (Donald, 1963). A sparse stand by withdrawing less water from the common pool at an early stage of growth, may 'save' water that will be available to the crop at a later, more sensitive stage. Any available light that is not intercepted by the canopy at a given moment, is lost to the crop. 'Light energy is instantaneously available and it must be instantaneously intercepted' (loc. cit.).

Competition for light is universal and is absent only for a short period after emergence, or in the very wide spacings that are characteristic of plant communities which have become adjusted to arid conditions. In the latter, leaf cover never reaches a density which ensures the most effective utilization of radiation (Blackman & Black, 1959). In contrast, with competition for water or nutrients, which increases in severity with decreasing availability, competition for light in a dense population will be equally acute under conditions of high light intensity and of overcast skies (Donald, 1963). Competition between plants is not a static process, and the intensity of competition will depend on the time when it occurs. In the early growth stages, there still be little mutual shading and even at relatively low light intensities the plant will be able to photosynthesize with full efficiency. As the plants develop, mutual shading increases, and light begins to become a limiting factor. When plants reach the flowering stage, they may even lose weight on cloudy days (Jackson, 1963). Competition for light may be between plants, when one casts a shadow over any other, or within a plant, when one leaf shades another.

Essentially, there are two basic ways of ensuring maximum interception of light by the canopy: by improving the foliage pattern, and by increasing plant density.

Improving the foliage pattern: The most efficient plant canopy is not that with the most leaves, but that in which the inter-plant and intra-plant competition for light is reduced to a minimum, so that the canopy as a whole intercepts a maximum of light.

Increasing plant density: The light intensity required to give a maximum rate of photosynthesis by the individual leaf is about 1500-2000 foot-candles, while light intensities in the field may reach 10,000 foot-candles (Donald, 1963). It is therefore possible to reduce the distance between individual plants, so as to increase the efficiency of the plant canopy as a whole in utilizing the available sunlight. However, there is an optimal ratio of leaf area to ground surface (LAI) beyond which increasing plant density will increase excessively the proportion of the foliage which is below the compensation point.

The general conclusion that can be drawn is that the more favourable the conditions, under which a crop is grown are, the greater will be the plants density required to exploit fully the potential and to achieve maximum yield; conversely, higher than average plant densities will require more favourable growing conditions.

Other effects of plant density

Root systems: The extent and distribution pattern of root systems are markedly influenced by plant density. Very widely spaced plants of maize, which were presumably free from competition, developed a circular distribution of the roots, with a radius of about 75 cm. At high densities, the root systems of the individual plants interpenetrated to a high degree. At a 2.5 cm spacing within rows, portions of no fewer than 32 overlapping root systems could be recorded at any one point beneath or near the row of plants, while at a 80 cm spacing there were only two overlapping systems (Haynes & Sayre, 1956).

Plant height: With increasing density and competition for light, plant height may be markedly increased. For example, the average heights of wheat plants grown in rows spaced 30, 15 and 7.5 cm apart were 63, 75 and 85 cm, respectively at the age of 16 weeks (Wassermann, 1963).

Lodging: The risk of lodging is markedly increased by high population levels (Dungan *et al.*, 1958).

Plant mortality: At very high densities, competition may be so severe among the plants of a population that a proportion of them will die. In wheat, at a density of 1078 plants/m^2, only 40 per cent of the plants survived to the age of 6 months (Puckridge, 1962). This 'self-thinning' did not reduce plant density to that giving the highest yield of grain per unit area. Thus, 'plant survival had precedence over total seed production per unit area' (Donald, 1963).

Disease incidence: When sorghum seeds were sown more closely in the rows, the more rapid spread of seedling diseases was assumed to be one of the reasons for the relatively smaller number of plants established, as compared with sowing more sparsely (Porter *et al.*, 1960). However, there are occasional instances in which very close planting is effective in reducing the incidence of disease—as is the case for rosette disease of peanuts.

Maturity: In maize hybrids, silking was found to be delayed by one day for each additional plant per m² (Lang *et al.*, 1956).

Planting patterns: Planting patterns can have a direct effect on yield, on the absorption of radiant energy, and on water evaporation and thus an indirect effect of water use efficiency. The following planting patterns might conceivably have such influence: square arrangements, rectangular arrangements, very elongated rectangles (wide row interval with very small intervals within rows), irregular spacings in the row (pockets or hills within the row), and the direction of the rows.

Adjusting Planting Patterns to Limited Moisture Supply

Plant population must be adjusted to available soil moisture levels, either within rows or between rows. Increasing the distance between sorghum plants, for example, within the row in order to adjust to low moisture levels generally defeats its own purpose: the young plants, with little or no intra-row competition, show excessive vegetative growth: soil moisture is rapidly depleted, and the plants are unable to form satisfactory panicles or to mature their grain normally. The alternative is to space plants more closely within the row, and to increase the distance between rows in order to compensate for low moisture levels. In the wide-spaced rows, the soil moisture supply is not exhausted as rapidly as in narrow rows (Brown & Shrader, 1959).

While working on relative water loss between crop rows, Larson and Willis (1957) found that soil moisture increased from within the row to the middle point between the rows. This was more pronounced in the wider rows, and apparently reflects decreasing root density as the distance from row increases. Intra-row competition prevents excessive vegetative growth. In addition, for individual plants, the normal circular root pattern changes to oblong as a consequence of inter-plant competition. Closely spaced plants show increased root elongation into the space not already occupied by roots (Haynes *et al.*, 1959), where the laterally developing roots have to grow to reach moisture. They, therefore, continue to find available moisture between the rows later in the season, when it can be used for grain production—provided the distance between the rows has been well-adjusted to the available soil moisture. The heads are small but relatively numerous under these conditions, and maturity is more uniform than with plantings in close-spaced rows.

An example of the effect of adjusting row width on yields under difficult moisture conditions is provided by an experiment in rain-fed groundnuts, grown in a dry region of India. In a poor rainfall season with a total precipitation of 186.8 mm (plus an equivalent of 75.1 mm stored in the soil up to a depth of 1 m, before sowing) the best WUE was obtained from a planting distance of 60 cm × 25 cm. In the following year, with more favourable moisture conditions due to a rainfall of 357.3 mm (plus 67.2 mm of stored water) the best WUE resulted from a spacing of 45 cm × 25 cm. In both seasons, the close spacing of 30 cm × 25 cm gave the lowest WUE (Bhan & Misra, 1970b).

It might be assumed that the wide row spacings, by exposing large areas of bare soil to radiation, would increase moisture losses due to evaporation thereby defeating the purpose of the wider spacings. However, under dryland conditions, evaporation is influenced more by the moisture supply at the soil surface than by radiation. Therefore, once the upper soil layer has dried, further moisture losses by evaporation become negligible. Under these conditions, wide rows are not more conducive to greater water loss by evaporation than are narrow rows.

Row direction

Very few investigations on the effect of row direction on yields have been conducted. The few results have been surprisingly similar with different crops grown under widely different conditions. In Australia, yield increases in dry matter production by wheat, of 6.5 and 11 per cent respectively, were obtained in two experiments with north-south sowings as compared to east-west sowings (Santhirasegaram, 1962). In the U.S.S.R. spring wheat sown N-S produced from 100 to 300 kg/ha more than when sown E-W. It is assumed that sunlight and moisture were used more fully in the N-S than in the E-W rows, and that the plants in the N-S rows were less subject to excess heat (Perekaljskii, 1951).

In India, it has been found that maize planted in a north-south direction yielded significantly more grain and forage than when it was planted in an east-west direction (Dungan et al., 1955). Similar results were obtained with wheat (Shekhawat et al., 1966). In Illinois, spring oats drilled in a north-south direction yielded slightly more grain than when it was drilled in an east-west direction; the advantage of the north-south row increased as inter-row spacings increased (Pendleton & Dungan, 1958).

While a full explanation for these results is not available, it is possible that sunlight and the amount of reflected light are influenced by row direction, with N-S rows enjoying better lighting than the northern exposure of the E-W rows.

Establishing a stand

The establishment of an adequate stand is a prerequisite for a successful crop; and depends on proper germination and emergence of the seedlings. This aim is not easily achieved under arid conditions. The soil surface is wetted intermittently, generally at relatively longer intervals; it dries out rapidly, often before the seeds have had the time to germinate or the young seedlings to establish themselves. Many of these soils form a hard crust on drying, especially after rains of high intensity, so characteristic of these regions. The seedlings are unable to emerge through the crust, and a large proportion may be smothered under the surface.

Germination and emergence: The physical and chemical conditions required for germination are an adequate supply of water, a favourable temperature, suitable aeration, illumination for certain species, and the absence of toxic or inhibitory substances. For a rapid and adequate emergence of seedlings both a high soil temperature and a sufficient moisture content are essential. However, under field conditions in arid regions, this combination is seldom obtained; because high temperatures are generally related to a rapid drying out of the upper soil layer which constitutes the seed-bed (Feddes, 1971).

Moisture relations: Water uptake in germination usually occurs in two distinct stages: (a) *imbibition stage,* during which water adsorption by the seeds is largely passive, and (b) *growth stage,* which begins with the appearance of a radicle, that becomes increasingly active in water uptake. Between these two stages there is generally a period of internal physiological processes (respiratory, enzymatic, etc.) that initiate the onset of actual growth (Hillel, 1972).

Typically, the moisture in the seed-bed may vary from saturation, shortly after a rain, to extremely dry, after a dry period. The germination and emergence of most field crops are progressively delayed and reduced as the soil water tension increases; however the response, and in particular the critical suction for germination varies with crop species and even with varieties within a given species.

For example, the total emergence of sorghum was found to decrease from about 96 to 86% as the soil moisture tension increased from 1/3 to approximately 8 atm. Thereafter, the total emergence decreased very rapidly (Lyles & Fanning, 1964). In cotton, total emergence was not affected by changes in soil water tension between 1/3 and 3 bars; it was however reduced significantly at 4 bars; a sharp decrease was observed at a tension of 8 bars and no emergence at all occurred at tensions greater than 12 bars (Jensen, 1971). The rate of emergence and growth rate of the cotton seedlings first decreased progressively as tension increased from 2 to 4 bars; thereafter, as tension increased still further, the time required for emergence increased rapidly, and the rate of growth decreased sharply (loc. cit.). Threshold soil water tensions reported for some other crops are: 12.5 bars for maize, 6.6 bars for soybeans and 3.5 bars for sugar beets (Hunter & Erickson, 1952).

Temperature requirements: Each crop species has definite minimal, optimal and maximal temperatures for germination. Above and below the optimal temperatures, the metabolic activity preceding germination is reduced (Sosebee & Herbel, 1969). However, some species germinate better at alternating temperatures (Cuddy, 1963). Too low temperatures prevent germination and are conducive to seed-rot. Higher than optimum temperatures may induce seed dormancy. Soil temperatures of 20 °C were found to be most suitable for all varieties of dwarf wheat tested in the Punjab. Both lower (15 °C) and higher (35 °C) temperatures reduced the elongation of the coleoptile and shoot, impaired the synthesis of chlorophyll, and caused an increase in the level of RNA. The increased level of RNA was, however, not conducive to protein synthesis at higher temperature (Singh & Gill, 1972). Treating the seeds with kinetin ensured good germination at the higher soil temperature levels (30-35 °C) and alleviated the negative effect of higher temperature on the level of chlorophyll (loc. cit.).

Gupta and Sarla Sharma (1974) studied the germination and early growth responses of tall, one- and two-gene dwarf wheat cultivars to temperature at 5 °C intervals from 5 to 35 °C. The dwarf cultivars with Norin genes are more tolerant to cold than the tall ones. Sonora 64 and P. V. 18 appear to possess more cold tolerance, and Kalyan Sona maximum heat tolerance out of the seven varieties studied. The optimum temperature for germination and seedling growth is 5 °C less for dwarf wheats.

In winter rainfall regions, low temperatures may limit germination and seedling growth at times though soil moisture conditions are highly favourable. Soil temperatures also have a considerable influence on seedling development. Unfavourable soil temperatures, in particular, reduce the rate of root penetration (Troughton, 1957). This reduced rate of root growth may be critical for the establishment of the seedlings before the upper soil layer dries out.

Aeration: As soon as the seeds start imbibing water, there is a steep increase in their respiration rate (Toole *et al.*, 1956) and most crop varieties require an adequate supply of oxygen during germination. There may be a conflict between the requirements of a high moisture supply to the seeds and adequate aeration. Oxygen can be taken up by the seeds only after passing through the water film surrounding them. The diffusion coefficient of oxygen in water is smaller by a factor of 10^4 than the diffusion coefficient in air (Hillel, 1972).

Importance of rapid germination and emergence

In the first stage, seeds that have not absorbed sufficient water for germination may dry again without loss of viability. However, when germination is delayed because of unfavourable environmental conditions, seeds and seedlings are generally debilitated or killed by diseases and insect pests. Fungal hyphae can develop at levels of soil moisture too low for germination or seedling growth (Griffin, 1963).

The time required for emergence has been found to be a good indicator of the vigour and yielding ability of cotton plants; as shown by the following figures (Wanjura et al., 1969).

Table 1.9. Effect of time required for emergence, on survival rate and yield of cotton (Wanjura et al., 1969)

Time from sowing to emergence (days)	Average survival rate (%)	Average relative yields (%)
5	87	100
8	70	46
12	30	20

These results illustrate the dangers inherent in the rapid drying of the seed-bed, after sowing, which is so characteristic of rain-fed agriculture in dry hot regions.

Crop rotations

A well-planned crop rotation should have the following advantages over monoculture or a haphazard succession of crops; it should:
1. Maintain, and even improve, soil fertility,
2. Prevent the build-up of pests, weeds, and soil-borne diseases,
3. Control soil erosion,
4. Ensure a balanced programme of work throughout the year,
5. Stabilize income, and
6. Conserve moisture from one season to the next.

Types of crop rotations adapted to semiarid regions

While crop rotations may vary considerably in different regions, depending on tradition, the type of crops grown, local economic factors, etc., certain prototypes have developed which will be discussed here, as well as the fundamental principles on which they are based.

Winter rainfall regions with mild winters: In the transition region between aridity and semiaridity, where the average precipitation fluctuates between 250 to 400 mm, rain-fed crop production becomes possible, but is fraught with great dangers. In favourable seasons, when precipitation is above average, exceptionally good yields of grain can be obtained as a result of fertility build-up during the season of low rainfall and crop failure. Large areas are usually ploughed up and sown, to become dust bowls when there is a succession of drought years.

The principal crop rotations followed in these areas are:

1.   Continuous wheat (or barley), with crop failures during the dry years serving as unplanned fallow periods.   If good yields are to be obtained during the favourable seasons, heavy nitrogenous fertilizer applications are essential.   Inputs are therefore high, with a low probability of success.

2.   Cereal fallow: In Australia, in the wheat growing regions with an annual precipitation of 250 to 375 mm, experience shows that the fallow-wheat sequence usually assures the farmer of a crop, whereas continuous wheat would generally be a complete failure (Callaghan & Millington, 1956).

In the low rainfall regions, a succession of drought years is of frequent occurrence and, therefore, even the additional moisture stored by the fallow may be insufficient to ensure a good crop.   Cultivated fallow may promote an initial stimulation of yields, but in the long run it usually has adverse effects of which wind and water erosion are the ultimate outcome.   This system also requires fairly high inputs (tillage, fertilizers, etc.) with, however, uncertain returns.

3.   Leguminous leys: In some countries with advanced agriculture, rotations have been adopted in which cultivated fallow is replaced by leguminous leys.   A ley rotation adapted to semiarid conditions is based on alternating periods of two or more years of annual, self-seeding legumes—grazed by cattle or sheep—with one or more years of grain crops.

This system has a built-in auto-regulatory device ensuring a yearly, albeit fluctuating, income.   In the good rainfall seasons, the legume and the stubble of the cereal crop produce year-round grazing (provided the number of head of stock is properly adjusted to the carrying capacity), while good grain yields are also harvested.   In the poor rainfall seasons, the relatively low production of the legumes is supplemented by grazing the cereal fields which have no prospect of producing a satisfactory grain crop.   What would have been a total loss in an exclusively grain producing system, will give a fair yield of forage—even in conditions under which no grain is formed.   The legumes may produce from 100 to 500 feed units per hectare even with a yearly rainfall of not more than 60-100 mm; with 200 mm, which is insufficient for grain production, the cereal may still produce 1000 to 1300 FU/ha.   In a good year, the legumes will produce around 2000 FU/ha and the grain stubble will provide another 300-500 FU/ha (Arnon, 1972).

This integrated system of animal husbandry and cereal cropping also has the advantage of relatively low inputs: the annual legumes are self-seeding, so that no tillage, or only a minimum, is required.   Only phosphatic fertilizers are needed, and if applied in excess of current requirements, the residues are not wasted.   The legumes provide all the nitrogen that is needed by the cereal crop, but in a very good year additional nitrogen may be top-dressed. The cereal can be seeded into the legume stand by a chisel-drill without additional tillage; excessive legume volunteer plants in the cereal can be controlled by herbicides. Grain volunteer plants in the legumes provide balanced grazing. Perennial weeds such as Jhonson grass and Couch grass, are kept in check both by the grazing and by the competition of the cereal crop.

The effectiveness of the whole system depends on how animal numbers are in balance with the fluctuating forage supply. It is estimated that in Australia, the use of clover leys in the cereal areas has contributed to a 50 per cent increase in yields of grain (Donald, 1960) with practically no application of fertilizer nitrogen. The fertility levels of originally poor soils have been dramatically raised to moderate and even high levels of fertility by sowing Subterranean clover fertilized with superphosphate, and, where deficiencies of micronutrients occur, with sources of copper, zinc and molybdenum. The effect of this cropping system on soil fertility is illustrated by the figures in Table 1.10.

Table 1.10. Effect of inclusion of a fertilized clover ley on soil fertility
(Donald & Williams, 1954)

Treatment	N (per cent)	P (per cent)	S (per cent)
Original soil	0.076	0.012	0.010
Subterranean clover (with fertilizer)	0.184	0.028	0.024

Semiarid regions with 400 mm rainfall and above

Traditional crop rotation: The main objective of arable farmers in these regions is usually the production of cereals, preferably wheat. In the more problematic areas, wheat is replaced by barley. Farmers are usually aware that continuous cereal growing invites disaster, and therefore most of the wheat—or barley in the drier regions—is grown in alternate years. As normally only a single crop can be grown each year, the two-course rotation predominates throughout the region. Some of the variations of these rotations are: wheat-weed-fallow; wheat-pulses (beans, lentils—chick peas); wheat-cultivated summer crops; and wheat-barley. When three- or four-course rotations are practised, they usually take the form of wheat-barley-fallow, or of wheat-pulses-barley-fallow.

The farmers do not usually adhere rigorously to any of these rotations. If the rains are early and abundant, and the season bodes well, they are usually tempted to sow a wider area than that allocated to wheat in the rotation. Cultivated summer crops help in the control of weeds, which pose serious problems in continuous wheat growing. However, when the summer crop has a detrimental effect on the moisture status of the soil, it may offset any beneficial effect in regions in which soil moisture is the limiting factor. For this reason, in western Kansas, yields from wheat that has been sown immediately after the harvesting of cultivated summer crops (sorghum, maize, etc.) are frequently lower than those obtained from 'continuous' wheat. Between the harvesting and seeding of two successive wheat crops, three months elapse, during which time cultivated fallow will conserve soil moisture that will remain available to the wheat crop (Laude *et al.*, 1955).

Improved crop rotation: The traditional crop rotations described above are all exhaustive and make no contribution to soil fertility. The basic problem is, therefore, to devise a type of crop rotation that will raise the level of soil fertility, thus making it possible for the following crop to benefit fully from the favourable moisture regime prevailing during its growing period.

It is frequently assumed that pulses are desirable preceding crops for winter cereals, and it was originally thought that extending the area under pulses would have a beneficial effect on soil fertility. Many Ministries of Agriculture in the semiarid regions have adopted the inclusion of pulses in the rotation as an official policy aimed at improving overall productivity. However, results are always disappointing, as harvesting a seed crop from the legume usually results in a drop of at least 30 per cent in the yield of the following wheat crop, as compared with wheat following fallow. The legume removes more nitrogen than the root nodules produce. The soil is also left in a very unfavourable physical condition, and weed infestation in the subsequent cereal crops is heavier than usual (Arnon, 1972).

Leguminous crops that are *not* allowed to mature seed, but are used for pasture, soiling, hay, silage, or for turning under as green manure, have been shown to be very important for improving soil fertility. They also enhance the response of the winter cereals to other factors affecting production.

Green manures

At first, green manures were considered the ideal solution for rapidly raising the level of soil fertility. On the whole, the results obtained in semi-arid conditions have been disappointing, and green manures have generally shown little, if any benefit over results derived from leguminous forage crops, as shown by long-term experiments. In regions with less than 375 mm precipitation, for example, in long-term experiments in Montana, where annual precipitation ranged from 290-375 mm, a green manure crop of sweet clover had no beneficial effect on dryland wheat yields (Army & Hide, 1959). The negative results may be ascribed to the kind of crop used for turning under (frequently a cereal), to the soil moisture depletion by the growing crop, to the drying out of the soil due to inversion when ploughing under the green manure, and, finally, to the decomposition of the mass of organic matter. Where green manures have been beneficial, the increase in yield rarely justified the loss of a cropping season or the risks and expenditure involved.

Thus, it may be said that the most promising approach towards raising the level of soil fertility in semiarid regions of sufficient rainfall (400 mm and above) is the inclusion in the rotation of a leguminous forage crop. When the legume is cut before seed is formed, the amount of plant nutrients removed from the soil is relatively small, while the soil is enriched in nitrogen and organic matter. Weeds are cut before flowering and are therefore well controlled. The soil can be ploughed when still moist and an excellent tilth is obtained. Residual soil moisture may be almost as high as after fallow.

As regards the types of rotation, the areas devoted to a soil improving crop may vary from one-third to one-sixth of the total area, with a tendency to devote as large an area as possible to the winter cereal in the crop rotation. Hence we get a plethora of three-, four-, and six-year crop rotations, with various sequences of crops, in which the winter cereals occupy an important position. The best overall results in Israel have been obtained with the following three-course rotation:

First year—winter cereals (wheat, barley, or oats).

Second year—summer crops (sorghum, maize, sunflowers, sesame, or chick peas).

Third year—leguminous forage crops (vetch, annual clover, etc.).

A different sequence is sometimes adopted, in which the winter cereal follows the summer crop. This is justified when the fields are infested by grassy annuals, such as *Phalaris* and wild oats. In such a case it is the summer crop which is assigned the best place in the rotation, thereby benefiting from residual moisture after the legume and the favourable nitrogen status resulting from the latter.

Summer rainfall regions in the middle latitudes

Continuous cereal growing: In the semiarid regions of the world in which grasslands have been ploughed up for crop production in modern times (as in the Great Plains of the U.S.A.) and rainfall is generally adequate, the general tendency is to practise monoculture with wheat grown continuously for long periods. In the areas with relatively favourable precipitation, alternate wheat-fallow is practised only occasionally—either when weed infestation has become a serious problem, or when exceptionally deficient soil moisture at sowing time makes wheat sowing too hazardous.

Experience has shown that the accumulated fertility of soils which have always been under native grass before they were ploughed up, enables continuous wheat cropping without declining yields for 30 years or more—provided weeds are kept under control (Harper, 1959). However, during this period, at least half the original organic matter and nitrogen will have disappeared, and so it is difficult to prophecy whether (and, if so, when) continued monoculture will start to have undesirable results. Even if a satisfactory level of soil fertility is maintained, sooner or later a build-up of grassy weeds occurs, which makes wheat growing unprofitable. Under these conditions, a 3-year rotation of fallow-wheat-sorghum was found to give good weed control, as well as providing for efficient use of water and nitrogen and giving satisfactory protection against wind erosion. It also gave a higher gross income than a fallow-wheat-wheat rotation (Ramig & Smika, 1964).

Summer rainfall regions in the low latitudes

In the semiarid zone of Africa, south of Sahara, the two principal crops—sorghum and millets—are extensively grown on freshly cleared brush. These are extremely sensitive to soil depletion in organic matter. After a relatively short period of continuous sorghum or millet, yields become too low even for primitive farming, and the land has to be abandoned.

The rapid degradation of the soil resulting from cereal monoculture is an almost irreversible process under the conditions of primitive agriculture employed in this region. The exhausted soil, abandoned by the farmer, is covered only sparsely with vegetation. The process of regeneration is delayed by overgrazing and brush fires, so that it takes many years to return to the original level of soil fertility. Non-cultivated fallow alternating with cereal production is therefore incapable of maintaining an acceptable level of production after brush-clearing. The situation is no better when groundnut, another important crop of the region, is sown continuously. Yields decline rapidly, and even mineral fertilizers are unable to maintain a satisfactory fertility level. Alternating a groundnut crop with two or more years of fallow (non-cultivated) alleviates the situations without, however, providing a radical solution, as illustrated by the example given in table 1.11 (Gillier, 1960).

Table 1.11. Effect of fallow on yields of groundnuts
(average rainfall 421.8 mm) (Gillier, 1960)

Duration of fallow (years)			Yields of unshelled groundnuts (kg/ha)	Increase over control (%)
On depleted soil (control)	..	..	355	—
2	..	..	440	+24
3	..	..	610	+72
6	..	..	640	+80

It is clear that simply alternating groundnuts with periods of fallow does not allow for the production of high yields. Even with mineral fertilizers, yields are increased by only 270 kg/ha. Further, the respite provided by fallow in the depletion process is very transitory: after two years of cropping, even if six successive years of fallowing is followed, the drop in yield is considerable (Gillier, 1960).

It has been found that an alternation of crops is the first essential to maintaining a reasonable level of fertility. Short cycles of sorghum-ground-nuts, with light doses of mineral fertilizers, alternating with fallow, have been found not only capable of maintaining the original level of soil fertility, but even of gradually increasing yields.

Thus alternation of crops, with short periods of cropping alternating with fallow periods of sufficient length and the use of mineral fertilizers at moderate doses, have given the possibility of economic production within the framework of traditional agriculture. But the inclusion of green manures in traditional farming has not been found to be justified (loc. cit.).

Mixed cropping

Mixed cropping is a characteristic of primitive agriculture dating from antiquity. It is a method which attempts to make the most of the potentialities of the environment. By planting together a number of crops with varying planting and harvesting times and growth habits, plant nutrients in different soil layers are better exploited and light energy is more effectively intercepted. Plants of the same species compete more intensively with each other than do plants of different species—mainly because of differences in the root systems and periods of peak water requirement, so that a limited water supply is used more efficiently in a mixed cropping system than in pure stands. The risks due to diseases, pests, and climatic factors, are reduced and also better distributed, while weeds more effectively smothered. When primitive varieties are used, the total yield from a given area under mixed cropping may be greater than from pure stands (Baldy, 1963).

A notable example of mixed cropping, practised by primitive people, is the maize-beans-squash complex, which originated in Mexico during the period 1500-900 B.C. It was so successful that it spread out from Mexico and became the basis of practically all prehistoric Indian agriculture and in all parts of America. The complex of three crops exploited the soil and light energy most effectively: the beans climbed on the maize stalks, exposing their leaves to the light without excessive shading of the maize leaves; the squash grew prostrate on the ground and choked out weed growth. The mixed cropping also produced a highly balanced diet: the maize supplied most of the carbohydrates and certain amino acids in which beans are deficient; the beans supplied the bulk of the protein, and also phosphorus, iron, and the vitamins—riboflavin and nicotinic acid. The squashes added calories and an increment of fat (Stakman et al., 1967).

Intercropping is still practised on a large scale in the Mediterranean region, in Africa, and in India. In east Africa, it is exceptional for peasants to sow pure stands. Evans (1960) doubts whether it will be possible to introduce a rotational system of agriculture based on pure stands so long as the hoe is the main agricultural implement. He found that intercropping maize or sorghum with groundnuts generally gave higher crop production per unit area than growing these crops in pure stands. This was found to hold true in two areas of contrasting fertility as well as under conditions of contrasting rainfall; namely low, irregularly distributed rainfall and favourable rainfall.

The combinations castorbean-groundnuts and castorbean-soybean also usually showed an overall gain in production per hectare. When severe attacks of mirids reduced castor yields drastically, the associated crop gave a compensating yield increase (Evans & Sreedharan, 1962). Intercropping of cotton, both rain-fed and irrigated, with a wide variety of crops, in varying proportions, is widely practised in India. Common combinations are of cotton with sorghum, pulses, sesame, cucurbits, ground-nuts, or castorbeans. Usually, one or two rows of the associated crop alternate with 8-10 rows of cotton. The mixed cropping generally gives a larger total yield than the pure crop of each does in the aggregate; it provides insurance against complete crop failure, and it reduces soil erosion— particularly if one of the two associated crops has a trailing habit. In an investigation on root-rot (*Rhizoctonia* sp.) conducted in the Punjab, it was found that cotton, when intercropped with beans (*Phaseolus aconitifolius*), was much less damaged by the disease than when grown in a pure stand (Sawhney & Sikka, 1960).

In a 5-year experiment at Kota (India) a mixture of wheat and chick peas or gram (*Cicer arietinum*) was found to give a significantly higher mone-tary return than when each crop was grown singly; in very dry years, the cereal failed completely, while the chick peas gave at least some yield; in good years, the mixture gave higher yields than each crop grown singly (Dayal *et al.*, 1967).

With very few exceptions, particularly among forage and pasture crops, modern agriculture is based on pure stands. Weed control, whether mechanical or chemical, as well as pest and disease control, are hindered in mixed stands. Rational fertilizer applications are difficult to adjust to a mixture of different crops. However, probably the main limitation to mixed cropping in modern farming is that efficient mechanical harvesting of a mixed crop is not possible.

The Moisture Regime in Dryland Crop Production

EVAPOTRANSPIRATION (ET)

Actual and Potential Evapotranspiration

Water is lost by evaporation from a bare, moist soil surface at about the same rate as from a free water surface having the same exposure and temperature. Paradoxically, in arid regions, losses of water by evaporation from the soil are relatively low, the main component of water loss being plant transpiration. The surface soil dries quickly; as the dry layer produced deepens, evaporation is reduced until it becomes almost imperceptible. This is because at a soil water potential of approximately 15 bars the continuity of the liquid films is broken, and water diffuses only in the form of vapour (Kramer, 1969). This movement is very slow; according to Gardner (1958) the rate at which water can be lost under these conditions is usually less than 20% of the rate of loss by evaporation from a moist soil surface.

After the upper soil layer has become too dry to contribute to evaporation, plants continue to take up water from the lower moist layers. The high conductivity of the plants for water makes up for reduced evaporation from the dry soil surface and the plant cover will therefore maintain the level of water loss for sometime; the more dense the plant cover is, the greater will be the water loss. As available water is exhausted, the decrease in availability counterbalances the effect of increased plant cover on water loss. Therefore, after a while, the density of plant cover has no further effect on water loss.

The leaf area of plant stands in often three to six times the area of the land in which they grow and most leaves lose water from both surfaces, nevertheless, transpiration from a crop never exceeds that from a similar area of wet soil or open water surface under the same environmental conditions (Kramer, 1969).

In field measurements it is difficult to distinguish between the two sources of losses; they are therefore usually estimated together and called evapotranspiration (ET), or consumptive use. When the water supply is unlimited, evapotranspiration is equal to the evaporation from a free water surface, and therefore reaches the highest level possible under the prevailing conditions of radiation, wind velocity, temperature, air humidity, etc. It is then called *potential evapotranspiration* (PET).

In the dry regions the rate of potential evapotranspiration, as contrasted with precipitation, varies relatively little from year to year. As a general rule, conditions that cause a reduction in the amount of precipitation will at the same time favour an increase in potential evapotranspiration. Therefore, the discrepancy between water requirements and water supply in arid regions is still further aggravated in years of deficient rainfall.

It is fairly common for potential evapotranspiration to exceed precipitation considerably in regions with limited rainfall as indicated by the following examples: at Las Cruces, New Mexico, average annual precipitation was found to be 216 mm, as compared with 2337 mm for potential evapotranspiration. At Yuma, Arizona, potential evapotranspiration is 55 times as great as rainfall (Koéppe & Long, 1958).

Relationship between Actual ET and PET

When soil moisture is at field capacity, the initial values of ET are approximately equal to PET. As the amount of available soil moisture decreases, relative to PET, there is a progressive decline in actual ET, for all crops. As soil moisture stress increases, differences between crops in the rate of decline in ET, become apparent (Fig. 1.16). Thus, sorghum with its extensive root system and greater ability to withstand atmospheric desiccation, maintains ET at a relatively high level for sometime, whereas in cotton, with its less extensive and efficient root system, ET is reduced almost immediately; soil-water depletion commences.

However, the cumulative seasonal evapotranspiration for grain sorghum, even under relatively favourable moisture conditions, may be only

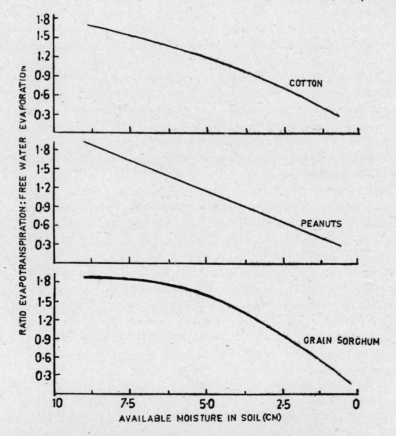

FIG. 1.16. Actual evapotranspiration in relation to potential evapotranspiration as a function of soil moisture (from Slatyer, 1958) (by courtesy of the Neth. J. agric. Sci.).

65% of PET (Jensen, 1968); in many farm crops seasonal water use may range from 55 to 75% of PET, under conditions in which in lucerne water use is 90% of the PET (Ripley, 1966).

IMPROVING THE WATER SUPPLY AVAILABLE TO THE CROP

Below a certain level of water supply, crop production is not possible. Relatively small increases in moisture supply may give quite marked increases in yield. Hence, even relatively small increments of water to the soil or reduced water losses may have disproportionally large effects on crop yields. Inevitably, ET will also be increased as a result of the improved moisture regime, but the effect on yields will always be greater under moisture deficient regimes, so that water use efficiency will be improved.

The improved moisture regime in the soil can be achieved in two ways:
(a) by increasing the amounts of water stored in the root zone, and
(b) by reducing losses due to evaporation and transpiration.
These two approaches can be complementary, and certain management practices, such as tillage, may have both effects concurrently. However, for convenience, the two approaches will be treated separately.

Increasing Water Storage in the Root Zone

The soil, up to the bottom of the root zone, constitutes a moisture reservoir of vital importance to agriculture. Water that infiltrates into this reservoir can be stored with relatively little loss for fairly long periods—longer than is generally realized. In the Mediterranean region, crops such as sorghum, melon and sesame, can be grown during the hot summer months, without receiving a drop of rainfall from sowing to harvest; they can produce high yields on the moisture stored in the soil during the winter months. In the Great Plains of North America, numerous investigations have proved that the amount of moisture stored in the soil, prior to the sowing of winter wheat, largely determines the yield level that can be expected.

The amount of precipitation taken in by the soil depends on runoff and infiltration. By reducing runoff and increasing infiltration, the amount of water stored in the soil can be increased—with beneficial effects on crop production, provided the total amounts of effective rainfall are sufficient.

Runoff control

It is somewhat paradoxical that the drier the climate is, the greater will be the havoc caused by rainfall. Precipitation in arid regions generally occurs as torrential rains, the sparse natural vegetation affords very little protection to the soil, and infiltration rates are rapidly reduced while run-off is increased. Most soil conservation methods, such as strip cropping, contour ploughing, terracing, etc. aim at reducing runoff, and are there-fore also effective in increasing the amount of water that is stored in the soil.

Studies on moisture conservation in India, on a shallow loam soil receiving 400 mm rainfall annually showed that bunding increased soil moisture content by 50 to 100%. Yield increases of up to 700% have been obtained as a result of the additional moisture stored in the soil (Misra & Mishra, 1966).

The protection provided by vegetation is usually a major factor in run-off control. Plants intercept part of the rainfall and reduce the velocity of rain drops; they also obstruct or slow down the movement of water on the soil surface. The indiscriminate destruction of the plant cover in water-sheds increases soil erosion and causes excessively rapid runoff that cannot be controlled.

Increasing infiltration

The maintenance of a high infiltration rate is an important objective of soil management; it reduces runoff and thereby increases the efficiency of rainfall, at the same time minimizing soil losses by erosion. The rate of infiltration of water into the soil depends on soil structure, soil cover, the degree of dryness of the soil, and the intensity and duration of the rainfall. As rain falls on a bare soil, the surface aggregates are destroyed by the impact of the drops of water and the pores of the soil surface become clogged with the particles; this rapidly reduces the rate of infiltration of the water.

The surface of many clay soils can be easily sealed and infiltration capacity reduced drastically, by a few minutes of heavy rainfall. Mulches of straw or crop residues, by breaking the impact of the rain drops, markedly improve infiltration (Fig. 1.17). Mulching was also found to reduce runoff by about half the amount that occurred without mulching.

Cultivated row crops, such as cotton, maize, and sorghum, usually afford less protection against the effects of rainfall on the soil than do densely-growing crops such as herbage and small grains, and therefore the former tend to lower infiltration rate. The frequent cultivations which they require also reduce soil aggregation. All factors that improve and maintain soil structure, also improve infiltration, and *vice versa*. However, if the subsoil is impervious, runoff will eventually occur even with a very permeable top-soil. Whenever the rate of water supply is in excess of the rate of infiltration, ponding or runoff will occur.

Water harvesting

In humid climates, runoff usually occurs only when rain falls on a saturated soil. The more arid the region, the rarer are situations in which the soil is saturated by rainfall, and the more frequent is the occurrence of runoff from soil that is not saturated, following rains that exceed a certain intensity. Under very arid conditions, reducing runoff and increasing infiltration rates are ineffective, as the amounts of moisture that can be stored in the soil do not, in any case, suffice for crop production. Rather efforts should be made in the opposite direction: to increase runoff and reduce infiltration in certain areas which can then serve as a source of water supply for other areas.

Water harvesting methods: In principle, water harvesting consists in using water derived from an area that has been treated to increase runoff of precipitation in order to supplement soil moisture in an adjacent area, situated at a lower elevation. In many dry regions, in which contemporary precipitation alone is not sufficient to ensure a crop, harvested water plus that accumulated in the soil will suffice, if a proper ratio between donor area and recipient area is established.

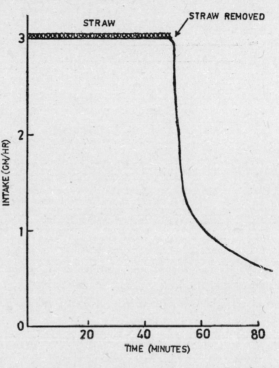

Fig. 1.17. Effect of straw mulch on intake of water by soil (from Duley, 1939) (by courtesy of the Soil Sci. Soc. Am.).

Water harvesting was developed to a fine art about 2000 years ago by the Nabateans; modern technology is attempting to develop more effective methods, aimed at reducing the ratio between donor and recipient areas. There are two main methods of water harvesting: conveying the water from barren hillsides to the adjacent relatively level land, and creating a micro-relief within a more or less level field.

Microwatersheds: Cropping systems have been developed in which run-off water from parts of a field are concentrated in strips in which crops are planted. The crop is sown in narrow strips between wide intervals that are ridged as artificial miniature watersheds. These latter are compacted to increase runoff of water to the crop rows. The relative widths of the water-shedding strips and of the crop-producing strips depend on the amount of annual precipitation that can be expected. The usual ratios are from 2 : 1 up to 4 : 1 (Fig. 1.18). This system is considered to be more efficient than following, in which water is conserved from one season to the other and the entire area is cropped in one year out of two.

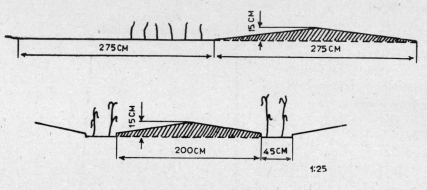

FIG. 1.18.   Microwatersheds:

Above—microwatersheds for small grains; *Below*—microwatersheds for row crops (from Kemper, 1964) (by courtesy of the U.S.D.A.).

Various methods for increasing the runoff from the water-supplying strips are being investigated in the arid west of the United States, in Israel, and elsewhere. The two main approaches used are (1) ground covers of plastic films, rubber or metal sheeting materials, and (2) waterproofing and stabilizing soil surfaces by spraying with low-cost materials can be used to reduce infiltration, by dispersing the soil colloids and sealing soil pores. Using sodium carbonate at the rate of 45 kg/ha, 70 per cent runoff was obtained from a cleared and smooth clay-loam soil. This method, too, is dependent on effective erosion control, in the absence of which the treated soil may be removed within one season. A number of water repellent treatments with materials such as silicone, to make the soil hydrophobic, have given encouraging results. Finally, sprayed asphalt appears to offer promise of providing a relatively low-cost and enduring sealing and binding coating (Myers, 1967).

The main disadvantages of the various films are the high cost and susceptibility to damage by winds. Research is continuing on developing new, less expensive and more durable materials, as well as methods of reducing damage—such as bonding the films to special asphalt pavements (Myers, 1967). Immediately, most promising approaches, however, appear to be the waterproofing and stabilizing of the soil surfaces. The simplest of these methods consists of creating a cleared smooth surface. On a well-structured clay-loam soil, with a 4 per cent slope, this method produced

21 per cent runoff of a 195 mm rainfall (Hillel *et al.*, 1967). However, this method is applicable only when erosion hazards are minimal.

Conservation bench terraces: A terrace system for semiarid regions has been designed by Zingg and Hauser (1959) that not only reduces water erosion, but also spreads runoff water over a levelled bench, where it is stored in the soil for use by the crop (see Fig. 1.19). Experience in the field with these terraces shows that good results can be achieved with this method, provided that (1) precision levelling is carried out, (2) there are adequate terrace outlets to handle excess water, and (3) fertilizers are applied so that the stored water is used efficiently. In a region with an average rainfall of 470 mm (mainly summer rainfall in the south-western Great Plains), it is recommended to use one-third of the field area for establishing the terraces, and the remaining two-third for watershed areas (Hauser & Cox, 1962).

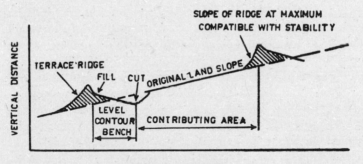

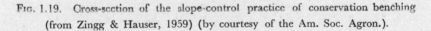

Fig. 1.19. Cross-section of the slope-control practice of conservation benching (from Zingg & Hauser, 1959) (by courtesy of the Am. Soc. Agron.).

Management Practices for Improving the Moisture Regime

Tillage

Role: Before the advent of mechanization, the general attitude towards tillage was that its importance could hardly be overstated. This attitude, equating a maximum number of tillage operations with good husbandry, was further strengthened by the fact that the cost of upkeep of draft animals was practically the same, whether they were working in the field or were stalled; farm labour was also cheap and plentiful.

The importance formerly attached to cultivation as an objective *per se*, is vividly reflected in the following quotation from the Standard Cyclopedia of Horticulture. 'It would have been a sorry thing for agriculture if there had been no weeds. They make us stir the soil, and stirring the soil is the foundation of good farming' (Bailey, 1950). In short, weeds justify their existence simply by obliging the farmer to cultivate the soil !

It was only following gradual replacement of draft animals by tractors, that these traditional concepts of tillage were submitted to close scrutiny. For cost of tillage operations had become a substantial part of the overall production cost. Changes in the number and depth of soil cultivations could make considerable saving possible. Many experiments on the effects of tillage on crop production have been carried out since the beginning of the present century, and the results obtained were most surprising to the early investigators. The overall picture that emerged was that the need and justification for numerous tillage operations had been grossly exaggerated in the past. As a result of the objective reappraisal of the effects of soil cultivation, a new understanding, new attitudes, and new methods, have been evolved.

Most of the classical concepts concerning tillage were first developed in north-west Europe, and later in the U.S.A., and they were naturally adapted to the temperate regions, and their aim was certainly not water conservation. Under the cool and humid conditions of these regions the soil is almost permanently moist; also rainfall is very rarely torrential and therefore is not conducive to erosion. Basic cultivation has been based on the mould-board plough, which cuts and inverts a furrow, completely covering all weeds, trash, stubble, and manure, and leaving a clean surface. Subsequently, disking, harrowing, and rolling, are needed to pulverize the furrow, compact the soil and prepare a seed-bed.

When these methods were transferred to arid lands, whether for the development of areas that had previously not been cultivated or to replace traditional cultivation methods, results were frequently disastrous. Optimum moisture conditions for cultivation are not encountered frequently in dry regions: during the rainy season, torrential downpours occur frequently and the soil may be too wet for heavy equipment; during the dry season, the soil generally dries out almost completely. European style ploughing shatters the soil, breaking the land into clods whose size and hardness depend mainly on the compaction caused by previous farming operations on land that was still moist; the heavy and frequent disking needed to break these clods pulverizes the soil into dust, breaking down soil aggregates, causing wind and water erosion. The soil is therefore easily eroded by water in winter and by wind in summer; soil compaction may cause hard-pans and reduce water infiltration.

With the advent of modern equipment, an entirely new concept of tillage methods developed in the dry regions—different from that of modern tillage in temperate humid climates and from traditional tillage in arid zones. Heavy equipment, drawn by tractors, made possible the cultivation of dry or almost dry soils. The effects achieved are entirely different from those of cultivating moist soil. The effects of tillage methods on crop growth and yields are to a large degree attributable to an increased soil moisture reservoir: (a) by creating soil conditions that favour root growth and penetration, and (b) by improving infiltration and conservation of water.

Water is lost by surface runoff, by infiltration beyond the root zone, through evaporation from the soil surface, and through transpiration by plants.

Tillage can be effective in reducing surface runoff if it is carried out according to approved soil conservation practices. These operations increase infiltration by reducing runoff and minimizing crust formation and may double the amount of water stored in the soil. These effects can be further enhanced by a mulch of crop residues which protects the soil from raindrop impact.

The influence of soil compaction on loss of water by evaporation depends on the moisture content of the soil. At high moisture levels, conduction of water to the soil surface, is greater in a compacted soil than in a loose one. When the soil surface is dry, however, water moves as vapour through the pore spaces, and evaporation will then be greater in a loose soil. Therefore, coarse tillage may increase water losses due to evaporation by leaving large cavities among clods, and thereby enabling an increase in vapour movement. On the other hand, by effectively destroying weeds, it may considerably reduce losses caused by transpiration.

Crop response to tillage will depend on the amount and seasonal distribution of the rainfall. In seasons during which precipitation provides adequate water to the crop throughout the growing period, differences in soil moisture regime due to tillage have little or no effect on yields. Conversely, tillage methods that increase available soil moisture are markedly beneficial to the crop in years of less than optimal rainfall. For example, in an investigation of tillage methods in Iowa, listed maize consistently out-yielded conventionally tilled maize in the six of eleven years that crop showed signs of severe water stress. The yield increases due to listing (which was conducive to water conservation) ranged from 308 kg/ha to as much as 2588 kg/ha; the average increase being 1324 kg/ha. In the other five years of the investigation, yields were above average because of favourable precipitation patterns and there was little difference in yields among different tillage methods.

The effects of the tillage treatments were most marked in years in which there was little soil-stored moisture at sowing time and when a large proportion of the early season precipitation occurred during the first six to seven weeks after planting (Amemiya, 1968).

Deep ploughing, carried out during the summer months in dry soil (see below), is probably the most effective means of controlling perennial weeds as 'couch grass' (*Cynodon dactylon*) and Johnson grass (*Sorghum halepense*), two almost ubiquitous weeds of the warm semiarid areas.

Depth of cultivation: Increasing the depth of ploughing and other tillage operations has a very marked effect on costs: for every additional centimetre of increased depth, the amount of soil to be moved or turned is increased by about 150 tonnes per hectare. The enormous additional effort required cannot be accomplished without a considerable expenditure of fuel. Much research, aimed at determining the most effective depth of tillage, has therefore been carried out, mostly in temperate climates. It was generally found that increasing the depth of ploughing beyond the minimum needed for a specific purpose—weed control, seed-bed preparation, shattering a plough-sole, etc.—did not improve yields.

Similar results were obtained in experiments in dry regions to that with a moist soil. Moisture loss is increased by the depth of tillage—especially if the tilled soil layer is inverted. When a dry soil is rewetted by rain, the proportion of the moisture conserved varies inversely as the depth of dry soil at the surface (Staple, 1964). Soils dry rapidly as the depth of cultivation increases; shallow tillage (up to 7 to 10 cm maximum) is less wasteful of rainfall than is deeper tillage.

The dry surface soil has to be wetted by rain to field capacity before any moisture can penetrate to at least 10-12 cm, at which depth it will be relatively safe from evaporation, and will contribute effectively to crop production. By avoiding tillage implements that invert the soil, subsurface moisture is not exposed and moisture losses are reduced. However, the cultivation of dry, or nearly dry soil, is typical of arid lands, and has no counterpart in temperate region cultivation. It has specific objectives and specific effects, and depth of ploughing has relevance to these effects. Deep tillage, to a depth of 50 cm and more, when carried out under the proper conditions, has marked beneficial effects that are difficult to achieve by other methods. These specific effects are sanitation, improvement of soil structure, and control of perennial weeds.

Exposing a ploughed soil to the effect of sun-rays for prolonged periods is an age-old practice in arid lands, and is still in present-day use both in countries using traditional agricultural methods and also in those using modern ones. This is accompanied by a considerable rise in temperature, which may exceed 74 °C, as recorded in black soils in Poona, India (Kasi Viswanath & Pillai, 1972). The effect of drying and wetting on the soil structure depends on the type of soil, temperature of drying, degree of dryness achieved and the intensity of the wetting process.

Drying the soil has complex chemical, physical and biological effects. For the black soils of India, the main beneficial effect on crop growth appeared to be due to an improvement in the physical properties of the soil (Sreenivasan & Aurangabadkar, 1940). This was confirmed by the more recent work of Kasi Viswanath and Pillai (1972) who found that the increase in size and percentage of water-stable aggregates could be considered as the immediate cause for the improved crop yields from dried and heated soils.

Deep ploughing of a sandy loam to a depth of 45 cm, improved soil structure and root penetration significantly (Subbarami & Dakshinamurti, 1971). A highly significant correlation between soil structure and root growth was observed.

In a dry tropical region of Africa deep ploughing of the soil (up to 60 cm) increased yields of millets and sorghum. This was also ascribed to improved macrostructure; as a result the root system was more extensive and water and nutrient uptake improved (Poulain & Tourte, 1970).

In order to achieve these beneficial results the soil has to be completely dried out before deep ploughing. The success of the deep ploughing depends, therefore, on the soil management during the year preceding the deep ploughing, and on the type of crop grown. The most desirable crop is one that withdraws all the available moisture by the time it is mature. A reasonable amount of soil compaction during seed-bed preparation and sowing of the crop is desirable, as it favours the formation of clods when the land is deep ploughed in the following summer. Deep-ploughing should not start before the land has dried out sufficiently, but should not be too late in the season as otherwise the time available for drying and weathering the clods will be too short. At least three months between the completion of ploughing and onset of the rains should be allowed for this purpose.

Deep ploughing is a very expensive operation, requiring special heavy apparatus; in modern dryland farming it has, however, been found to be an important practice for maintaining a high level of yields. Practical experience has shown that a time interval of five to six years between one deep ploughing and the next, strikes a proper balance between the cost and the benefits of the operation.

Newer concepts in tillage methods: The traditional concept of 'clean' cultivation, in which the farmer equated good farming practice with the complete burying of crop residues and weeds, has had to be abandoned in dry regions. Instead, a different approach has been developed—stubble-mulch farming, which aims at keeping the soil protected at all times, whether by a growing crop, or by crop residues left on the surface during fallow periods (Mishra & Misra, 1967).

In experiments in Nebraska it was found that the rates of erosion of a mulched surface were about one-fifth of those resulting from 'clean tillage' with mould-board ploughing. Wind erosion was also substantially reduced; residues of various amounts and types, reduced the force of the wind immediately above the soil surface by 5 to 99 per cent. The crop (and weed) residues left on the surface of the soil not only offered protection against erosion, but improved water penetration and reduced losses from evaporation (Zingg & Whitefield, 1957). In a three-year grain rotation in Nebraska, a clean-ploughed loess soil lost 2 to 6 times as much runoff water and 4 to 8 times as much soil by erosion as did the stubble-mulched land.

Within certain limits, the control of runoff and erosion is proportional to the amounts of crop residues left on the soil surface; small amounts are more effective against wind erosion than against water erosion. When the total straw production of the crop does not exceed one tonne per hectare, very little protection can be expected from the residues left on the surface.

Stubble-mulch tillage was found to improve moisture conditions in the seed zone significantly, when compared with disk tillage in years with high intensity rainfall. In the central Great Plains (Kansas), soil moisture at seeding time was significantly greater under stubble-mulch than on clean tilled plots in 3 out of 6 years, in a fallow-wheat crop rotation. This improvement occurred in years with high intensity rainfall or when 4 to 6 days of consecutive precipitation occurred more frequently than usual. On the other hand, stubble-much tillage had no influence on soil moisture storage at a depth of 1.30 m (Army et al., 1961).

Mulches may reduce soil temperature for a period of 3 to 6 months, by as much as 3 to 6 °C at 2-5 cm depth, and by 2 to 4 °C at a 10 cm depth (McCalla & Duley, 1946).

The high C/N ratio of the crop residues may depress nitrification, especially in the early growth period, and thereby adversely affect the growth of the crop and, ultimately, its yield. Research data appear to indicate that the response to stubble-mulch tillage is intimately linked with nitrogen availability, as is indicated by the greater response to nitrogen of cereals growing on stubble-mulch tilled plots as compared with conventional tillage, and also by the reduction in protein content of the grain and the reduced straw production of mulched plots. Soil analysis also showed reduced nitrates under stubble-mulching. The lower rate of nitrification under stubble-mulch, as compared to 'clean-tilled' plots, may be due to lower temperature, less effective aeration, and most important to nitrogen fixation by the crop residues, which decompose more slowly on the soil surface than when incorporated in the soil.

The obvious conclusion to be drawn from these observations is that a favourable effect from stubble-mulching can be expected only if nitrogen applications are made in the quantities and at the times required to offset the negative effect of the mulch on available nitrate supply.

Stubble-mulch tillage, however, presents practical problems: the residues left on the surface interfere with seed-bed preparation, weed control and sowing operations. The traditional tillage and sowing equipment is not suitable under these conditions, and a whole new class of equipment had to be developed before the new system became practical.

Stubble-mulch farming has been found to be most effective and beneficial in regions and seasons of low rainfall, and is critically needed where wind erosion presents a considerable hazard. Under conditions of higher rainfall, negative results have been reported; apparently, the stubble-mulch is then conducive to excessive soil moisture, with its resultant ill-effects.

Minimum tillage: Research in recent years has repeatedly shown that frequent tillage operations are rarely beneficial, and frequently detrimental, in addition to being costly. It is a paradox that the modern heavy equipment used for tillage, cultivation, and harvesting, damage the soil structure and increase soil compaction, thereby reducing water infiltration and storage capacity. 'Minimum tillage' can be defined as a method aimed at reducing tillage to the minimum necessary for ensuring a good seed-bed, rapid germination, satisfactory stand, and favourable growing conditions.

In recent years, studies of soil structure in the root zone of maize have shown that the optimum conditions in the row are different from what is optimum in the region between the rows. From this we may conclude that fields in which row crops are grown should be managed as two distinct zones, called by Larson (1962) "seedling environment zone" and "water management zone" and by Shear (1965) "seed-bed zone" and "root-bed zone," respectively. One example of the several minimum tillage methods developed, is *wheel-track planting*.

Wheel-track planting: In this method, the field is ploughed as usual, but instead of using the conventional methods of seed-bed preparation, the seeds are planted in the area compacted by the wheels of the tractor. Experience has shown that tractor wheels make a firm, satisfactory seed-bed even on cloddy soil, ensuring rapid and even germination. The soil between the rows remains rough and loose and is, therefore, better able to absorb moisture and to reduce runoff. Weed seeds lie dormant in the loose soil until rain falls.

Wheel-track planting was found to save about 40 per cent of tillage costs (Peterson *et al.*, 1958). By adding two extra rear wheels to the tractor, it is possible to use a 4-row planter. Experience has shown that the optimal soil moisture for ploughing is also optimal for seed germination (Hansen *et al.*, 1958). Any delay between ploughing and sowing always reduces soil moisture, which may become too low for seed germination. In order to prevent the top-soil from drying out and becoming hard before sowing, it is essential to plough and plant the field in one and the same day.

Certain problems related to the use of minimum tillage have not yet been resolved, in particular those concerning chemical weed control with which minimum cultivation has to be associated.

Fallow: The favourable effect of fallow can be attributed to : better seed-bed preparation, weed control, improved supplies of N and the extra water available to the crop. In Australia, it was found that the two factors of greater importance were water, which accounted for 62% of the variation in grain yield, and nitrogen, which accounted for 29% (French, 1966).

In the rainfall deficient areas, the main importance of cropping sequence is to provide the minimal quantity of moisture required by the wheat crop; hence alternate wheat-fallow is almost inevitably the standard practice. By sacrificing a crop, moisture is conserved from one season to the next, so that the combined precipitation of two rainy seasons may suffice for producing one satisfactory crop. Fallow is considered essential for wheat production in the summer rainfall areas of the middle latitudes when annual precipitation is less than 350-375 mm (Mathews, 1951).

Fallow is effective in conserving soil moisture only if the amount and, in particular, the distribution of rainfall during the fallow period is such as to permit moisture penetration in depth. Practically all available moisture in the upper 20 cm of the soil will be lost by evaporation. Therefore, total seasonal rainfall must not only be sufficient, but individual rains must be sufficient to penetrate in depth. As losses by evaporation are confined mainly to the upper 10-20 cm of the soil surface, a far greater proportion of the total precipitation is lost from a relatively large number of light rains than from a smaller number of heavy rains. In an average season in southern Saskatchewan, less than 10 showers contribute to water storage in fallowed fields from May to October. In a wet season, twice as many showers contribute, but in drought years the storage is almost nil (Staple, 1964).

Conditions for infiltration must be satisfactory, and runoff must be minimized by proper cultivation measures. Moreover, the loss of the stored moisture must be minimized by effective weed-control.

However, even with the best management practices, fallow is usually not efficient in moisture storage, as the following examples demonstrate. In the Great Plains of North America, under an alternate crop-fallow system, the average amount of moisture conserved in the soil during the fallow year was only 16.3 per cent of the total precipitation under conditions in which losses due to runoff and deep percolation were negligible and weeds were well-controlled (Mathews & Army, 1960). In North Dakota, in a region with an average annual precipitation of 400 mm; the average moisture storage efficiency over a 19-year period was 20 per cent (Evans & Lemon, 1957).

However inefficient, the additional 80-100 mm or so of water stored in the soil by fallowing may make the difference between success and complete failure of the succeeding crop in regions with marginal precipitation. Long-term weather records indicate that, in the southern High Plains of the United States, a wheat-fallow rotation will produce yields in excess of 700 kg/ha in approximately eight summers out of ten, while with continuous cropping to wheat the chances of obtaining such yields are in only five seasons out of ten (Army et al., 1959).

In a cereal farming system, an increase of 100 per cent in yield on fallowed land, to compensate for the loss of a cropping year, is not a precondition for making fallow economically justified. Stability of production, distribution of labour, and economy in weed control, may justify fallow even under conditions of lesser response.

Where precipitation is too low for successful crop production, fallow is indispensable. Where crops can be grown with a reasonable prospect of success, fallow is optional; its value is determined by other factors in addition to the degree of crop response, and the areas under fallow will vary from year to year—depending inter alia on economic factors and soil moisture conditions. It is therefore far easier to decide in which regions fallow is essential and where its use is optional.

Fallow and soil fertility: Fallow may have adverse effects on soil fertility which need to be taken into account. In southern California, from 30 to 40 per cent of the organic matter has been lost from the surface 25 cm after 50 to 70 years of grain cropping, mostly in the alternate fallow-grain system (Luebs & Laag, 1964). In south Australia, the inherent fertility of the redbrown soils was quite rapidly depleted by the bare fallow-wheat rotation which was at first widely practised. The situation improved only after the introduction of Subterranean clover pastures into the rotation, which rapidly restored the productivity of worn out wheat soils.

Simply resting the soil, even for a period of only one year ('weedy' fallow) is detrimental to yields and a very poor antecedent for the winter cereals. The depressant effect is due mainly to weed competition, for a cultivated fallow does not show the same negative influence.

Part of the value of fallow is that satisfactory moisture conditions may coincide with temperatures that are favourable for nitrification, so that sufficient amounts of nitrate nitrogen may be made available for the fallowing crop. Fallow is also effective in accumulating nitrate in the soil. In a semiarid winter rainfall area, fallow increased available nitrogen from five- to six-fold over recent cropping (Littlejohn, 1956).

Forage legumes in the rotation: The benefits of cultivated fallow in regions of adequate rainfall are usually overrated and, except in years of unusually low rainfall, the yields obtained after a leguminous forage crop are generally higher than those obtained after a cultivated fallow. Under conditions in which the inclusion of annual forage legumes in the rotation increased the yields of the subsequent cereal crop, residual soil moisture after removal of the legume may be high, and not much less than after fallow, as is shown in Table 1.12.

The earlier the legume was harvested, the higher was the amount of residual moisture (Fig. 1.20). Green manure and silage were as effective or nearly as effective in conserving moisture as was cultivated fallow. By contrast, when a deep rooted legume crop such as lucerne or sweet clover was grown, the soil usually dried out to a considerable depth. For example, in Nebraska it was found that lucerne, a deep rooted, drought resistant crop, made excellent growth the first three years after seeding, quite independently of

Table 1.12. Effect of fallow and legumes in the rotation, on amount of residual moisture at the time of sowing the following wheat crop

(Arnon, 1961)

Preceding crop		Amount of residual moisture in soil (30 to 120 cm depth)	
		m³ per ha	in percentage of control
Fallow	..	3500	100
Green manure (fenugreek)	..	3500	100
Silage (horse-beans)	..	3230	92
Hay (vetches)	..	2950	84
Grain (fenugreek)	..	2520	72

current rainfall, because it was drawing on the water reserves in the soil to a depth of up to 9 m. Subsequently, after the available water in the subsoil was depleted, yields declined and became closely associated with current rainfall. When cereals followed lucerne, it was found that subsoil moisture

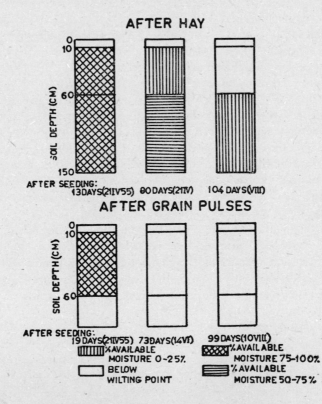

Fig. 1.20. Effect of the stage at which a legume is harvested on the amount of residual soil moisture available to the following sorghum crop (Arnon, 1961).

was not replaced to a marked degree in the course of 15 years (Kramer, 1969).

A fallow-crop system, will reduce the organic matter content of the soil far more rapidly than does a continuous cropping system, and will eventually result in lower yields. The time required to reach this condition depends on the original level of soil fertility, the net quantity of nutrients removed annually, management practices (such as burning stubble, stubble-mulch farming, etc.), and the amount of precipitation.

Better results both from the point of view of soil fertility and moisture regime can generally be achieved by including annual or leguminous forage crops in the crop rotation.

Reducing Losses due to Evapotranspiration

Reducing losses due to transpiration by the crop

Role of transpiration: There are two schools of thought regarding the role of transpiration. The one considers transpiration as a necessary evil, the other as an unavoidable evil. Transpiration is to some extent an evil, because inevitably absorption of water lags behind transpiration, causing water deficits in the plant tissues—with adverse effects on photosynthesis and growth, disruption of metabolic processes, and in extreme cases results in death of the plants.

Transpiration is considered a necessary evil, because the foliage of a crop intercepts a quantity of radiation that is far in excess of its ability to utilize effectively. Leaves subjected to such a radiation load must be able to dissipate the excess energy quickly, or else their temperature would rise to lethal levels within less than one minute (Idso et al., 1966). This dissipation of excess heat is made possible by three mechanisms: thermal radiation of the leaf, removal of heat by convection currents, and transpiration. The literature is full of conflicting claims regarding the relative importance of these mechanisms in dissipating excess heat from leaves.

One group of authors maintain that, for most cultivated crops, the transpiration of large quantities of water is the main mechanism for this purpose (Thornthwaite & Mather, 1954), each gram of water evaporated removing the energy equivalent to 580 calories.

Another school of thought states that the role of transpiration in cooling plants has little practical significance. Many research workers have shown that there is little relationship between leaf temperature and the rate of transpiration. The temperature of wilted leaves was found to increase by only 2-5 °C, when transpiration was slowed down. For them, the main factor in preventing an excessive rise in leaf temperature is the removal of heat by air movement (Ansari & Loomis, 1959).

There is no doubt that transpiration participates in dissipating excess heat; when leaf temperature approaches a lethal level, transpiration—by reducing leaf temperature by only a few degrees—may swing the difference between survival and death (Gates, 1964). When transpiration is reduced, however, convective cooling increases; only under extreme conditions of high radiation incidence and very low velocity, would there be a danger of excessive leaf temperatures as a result of reduced transpiration (Gale & Hagan, 1966). Moreover in hot, arid regions, the stomata of plants close during the hottest hours of the day, when the cooling effect of transpiration would be most needed.

Transpiration is also an extremely important physiological process, because water movement in the xylem is essential to nutrient distribution in the plants. Transpiration produces the energy gradient which causes movement of water into and through plants, and the translocation of organic and inorganic materials between cells. However, water movement in the xylem is considerably in excess of that required for adequate nutrient transport (Crafts, 1968). Transpiration can also have considerable effects on respiration rates and various biochemical activities of the plant (Gates, 1964).

Transpiration is considered an unavoidable evil, because the entrance of carbon dioxide into the leaf for photosynthesis is essential; a plant structure that makes this possible will inevitably make possible water loss through transpiration. It has been shown that most plants which have very low rates of transpiration also have low rate of photosynthesis and grow slowly (Hygen, 1953). Maximum rates of photosynthesis and growth are related to a maximum rate of transpiration (Penman, 1952).

All this does not imply that it might not be possible to reduce transpiration to some extent, and without adverse effects. For example, it has been found that small increases in carbon dioxide concentration can cause large decreases in stomatal apertures, and in transpiration, while net photosynthesis is increased (Moss *et al.*, 1961).

Methods for decreasing transpiration: In principle, transpiration can be reduced in the field in four ways:

(a) Increasing leaf resistance to water vapour loss by applying materials that tend to close or cover the stomata (antitranspirants). —see the chapter by Davenport and Hagan in this volume.

(b) Reducing the net energy uptake by the leaves, by increasing leaf reflectance.

(c) Reducing top growth by growth retardants (Papadakis, 1974).

(d) Increasing the air resistance to water vapour transfer, by using windbreaks—see the chapter by Sturrock in this volume.

Stomatal closure: The two types of gas exchange between plant and atmosphere: transpiration and CO_2 assimilation (appat. photosynthesis) are intimately linked. Stomatal resistance slows down simultaneously both processes, the loss of water to the atmosphere and entry of CO_2 into the plants (Mingeau, 1969).

The main objection to antitranspirants is that, by reducing transpiration, they might cause an increase in leaf temperature to critical levels. It has, however, been estimated that under field conditions, transpiration cannot reduce the temperature of leaves by more than 5 per cent, and that under most conditions the higher temperature would not be critical (Gale & Poljakoff-Mayber, 1965). The best antitranspirants reduce transpiration by 30 to 40 per cent at the most.

The possibility of inducing stomatal closure in such a way as to decrease transpiration to a greater degree than photosynthesis, has been given much attention.

Inducing stomatal closure: Spray materials used for various purposes, such as certain herbicides, fungicides, metabolic inhibitors, and growth hormones, have been found to cause the closure of the guard cells of the stomata and thereby reduce transpiration (Gale & Hagan, 1966), and an extensive study of compounds to be used for this purpose has been made in the last decade (Poljakoff-Mayber & Gale, 1972).

The main practical problem is to obtain materials that induce stomatal closure without toxic effects and that are long-lasting. This has not yet been achieved. For example, one of the initially most promising materials phenylmercuric acetate (PMA), a fungicide that also causes stomatal closure, was found to cause direct inhibition of mesophyll photosynthesis, making it unsuitable for use as an antitranspirant (Squire & Jones, 1971).

Film-type antitranspirants: Plastic and waxy materials that cover the stomata with a film which has more resistance to the passage of water than to that of CO_2, are being sought. The characteristics required, in addition to selective gas-permeability, are easy application, inexpensiveness, and non-phytotoxicity—also the ability to form a continuous film on the leaf surface, to resist degradation, and to retain elasticity (Gale & Hagan, 1966).

Film-type antitranspirants which present selectively permeable barriers to water vapour and carbon dioxide diffusion in the required direction have not yet been found. Those available are many times more permeable to water vapour than to CO_2; however, as in practice they only cover part of the leaf, transpiration and photosynthesis are reduced to about the same degree (Poljakoff-Myber & Gale, 1972). In brief, methods for reducing transpiration have not yet proved to be of practical application. Should effective, non-toxic antitranspirants become available, their most promising use would possibly be during relatively short periods of extreme drought susceptibility, such as during flowering of maize, for example (Waggoner, 1966).

Increasing leaf reflectance (leaf albedo): Among other moisture saving characteristics of desert vegetation, is the commonly light grey colour of the foliage, which has a high albedo and is considered by Thornthwaite (1958) to be one of the most important moisture conserving properties of such plants.

Photosynthesis of leaves of many crops completely exposed to sunlight is usually saturated at relatively low light intensities. Furthermore, 60% of the solar radiation is of a wavelength longer than 0.7μ, and is not used in photosynthesis (Gates, 1962). Therefore, the greater the average overall radiation in the dry regions, the higher is the transpiration/photosynthesis ratio (Wit, 1958). Reflective materials, which reduce the amount of solar radiation absorbed by the leaves, could therefore reduce the transpiration rate considerably more than photosynthesis. It has been calculated that increasing natural albedo from 0.25 to 0.4 of the incident short wave radiation, would enable a 30% saving in water use by the crop (Seginer, 1969).

Under laboratory conditions, it was found that the application of kaolinite to leaves of different plant species induced a reduction in leaf temperature of 3-4 °C and a decrease in transpiration of 22-28%. Photosynthesis was reduced only at low light intensities (Abu-Khaled *et al.*, 1970). Similar trials under field conditions do not appear to have been carried out. Selective materials, which reflect only wavelengths which are not used in photosynthesis (i.e. above 0.7μ) are not known at present (Poljakoff-Mayber & Gale, 1972).

Growth retardants: Certain growth retardants have been found to reduce the plant susceptibility to water stress. Untreated plants wilted much more quickly and severely than did plants treated with growth retardants and they died sooner when exposed to stress. In view of the known antagonism between gibberellic acid and growth retardants, Livne and Vaadia (1972) propose the view that the apparent increase in drought tolerance of plants treated by growth retardants might be related to interference of these compounds with biosynthesis of gibberellic acid. A reduced level of gibberellic acid in the treated plants could result in reduced stomatal opening and hence lowered transpiration. However, Plaut *et al.* (1964) did not find that the treatments with growth retardants decreased the transpiration rate per unit leaf area.

Although (2-chloroethyl) trimethyl ammonium chloride (CCC) is used to reduce lodging, numerous instances are cited in the literature in which increases in yield were recorded, even when no or negligible lodging occurred (Pinthus & Rudich, 1967; Humphries, 1968; Papadakis, 1968, 1972, 1974).

In trials in Australia, in which CCC gave large increases in yield, the yield increases were not ascribed to lodging as the latter occurred late

in the life of the untreated plants and was not severe. The yield increment was due to an increase in the number of grains per ear indicating a
favourable effect of CCC prior to grain setting, at a time when drought
occurred. Subsequently, summer rains relieved the moisture stress and
provided moisture for grain filling (Philpotts, 1972). Lowe and Carter
(1970) in Australia, also imputed yield increases obtained from CCC-
treated wheat to a delay in ear emergence which could result in more
florets per spikelet.

In trials in Israel, bean plants treated with CCC remained turgid and
survived longer under stress conditions than control plants. At a moisture
regime maintained near wilting point, the growth of the treated plants
exceeded that of the untreated ones (Halevy & Kessler, 1963). In India
too, it was found that foliar applications of CCC increased yields of wheat
significantly, though the yield levels were generally low due to late sowing
(Shrivastava *et al.*, 1968).

CCC was found to increase root growth at all depths (Hanus, 1967).
Humphries (1968) also attributes the improved yields obtained from
treating wheat plants with CCC, when no lodging occurred in the control,
to the increased root growth. The increase in root growth in depth may
enable more shoots of the treated plants to survive dry periods, especially
at the time of ear emergence (loc. cit.), when drought is most critical.
Plaut and Halevy (1966) ascribed increased yields of treated plants to
their increased ability to regenerate new shoots on watering after wilting,
but found no increase in root growth of the treated plants.

Another effect of growth retardants (CCC & B-995) that has been
recorded, is a considerable delay in the senescence of detached leaves
(Halevy & Wittwer, 1965). This delay in senescence may explain the
increased ability of the treated plants to withstand drought.

While growth retardants usually decrease the top/root ratio and have
frequently proved effective in increasing yields under conditions of moisture stress, there is little evidence that their beneficial effect can be ascribed
to a reduction in the transpiration rate of the treated plants.

Windbreaks: Much work has been done on the effect on crop production
in the semiarid steppes of the U.S.S.R. of planting shelter-belts of trees
(Albenskii & Nikitin, 1956). Many shelter-belts were also planted in
the semiarid plains of the United States. While some conflicting results
have been recorded, the vast majority of reports indicate beneficial effects
due to windbreaks, and their value in the semiarid regions of the world
is well-documented (Rosenberg, 1967; Sturrock, 1974).

In the U.S.S.R. it was found that the yields of grain crops were increased
by 20-30 per cent, and those of some grasses by 100-200 per cent, in the
sheltered zone. The advantages of the shelter-belts were most marked in
years of drought, as utilization of the limited water available for transpiration

was more efficient by the sheltered crops than by others (Albenskii & Nikitin, 1956).

Wind strip cropping: Wind strip cropping consists in growing annual crops between strips of perennial grasses, and has been found to be an effective method for efficient wind erosion control and moisture conservation in trials carried out at the Central Arid Zone Research Institute, Jodhpur (Misra, 1964 a,b). The width of the protective strips depends on soil and wind characteristics and the type of farm machinery used (Mishra *et al.,* 1968). Grass strips of *Lasiurus sindicus, Panicum antidotale* and *P. turgidum* gave good results. (For a detailed study on the effect of wind on crop production, readers are advised to refer the chapter by Dr. J. W. Sturrock in this volume.)

The control of weeds

Since time immemorial, controlling weeds has been known to be one of the most effective means of increasing the amount of water available to the crops and, therefore, of increasing water use efficiency. Weeds frequently transpire greater amounts of water per unit of dry matter produced than do the plants with which they grow in association. The leaf area of a single plant of *Sinapis arvenis* (Wild Mustard or Charlock) at blooming stage was found to be 7300 sq cm, as compared with 140 sq cm for a single wheat plant with which it was growing in association (Pavlychenko, 1949). This disproportion in leaf area gives an indication of the relative demands of the weed and of the cultivated crop on soil moisture supplies, as well as on the amount of radiant energy intercepted by the weed, with its concomitant reduction of photosynthesis in the cultivated crop. It has been estimated that the amount of water saved by eliminating weeds in a maize field is equivalent to providing an entire irrigation at the time of maximum need (Mangelsdorf, 1966).

The effects of weed competition are mainly felt in the young crop; the much more rapid rate of growth of both the aerial parts and the roots of many weeds gives them a considerable advantage in depressing and even crowding out the crop plants among which they are growing.

Weeds are naturally endowed with a number of characteristics which increase their survival rate and their ability to compete with crop plants. Their vitality frequently helps them to overcome the ill-effects of herbicides. They produce enormous quantities of seeds. In many species the seeds germinate only when conditions favourable to the survival of the seedlings are assured. In others, the seeds have various periods of dormancy; only a fraction of the total quantity of seeds germinate at a given time, so that seed reserves are always available in the soil even if one or more germinations are destroyed by natural causes or by the efforts of the cultivator.

Causes and prevention: Farmers are frequently responsible in the first place for causing the weed infestation of their fields. The most obvious way in which weeds are introduced is by the use of contaminated seed supplies. Hence, the importance of seed laws to safeguard the farmer against unscrupulous or negligent seed suppliers, and of seed certification schemes to ensure proper supervision of seed production and distribution.

The use of manure, especially that of sheep that have grazed in weedy areas, unless properly decomposed, can contribute enormous amounts of seeds to the fields.

The introduction of combine harvesting has also favoured the spread of weed seeds. When cereals are harvested by hand or by binders and thrashing is concentrated in a single place, weed seeds can be collected and destroyed. The combine-harvester does a preliminary cleaning job, separates a large proportion of weed seeds, and scatters them in the field behind the combine.

Irrigation and drainage ditchbanks, uncultivated patches, fence rows, weedy banks of roadsides, and country lanes, are also permanent sources of weed reinfestation.

Inappropriate tillage methods help to divide and disperse the roots and rhizomes of perennial weeds. Delays in tillage, in mowing, or in the harvesting of crops, may provide the weeds with an additional opportunity to disperse their seeds. Controlling the weeds in one crop, and neglecting weed control in the next, gives a new start to weed infestation. It is estimated that if only 1 per cent of a typical stand of weeds survive control methods, it is capable of producing over 100 million new weed seeds per hectare (Day, 1966).

Mechanical control: Even with the effective modern chemical methods available, mechanical methods of weed control are still frequently justified, as they may be less expensive and less dangerous to neighbouring crops or orchards. However, even intensive cultivations, planned for effective weed control, cannot destroy in a single year more than about 50 per cent of the viable seeds. It is estimated that a 10-year control programme will reduce a typical weed seed population of 500 millions per hectare, to about half-a-million (Day, 1966).

Hoeing and hand-weeding: Hoeing and hand-weeding are probably the oldest agricultural occupations, and the back-breaking work involved still forms a considerable and inevitable part of the human effort involved in primitive agriculture.

Tillage

Even after the advent of chemical weed-killers, tillage methods are still, for many situations, the most effective and economical means of weed control. Ploughing, cultivating, and harrowing, make possible weed control before sowing the crop, and there are appropriate tools that can do a satisfactory job even after its emergence. The younger and smaller the weeds are, the more efficient and economical will be their control.

The role of tillage in weed control consists in:

(a) provoking the germination of weed seeds, which can then be easily destroyed by mechanical or chemical means;

(b) bringing roots or stolons to the surface, where they will dry out under the sun;

(c) repeated cultivation, depletes the food reserves of the plant; and

(d) uprooting or smothering the weeds with soil.

Tillage may consist of cultivating a field between cropping periods (clean tillage), in passing through a sown field with special equipment that destroys the weeds without severely damaging the crop (blind tillage), accomplished by harrows, rotatory hoes, finger weeders etc., or in inter-tillage of row-crops.

The disturbance of the soil surface stimulates many weeds to germinate (King, 1966). Therefore, the first tillage operation usually stimulates the reappearance of a new wave of weeds, and needs to be followd by a second operation for their destruction. The implement chosen should be the one that under the given circumstances—soil condition, weed size, age of crop, etc.—will destroy weeds efficiently at the least cost to the farmer. Tillage operations should be as superficial as possible, and adjusted to the minimum depth needed for effective weed control. Deeper tillage is more expensive, brings a new supply of weed seeds to the surface, and in intertillage damages the roots of the cultivated crop unnecessarily.

Chemical control: The development of the selective organic herbicides is probably the most significant advance in agriculture since World War II. A whole array of new techniques and chemicals—low volume spraying, improved surfactants, the precision application of herbicides to the soil, and granular formulations; new approaches such as presowing and pre-emergence weed control; the discovery of new herbicides that kill grasses selectively, and of chemicals that are converted into herbicides by the plant or in the soil—have supplied the farmer with means for selective control of weeds in most crops, even including those that were considered to be most susceptible to the hormonal herbicides.

Kinds of herbicides: The number and variety of herbicides have increased enormously in recent years; some disappear after a relatively short period of use, to be replaced by other, more effective compounds. New compounds are constantly being added to the list. Up to the present, about 30 groups of herbicides have been investigated, including several thousands of active compounds, of which about 100 are already in commercial use (Day, 1966).

It is interesting to note that most of the current weed control is actually being achieved with a very small number of chemicals. In 1964, three basic chemicals—2,4-D, Simazine and Diuron, and their homologues and analogues—accounted for 75 per cent of all weed control by chemicals. Only two fundamental physiological effects on plants are involved in the action of these herbicides: 2,4-D causes abnormal plant growth, while Simazine and Diuron interfere with photosynthesis, and, for this reason, their herbicidal effectiveness depends to a large degree on light intensity (Overbeek, 1964).

Problems resulting from the use of herbicides

Persistence of herbicides in the soil: Herbicides in the soil may be destroyed by microorganisms, may decompose chemically or by photodecomposition, may be inactivated by adsorption on the soil colloids, or may be lost by leaching or volatilization (Klingman, 1961). The principal factor involved in the degradation of the herbicides is biological. Decomposition of herbicides to subtoxic levels by soil microorganisms may require a few days or up to a year or more.

The problem of the persistence of herbicides in the soil has two contradictory aspects: persistence is desirable in order to ensure a weedfree environment for as long as possible, but it is undesirable if it interferes with the sowing of a susceptible crop following the crop for which it had been used. In addition, the build-up of residues may reach toxic levels for most, if not all, crops.

The detrimental effects of herbicide residues are usually more serious in arid than in humid regions, and in rain-fed agriculture more than under irrigation. The erratic unpredictable rainfall of the semiarid regions makes it difficult to forecast the time that will be required for breakdown of a herbicide to innocuous levels. The long dry periods may permit persistence of herbicidal activity, which may then interfere with cropping schedules.

In Nebraska, phytotoxic concentrations of Simazine and Atrazine were found to have accumulated in the subsoil, 16 months after treatment (Burnside *et al.*, 1963). 2, 3, 6-TIBA (2, 3, 6-trichlorobenzoic acid) was found to destroy soybeans five seasons after application. Monuron reduced oat yields in the third growing season after its application (Burnside *et al.*, 1965).

The introduction of new, effective and selective weed control measures, has had a considerable impact on traditional management practices. A new criterion in the choice of varieties is their relative susceptibility to the standard herbicides. Varieties such as dwarf wheats, which could not have held their own against broad-leafed weeds, can now be sown safely. When pre-emergence treatments are anticipated, the seed-bed has to be prepared accordingly; direct seeding can replace planting, and rates of sowing based on the need for subsequent thinning are no longer necessary. In general, rates of sowing and distances between rows can be reduced when the farmer is certain of a relatively weedfree stand.

Chemical fallowing: Weeds and volunteer wheat often germinate during the fallow year and are difficult to control, especially with stubble-mulch tillage; appropriate herbicides can be used successfully for this purpose and it is this use that makes stubble-mulching practicable (Oveson & Appleby, 1971).

As a result of numerous studies on methods of utilizing herbicides in semiarid areas of weed control during fallow periods, 'chemical fallowing' is in many cases replacing the traditional clean-tilled fallow and even the newer methods of mechanical stubble-mulch farming (Wiese *et al.*, 1967). With chemical control of weeds in fallow, yields were identical to those obtained from conventional tillage (Baker *et al.*, 1956). Chemical fallow greatly increases the crop residues that are available for wind erosion control. With an initial amount of residue after harvest of approximately $2\frac{1}{2}$ tonnes/ha, after 11 months chemical fallow left 80 per cent of this, sweep tillage left 66 per cent, and disking left less than 3 per cent (Wiese & Army, 1958).

Chemical fallow reduces tillage operations, not only during the fallow period, but also subsequently in the growing crop. For example, when Propazine was applied to wheat stubble, it was found that three tillage operations during the fallow period were eliminated, as was one in the fallowing sorghum crop. Soil moisture storage and sorghum yields were the same as those obtained by traditional tillage during fallow and inter-row cultivation of the sorghum crop (Wiese *et al.*, 1967).

Chemical fallow has also been shown to reduce costs of production. When atrazine was used for weed control in the fallow after wheat and a subsequent sorghum crop, net returns were markedly increased over those obtained with mechanical weed control methods (Phillips, 1964). Following chemical fallowing, mechanical harvesting has been facilitated in weedfree crops such as cotton, and is much improved in efficiency in other crops.

Reducing evaporation losses from the soil

Lemon (1956) has described three stages of evaporation from soils. The first stage is characterized by a rapid and steady loss of water with the rate dependent on the net effects of water transmission rate through the soil and the above ground boundary conditions, such as wind speed, temperature, relative humidity and radiant energy. The second stage is one of rapid decline in the rate of loss as the soil reservoir becomes depleted. Here the above ground conditions are no longer as important, and intrinsic soil factors assume a dominant role in governing the rate of moisture flow to the surface. The third stage is extremely slow and is governed by adsorptive forces of molecular distances at the liquid-solid interface.

The greatest potentials for suppressing evaporation from soil lie within the first and second stages; these include methods for (i) decreasing turbulent transfer of water vapour to the atmosphere by plants, wind breaks, straw mulches etc., (ii) decreasing capillary continuity by rapid drying of the surface layer, and (iii) decreasing capillary flow and moisture holding capacity of the surface soil layers. Some applications in practice will now be considered.

Soil mulches: At the beginning of the century, King (1914) carried out his 'classical' experiment from which he claimed that a surface mulch of dry soil 5-8 cm deep, by obstructing the rise of water to the surface through capillary action, effectively reduced loss of water as compared with a soil having an undisturbed surface. Following King's experiment and conclusions, a soil mulch for moisture conservation became standard procedure in dry regions, and dicta such as: 'two cultivations can replace one irrigation' became very popular. The too-frequent cultivations impaired soil structure, however, and increased soil losses by erosion. These effects were most pronounced on the rowcrops, such as cotton, maize, and soybeans, which, for this reason, gained the reputation of being soil destroying crops.

It has since been shown that after a rainfall, the top 7-10 cm of the soil dry out rapidly; in any case it would be impossible to prevent this loss by cultivation, because the drying out had already taken place by the time the soil surface was sufficiently dry for cultivation to be possible. Below the dry layer, moisture loss by evaporation from the soil becomes minimal, and further water losses are mainly due to plant transpiration—hence the favourable effect of weed control on water losses which are thereby reduced.

An important benefit from maintaining a loose layer on the surface of the soil is obtained on soils that tend to shrink and crack deeply on drying. Such cracks, which penetrate deeply, may cause the loss of considerable amounts of moisture through much of the root zone. In Texas, it was found that the evaporation from the side walls of shallow shrinkage cracks in a clay soil varied from 33 to 91 per cent of that from a comparable area of surface soil (Adams & Hanks, 1964). These cracks are filled and covered by the loose layer that is formed during cultivation of the soil surface.

Straw mulches: As opposed to the effectiveness of creating a 'dust mulch' by cultivation, in order to reduce evaporation, straw and the other residues left on the soil surface have proved to be very effective. Where mulching is practiced both the amount of energy absorbed by the soil and air movement immediately above the soil are decreased and hence evaporation reduced. It has been estimated that a straw mulch saved the equivalent of 50 to 75 mm of rainfall in dry weather (Stephenson & Schuster, 1946).

Chemical treatments: Experiments have been carried out with the object of reducing evaporation from the soil by using suitable chemicals.

It has been found that Hexadecanol, a long chain alcohol mixed with the surface 1/4 inch of the soil, reduced evaporation by 43 per cent (Olson *et al.*, 1964b). This material, which is resistant to microbial activity, remained effective for more than a year. The surface layer of treated soil dried out more rapidly than that of untreated soil, creating a diffusional barrier to evaporation. Fewer cracks developed in the treated than in untreated soil, and the Hexadecanol also increased aggregate stability. (For a detailed study on mulches, the readers are advised to refer the chapter on "Role of mulches in dryland agriculture" by Dr. P. W. Unger in this volume.)

REFERENCES

AAMODT, O. S. and W. A. JOHNSTON, 1936. Studies on drought resistance in spring wheat. Can. J. Res. 14 : 122-52.

ABU-KHALED, A.; R. M. HAGAN and D. C. DAVENPORT, 1970. Effect of kaolinite as a reflective antitranspirant, on leaf temperature, transpiration, photosynthesis and water use efficiency. Water Resour. Res. 6: 280.

ADAMS, F.; F. J. VEIHMEYER and N. BROWN, 1942. Cotton irrigation investigations in San Joaquin Valley, California, 1926-35. Calif. agric. Exp. Sta. Bull. 668.

ADAMS, J. E. and R. J. HANKS, 1964. Evaporation from soil shrinkage cracks. Proc. Soil Sci. Soc. Am. 28: 281-4.

ALBE, E. M. and D. FOURNIER, 1958. The modification of microclimates. Arid Zone Res. 10: 126-46.

ALBENSKII, A. V. and P. D. NIKITIN, 1956. "Handbook of Afforestation and Soil Amelioration," State Publishing House for Agriculture, Moscow (Translated from Russian by Israel Programme for Scientific Translation, Jerusalem).

AMEMIYA, M. 1968. Tillage soil water relations of corn as influenced by weather. Agron. J. 60: 534-7.

ANSARI, A. Q. and W. E. LOOMIS, 1959. Leaf temperatures. Am. J. Bot. 46: 713-7.

ARMY, T. J.; J. J. BOND and C. E. DOREN VAN, 1959. Precipitation yield relationships in dryland wheat production on medium- to fine-textured soils of the southern High Plains. Agron. J. 51: 721-4.

ARMY, T. J. and J. C. HIDE, 1959. Effect of green manure crops on dryland production in the Great Plains area of Montana. *Ibid.* 51: 196-8.

ARMY, T. J.; A. F. WIESE and R. J. HANKS, 1961. Effect of tillage and chemical weed control practices on soil moisture losses during the fallow period. Proc. Soil Sci. Soc. Am. 25: 410-13.

ARNON, I. 1961. "Some Aspects of Research on Field Crops in Israel", Div. of Publ., Nat. & Univ. Inst. of Agric., Rehovot, Iarael. Abstract of Publication 372-E.

ARNON, I. 1972. "Crop Production in Dry Regions" (2 vols.), Leonard Hill, London.

ARNON, I. and A. BLUM, 1964. Response of hybrid and self pollinated sorghum varieties to moisture regime and intra-row competition. Israel J. agric. Res. 14: 45-53.

ASANA, R. D. 1957. The problem of assessment of drought resistance in crop plants. Indian J. Genet. Pl. Breed. 17: 371-8.

ASANA, R. D. 1962. Analysis of drought resistance in wheat. Arid Zone Res. 16: 183-90.

ASANA, R. D.; P. N. BAHL; P. N. SHARMA and B. KUMAR, 1968. Grain weight of main shoot as an index of yield for non-irrigated wheat. Indian J. Genet. Pl. Brced. 28: 85-90.

ASANA, R. D. and V. S. MANI, 1949. Photosynthesis in the ears of five varieties of wheat. Nature 163: 450-1.

ASANA, R. D.; A. D. SAINI and D. RAY, 1958. Studies in physiological analysis of yield. III. The rate of grain development in wheat in relation to photosynthetic surface and soil moisture. Physiol. Pl. 2: 655-65.

ASANA, R. D. and D. N. SINGH, 1967. On the relation between flowering time, root growth and soil moisture extraction in wheat under non-irrigated cultivation. Indian J. Pl. Physiol. 10: 154-69.

ASHTON, F. M. 1956. Effect of a series of cycles of alternating low and high soil water contents on the rate of apparent photosynthesis in sugarcane. Pl. Physiol. 31: 226-34.

ASHTON, T. 1948. "Technique of Breeding for Drought Resistance in Crops", Commonwealth Bureau of Plant Breeding and Genetics, Technical Communication No. 14.

ASPINALL, D.; P. B. NICHOLLS and C. H. MAY, 1964. The effect of soil moisture stress on the growth of barley. I. Vegetative development and grain yield. Aust. J. agric. Res. 15: 729.

AZIZBEKOVA, Z. S. 1962. The effect of sulphate salination-hardening on the productivity of some agricultural plants (in Russian with English summary). Fiziol. Rast. 9: 741-6.

BAGGA, A. K.; K. N. RUWALI and R. D. ASANA, 1970. Comparison of the responses of some Indian and semidwarf Mexican wheats to unirrigated cultivation. Indian J. agric. Sci. 40: 421-7.

BAGNOLD, R. A. 1954. The physical aspects of dry deserts. In: Biology of Deserts, Cloudsley-Thompson, J. L. (ed), Inst. of Biol., London.

BAILEY, L. H. 1950. "The Standard Cyclopedia of Horticulture". Vol. III. Macmillan, New York.

BAKER, D. N.; J. D. HESKETH and R. E. C. WEAVER, 1974. Crop architecture in relation to yield. *In:* Crop Physiology, Gupta, U. S. (ed), Haryana Agric. Univ., Hissar, India.

BAKER, D. N. and R. B. MUSGRAVE, 1964. The effects of low level moisture stress on the rate of apparent photosynthesis in corn. Crop Sci. 4: 249-53.

BAKER, L. O.; J. L. KRALL; T. S. AESHEIN and T. T. HARTMAN, 1956. Chemical summer fallow in Montana. Down to Earth 11:21-23.

BALDY, C. 1963. Cultures associées et productivitè de l'eau. Ann. Agron. 14: 489-534.

BARBER, S. A. 1959. Relation of fertilizer placement to nutrient uptake and crop yield. II. Effects of low potassium soil level and precipitation. Agron. J. 51: 97-9.

BHAN, S. and D. K. MISRA, 1970a. Effects of variety, spacing and soil fertility on root development in groundnut under arid conditions. Indian J. agric. Sci. 40: 1050-55.

BHAN, S. and D. K. MISRA, 1970b. Water utilization by groundnut (*Arachis hypogea* L.) as influenced due to variety, plant population and soil fertility level under arid zone conditions. Indian J. Agron. 15: 258-63.

BINGHAM, J. 1966. Varietal response in wheat to water supply in the field, and male sterility caused by a period of drought in a glass house experiment. Ann. app. Biol. 57: 365-77.

BLACK, C. A. 1968. Crop yields in relation to water supply and soil fertility. *In:* Plant Environment and Efficient Water Use, pp. 177-206, Pierre, W. H.; D. Kirkham; J. Pesek and R. Shaw (eds), Am. Soc. Agron. & Soil Sci. Soc. Am., Madison, Wisconsin.

BLACKMAN, C. E. and J. N. BLACK, 1959. Physiological and ecological studies in the analysis of plant environment. XII. The role of light as a limiting factor. Ann. Bot. (N. S.) 23: 131-45.

BLUM, A. 1972. Effect of planting date on water use and its efficiency in dryland grain sorghum. Agron. J. 64: 775-8.

BOND, J. J.; J. F. POWER and W. O. WILLIS, 1971. Soil water extraction by N-fertilized spring wheat. Agron. J. 63: 280-3.

BONNER, J. 1962. The upper limit of crop yield. Science 137: 11-5.

BOYER, J. S. 1970. Differing sensitivity of photosynthesis to low leaf water potentials in corn and soybean. Pl. Physiol. 46: 236-9.

BRAG, H. 1972. The influence of potassium on the transpiration rate and stomatal opening in *Triticum aestivum* and *Pisum sativum*. Pl. Physiol. 26: 250-57.

BROUWER, R. 1964. Response of bean plants to root temperatures. I. Root temperatures and growth in the vegetative stage. Jaarb. I. B. S. 11-22.

BROWN, B. L. and W. D. SHRADER, 1959. Grain yields, evapotranspiration and water use efficiency of grain sorghum under different cultural practices. Agron. J. 51: 339-43.

BROWN, D. A.; G. A. PLACE and J. V. PETTIET, 1960. The effect of soil moisture upon cation exchange in soils and nutrient uptake by plants. Trans. 7th Int. Congr. Soil. Sci. 3: 443-9.

BROWN, P. L. 1972. Water use and soil water depletion by dryland wheat as affected by nitrogen fertilization. Ibid. 63: 43-6.

BUCHINGER, A. 1930. Die Bedeutung der Selektion nach der Saugkraft fur die Pflanzenzuchtung. Z. Zucht. 15: 101-14.

BUNTING, A. H. and D. S. H. DRENNAN, 1966. Some aspects of the morphology and physiology of cereals in the vegetative phase, pp. 20-38. In: The Growth of Cereals and Grasses, Milthorpe, F. L. and J. D. Ivins (eds), Butterworths, London.

BURNSIDE, O. C.; C. R. FENSTER and G. A. WICKS, 1963. Dissipation and leaching of Monuron, Simazine and Atrazine in Nebraska soils. Weeds 11: 209-13.

BURNSIDE, O. C.; G. A. WICKS and C. R. FENSTER, 1965. Herbicide longevity in Nebraska soils. Ibid. 13: 277-8.

CALDER, D. M. 1966. Inflorescence, induction and initiation in the Graminae, pp. 59-73. In: The Growth of Cereals and Grasses, Milthorpe, F. L. and J. D. Ivins (eds), Butterworths, London.

CALLAGHAN, A. R. and A. J. MILLINGTON, 1956. "The Wheat Industry in Australia", Angus and Robertson, Sydney.

CAMPBELL, C. A.; D. S. McBEAN and D. G. GREEN, 1969. Influence of moisture stress, relative humidity and oxygen diffusion rate on seed-set and yield of wheat. Can. J. Pl. Sci. 49: 29-37.

CHARLES, C. A. and G. W. TODD, 1968. Ribonucleotide compositional changes in wheat leaves by water stress. Crop Sci. 8: 319-21.

CHEN, D.; A. SARID and E. KATCHALSKI, 1968. The role of water stress in the inactivation of mRNA of germinating wheat embryos. Proc. Nat. Acad. Sci. U.S. 61: 1378-83.

CHINOY, J. J. 1960. Physiology of drought resistance in wheat. I. Effect of wilting at different stages of growth on survival values of eight varieties of wheat belonging to seven species, Phyton 14: 147-57.

COCHEMÉ, J. and P. FRANQUIN, 1967. "A Study of the Agroclimatology of the Semiarid Area South of the Sahara in West Africa." Tech. Rep. F.A.O., Rome.

COMMONWEALTH AGRICULTURAL BUREAUX, 1971. Drought resistance in cereals induced by seed treatment. Annotated Bibliography No. 1294.

CRAFTS, A. S. 1968. Water deficits and physiological processes, pp. 85-133. In: Water Deficits and Plant Growth. Vol. II. Kozlowski, T. T.

(ed), Academic Press, New York.

CRAFTS, A. S.; H. R. CURRIER and C. R. STOCKING, 1949. "Water in the Physiology of Plants", Ronald Press, New York.

CRITCHFIELD, H. J. 1966. "General Climatology", Prentice-Hall, Englewood Cliffs, New Jersey.

CUDDY, T. F. 1963. Germination of the blue grasses. Proc. Assoc. Seed Anal. 53: 85-90.

CURRIER, H. B. 1967. Nature of plant water, pp. 307-19. In: Irrigation of Agricultural Lands, Hagan, R. M.; H. R. Haise and T. W. Edminster (eds), Agronomy Series, Am. Soc. Agron., Madison, Wisconsin.

DAY, B. E. 1966. The scientific basis of weed control, pp. 102-44. In: Scientific Aspects of Pest Control, Nat. Acad. Sci., Washington.

DAYAL, R.; G. SINGH and R. C. SHARMA, 1967. Growing of legumes and cereal mixture under dryfarming conditions. Indian J. Agron. 12: 126-31.

DENMEAD, O. T. and R. H. SHAW, 1960. The effects of soil moisture stress at different stages of growth on the development and yield of corn. Agron. J. 52: 272-4.

DERERA, N. F.; D. R. MARSHALL and L. N. BALAAM, 1969. Genetic variability in root development in relation to drought tolerance in spring wheats. Exp. Agric. 5: 327-37.

DITTMER, H. J. 1938. A quantitative study of the subterranean members of three field grasses. Am. J. Bot. 25: 654-7.

DONALD, C. M. 1954. Competition among pasture plants: the influence of density of flowering and seed production in annual pasture plants. Aust. J. agric. Res. 5: 585-97.

DONALD, C. M. 1960. The impact of cheap nitrogen. J. Aust. Inst. agric. Sci. 26: 319-38.

DONALD, C. M. 1961. Competition for light in crops and pastures, pp. 282-313. In: Symp. Soc. exp. Biol. No. XV. Mechanisms in Biological Competition, University Press, Cambridge.

DONALD, C. M. 1963. Competition among crop and pasture plants. Adv. Agron. 15: 1-118.

DONALD, C. M. and C. H. WILLIAMS, 1954. Fertility and productivity of podzolic soil as influenced by subterranean clover and superphosphate. Aust. J. agric. Res. 5: 664-87.

DOWNES, R. W. and J. D. HESKETH, 1968. Enhanced photosynthesis at low oxygen concentrations: differential response of temperature and tropical grasses. Planta 78: 79-84.

DOWNTON, W. J. S. and E. B. TREGUNNA, 1968. Carbon dioxide compensation—its relation to photosynthetic carboxylation reaction, systematics of the Graminae and leaf anatomy. Can. J. Bot. 46: 207-15.

DUNGAN, G. H.; U. S. SISODIA and G. D. SINGH, 1955. The benefit of sowing maize for fodder in north and south lines. Allahabad Farmer (India) 29: 8-13.

DUNGAN, G. H.; A. L. LANG and J. W. PENDLETON, 1958.   Corn plant population in relation to soil productivity. Adv. Agron. 10: 335-73.

EATON, F. M. and D. R. ERGLE, 1952.   Fibre properties and carbohydrate and nitrogen levels as affected by moisture supply and fruitfulness. Pl. Physiol. 27: 541-62.

ECK, H. V. and B. A. STEWART, 1954.   Wheat fertilization studies in western Oklahoma. Okl. agric. Exp. Sta. Bull. 432.

ECKARDT, F. 1953.   Transpiration et Photosynthése chez un xérophyte mesomorphe. Physiol. Pl. 6: 253-61.

EKERN, P. C. 1965.   Evapotranspiration of pine apple in Hawai. Pl. Physiol. 40: 736-9.

EL-SHARKAWY, M. and J. D. HESKETH, 1965.   Photosynthesis among species in relation to characteristic of leaf anatomy and CO_2 diffusion resistances. Crop Sci. 5: 517-21.

EL-SHARKAWY, M.; R. S. LOOMIS and W. A. WILLIAMS, 1968.   Photosynthetic and respiratory exchanges of carbon dioxide by leaves of the grain amaranth.   J. appl. Ecol. 5: 243-51.

EMBERGER, L. and G. LEMÉE, 1962.   Plant Ecology. Arid Zone Res. 18: 197-212.

EPHRAT, Y.; Z. KARCHI; A. GRAMA and Z. GERECHTER, 1964.   "Experiments with dwarf and semidwarf wheat varieties in the seasons 1961/62 and 1962/63"—in Hebrew with English summary, Prelim. Rep. Nat. Univ. Inst. Agric., Rehovot, No. 453.

Evans, A. C. 1960.   Studies of intercropping. I. Maize or sorghum with groundnuts. E. Afr. agric. J. 26: 1-10.

EVANS, A. C. and A. SREEDHARAN, 1962.   Studies of intercropping. II. Castorbean with groundnuts or soybean. Ibid. 28: 7-8.

Evans, C. E. and E. R. LEMON, 1957.   Conserving soil moisture, pp. 340-59. In: Soil: The Year Book of Agriculture, U.S.D.A., Washington, D.C.

EVENARI, M. 1962.   Plant physiology and arid zone research. Arid Zone Res. 18: 175-96.

FEDDES, R. A. 1971.   Water, Heat and Crop Growth, Med. Landbouwhoogs, Wageningen, 12.

FISHER, R. A. and R. M. HAGAN, 1965.   Plant-water relations, irrigation management, and crop yield. Expl. Agric. 1: 161-77.

FRANKEL, O. H. 1935.   Analytical yield investigation in New Zealand. II. Five Years' Analytical Variety Trials. J. agric. Sci., Camb. 25: 466-509.

FRENCH, R. J. 1966.   The effect of fallowing on water and nitrate supply and on the yield of wheat in south Australia. M. Agric. Sci. Thesis Univ. of Adelaide.

FREY-WYSSLING, A. and M. S. BUTTROSE, 1959. Plant physiology, photosynthesis in the ear of barley. Nature 184: 2031.

FUCHS, H. and K. ROSENSTIEL, 1958. Ertragsicherheit, pp. 365-442. *In:* Handbunch der Pflanzenzuchtung, Kappert, H. and W. Rudorf (eds), Paul Parey Verlag, Berlin.

GAASTRA, P. 1963. Climatic control of photosynthesis and respiration, pp. 113-18. *In:* Environmental Control of Plant Growth, Evans, L. T. (ed), Academic Press, New York.

GALE, J. and R. M. HAGAN, 1966. Plant antitranspirants. Ann. Rev. Pl. Physiol. 17: 269-82.

GALE, J. and A. POLJAKOFF-MAYBER, 1965. Effect of antitranspirant treatment on leaf temperatures. Pl. & Cell Physiol. 6:111-5.

GARDNER, W. H. 1964. Research for more efficient water use: soil physics, pp. 85-94. *In:* Research on Water, Soil Sci. Soc. Am., Madison, Wisconsin.

GARDNER, W. R. 1958. Some steady-state solutions of the unsaturated moisture flow equation with application to evaporation from a water table. Soil Sci. 85: 228-32.

GARG, O. K.; B. C. MISRA and B. P. SINGH, 1972. Effect of pretreating of seeds to gamma-radiation on the drought resistance behaviour of barley plants (*Hordeum vulgare* L.) Plant & Soil 36: 39-45.

GATES, C. T. 1968. Water deficits and growth of herbaceous plants, pp. 135-90. *In:* Water Deficits and Plant Growth. Vol. II. Kozlowski, T. T. (ed), Academic Press, New York.

GATES, C. T. and W. MUIRHEAD, 1967. Studies of the tolerance of *Atriplex* species. I. Environmental characteristics and plant response of *A. vasicaria, A. nummularia* and *A. semibassata.* Aust. J. expt. Agric. An. Husb. 7: 39-49.

GATES, D. M. 1962. "Energy Exchange in the Biosphere", Harper, New York.

GATES, D. M. 1964. Leaf temperature and transpiration. Agron. J. 56: 273-7.

GAUTREAU, J. 1970. Etude comparative de la transpiration relative chez deux varieties d'ara chide. Oleagineux 25: 23-28.

GENKEL, P. A. and P. A. HENCKEL, 1961. Drought resistance of plants: methods of recognition and of intensification. Arid Zone Res. 16: 167-74.

GILLIER, P. 1960. La reconstitution et el mainten de la fertilité des sols du Sénegal et le problème des jachères. Oléagineux 15: 637-43, 699-704.

GINGRICH, J. R. and M. B. RUSSELL, 1956. Effect of soil moisture tension and oxygen concentration on the growth of corn roots. Agron. J. 48: 517-20.

GLOVER, J. 1959. The apparent behaviour of maize and sorghum stomata during and after drought. J. agric. Sci., Camb. 53: 412-16.

GOLDSWORTHY, A. 1974. Photorespiration in relation to crop yield. *In:* Physiological Aspects of Dryland Farming, Gupta, U. S. (ed), Haryana Agric. Univ., Hissar, India.

GRAFIUS, J. E. 1956. Components of yield in oats: a geometrical interpretation. Agron. J. 48: 419-23.

GRAFIUS, J. E. 1959. Heterosis in barley. *Ibid.* 51: 551-5.

GRIFFIN, D. M. 1963. Soil moisture and the ecology of soil fungi. Biol. Rev. 38: 141-66.

GRIMES, D. W.; R. J. MILLER and L. DICKENS, 1970. Water stress during flowering of cotton. Calif. Agric. 24: 4-6.

GRUNDBACHER, F. J. 1963. The physiological function of the cereal awn. Bot. Rev. 29: 366-81.

GUPTA, U. S. and SARLA SHARMA, 1974. Germination and early growth of tall and one- and two-gene dwarf wheat cultivars under low and high temperature incubation. Biochem. Physiol. Pflanzen. (communicated).

HAISE, H. R.; L. R. JENSEN and J. ALLESSI, 1955. The effect of synthetic soil conditioners on soil structure and production of sugar beets. Proc. Soil Sci. Soc. Am. 19: 17-19.

HALEVY, A. H. and B. KESSLER, 1963. Increased tolerance of bean plants to soil drought by means of growth retarding substances. Nature 197: 310.

HALEVY, A. H. and S. H. WITTWER, 1965. Chemical regulation of leaf senescence. Quart. Bull. Mich. agric. Exp. Sta. 48: 30-35.

HANSEN, C. M.; L. S. ROBERTSON and B. H. GRIGSBY, 1958. The practicality of ploughing for and planting corn in one operation. *Ibid.* 40: 549-54.

HANUS, H. 1967. Die Beeinflussung des Wurzelstems von Weizen durch CCC. Z. Acker-Pflanzenbau 125: 40-6.

HARPER, H. J. 1959. 65 years of continuous wheat. Bull. Oklahoma agric. Exp. Sta. B-531.

HARPER, J. L. 1961. Approaches to the study of plant competition. *In:* Mechanism in Biological Competition, pp. 1-39. Milthorpe, F. L. (ed), 15th Symp. Soc. exp. Biol.

HARRINGTON, J. B. 1935. Cereal crop improvement for dryfarming conditions. Aci. agric. 16: 113-20.

HARTT, C. E. 1967. Effect of moisture supply upon translocation and storage of ^{14}C in sugarcane. Pl. Physiol. 42: 338-46.

HATCH, M. D. and C. R. SLACK, 1970. Photosynthetic CO_2-fixation pathways. Ann. Rev. Pl. Physiol. 21: 141-62.

HATCH, M. D.; C. R. SLACK and H. S. JOHNSON, 1967. Further studies on a new pathway of photosynthetic CO_2-fixation in sugarcane and its occurrence in other plant species. Biochem. J. 102: 417-22.

HAUSER, V. L. and M. B. COX, 1962. Evaluation of Zingg conservation bench terraces. Agric. Engg., London 43: 462-4, 467.

HAYNES, J. L. and J. D. SAYRE, 1956. Response of corn to within-row competiton. Agron. J. 48: 362-4.

HAYNES, J. L.; C. H. STRINGFIELD and W. A. JOHNSON, 1959. Effect of corn planting pattern on yield, root extension and interseeded cover crops. *Ibid.* 51: 454-6.

HEICHEL, G. H. and R. B. MUSGRAVE, 1969. Varietal differences in net photosynthesis of *Zea mays* L. Crop Sci. 9: 483-6.

HENCKEL, P. A. 1964. Physiology of plants under drought. Ann. Rev. Pl. Physiol. 15: 363-86.

HILLEL, D. 1972. Soil moisture and seed germination, pp. 65-89. *In:* Water Deficits and Plant Growth, Vol. III. Kozlowski, T. T. (ed), Academic Press, New York.

HILLEL, D.; R. RAWITZ and R. STEINHERDT, 1967. "Runoff Inducement in Arid Land." Ann. Res. Rept., Volcani Inst. agric. Res., Bet Dagan, Israel.

HOLLIDAY, R. 1960. Plant population and crop yield. Field Crop Abstr. 13: 159-67, 247-54.

HUBAC, C. 1962. La reviviscence en aptitude a l'hydrobiose et ses variations naturalles et experimentales chez les embryos et les plantules. Arid Zone Res. 16: 271-4.

HUMPHRIES, E. C. 1968. The beneficial effects of CCC on wheat yields in dry conditions. Euphytica (Suppl. No. 1) : 275-9.

HUNTER, A. S. and O. J. KELLEY, 1946. Extension of plant roots into dry soil. Pl. Physiol. 21:445-51.

HUNTER, J. R. and A. E. ERICKSON, 1952. Relation of seed germination to soil moisture tension. Agron. J. 44: 107-10.

HURD, E. A. 1971. Can we breed for drought resistance? pp. 77-88. *In:* Drought Injury and Resistance in Crops. CSSA Special Publ. No. 2, Madison, Wisconsin.

HUSAIN, I.; L. H. MAY and D. ASPINALL, 1968. Effect of soil moisture stress on the growth of barley. Aust. J. agric. Res. 19: 213-20.

HYGEN, G. 1953. Studies in plant transpiration. II. Physiol. Pl. 6: 106-33.

IDSO, S. B.; D. G. BAKER and D. M. GATES, 1966. The energy environment of plants. Adv. Agron. 18: 171-218.

ITAI, C. and Y. VAADIA, 1965. Kinetin-like activity in root exudate of water-stressed sunflower plants. Physiol. Pl. 18: 941-4.

JACKSON, J. E. 1963. Relationship of relative leaf growth rate of net assimilation rate. Nature 200: 909.

JACKSON, W. A. and R. J. VOLK, 1970. Photorespiration. Ann. Rev. Pl. Physiol. 21: 385-432.

JACOBY, B. and H. R. OPPENHEIMER, 1962. Presowing treatment of sorghum grains and its influence on drought resistance of the resulting plants. Phyton 19: 109-13.

JARVIS, P. G. and M. S. JARVIS, 1964. Presowing hardening of plants to drought. *Ibid.* 21: 113-7.

JENSEN, M. E. 1968. Water consumption by agricultural plants, pp. 1-22. *In:* Water Deficits and Plant Growth. Vol. II. Kozlowski, T.T. (ed), Academic Press, New York.

JENSEN, R. D. 1971. Effects of soil water tension on the emergence and growth of cotton seedlings. Agron. J. 63: 766-8.

JEWITT, T. N. 1966. Soils of arid lands, pp. 103-24. *In:* Arid Lands: A Geographical Appraisal, Hills, E. S. (ed), UNESCO, Paris.

KASI VISWANATH, G. and S. C. Pillai, 1972. Significance of heating agricultural soils. Indian J. agric. Sci. 42: 75-80.

KASSAS, M. 1966. Plant life in deserts, pp. 145-80. *In:* Arid Lands: A Geographical Appraisal, Hills, E. S. (ed), UNESCO, Paris.

KAUFMANN, M. R. 1972. Water deficits and reproduction growth, pp. 91-124. *In:* Water Deficits and Plant Growth, Vol. III. Kozlowski, T. T. (ed), Academic Press, New York.

KAUL, R. 1965. Effect of water stress on respiration of wheat. Can. J. Bot. 44: 623-32.

KAUL, R. 1969. Relation between water status and yield of some wheat varieties. Z. fur Pflanzenzuchtung 62: 145-54.

KEMPER, A. 1964. Experiments on the application of chemical soil disinfectants in the field. Mitt. *biol.* Bund Anst Berlin III: 50-4.

KESSLER, B. 1961. Nucleic acids as factors in drought resistance in higher plants. Recent Adv. Bot 2: 1153-9.

KHAN, R. A. and H. M. LAUDE, 1969. Influence of heat stress during seed germination on germinability of barley seed at harvest. Crop Sci. 9: 55-8.

KILLIAN, C. and G. LEMÉE, 1956. Les xérophytes: leur économie d'eau, pp. 787-824. *In:* Handbuch der Pflanzenphysiologie, Ruhland, W. (ed), Springer Verlag, Berlin, Band III.

KING, F. M. (ed) 1914. "Physics of Agriculture", Publ. F. H. King, Madison, Wisconsin.

KING, J. C. and J. W. COLLIER, 1961. "Performance of Grain Sorghum Hybrids and Varieties", 1957-60. Progr. Rep. agric. Exp. Sta. No. 2183, pp. 5 (mimeographed).

KING, L. J. 1966. "Weeds of the World: Biology and Control" Plant Science Monographs, Polunin, N. (ed), Leonard Hill, London, and Interscience, New York.

KLINGMAN, G. C. 1961. "Weed Control as a Science" John Willey, New York.

KMOCH, H. G.; R. E. RAMIG; R. L. Fox and F. E. KOEHLER, 1957. Root development of winter wheat as influenced by soil moisture and nitrogen fertilization. Agron. J. 49: 20-5.

KNOERR, K. 1966. Contrasts in energy balances between individual leaves and vegetated surfaces, pp. 391-401. *In:* International Symposium in Forest Hydrology, Sopper, W. L. and H. W. Lull, (eds) Pergamon Press, New York.

KOÉPPE, C. E. and G. C. LONG, DE, 1958. "Weather and Climate", McGraw-Hill Book Co., New York.

KOZLOWSKI, T. T. 1964. "Water Metabolism in Plants", Harper & Row, New York.

KRAMER, P. J. 1959. Transpiration and the water economy of plants, pp. 607-726. *In:* Pl. Physiol. Vol. II. Steward, F. C. (ed), Academic Press, New York.

KRAMER, P. J. 1969. "Plant and Soil Water Relationships: Modern Synthesis." McGraw-Hill Book Co., New York.

KURTZ, E. B. 1958. A chemical basis for the adaptations of plants, pp. 23-9. *In:* Bioecology of the Arid and Semiarid Lands of the Southwest, Lora, M. S. and L. J. Gardner (eds), New Mexico Highlands University Bulletin.

LAETSCH, W. M. 1968. Chloroplast specialization in dicotyledons possessing the C_4-dicarboxylic acid pathway of photosynthetic CO_2 fixation. Am. J. Bot. 55: 875-83.

LAHIRI, A. N. and S. SINGH, 1969. Effect of hyperthermia on the nitrogen metabolism of *Pennisetum typhoides*. Proc. Nat. Inst. Sci., India, Part B 35: 131-8.

LANG, A. L.; J. W. PENDLETON and G. H. DUNGAN, 1956. Influence of population and nitrogen levels on yield and protein and oil contents of nine corn hybrids. Agron. J. 48: 284-9.

LARSON, W. E. 1962. Tillage requirements for corn. J. Soil Wat. Conserv. 17: 3-7.

LARSON, W. E. and W. O. WILLIS, 1957. Light, soil temperature, soil moisture and alfalfa red clover distribution between corn rows of various spacings and row directions. Agron. J. 49: 422-6.

LAUDE, H. M.; J. A. HOBBS; F. W. SMITH; F. G. HEYNE; A. L. CLAPP and J. W. ZAHNLEY, 1955. Growing wheat in Kansas. Kan. agric. Exp. Sta. Bull. 370.

LEMON, E. 1956. The potentialities for decreasing soil moisture evaporation loss. Soil Sci. Soc. Am. Proc. 20: 120-5.

LEMON, E. 1963. Energy and water balance of plant communities, pp. 55-79. *In:* Environmental Control of Plant Growth, Evans, L. T. (ed), Academic Press, New York.

LEVITT, J. 1951. Frost, drought and heat resistance. Ann. Rev. Pl. Physiol. 2: 245-68.

LEVITT, J. 1956. Significance of hydration of the state of protoplasm, pp. 650-51. *In:* Handbuch der Pflanzenphysiologie, Ruhland, W. (ed), Springer Verlag, Berlin, Band III.

LEVITT, J. 1958. Frost, drought and heat resistance. Protoplasmatologia 6: 87.

LEVITT, J. 1972. "Responses of Plants to Environmental Stresses," Academic Press, New York.

LINGEGOWDA, B. K.; S. S. INAMDAR and K. KRISHNAMURTHY, 1971. Studies on the split application of nitrogen to rain-fed hybrid sorghum. Indian J. Agron. 16: 157-8.

LITTLEJOHN, L. 1956. Some aspects of soil fertility in Cyprus. Emp. J. exp. Agric. 14: 123-34.

LIVNE, A. and Y. VAADIA, 1972. Water deficits and hormone relationship, pp. 255-75. *In:* Water Deficits and Plant Growth. Vol. III. Kozlowski, T. T. (ed), Academic Press, New York.

LOMMASSON, T. 1947. The influence of rainfall on prosperity in eastern Montana, 1878-1946. Mimeographed Rep., 7, Region I, U. S. Forest Service.

LONG, I. F. 1958. Some observations on dew. Met. Mag. 87: 161-8.

LOOMIS, R. S. and W. A. WILLIAMS, 1963. Maximum crop productivity. Crop Sci. 3: 67-72.

LOOMIS, R. S.; W. A. WILLIAMS and W. G. DUNGAN, 1967. Community architecture and the productivity of terrestrial plant communities, pp. 291-308. *In:* Harvesting the Sun—Photosynethesis in Plant Life. Pictro, A. S.; F. A. Greer and T. J. Army (eds), Academic Press, New York.

LOOMIS, R. S.; W. A. WILLIAMS and A. E. HALL, 1971. Agricultural productivity. Ann. Rev. Pl. Physiol. 22: 431-68.

LOWE, L. B. and O. G. CARTER, 1970. The influence of (2-chloroethyl) trimethyl-ammonium chloride (CCC) and gibberellic acid in wheat yields. Aust. J. exp. Agric. & An. Husb. 10: 354-9.

LUEBS, R. E. and A. E. LAAG, 1964. Tillage and nitrogen for dryland grain in a winter rainfall climate. Bull. Calif. agric. Exp. Sta. 805.

LYLES, L. and C. D. FANNING, 1964. Effects of presoaking, moisture tension and soil salinity on emergence of grain sorghum. Agron. J. 56: 518-20.

MANGELSDORF, P. C. 1966. Genetic potentials for increasing yields of food crops and animals. pp. 66-71. *In:* Prospects of the World Food Supply—A Symposium. National Academy of Science, Washington, D.C.

MANOHAR, M. S. and M. K. MATHUR, 1966. Effect of succinic acid treatment on the performance of Pearl millet. Adv. Front. Plant Sci. 17: 133-48.

MARTIN, R. E. and S. D. MIKKELSEN, 1960. Grain fertilization in

California. Bull. Calif. agric. Exp. Sta. 775.

MATHEWS, O. R. 1951. Place of summer fallow in the agriculture of the western states. Circ. U.S. Dep. Agric. 887: 1-17.

MATHEWS, O. R. and T. J. ARMY, 1960. Moisture storage on fallowed wheatland in the Great Plains. Proc. Soil Sci. Soc. Am. 24: 414-18.

MAY, L. H. and F. L. MILTHORPE, 1962. Drought resistance of crop plants. Field Crop Abstr. 15: 171-9.

McALISTER, D. F. 1944. Determination of soil drought resistance in grass seedlings. J. Am. Soc. Agron. 36: 324-36.

McCALLA, I. M. and F. L. DULEY, 1946. Effect of crop residues on soil temperature. *Ibid.* 38: 75-89.

McDONOUGH, W. T. and H. G. GAUCH, 1959. The contribution of the awns to the development of the kernels of bearded wheat. Bull. Md. agric. Exp. Sta. 103.

McWILLIAM, J. R. and P. J. KRAMER, 1968. The nature of the perennial response in Mediterranean grasses. I. Water relation and summer survival in *Phalaris.* Aust. J. agric. Res. 19: 381-95.

MIGAHID, A. M. 1962. The drought resistance of Egyptian desert plants. Arid Zone Res. 18: 213-23.

MILTHORPE, F. L. 1950. Changes in the drought resistance of wheat seedlings during germination. Ann. Bot., N. S. 14: 79-89.

MINGEAU, M. 1969. Action de la nutrition minérale sur l'économie de l'eau daus la plante. Ann. Agron. 20: 263-76.

MISHRA, M. N. and D. K. MISRA, 1967. Stubble-mulching for wind erosion control in arid zone. North Zonal Workshop in Soil Sci., Punjab Agric. Univ., India.

MISHRA, M. N.; R. PRASAD and S. BHAN, 1968. Arid zone agriculture. World Crops 20: 66-8.

MISRA, D. K. 1964a. Arid zone research work. Indian Fmg. 14: 18-19.

MISRA, D. K. 1964b. Agronomic investigation in arid zone, Gen. Symp., Problems of Indian Arid Zone, Jodhpur, India.

MISRA, D. K. and M. N. MISHRA, 1966. Moisture conservation, Scientific Prog. Rep. CAZRI, Jodhpur, India.

MIZRAHI, Y.; A. BLUMENFELD and A. E. RICHMOND, 1970. Abscisic acid and transpiration in leaves in relation to osmotic root stress. Pl. Physiol. 46: 169-71.

MOLDENHAUER, W. C. and F. C. WESTIN, 1959. Some relationships between climate and yields of corn and wheat in Sprink Counry, S. D., and yields of milo and cotton at Big Spring. Tex. Agron. J. 51: 375-6.

MONTEITH, J. L. 1963. Dew: facts and fallacies, pp. 37-56. *In:* The Water Relations of Plants, Rutter, A. J. and F. H. Whitehead (eds), Blackwell, Oxford.

MOSS, D. N. 1962. The limiting carbon dioxide concentration for photosynthesis. Nature 193: 587.

Moss, D. N. and H. P. Rasmussen, 1969. Cellular localization of CO_2 fixation and translocation of metabolites. Pl. Physiol. 44: 1063-78.

Moss, D. N.; R. B. Musgrave and E. R. Lemon, 1961. Photosynthesis under field conditions. III. Some effects of light, carbon dioxide, temperature and soil moisture on photosynthesis, respiration and transpiration of corn. Crop Sci. 1: 83-7.

Mothes, K. 1956. Der Einfluss des Wasserzustandes auf Fermentprozesse und Stoffumsatz, pp. 656-63. In: Handbuch der Pflanzenphysiologie. Band III. Ruhland, W. (ed), Springer Verlag, Berlin.

Mothes, K. and A. Romeike, 1958. Die Alkaloide, pp. 989-1059. In: Handbuch der Pflanzenphysiologie. Band III. Ruhland, W. (ed), Springer Verlag, Berlin.

Murata, Y. and J. Iyama, 1963. Studies on the photosynthesis of forage crops. II. Influence of air-temperature upon the photosynthesis of some forage and grain crops. Proc. Crop Sci. Soc. Japan 31: 315-22.

Myers, L. E. 1967. New water supplies from precipitation harvesting, pp. 631-40. In: Water for Peace (2 vols.), U.S. Govt. Printing Office, Washington, D.C.

Newman, E. I. 1966. Relationship between root growth of flax (Linum usitatissimum) and soil water potential. New Phytol. 65: 273-83.

Nichiporovic, A. A. 1960. Photosynthesis and the theory of obtaining high crop yields. Field Crop Abstr. 13: 169-75.

Nichiporovic, A. A. 1966. "Photosynthesis and Productive Systems". Nauka Publ. House, Moscow (Translated from Russian by Israel Programme for Scientific Translations).

Norum, E. B. 1963. Fertilized grain stretches moisture. Bett. Crops 47: 40-44.

Olson, R. A.; C. A. Thompson; P. E. Grabouski; K. D. Stukenholtz; K. D. Frank and A. F. Dreier, 1964a. Water requirement of grain crops as modified by fertilizer use. Agron. J. 56: 427-32.

Olson, S. R.; F. S. Watanabe; F. E. Clark and W. D. Kemper, 1964b. Effect of hexadecanol on evaporation of water from soil. Soil Sci. 97: 13-18.

Oppenheimer, H. R. 1960. Adaptation to drought: xeromorphysm. Plant-water relationships in arid and semiarid conditions. Arid Zone Res. (UNESCO, Paris) 15: 105-38.

Orazem, F. and R. B. Herring, 1958. Economic aspects of the effects of fertilizers, soil moisture and rainfall on the yields of grain sorghum in the sandy lands of south-west Kansas. J. Fm. Econ. 40: 697-708.

Overbeek, J. van, 1964. Survey of mechanisms of herbicide action, pp. 387-400. In: The Physiology and Biochemistry of Herbicides, Audus, L. J. (ed), Academic Press, London.

OVESON, M. M. and A. P. APPLEBY, 1971. Influence of tillage management in a stubble mulch fallow-winter wheat rotation with herbicide weed control. Agron. J. 63: 19-20.

PAAUW, F. VAN DER, 1958. Relation between the potash requirement of crops and meteorological conditions. Plant & Soil 9: 245-68.

PALLAS, J. E. IR.; R. B. ANSON; D. G. HARRIS; C. B. ELKINS and C. L. PARKS, 1962. Research in plant transpiration. Prod. Res. Rep. U.S. Dep. Agric. 87.

PAPADAKIS, J. 1968. "Growth Retardants and Fertilizers". Buenos Aires, 20 pp.

PAPADAKIS, J. 1972. "Auxins, Biochemical Plant Interaction, Growth Retardants and Dense High Yielding Crops". Buenos Aires, 32 pp.

PAPADAKIS, J. 1974. Root toxins and crop growth. *In:* Crop Physiology, Gupta, U. S. (ed), Haryana Agric. Univ., Hissar, India.

PARKER, J. 1968. Drought resistance mechanisms, pp. 195-234. *In:* Water Deficits and Plant Growth, Kozlowski, T. T. (ed). Vol. I. Academic Press, New York.

PASTERNAK, D. and G. L. WILSON, 1969. Effects of heat waves on grain sorghum at the stages of head emergence. Aust. J. exp. Agric. An. Husb. 9: 636-8.

PAVLYCHENKO, T. K. 1949. Plant competition and weed control. Agric. Inst. Rev. 4: 142-5.

PELTON, W. L. 1969. Influence of low seeding rates on wheat yield in south-western Saskatchewan. Can. J. Pl. Sci. 49: 607-14.

PENCIC, M.; L. J. RUDNJANJIN and B. KERECKI, 1966. Effect of preplanting treatment of seed with different temperatures with yields and moisture conditions in maize crops. Savr. Poljopr. 14: 23-30.

PENDLETON, J. W. and G. H. DUNGAN, 1958. Effect of row direction on spring oat yield. Agron. J. 50: 341-3.

PENMAN, H. L. 1952. The physical bases of irrigation control. 13th Intern. Hort. Congr., London, pp. 913-24.

PEREKALJSKII, F. M. 1951. Direction of the drills of a sown area—in Russian. Selek Semenovod 18: 70-77.

PETERS, D. B. and J. R. RUNKLES, 1967. Shoot and root growth as affected by water availability, pp. 373-86. *In:* Irrigation of Agricultural Lands, Hagan, R. M.; R. H. Haise and T. W. Edminster (eds), Agronomy series, Am. Soc. Agron., Madison, Wisconsin.

PETERSON, A. E.; O. K. GERGE; S. T. MURDICK and D. R. PETERSON, 1958. Wheel-track corn planting. Circ. Wisc. Ext. Serv. 559.

PETINOV, N. S. 1961. Physiological principles of raising plants under irrigated agriculture. Arid Zone Res. 16: 81-92.

PETINOV, N. S. and U. G. MOLOTKOVSKY, 1962. The protective processes of heat resistant plants. *Ibid.* 16: 275-83.

PHILLIPS, W. M. 1964. A new technique for controlling weeds in sorghum in a wheat-sorghum-fallow rotation in the Great Plains. Weeds 12: 42-4.

PHILPOTTS, H. 1972. The effect of (2-chloroethyl) trimethyl-ammonium chloride (CCC) and presowing drought hardening on growth and grain yield of wheat. Aust. J. exp. Agric. & An. Husb. 12: 70-74.

PINTHUS, M. J. and J. RUDICH, 1967. Increase in grain yield of CCC-treated wheat (*Triticum aestivum*) in the absence of lodging. Agrochimica 11: 565-70.

PIPER, C. S. and M. P. C. VRIES, DE, 1964. The residual value of super-phosphate on a redbrown earth in south Australia. Aust. J. agric. Res. 15: 234-72.

PLAUT, Z. and A. H. HALEVY, 1966. Regeneration after wilting, growth and yield of wheat plants, as affected by two growth retarding compounds. Physiol. Pl. 19: 1064-72.

PLAUT, Z.; A. H. HALEVY and E. SHMUELI, 1964. The effect of growth retarding chemicals on growth and transpiration of bean plants grown under various irrigation regimes. Isr. J. agric. Res. 14: 153-8.

POLJAKOFF-MAYBER, A. and J. GALE, 1972. Physiological basis and practical problems of reducing transpiration. *In:* Water Deficits and Plant Growth. Vol. III. Kozlowski, T. T. (ed), Academic Press, New York and London.

POLUNIN, N. 1960. "Introduction to Plant Geography and Some Related Sciences", Longmans Green, London, and Barnes and Noble, New York.

PORTER, K. B.; M. E. JENSEN and W. A. SLETTEN, 1960. The effect of row spacing, fertilizer and planting rate on the yield and water use of irrigated grain sorghum. Agron. J. 52: 431-4.

POULAIN, J. F. and R. TOURTE, 1970. Influence de la préparation profonde du sol en sec sur la résponse des mils et sorghos à la fumure azotée (sols sableux de la zone tropicale sèche). Sols Africains 15: 517-86.

PUCKRIDGE, D. W. 1962. Thesis, Deptt. of Agronomy, Univ. of Adelaide, Adelaide, Australia, cf. Donald, C. M. 1963.

PUNTAMKAR, S. S.; P. C. MEHTA and S. P. SETH, 1971. Note on the inducement of salt resistance in two wheat (*Triticum aestivum* L.) varieties by presoaking with different salts of varying concentrations. Indian J. agric. Sci. 41: 717-18.

RAMIG, R. E. and H. F. RHOADES, 1963. Interrelationships of soil moisture level at planting time and nitrogen fertilization on winter wheat production. Agron. J. 55: 123-7.

RAMIG, R. E. and D. E. SMIKA, 1964. Fallow-wheat-sorghum: an excellent rotation for dryland in Central Nebraska. Bull. Nebr. agric. Exp. Sta. 483.

Rawson, H. M. and P. M. Bremner, 1974. Development in relation to grain yield in the temperate cereals. *In:* Crop Physiology, Gupta, U. S. (ed), Haryana Agric. Univ., Hissar, India.

Richards, L. A. and C. H. Wadleigh, 1952. Soil water and plant growth, pp. 73-225. *In:* Soil Physical Conditions and Plant Growth, Shaw, B. (ed), Academic Press, New York.

Ripley, P. F. 1966. The use of water by crops. Proc. Intern. Comm. Irrigation & Drainage, New Delhi, Jan. 1966, Spec. Session Rept. 2: 59.

Robins, J. S. and C. E. Domingo, 1953. Some effects of severe soil deficits at specific growth stages of corn. Agron. J. 45: 618-21.

Rosenberg, N. J. 1967. The influence and implications of windbreaks on agriculture in dry regions, pp. 327-49. *In:* Ground Level Climatology, Shaw, R. H. (ed), Am. Ass. Adv. Sci., Washington, D.C.

Russell, J. S. 1967. Nitrogen fertilizer and wheat in a semiarid environment. Aust. J. exp. Agric. & An. Husb. 7: 453-62.

Salim, M. H. and G. W. Todd, 1968. Seed soaking as a presowing, drought hardening treatment in wheat and barley seeds. Agron. J. 60: 179-82.

Salim, M. H.; G. W. Todd and A. M. Schlehuber, 1965. Root development of wheat, oats and barley under conditions of soil moisture stress. *Ibid.* 57: 603-7.

Santhirasegaram, K. 1962. Thesis, Waite Inst., Univ. of Adelaide, Adelaide, Australia, cf. Donald, C. M. 1963.

Sawhney, K. and S. M. Sikka, 1960. Agronomy, Vol. 1. pp. 106-63. *In:* Cotton in India, Examiner Press, Bombay.

Schmidt, H.; K. Diwald and O. Stocker, 1940. Plasmatische Untersuchungen an Durrempfindlichen und Durreresistenten Sorten Landwirtschaflicher Kulturpflanzen. Planta 31: 559-96.

Seginer, I. 1969. The effect of albedo on the evapotranspiration rate. Agric. Meterol. 6: 5-31.

Sharma, K. C.; R. D. Misra; B. C. Wright and B. A. Krantz, 1970. Response of some dwarf and tall wheats to nitrogen. Indian J. Agron. 15: 97-105.

Sharma, K. C.; S. P. Singh and V. Kumar, 1966. Comparative study of soil versus foliar application of urea on wheat. *Ibid.* 11: 219-22.

Shaw, R. H. and W. C. Burrows, 1966. Water supply, water use and water requirement, pp. 122-42. *In:* Advances in Crop Production, Pierre, W. H.; S. A. Aldrich and W. P. Martin (eds), Iowa State Univ. Press, Ames, Iowa.

Shaw, R. H. and D. R. Laing, 1968. Moisture stress and plant response, pp. 73-94. *In:* Plant Environment and Efficient Water Use, Pierre, W. H.; D. Kirkham; J. Pesek and R. Shaw (eds), Am. Soc. Agron. & Soil Sci. Soc. Am., Madison, Wisconsin.

SHEAR, G. M. 1965. The role of herbicides in no-tillage crop production. Agric. Chem. 20: 31-6.

SHEKHAWAT, G. S.; D. C. SHARMA and M. B. GUPTA, 1966. Wheat growth and production in relation to row spacing and direction of sowing. Indian J. Agron. 11: 62-5.

SHIELDS, L. M. 1958. Morphology in relation to xerophytism, pp. 15-22. In: Bioecology of the Arid and Semiarid Lands of the South-west, Lora, M. S. and L. J. Gardner (eds), New Mexico Highlands Univ. Bull.

SHIMSHI, D. and Y. EPHRAT, 1970. A study of intervarietal differential of stomatal behaviour in wheat, in relation to transpiration and potential yield. Report to Ford Foundation.

SHRIVASTAVA, M. S.; S. M. SHARMA and S. P. SINGH, 1968. A note on the effect of Cycocel on growth and yield of wheat. Indian J. Agron. 13: 192-4.

SHRIVASTAVA, S. P. and A. SINGH, 1970. Maturity of hybrid sorghum as influenced by fertilizer application and intra-row spacing. Indian J. agric. Sci. 40: 1056-60.

SIMONIS, W. 1952. Untersuchungen zum Durreeffekt. I. Morphologische Struktur, Wasserhaushalt, Atmung und Photosynthese feucht und trocken gezogener Pflanzen. Planta 40: 313-32.

SIMPSON, G. M. 1968. Association between grain yield per plant and photosynthetic area above the flag-leaf node in wheat. Can. J. Pl. Sci. 48: 253-60.

SINGH, O. S. and K. S. Gill, 1972. Some physiological aspects of the effects of kinetin, depth of seedling and soil temperature on seedling establishment and metabolism of dwarf wheats. Indian J. agric. Sci. 42: 205-10.

SINGH, T. N.; D. ASPINALL and L. G. PALEG, 1972. Proline accumulation and varietal adaptation to drought in barley; a potential metabolic measure of drought resistance. Nature New Biology 236: 188-90.

SKERMAN, P. J. 1956. Heat waves and their significance in Queensland's primary industries. Arid Zone Res. 11: 195-8.

SLATYER, R. O. 1958. Availability of water to plants. Ibid. 11: 159-64.

SLATYER, R. O. 1967. "Plant-Water Relations", Academic Press, New York.

SMITH, G. E. 1954. Soil fertility—the basis for high crop production. Bett. Crops 38: 22-30.

SNEVA, F. A.; D. N. HYDER and C. S. COOPER, 1958. The influence of ammonium nitrate on the growth and yield of crested wheat grass in the Oregon high desert. Agron. J. 50: 40-44.

SOSEBEE, R. E. and C. A. HERBEL, 1969. Effects of high temperatures on emergence and initial growth of range plants. Ibid. 61: 621-4.

SQUIRE, G. R. and M. B. JONES, 1971. Studies on the mechanisms of action of the antitranspirant phenylmercuric acetate and its penetration into the mesophyll. J. exp. Bot. 22: 980-91.

SREENIVASAN, A. and K. K. AURANGABADKAR, 1940. Effects of fire-heating on the properties of black cotton soils in comparison with those of gray and of humus-treated soil. Soil Sci. 50: 449-62.

STAKMAN, E. C.; R. BRANDFIELD and P. C. MANGELSDORF, 1967. "Campaigns Against Hunger", Harvard Univ. Press, Cambridge, Massachusetts.

STALFELT, M. G. 1956. Die Stomatare Transpiration und die Physiologie der Spaltoffnungen, pp. 351-426. In: Handbuch der Pflanzenphysiologie. Band III. Ruhland, W. (ed), Springer Verlag, Berlin·

STAPLE, W. J. 1964. Dryland agriculture and water conservation, pp. 15-30. In: Research on Water, ASA Spec. Publ. Soil Sci. Soc. Am., Madison, Wisconsin.

STEPHENSON, R. E. and G. E. SCHUSTER, 1946. Straw mulch for soil improvement. Soil Sci. 61: 219-30.

STOCKER, O. 1960. Physiological and morphological changes in plants due to water deficiency. Res. Rev. 15: 63-104.

STOUGHTON, R. H. 1955. Light and plant growth. J. Royal hort. Soc. 80: 454-66.

STOY, V. 1963. Some plant physiological aspects of the breeding of high-yielding varieties, pp. 264-75. In: Recent Plant Breeding Research, Wiley, New York.

STURROCK, J. W. 1974. Effect of wind and their amelioration in crop production. In: Physiological Aspects of Dryland Farming, Gupta, U. S. (ed), Haryana Agric. Univ., Hissar, India.

STUTTE, C. A. and G. W. TODD, 1967. Effects of water stress on soluble leaf proteins in Triticum aestivum L. Phyton 24: 67-75.

SUBBARAMI, R. D. and C. DAKSHINAMURTI, 1971. ` Root growth and soil structure under different tillage operations and uniform application of fertilizer. Indian J. agric. Sci. 41: 413-22.

SYME, J. R. 1969. A comparison of semidwarf and standard height wheat varieties at two levels of water supply. Aust. J. exp. Agric. & An. Husb. 9: 528-31.

TADMOR, N. H.; S. DASBERG; S. J. ELLERN and Y. HARPAZ, 1964. Establishment and maintenance of seeded dryland range under semiarid conditions. Res. Rep. for April 1963 to March 1964 to U. S. D. A.

TANNER, J. W. and C. J. GARDNER, 1965. Leaf position important in barley varieties. Crops & Soils 18: 17.

THORNE, G. N. 1962. Survival of tillers and distribution of dry matter between ear and shoot of barley varieties. Ann. Bot. N. S. 26: 37-54.

THRONE, G. N. 1966. Physiological aspects of grain yield in cereals, pp. 88-105. In: The Growth of Cereals and Grasses, Milthorpe, F. L.

and J. D. Ivins (eds), Butterworths, London.

THORNTHWAITE, C. W. 1956. Climatology in arid zone research, pp. 67-84. *In:* The Future of Arid Lands, White, G. F. (ed), Am. Soc. Adv. Sci., Washington, D.C.

THORNTHWAITE, C. W. 1958. Introduction to arid zone climatology. Arid Zone Res. 11: 15-22.

THORNTHWAITE, C. W. and J. R. MATHER, 1954. Climate in relation to crops: Recent studies in biology. Am. Met. Soc. Meteorological Monograph 2: 1-10.

TISDALE, S. L. and W. L. NELSON, 1966. "Soil Fertility and Fertilizers", Macmillan, New York.

TIVER, N. S. and R. F. WILLIAMS, 1943. Studies of the flax plant. II. The effect of artificial drought on growth and soil production in a linseed variety. Aust. J. exp. Biol. Med. Sci. 21: 201-9.

TODD, G. W. 1972. Water deficits and enzymatic activity, pp. 177-216. *In:* Water Deficits and Plant Growth. Vol. III. Kozlowski, T. T. (ed), Academic Press, New York.

TODD, G. W. and D. L. WEBSTER, 1965. Effect of repeated drought periods on photosynthesis and survival of cereal seedlings. Agron. J. 57: 399-404.

TOOLE, E. H.; S. B. HENDRICKS; H. A. BORTHWICKS and V. K. TOOLE, 1956. Physiology of seed germination. Ann. Rev. Pl. Physiol. 7: 299-325.

TRANQUILLINI, W. 1963. Die Abhangigkeit der Kohlensaure-assimilation junger Larchen, Fichten und Zirben von der luft und Bodenfeuchte. Planta 60: 70-94.

TREWARTHA, J. T. 1954. "An Introduction to Climate", McGraw-Hill Book Co., New York.

TROLL, C. 1958. Climatic seasons and climatic classification. Orient. Geogr. 2: 141-65.

TROUGHTON, A. 1957. The underground organs of herbage grasses. Distribution of roots in the soil. Bull. Commonwealth Bur. Pastures Field Crops 44: 41-6.

TYANKOVA, L. A. 1967. Influence of proline on the sensitivity of wheat plants to drought. Chem. Abstr. 66: 100902.

VAADIA, Y. and Y. WAISEL, 1967. Physiological processes as affected by water balance, pp. 354-68. *In:* Irrigation of Agricultural Lands, Hagan, R. M.; R. H. Haise and T. W. Edminster (eds), Agron. Series, Am. Soc. Agron., Madison, Wisconsin.

VEGIS, A. 1963. Climatic control of germination, bud break and dormancy, pp. 265-88. *In:* Environmental Control of Plant Growth, Evans, L. T. (ed), Academic Press, New York.

VERHAGEN, A. M. W.; J. H. WILSON and E. J. BRITTEN, 1963. Plant production in relation to foliage illumination. Ann. Bot. N. S. 27: 627-40.

VIETS, F. G. JR. 1967. Nutrient availability in relation to soil water, pp. 458-67. *In:* Irrigation of Agricultural Lands, Hagan, R. M.; R. H. Haise and T. W. Edminster (eds), Agron. Series, Am. Soc. Agron., Madison, Wisconsin.

VIETS, F. G. JR. 1972. Water deficits and nutrient availability, pp. 217-39. *In:* Water Deficits and Plant Growth, Vol. III. Kozlowski, T. T. (ed), Academic Press, New York.

WAGGONER, P. E. 1966. Decreasing transpiration and the effect upon growth, pp. 49-72. *In:* Plant Environment and Efficient Water Use, Pierre, W. H.; D. Kirkham; J. Pesek and R. Shaw (eds), Am. Soc. Agron. & Soil Sci. Soc. Am., Madison, Wisconsin.

WAISEL, Y. 1958. Dew absorption by plants of arid zones. Bull. Res. Coun. Israel, 6D: 180-86.

WAISEL, Y. 1962. Presowing treatments and their relation to growth and to drought, frost and heat resistance. Physiol. Pl. 15: 43-6.

WANG, J. Y. 1963. "Agricultural Meteorology", Pacemaker Press, Milwaukee, Wisconsin.

WANJURA, E. F.; E. B. HUDSPETH and J. D. BILBRO, 1969. Emergence time, seed quality and planting depth effects on yield and survival of cotton. Argon. J. 61: 63-9.

WARDLAW, I. F. 1967. The effect of water stress on translocation in relation to photosynthesis and growth. I. Effect during grain development in wheat. Aust. J. biol. Sci. 20: 25-39.

WASSERMANN, V. D. 1963. Thesis, Deptt. of Agronomy, Univ. of Adelaide, Adelaide, Australia, cf. Donald, C. M. 1963.

WASSINCK, E. C. 1954. Remarks on energy relations in photosynthesis processes. Proc. 1st. Int. Photobiol. Congr., Amsterdam, Biology Sect. V.

WATSON, D. J. 1947. Comparative physiological studies on the growth of field crops. I. Variations in net assimilation rate and leaf area between species and varieties and within and between years. Ann. Bot. N. S. 11: 41-76.

WATSON, D. J. 1967. Physiological characteristics of the growth of sugar beet crops on different soils. J. Intern. Sugar Beet Res. 2: 225-9.

WEISER, V. 1960. "North Dakota Fertilizer Guide", North Dakota Ext. Circ. A-350.

WELLS, S. A. and S. DUBETZ, 1966. Reaction of barley varieties to soil water stress. Can. J. Pl. Sci. 46: 507-12.

WENT, F. W. 1952. The effect of rain and temperature on plant distribution in the desert, pp. 232-7. *In:* Desert Research, Research Council of Israel.

WEST, S. H. 1962. Protein, nucleotide and ribonucleic acid metabolism in corn during germination under water stress. Pl. Physiol. 37: 565-71.

WHITE, G. F. 1966. The World's Arid Areas, pp. 15-30. *In:* Arid Lands:

A Geographical Appraisal, Hills, E. S. (ed), UNESCO, Paris.

WHITEMAN, P. C. and G. L. WILSON, 1965. Effects of water stress on the reproductive development of *Sorghum vulgare* Pers. Univ. of Queensland Papers 4: 233-9.

WIESE, A. F. and T. J. ARMY, 1958. Effect of tillage and chemical weed control practices on soil moisture storage and losses. Agron. J. 50: 465-8.

WIESE, A. F.; E. BURNETT and J. E. Box, Jr. 1967. Chemical fallow in dryland cropping sequences. *Ibid.* 59: 175-7.

WILLIAMS, M. S. and J. W. COUSTON, 1962. "Crop Production Levels and Fertilizer Use", F.A.O., Rome.

WILSON, C. C. 1948. Diurnal fluctuations of growth of length of tomato stem. Pl. Physiol. 23: 156.

WILSON, J. W. 1969. Maximum yield potential, pp. 34-56. *In:* Transition from Extensive to Intensive Agriculture, Proc. 7th Coll. Int. Potash Inst., Israel.

WIT, C. T. DE, 1958. Transpiration and crop yields. Versl. Landbouwk. Onderzok. 64: 1-88.

WIT, C. T. DE, 1967. Photosynthesis: its relationship to overpopulation, pp. 315-20. *In:* Harvesting the Sun: Photosynthesis in Plant Life, Pietro, A. S.; F. A. Greer and T. J. Army (eds), Academic Press, New York.

WITTWER, S. H. 1974. Production potential of crop plants, *In:* Crop Physiology, Gupta, U. S. (ed), Haryana Agric. Univ., Hissar, India.

WOODRUFF, D. R. 1969. Presowing drought hardening of wheat. Aust. J. agric. Res. 20: 13-24.

WRIGHT, S. T. C. 1969. An increase in the "Inhibitor-β" content of detached wheat leaves following a period of wilting. Planta 86: 10-20.

ZINGG, A. W. and V. L. HAUSER, 1959. Terrace benching to save potential runoff for semiarid land. Agron. J. 51: 289-92.

ZINGG, A. W. and C. L. WHITEFIELD, 1957. Stubble-mulch farming in the western states. Tech. Bull. U.S. Dept. Agric. 1166.

Prof. Kenneth L. Larson

Dr. Larson was born on an Iowa farm during the drought year of the 1930. Educated during his earlier years in a rural elementary school and small town high school, he sought further agricultural training at Iowa State University (BS, 1954) and University of Wisconsin (MS, 1959; PhD., 1961). From 1954 to 1957 he served as a pilot in the United States Air Force. From 1961 to 1970, he was employed in the Department of Agronomy at North Dakota State University, where his primary responsibilities were in forage management, production, and physiology. From 1970 to the present he has been Professor of Agronomy in the Department of Agronomy at University of Missouri, where he teaches *Introductory Plant Science* and *Forage Crops*. His primary research interests are plant responses to drought stresses, and in 1971 he co-edited *Drought Injury and Resistance in Crops*, published by the Crop Science Society of America. In 1973 Dr. Larson co-authored "Cold, drought and heat tolerance" in *Alfalfa Science and Technology*, published by the American Society of Agronomy. The author was a member of the Board of Directors, Crop Science Society of America, 1968-70, and is a member of Alpha, Zeta, Gamma, Sigma, Delta, Sigma Xi, American Society of Plant Physiologists, Missouri Academy of Science, and American Society of Agronomy.

2. DROUGHT INJURY AND RESISTANCE OF CROP PLANTS

KENNETH L. LARSON
Department of Agronomy
University of Missouri

Introduction

Drought is a hazard to successful crop production throughout the world. It occurs when various combinations of the physical factors of the environment produce an internal water stress in crop plants sufficient to reduce their productivity. This reduction in productivity is brought about by a delay or prevention of crop establishment, weakening or destruction of established crops, predisposition of crops to insects and diseases, alteration of physiological and biochemical metabolism in plants, and alteration of the quality of the grain, forage, fibre, oil and other sought-for products (Larson & Eastin, 1971). Drought is often a factor in yield reduction even when the damage is not apparent.

Role of Water

Several functions of water in plants have been well-established (Russell *et al.*, 1959). Water is a major constituent of tissue, a reagent in photosynthetic and hydrolytic processes, the solvent for and mode of translocation for metabolites and minerals within plants, and is essential for cell enlarge-

ment and growth.   Cell enlargement is correlated to turgor pressure which
is reduced as water deficits occur.   With occurrence of water deficits, many
of the physiological processes associated with growth are affected, and
under severe deficits, death of plants may result.

Growth is reduced by a decrease of relative turgidity below 90%, and
is approximately half of the normal growth rate when the relative turgidity
reaches 85 to 83% (Mitchell, 1970).   Nevertheless, limited growth will
occur in some species even at a relative turgidity of 62%, which corresponds
closely with the appearance of permanent wilting.

In addition to the role of water in total growth, it is apparent, a deficiency of water will influence the growth of different organs in various ways.
Among these are: (1) a decrease in the ratio of shoot to root growth, (2) a
decrease in the proportion of lateral roots to total root length, and (3) a
decrease in ratio of leaf to stem.

Drought has generally been accepted as a deficiency of available
soil moisture which produces water deficits in the plant sufficient to cause a
reduction in growth.   However, such a definition provides a qualitative
indication of the amount of available water in the soil but does not take
into consideration the water status within the plant.   There occasionally
are periods when the rate of transpiration exceeds the rate of absorption of
water due to low relative humidities, high temperatures, and moderate wind
velocities, even though the available soil moisture in the root zone is high.
Progress in drought research has lagged because much of the past research
on plant response to drought stress has been based on soil moisture rather
than plant water status.

Plant Response to Drought

Total drought resistance consists of several complex mechanisms and
interactions.   It has been suggested that there are only two basic resistance
mechanisms—these being avoidance and tolerance (Levitt, 1969, 1972).
However, the plant may also exclude the drought stress from its tissues
by its ability to complete its life cycle before the advent of environmental conditions causing drought stress.   Such a plant is called a drought escaper
instead of a drought avoider, and as such does not represent a resistance
mechanism.

Plants may resist drought stress by their ability to maintain a high
internal water content.   This is accomplished by a deep and extensive root
system or a reduced rate of transpiration.   Transpiration can be reduced
by the presence of a very thick and highly impermeable cuticle and the
closure of stomata during the hot and dry periods of the day.   Severe
desiccation may still be avoided when the stomata close, but diffusive resistance to carbon dioxide exchange increases, photosynthesis decreases, and

the yield is usually reduced. Such a plant has drought resistance because of avoidance.

The plant may survive the drought stress even though it has a low internal water content. This resistance mechanism is tolerance (or hardiness), and plants possessing tolerance exhibit the ability to recover and grow when soil water becomes available. The main method of survival in vegetative lower plants and in seed, pollen grains and other dormant parts of higher plants is through drought tolerance. However, in vegetative higher plants drought avoidance appears to be the major mechanism of survival. Tolerance seems to be more primitive of the two mechanisms because it is the only kind of resistance developed by lower plants.

Environmental Stresses

Crop plants may be subjected to stresses other than drought as the growth and development of plants are constantly under the control of the environment. Temperature, radiation, nutrients, and gases, as well as moisture, can either enhance or retard growth and development, depending on the magnitude of these factors within the environment (Levitt, 1972). When these factors exist in an abnormal amount or concentration sufficient to place a strain or stress on the plant or its component parts, the strain may be elastic and reversible, or it may be irreversible. Strains do occur as a result of the environmental stresses but in the resistant plants these are always reversible. Each environmental stress may produce its own kind of irreversible strain or stress injury.

Temperature stresses can occur at temperatures being either too low or too high. Most actively growing plants are killed and some dormant overwintering plants may be injured by freezing. This injury is called freezing or frost injury. Some warm season plants, such as corn and sorghum, may be injured or killed by continued exposure to temperatures slightly above freezing. This injury is called chilling injury. Plants have a thermal death point under high temperatures, and when injury or death occurs from high temperatures, this is called heat injury. Injury due to heat or drought stress is difficult to assess because high temperatures are generally associated with low moisture. Whether the injury is due to heat or drought stress or from a combination of the two stresses has made the study of drought injury and resistance extremely complex under field conditions.

Excess moisture may injure or kill plants because of insufficient oxygen in the soil required by root cells for respiration and release of energy used in growth and development. This injury is called flooding injury.

Radiation stress has not been a limiting factor in crop production although radiation injury can result from ultraviolet radiation. Fortunately, ultraviolet radiation from the sun is usually effectively screened by the atmosphere and thus is of low intensity and seldom injures most plants.   Injury due to the longer wavelengths of infrared radiation is a form of heat injury.

Salt stress will occur in plants growing in soils high in any one of a large number of salts.   Toxicity from these salts can directly limit plant growth and development, and the same salts can influence the movement of water, or the lack of water movement, into the roots from the soil.   The latter response will cause a drought stress within the plant.

Of these environmental stresses, cold and drought injury and resistance have received the greatest attention, with cold temperature stress being studied considerably more than drought stress.   Nevertheless, present-day evidence suggests that the mechanism(s) responsible for cold and drought resistance (tolerance) is probably similar since both stresses desiccate cells. Supporting evidence for a similar mechanism(s) is as follows: (1) plants hardened to cold also become drought hardened and *vice versa*; (2) drought and cold tolerance are both associated with small cell size; (3) species, and occasionally varieties, have parallel rankings for drought and cold tolerance; (4) changes in drought and cold tolerance are associated with plant development and growth; and (5) many physiological changes that occur during hardening to drought and cold are similar (Levitt, 1956).

Mechanism of Stress Injury and Resistance

The correlation between cold and drought tolerance suggests that freezing and drought injury in plants are the result of the dehydration process. The cause for injury by this process is not known although several suggestions for the cause(s) have been made:

(1) Removal of water may concentrate the salts and other solutes to the extent that they become toxic to the protoplasmic constituents.

(2) The cell through the lack of turgor may collapse to the point that a physical tension is exerted on the protoplasm sufficient to injure some sensitive component.

(3) Proteins are forced into an irreversible aggregation as dehydration brings the proteins close enough together to form intermolecular bonds. In the dehydration process, the bound (protective) water which provides stability and protection for the protein molecule is removed, allowing for new chemical bonds to form among the protein molecules.

Plants respond to progressive dehydration by changing the colloidal-chemical state of the protoplasm by increasing hydration and hydrophyllic activity of the colloids of the protoplasm.   The same changes in the colloidal system occur from dehydration as from cell aging in that they lower the water-holding capacity of the colloids and their ability to swell.

Permeability of the protoplasm has become much higher with increasing dehydration (Henckel, 1964). Protoplasmic viscosity has been shown to first decrease and then increase in response to dehydration. The level in protoplasmic viscosity remains much higher after a drought than if no drought stress was imposed. This response of a higher protoplasmic viscosity in plants surviving drought, in all probability, is a protective-adaptive reaction of the plant to the effects of dehydration (Table 2.1). Abscisic acid (ABA) has been shown to have a marked increase on the permeability of plant tissues to water (Glinka & Reinhold, 1971). Water stress has led to a significant increase in abscisic acid concentration in leaves (Mizrahi et al., 1970; Zeevaart, 1971). When water was withheld from spinach plants until wilting symptoms appeared, the abscisic acid content increased more than 10-fold over that of turgid plants (Zeevaart, 1971). Furthermore, treatment with ABA has reduced transpiration rates, probably through stomatal closure (Jones & Mansfield, 1970; Zeevaart, 1971). These results suggest an association between drought and permeability of membranes through ABA.

Table 2.1. Changes in viscosity (time for plasmolysis) of protoplasm in tomato leaves subjected to drought stress[1]

Stress condition			Plasmolysis occurrence (minutes)
Control	..	..	21
Soil drought	..	..	27
Dry winds	..	..	36
Soil drought and dry winds	..	..	43

[1] Adapted from Henckel (1964).

Drought and Physiological Processes

The deleterious effects of drought are generally more pronounced in cells and tissues which are in stages of most rapid growth and development. There are periods of growth when plants have a great sensitivity to water stress as far as quantity and quality of the harvested crop are concerned (Denmead & Shaw, 1960; Reed, 1966). For example, drought stress during anthesis in corn (*Zea mays*) provides for little to no fertilization of the ovules which results in an ear void of grain (Table 2.2). Drought stress during the boot stage in barley (*Hordeum vulgare*) results in a low yield of grain which has a high protein percentage, a condition undesirable in the malting of barley (Table 2.3).

Since water plays an important role in plants, as previously described,

Table 2.2. Production of stover and grain of corn plants subjected to various moisture stress periods[1]

Stress period				Dry matter yield (g)		
				Stover	Grain	Stover+Grain
Vegetative	..	..	..	151	273	424
Silking	..	..	..	153	183	336
Ear	..	..	..	183	289	472
Vegetative+Silking	..	..	..	95	154	249
Vegetative+Ear	..	..	..	121	243	364
Silking+Ear	..	..	..	113	179	292

[1] Adapted from Denmead and Shaw (1960).

Table 2.3. Per cent nitrogen and protein in the grain of Trophy barley subjected to drought stress at different stages of growth[1]

Stage of growth		% Nitrogen	% Protein
Control	..	1.36	8.5
Tillering	..	1.50	9.4
Boot	..	2.16	13.5
Heading	..	1.68	10.5
Mature	..	1.56	9.8

[1] Adapted from Reed (1966).

it is not surprising that reduced water absorption and dehydration can have a deleterious effect on most physiological processes.

Cell division and enlargement are very sensitive to drought stress. However, it has been observed that leaves of plants which have been exposed to drought stresses may contain a similar number of cells as leaves of non-stressed plants. Cell division may continue during stress at a reduced rate but upon removal of the drought stress a relatively rapid resumption of expansion growth or cell enlargement may occur. Nevertheless, during drought stress cell enlargement is affected and is the primary cause of plant stunting commonly observed under field conditions. Stem elongation or leaf enlargement can be inhibited by small diurnal water deficits that occur even with well-watered plants on days of high radiation incidence. The effect of inhibited leaf enlargement is a reduction in the size of the photosynthesizing surface causing a reduced crop growth.

The effect of drought stress can be shown on nutrient absorption, carbohydrate and protein metabolism, and translocation of ions and metabolites. Little is known about the effects of drought on root development although it has been suggested that root development is enhanced relative to shoot development during and following drought stress (Slatyer, 1969). When stem cuttings of alfalfa taken from control and drought stressed plants were placed in a propagation media under favourable growing conditions, the drought stressed cuttings rooted quickly, whereas control cuttings rooted poorly (Jung & Larson, 1972). Most research has shown a progressive reduction in rate of root elongation as drought is imposed, and in some cases root elongation ceases before shoot growth. In addition, as rates of root elongation are reduced the rate of suberization exceeds the rate of elongation. The non-suberized zone is reduced until it is virtually eliminated in non-elongating roots. Such a response to severe drought stress greatly reduced the absorbing ability of roots.

Stomatal closure is influenced by water deficits as turgidity of the guard cell is dependent on water content (Brix, 1962). Such a response has a significant effect in crop productivity as the amount of carbon dioxide taken into the leaf can directly regulate photosynthesis (Table 2.4).

Table 2.4. **Influence of drought stress on photosynthetic rates in tomato and loblolly pine[1]**

Stress (DPD atm)			% Photosynthetic rate[2]	
			Tomato	Loblolly pine
2	..	..	100	100
6	..	..	100	60
8	..	..	74	25
10	..	..	36	6
12	..	..	12	0
14	..	..	2	0
18	..	..	0	0
22	..	..	0	0

[1] Adapted from Brix (1962).
[2] Based on photosynthetic rate in plants grown in soil at field capacity.

Mineral uptake is frequently reduced in drought stressed plants (Slatyer, 1969). One of the earliest signs of drought stress is the translocation of phosphorus from older leaves to the stems and meristematic tissues. The translocation of nitrogen closely follows that of phosphorus, suggesting the occurrence of protein hydrolysis and alteration of normal cell function.

A recent inference supports the hypothesis that the uptake of phosphorus is influenced by the dieback of the absorbing roots during drought. Forde (1972) found that uptake of ^{32}P by surface roots of oil palm (*Elaeis guineenis* Jacq.) was reduced under drought stress conditions. He concluded that this inference has a direct bearing on the accepted mode of making fertilizer applications to the oil palm in West Africa. Broadcasting around the base of the palms early in the rainy season has been a sound recommended practice based on his study.

Interruption of protein synthesis and proteolysis generally occur under drought stress (Slatyer, 1969). There is a close relationship between protein synthesis and ribonucleic acid (RNA) levels. Drought stress has been shown to impair the nucleic acid system intimately correlated with protein synthesis. Others have shown that a decline in protein synthesis in droughted leaves is due to a deficiency of cytokinins (Richmond & Lang, 1957; Osborne, 1965). Addition of cytokinins to leaves of a number of annual plants has been shown to retard chlorophyll degradation and has promoted amino acid incorporation and protein synthesis. Nevertheless, it has been suggested that the protein breakdown injures the drought stressed plant due to the accumulation of a toxic product of protein breakdown, such as ammonia, rather than due to a protein deficiency.

High levels of free amino acids and amides have been associated with drought stress in plants (Barnett & Naylor, 1966). Proline has been especially high in stressed plants although understanding for this response is unknown (Table 2.5). It has been suggested that free proline serves as a storage compound for carbon and nitrogen during drought, when both starch and protein syntheses are inhibited.

Table 2.5. Changes in amounts of several free amino acids in Bermuda grass (*Cynodon dactylon* (L.) **Pers.**) **subjected to drought stress**[1]

Amino acid			μ moles/gram dry weight		
			Control	Moderate stress	Severe stress
Common					
Aspartic acid	..	..	..	11.8	4.5	8.4
Proline	..	..	..	2.7	30.5	69.3
Glycine	..	..	..	1.8	1.7	1.2
Alanine	..	..	..	31.9	15.2	11.6
Total		..	211.5	192.9	246.5
Coastal					
Aspartic acid	..	..	..	7.0	9.0	9.7
Proline	..	..	..	1.1	138.0	126.0
Glycine	..	..	..	0.8	2.7	1.8
Alanine	..	..	..	21.4	17.3	13.1
Total		..	128.0	377.4	302.5

[1] Adapted from Barnett and Naylor (1966).

Carbohydrate metabolism is affected by drought through direct and indirect effects on photosynthesis and through several intermediate components and processes (Slatyer, 1969). Net photosynthesis is reduced by water stress, partially by insufficient carbon dioxide supply following stomatal closure and by a direct effect of dehydration on the photosynthetic system. Under drought stress (Eaton & Ergle, 1948), there is a conversion of starch to sugar (Table 2.6). This conversion is frequently associated together although there are reports of reduced polysaccharide levels not being associated by an increase in sugar content. Reduced starch levels have been attributed to reduced photosynthesis and increased hydrolysis as well as to decreased synthesis. Starch content of wilted excised leaves of *Phaseolus vulgaris* decreased faster than it did in turgid leaves (Stewart, 1971). The accelerated starch loss was accompanied by an increase in free (alcohol-soluble) sugars, primarily sucrose, in stressed leaves whereas no similar increase was observed in the turgid leaves. Total carbohydrate decreased at the same rate in both wilted and turgid leaves during dark incubation. This accelerated loss of starch due to wilting is a common occurrence. According to Stewart (1971) the rate of respiration was not affected greatly by wilting insofar as the rate of total carbohydrate loss was the same in the wilted as turgid leaves. Nevertheless, measurements of oxygen uptake using standard Warburg-technique indicated that wilting resulted in a decrease in respiration rate of about 10%. The effect of wilting

Table 2.6. Influence of drought on hexoses, sucrose
and starch in two cotton varieties[1]

Stress				% Hexoses	% Sucrose	% Starch
				Acala		
Check	..	..	..	0.88	0.53	3.95
Drought	..	..	..	1.40	0.18	0.43
				Stonville		
Check	..	..	..	0.61	0.72	3.05
Drought	..	..	..	1.60	0.36	0.94

[1] Adapted from Eaton and Ergle (1948).

may be different in plants under natural moisture stress, whereas the above investigations were with excised leaves maintained in the dark after rapid wilting. Sugars serve to stabilize protoplasmic colloids, preventing their denaturation by replacing water molecules from the hydration shells. Artificial application of sugar solutions during desiccation has been shown to reduce desiccation injury.

Abscission of leaves, fruits and seeds can be induced by plant water deficits. For example, the yield of cotton can be reduced up to 70% of the yield potential by premature shedding of squares and young bolls. This response has been demonstrated insofar as low water content in plants and soil will increase shedding.

The relation of plant water deficit to the abscission process is not understood although McMichael *et al.* (1972, 1973) present data that greater-than-normal rates of ethylene production by intact cotton petioles are associated with severe plant water deficits. Ethylene is able to block basipetal transport of auxin in cotton petioles (Beyer & Morgan, 1971) which is considered to regulate natural leaf abscission. These results suggest that shedding of squares and bolls can possibly be explained by water-stress-induced ethylene production by petioles.

The influence of drought stress on the respiration of plants has been presented in several reviews (Crafts, 1968; Henckel, 1964) and it is generally agreed that under severe water stress respiration is drastically reduced. Nevertheless, the influence of limited stress on respiration is debatable because some investigators have reported an initial stimulation in rates of respiration at low levels of stress (Schneider & Childers, 1941; Street & Opik, 1970) whereas others have reported a continuous reduction in respiration with stress (Boyer, 1970; Brix, 1962; Flowers & Hanson, 1969). Bell *et al.* (1971) isolated mitochondria from etiolated corn shoots and found that drought had a marked effect on the respiratory capacity of mitochondria. Previous work (Miller *et al.*, 1971) had shown that alterations of mitochondrial membrane function occur with increasing water stress. Bell *et al.* (1971) concluded that since membranes are the site of mitochondrial respiration and a structure-function relationship exists between membrane and respiration, changes in the phospholipid or protein structure of the mitochondrial membrane may cause the suppression of oxidation rates of succinate, malate-pyruvate, and exogenous NADH in water stressed tissues. Therefore, the ultimate cause of the inhibited oxidation of respiratory substrates measured in mitochondria isolated from drought stressed corn may be due to altered membrane structure caused by depletion of water.

Drought Stress and Grain Yield

Three important stages of growth in relation to drought stress should be considered. These are stages of floral initiation and inflorescence development, anthesis and fertilization, and grain filling (Slatyer, 1969).

Good evidence exists that a slight drought stress can reduce the rate of appearance of floral primordia. However, removal of a slight drought stress in barley has been shown to cause a more rapid rate of primordial initiation than for non-stressed plants (Nicholls & May, 1963). When a severe drought stress was imposed, the recovery from drought was unsatisfactory and the total spikelet number was greatly reduced. Primordial initiation is more affected by drought stress than spikelet development, and thus, stress at the former stage can alter grain number more than at the latter stage.

Drought stress at anthesis and fertilization will reduce the number of kernels because of the dehydration of pollen grains. Another factor is that pollen grain germination and pollen tube growth down the style into the ovary and ovule are affected. Wilting of the styles interferes with pollen tube growth, and one might expect such a response to be more pronounced in species possessing long styles, such as corn. Crop plants which shed pollen over an extended period of time will be more likely to avoid the influence of drought at this stage of growth than crop plants which shed pollen in a relatively short period of time.

Drought stress at the stage of grain filling is pronounced as yield development, expressed by weight per grain, requires the accumulation of photosynthate in the grain. The two sources for the accumulation of these assimilates are photosynthesis in the grain itself and translocation from other plant parts. A portion of the photosynthate is synthesized prior to anthesis, stored in the stem or other organ and later translocated to the developing grain, but the greatest accumulation is synthesized after anthesis. Drought stress has been shown to reduce translocation from the leaves, and as drought hastens maturation, this response in addition to reduced photosynthesis contributes to lower grain yield.

Antitranspirants

Antitranspirants have received attention in recent years as a means to decrease water loss from plant leaves by reducing the size or number of stomatal openings, and thus decreasing the rate of diffusion of moisture vapour (Fuehring, 1973). However, a supply of carbon dioxide diffusing into the stomatal cavity is necessary for the occurrence of photosynthesis, and if the reduction in openings results in a restriction of actual photosynthesis, yield reduction will result. Successful antitranspirant use must achieve a favourable balance in restricting moisture loss from leaves without restricting photosynthesis. Reducing the use of soil moisture during periods of drought will extend the period of time before growth is seriously affected.

Another aspect in the use of antitranspirants which should be considered is the importance of transpirational cooling on leaf temperature. Williamson (1963) has shown that antitranspirants have resulted in a rise in leaf temperature of tobacco by as much as 9 °F above the controls. Likewise, when determining heat injury in a temperature-controlled chamber, a doubling in injury was obtained by increasing the relative humidity from 50 to 75% or from 75 to 100%, when heated to 43 °C for 8 hours (Kinbacher, 1969).

Two means by which antitranspirants can be effective are through films that coat the leaf and chemicals that close the stomata (Davenport *et al.*, 1972). Synthetic films that are sprayed on a leaf should ideally be resistant to water and completely permeable to carbon dioxide. Such specification is difficult to achieve. Gale and Hagan (1966) refer to polymer emulsions as materials forming relatively thick films, and have concluded that a major factor in their value as antitranspirants is their relative resistance to CO_2, O_2 and water vapour transmission. They further concluded that one of the main practical problems in the development of improved film-forming antitranspirants is finding greater selectivity to gases and vapour. Their review cites numerous references where antitranspirants have been studied. Latex has been used successfully in reducing water usage by potted sweet orange seedlings (Malcolm & Stolzy, 1968).

Davenport *et al.* (1972) used a commercially available wax emulsion (Mobileaf) manufactured by the Mobil Oil Company, on peach trees and found resistance to water vapour diffusion from the leaves and also the water potential of those leaves increased.

Stomatal closure by chemical sprays has been investigated and one of the most reliable inhibitors is phenylmercuric acetate (PMA) (Zelitch, 1969). PMA has several desirable properties which make it useful as the chemical: (1) closes stomata when sprayed on leaves at low concentrations, (2) affects only the stomata in the sprayed area and is not likely to be trans-located, and (3) will inhibit stomatal opening for at least 4 days without apparent toxicity in many species. Fuehring (1973) studied the use of PMA, Atrazine, and Folicote (a hydrocarbon emulsion) on grain sorghum under limited irrigation. Mean grain yield increases of 5 to 17% were obtained with rates of approximately 60 g/ha for PMA, 130 g/ha for Atrazine, and 2 litres/ha for Folicote. Application just prior to the boot stage was more effective than a later application. Zelitch (1969) cites numerous references on the use of inhibitors of stomatal opening as antitranspirants.

Sij *et al.* (1972) found that it was necessary to apply at least 360 μM PMA in field-grown sorghum to maintain increased stomatal resistance up to 20 days. Their preliminary data showed that in short-term studies of 3 to 4 days post-treatment, photosynthesis was temporarily reduced more than was transpiration by PMA concentrations that produced prolonged effects on stomata.

Waggoner (1969) refers to the use of antitranspirants as stomatal management and has indicated that PMA is toxic to leaves and that the failure to increase yields by stomatal management may be caused by stomatal resistance to CO_2 or by the toxicity of PMA. Although PMA is still one of the most effective chemicals used at low concentrations for inducing stomatal closure, its effectiveness in increasing water use efficiency (photosynthesis/transpiration) has been inconsistent.

Drought Hardening

Plants subjected to slight drought conditions will upon recovery be more resistant to the influences of further drought stresses. The drought hardened plant exhibits increased viscosity of the protoplasm, higher rates of photosynthesis, lower rates of respiration, higher root-to-top ratio, and less yield reduction when subjected again to drought as compared to a non-drought hardened plant. Some other changes that have occurred in plants subjected to conditions favouring the development of drought hardiness are: (1) decreased relative turgidity and moisture content, (2) decreased nitrate reductase activity, (3) accumulation of nitrate, (4) increased total nitrogen per plant, and (5) decreased molybdenum levels in plants (Mattas & Pauli, 1965).

Effective Drought Control

Successful crop production in regions of frequent drought requires methods and practices for providing or maintaining sufficient available water for crop growth. Among these methods and practices are selection of crops that evade or endure periods of insufficient moisture, utilization of cultural and soil management techniques that increase soil water storage or decrease the rate of use of the limited soil water supply, and development of methods that reduce evapotranspiration (Viets, 1971).

The selection of crops depends on the total water demand, timing of the need for water in relation to the supply, and the ability of the crop to endure drought without damage. Even varieties within a crop species differ in ability to endure drought. Mederski and Jeffers (1973) reported that under high moisture stress conditions, the yield of the most stress resistant varieties of soybeans was reduced by about 20% while the yield of the least stress resistant varieties was reduced by about 40%. The absolute reduction in yield for the most stress sensitive varieties was approximately 1000 kg/ha, while the yield of the least stress sensitive varieties was reduced by about 200 to 400 kg/ha. Total water requirements of crops vary because of the length and timing of their growth periods in relation to the evaporative demand. Crops which demand a long growing season, such as soybean and corn, generally do poorly in regions of low rainfall. Depletion of moisture during peak water use or before the usable part of the crop is produced results in crop failure. Most crops have a critical stage of peak water use when the plant cannot withstand drought stress without considerable injury and yield reduction. For example, corn is subjected to great yield reduction when drought stress occurs at anthesis (tasseling and silking) (Shaw & Laing, 1966). The critical stage in wheat is at heading and filling of the grain (Slatyer, 1969). The boot stage is critical for barley as stress at this time greatly reduces grain yield and quality, and increases the protein content which is undesirable in the malting industry (Reed, 1966). Drought stress during the period of fruit or grain growth leads to small fruit or grain size, primarily by a direct effect on photosynthesis or more likely by an indirect effect on the oxidative respiration system. It does appear that the total yield of grain is not reduced as much by drought at later stages of growth than at the earlier stages.

Most cells are killed when 50-70% of their water content is lost. However, in flowering plants meristematic cells can withstand desiccation better than extended cells.

Various cultural practices are available to reduce the hazards of drought, in addition to selection of crops with tolerance and growing those adapted to the timing of soil moisture availability (Viets, 1971). One practice is to plant crops more thinly so that the transpiration and evaporation (ET) from plant and soil are less than the potential ET. Row spacing can be increased and plant populations decreased in order to utilize water more slowly to have an available supply when environmental conditions favour drought. A common practice is the use of a seeding rate of 44.8 kg of winter wheat per hectare on dryland, whereas 134.4 kg/ha are used under irrigation. In the case of corn, row spacings of 91.4 to 106.7 cm and populations of 19,750 to 29,630 plants per hectare are used on dryland, whereas under irrigation row spacings of 61 to 76 cm and populations of 49,380 to 61,730 plants per hectare are common. Lower planting rates are possible when plant pests, such as weeds, insects, diseases and nematodes are chemically controlled. Weeds are especially competitive in thin stands and need to be controlled for successful crop production. With control of plant pests, low planting rates generally produce significantly more grain per plant than higher planting rates, with the greatest increases occurring in drought years.

Soil fertility needs to be considered as a cultural practice to minimize drought injury. Correcting nutrient deficiencies that exist in the soil will increase the efficiency of water use. A plant with a limited supply of water has the potential to grow but because of a lack of essential nutrients no new growth is produced. The recommended use of fertilizer is a cheap and profitable way to increase water use efficiency.

Modification of the microclimate to reduce the hazards of drought has received attention. The use of shelter-belts and artificial barriers to reduce evapotranspiration and wind movement has occasionally provided yield increases under dryland conditions.

Practices which lead to increased water storage in the soil and the collection of runoff for crop production have been successful. Soil moisture storage at time of planting is an important consideration in deciding whether to plant, the best planting rate, and the rate of fertilizer application. In some areas of rainfall less than 50 cm annually clean or weedless fallow is practised for the saving of rain in one summer for use in the next season. Summer fallow under extreme dryland conditions has often more than doubled wheat yields, although the use of fallow is recognized as being an inefficient process in conserving moisture. Only approximately 20 per cent of the precipitation which falls during the fallowing period is saved for next year's crop. Nevertheless, an additional 2-5 cm of water, available at the critical stages of growth, can be extremely beneficial.

Fallow controls weeds which has an added effect in conserving moisture. However, herbicides are now available which can be used for weed control. The practice has allowed mineralization of soil nitrogen which is an advantage of fallow, but the availability of relatively cheap nitrogen fertilizers has lessened this advantage. Wind and water erosion has been a hazard to clean summer fallow. A method to alter this disadvantage is stubble-mulch, a practice to keep crop residues on the soil surface. The extra moisture retained by stubble-mulching has increased wheat yields in seasons with warm dry springs but have decreased yields in seasons with cool, wet springs.

Practices have been developed to reduce water runoff and to increase infiltration of water. One method includes pitting of rangelands with heavy disks or similar equipment to make for a more rapid and complete infiltration of water. In sandy soils these pits have a life span of approximately 4 years. Pitting has not been widely accepted. Another method is the construction of contour ridges which run horizontally around the hills to reduce water runoff.

In regions of snowfall, methods of intercepting snow and preventing it from blowing off the fields have been devised. Use of snow fences, spaced row crops (corn, sunflower, sorghum), and shelter-belts have been used for this purpose.

Shaping of land so that the water stays where it falls or runs off from a

Table 2.7. Crop yield on level benches for several crops at Mandan, North Dakota[1]

Treatment		Wheat	Corn	Alfalfa	Brome grass
		1962-65			
Check	..	30.5 bu/A	38.2 bu/A		
Level benches	..	34.0 ,,	40.4 ,,		
		1963-66			
Check	..			1800#/A	1890#/A
Level benches	..			3890 ,,	3140 ,,

[1] Adapted from Haas and Willis (1968).

slope to irrigate a level bench below the slope has received attention. This method looks promising for more stable crop production in times of drought. Data collected in North Dakota have shown a yield advantage for wheat, corn, alfalfa, and bromegrass grown on benches (occasionally called level terraces). However, conservation benching has been more favourable for alfalfa and bromegrass than for corn and wheat (Table 2.7).

This chapter has been devoted to drought injury and resistance in crop plants. It would have been desirable to precisely state the causes for injury and resistance of plants to insufficient water stress, but this is not possible because of inadequate drought research and knowledge, varied interpretations of results among drought researchers, differences existing among species, and even differences existing among growth stages within a given species. Nevertheless, the author hopes that students using this chapter will have a better understanding of drought injury and resistance in crop plants and ways to overcome this hazard to crop production.

REFERENCES

BARNETT, N. M. and A. W. NAYLOR, 1966. Amino acid and protein metabolism in Bermuda grass during water stress. Pl. Physiol. 41: 1222-30.

BELL, D. T.; D. E. KOÉPPE and R. J. MILLER, 1971. The effect of drought stress on respiration of isolated corn mitochondria. Pl. Physiol. 48: 413-15.

BEYER, E. M. JR. and P. W. MORGAN, 1971. Abscission: the role of ethylene modification of auxin transport. Pl. Physiol. 48: 208-12.

BOYER, J. S. 1970. Leaf enlargement and metabolic rates in corn, soybean, and sunflower at various leaf water potentials. Pl. Physiol. 46: 233-5.

BRIX, H. 1962. The effect of water stress on the rates of photosynthesis and respiration in tomato plants and loblolly pine seedlings. Physiol. Pl. 15: 10-20.

CRAFTS, A. S. 1968. Water deficits and physiological processes. In: Water Deficits and Plant Growth. Vol. II. Kozlowski, T. T. (ed), pp. 85-133, Academic Press, New York.

DAVENPORT, D. C.; M. A. FISHER and R. M. HAGAN, 1972. Some counteractive effects of antitranspirants. Pl. Physiol. 49: 722-4.

DENMEAD, O. T. and R. H. SHAW, 1960. The effects of soil moisture stress at different stages of growth on the development and yield of corn. Agron. J. 52: 272-4.

EATON, F. M. and D. R. ERGLE, 1948. Carbohydrate accumulation in the cotton plants at low moisture levels. Pl. Physiol. 23: 169-87.

FLOWERS, T. J. and J. B. HANSON, 1969. The effect of reduced water potential on soybean mitochondria. Pl. Physiol. 40: 1033-40.

FORDE, ST. C. M. 1972. Effect of dry season on uptake of radioactive phosphorus by surface roots of the oil palm (*Elaeis guineenis* Jacq.). Agron. J. 64: 622-3.

FUEHRING, H. D. 1973. Effect of antitranspirants on yield of grain sorghum under limited irrigation. Agron. J. 65: 348-51.

GALE, J. and R. M. HAGAN, 1966. Plant antitranspirants. Ann. Rev. Pl. Physiol. 17: 269-82.

GLINKA, Z. and L. REINHOLD, 1971. Abscisic acid raises the permeability of plant cells to water. Pl. Physiol. 48: 103-5.

HAAS, H. J. and W. O. WILLIS, 1968. Conservation bench terraces in North Dakota. Trans. ASAE 11: 396-8.

HENCKEL, P. A. 1964. Physiology of plants under drought. Ann. Rev. Pl. Physiol. 15: 363-86.

JONES, R. J. and T. A. MANSFIELD, 1970. Suppression of stomatal opening in leaves treated with abscisic acid. J. exp. Bot. 21: 714-9.

JUNG, G. A. and K. L. LARSON, 1972. Cold, heat and drought tolerance. *In*: Alfalfa Science and Technology, Hanson, C. H. (ed), American Society of Agronomy, Madison, Wisconsin, pp. 185-209.

KINBACHER, E. J. 1969. The physiology and genetics of heat tolerance. *In*: Physiological Limitations on Crop Production under Temperature and Moisture Stress, Lemon, E.R. *et al.*, (eds), Nat. Acad. Sci. Washington, D. C.

LARSON, K. L. and J. D. EASTIN (ed), 1971. Drought Injury and Resistance in Crops. CSSA Special Publication No. 2. Crop Science Society of America, Madison, Wisconsin.

LEVITT, J. 1956. The hardiness of plants. Academic Press Inc., New York, pp. 278.

LEVITT, J. 1969. Introduction to Plant Physiology. The C. V. Mosby Company, Saint Louis, Missouri.

LEVITT, J. 1972. Responses of Plants to Environmental Stresses. Academic Press, New York.

MALCOLM, C. V. and L. H. STOLZY, 1968. Effect and mode of action of latex and silicone coatings on shoot growth and water use by citrus. Agron. J. 60: 598-601.

MATTAS, R. W. and A. W. PAULI, 1965. Trends in nitrate reduction and nitrogen fractions in young corn plants during heat and moisture stress. Crop. Sci. 5: 181-4.

McMICHAEL, B. L.; W. R. JORDAN and R. D. POWELL, 1972. An effect of water stress on ethylene production by intact cotton petioles. Pl. Physiol. 49: 658-60.

McMICHAEL, B. L.; W. R. JORDAN and R. D. POWELL, 1973. Abscission process in cotton: Induction by plant water deficit. Agron. J. 65: 202-4.

MEDERSKI, H. J. and D. L. JEFFERS, 1973. Yield response of soybean varieties grown at two soil moisture stress levels. Agron. J. 65: 410-12.

MILLER, R. J.; D. T. BELL and D. E. KOÉPPE, 1971. The effects of water stress on some membrane characteristics of corn mitochondria. Pl. Physiol. 48: 229-31.

MITCHELL, R. L. 1970. Crop Growth and Culture. The Iowa State University Press, Ames, Iowa.

MIZRAHI, Y., A. BLUMENFELD and A. E. RICHMOND, 1970. Abscisic acid and transpiration in leaves in relation to osmotic root stress. Pl. Physiol. 46: 169-71.

NICHOLLS, P. B. and L. H. MAY, 1963. Studies on the growth of the barley apex. I. Interrelationship between primordium formation, apex length and spikelet development. Aust. J. biol. Sci. 16: 561-71.

OSBORNE, D. J. 1965. Interactions of hormonal substances in the growth and development of plants. J. Sci. Food Agr. 16: 1-13.

REED, A. J. 1966. Associations of various nitrogenous constituents and drought in alfalfa and barley. M. S. Thesis, North Dakota State University, Fargo.

RICHMOND, A. E. and A. LANG, 1957. Effect of kinetin on protein content and survival of detached Xanthium leaves. Science 125: 650-51.

RUSSELL, M. B.; L. W. HURLBUT; D. E. ANGUS; D. WIERSMA; P. J. KRAMER; R. M. HAGAN; Y. VAADIA; D. W. HENERSON and G. W. BURTON, 1959. Water and its relation to soils and crops. Adv. Agron. 11: 1-131.

SCHNEIDER, G. W. and N. F. CHILDERS, 1941. Influence of soil moisture on photosynthesis, respiration and transpiration of apple trees. Pl. Physiol. 16: 565-83.

SHAW, R. H. and D. R. LAING, 1966. Moisture stress and plant response. In: Plant Environment and Efficient Water Use. Pierre, W. H.; D. Kirkham; J. Pesek and R. Shaw (eds), American Society of Agronomy and Soil Science Society of America, pp. 73-94.

SIJ, J. W.; E. T. KANEMASU and I. D. TEARE, 1972. Stomatal resistance, net photosynthesis and transpiration in PMA-treated sorghum: A field study. Crop Sci. 12: 733-5.

SLATYER, R. O. 1969. Physiological significance of internal water relations to crop yield. In: Physiological Aspects of Crop Yield, pp. 53-88, Eastin, J. D.; F. A. Haskins; C. Y. Sullivan and C. H. M. van Bavel (eds), American Society of Agronomy and Crop Science Society of America, Madison, Wisconsin, pp. 53-83.

STEWART, C. R. 1971. Effect of wilting on carbohydrates during incubation of excised bean leaves in the dark. Pl. Physiol. 48: 792-4.

STREET, H. E. and H. OPIK, 1970. The physiology of flowering plants:

their growth and development. American Elsevier Publishing Company, Inc., New York.

VIETS, F. G. JR. 1971. Effective drought control for successful dryland agriculture. *In*: Drought Injury and Resistance in Crops, Larson, K.L. and J.D. Eastin (eds), Crop Science Society of America, Madison, Wisconsin, pp. 57-76.

WAGGONER, P. E. 1969. Environmental manipulation for higher yields. *In*: Physiological Aspects of Crop Yield, Eastin, J. D. *et al.* (eds), American Society of Agronomy and Crop Science Society of America, Madison, Wisconsin, pp. 343-73.

WILLIAMSON, R. E. 1963. The effect of a transpiration-suppressant on tobacco leaf temperature. Soil Sci. Soc. Am. Proc. 27: 106.

ZEEVAART, J. A. D. 1971. Abscisic acid content of spinach in relation to photoperiod and water stress. Pl. Physiol. 48: 86-90.

ZELITCH, I. 1969. Stomatal control. Ann. Rev. Pl. Physiol. 20: 329-50.

Dr. E. A. "Ted" Hurd

Born in Saskatchewan and spent early years on a prairie farm. Joined Royal Canadian Air Force and travelled extensively on Ferry command over five year period. B.S.A. (1950), M.Sc. (1951) from University of Saskatchewan, and Ph.D. (1960) from University of Manitoba. Wheat Breeder 1950 to 1967, Regina, Sask., Wheat Breeder 1967 to 1970, Njoro, Kenya. Breeder and coordinator of South Saskatchewan Wheat Programme 1970 to present. Director and President of four Scientific or Professional organizations. Published over 40 scientific and related papers.

Dr. E. D. Spratt

Dr. E.D. Spratt was born in Saskatchewan and was raised on a farm. He obtained B.S.A. (Soils) in 1958 and M.Sc. (Soil Chemistry) in 1960 from the University of Saskatchewan, Saskatoon. He worked as Pedologist (1960-61) in South Saskatchewan Irrigation Project, Soil Survey Unit, Saskatoon, and as Research Officer (1961-66), Canada Department of Agriculture Experimental Farm. From 1966 to 1968 he was on educational leave from the Canada Department of Agriculture to work at Rothamsted Experimental Station, Chemistry Department, leading to Ph.D. degree from the University of London in 1968.

From 1968-72 he worked as Research Scientist, Canada Department of Agriculture, Brandon, Manitoba. He served as Chairman of the Research Station agronomy group and Member of the Research Station Executive Committee. In 1971 he visited Ghana and Nigeria under the Commonwealth Foundation-Scientist Exchange programme. In 1972-73 he served as Head of the Plant Science Section at the Research Station, Brandon, and is at present working as Joint Coordinator, All India Coordinated Research Project for Dryland Agriculture with headquarters at Andhra Pradesh Agricultural University, Rajendranagar, Hyderabad. He has published 25 research papers relating to soil fertility and plant nutrition.

Dr. E. A. "Ted" Hurd

Dr. E. D. Spratt

3. ROOT PATTERNS IN CROPS AS RELATED TO WATER AND NUTRIENT UPTAKE

E. A. HURD
Research Station
Research Branch, Agriculture Canada
Swift Current, Saskatchewan

E. D. SPRATT[1]
Research Station
Research Branch, Agriculture Canada
Brandon, Manitoba

Introduction

Grain crops can be considered as factories whose production is for the purpose of producing carbohydrate and protein which are stored in the seed. The raw materials are carbon dioxide from air and water and nutrients from soil. Water is also a medium for transport of materials within roots, phloem and xylem in plants. Chloroplasts in the leaves convert raw materials into storable products with the aid of sunlight as the source of energy. Plant roots gather minerals and water from soil and transport them to the stem through which they move to the green leaves. Stems and roots transport the photosynthate formed in the leaves to the growing parts including root tips.

While this account is over simplified to the point of error, it does indicate the primary function of plant parts in the production of seed; usually the end product in grain crop production. The task of the plant breeder and the agronomist, the applied researchers, is to produce more and better quality grain per unit area. This means increasing the efficiency of the plant factory. Plants are grown in different environments and there is not only a fine balance between the various parts of the plant (MacKey, 1973) but between the plant and the environment. If any physical part, or chemical pathway of a plant is changed, even to a character as simple as height, it will affect the functioning of many other parts.

So as to select for optimum balance the breeder has no alternative but to select for yield in the environment for which the crop will be grown. Most of the cereal crops of the world are grown in semiarid climates where moisture is the main limiting factor. Thus the ability of the plant to utilize all available moisture is usually of primary importance and this largely depends on the root system. In spite of the importance of roots in the crop production, little practical research on roots has been carried out. This chapter brings together a considerable body of *ad hoc* root research. Since the main function of the root system is water movement and nutrient uptake, the principles involved will be considered prior to the discussion of the root system and its relationship to moisture stress. An understanding of the plant and its reaction to drought stress will greatly help the plant breeder in combining a number of advantageous characters from different parents into superior cultivars.

Water Movement

ENERGY AND WATER MOVEMENT

Crop plants survive and produce seed under drought because of factors affecting their intake or loss of water, or because they survive desiccation. The physiological process of water movement has been studied by many researchers (Slatyer & Gardner, 1965; Fogg, 1965; Feddes & Rijtema, 1972; Gardner, 1960a, b, 1965, 1968; Slatyer, 1957, 1960, 1967, 1973b; Kramer, 1963; Dainty, 1969; Russell, 1957). These reports have been freely used in the preparation of this discussion. An attempt has been made to avoid details and to present instead a review that will be of use in understanding the role of roots in plant growth under moisture stress.

Water moves in response to a thermodynamic force. The free energy of a system (i.e. a plant) is the ability to do useful work. The authors do not intend to discuss the thermodynamics or the nature of the force. Good reviews have been presented by Dainty (1969), Slatyer (1967, 1973a, b), and others. If, for example, we consider two parts of a system, the root and the soil, and find that the chemical energy of each is equal, the system will be in equilibrium and no movement will occur. If the potential of one is greater than the other, water will flow and the relative amounts of free energy will change proportionately to the amount of water moved. More commonly used terminology is water potential gradient. Pure water flows freely but when it contains nutrients, they cause resistance in the system. Sometimes the transport of solutes is against the chemical potential gradient. Slatyer (1967) questions the movement of water against a gradient. In growing plants, the soil-plant-air system moves water through the soil to the root surface, into the root, through the root to xylem vessel, up the vessel to the leaf, through the leaf to the evaporating surface and through vapour to air. This is a gradient with resistances at various places in the system.

Soil to Plant Water Movement

Where the soil is near field capacity water fills both the large and small pores—and is in close contact with solids and air. Since there are no membranes in the soil, water moves freely regardless of solutes. In wet soil, roots require a very low water potential (-1 bar) in order to maintain an adequate flow of water to the root (Gardner, 1960a). When soil dries out water disappears from the large pores and then from the small pores. In so doing the resistance increases, making the water potential required to move water high. If the soil potential were -15 bar, the water potential at the root surface would be about -30 bar (Dainty, 1969; Gardner, 1960a). If drying continues, the water potential at the root may be so low that the root cannot overcome it.

Water, in moving across the root, has to pass various membranes that act as resistances. Thus a gradient in water potential exists if water is to move. Root hairs increase the root surface layer by three or four times (Dainty, 1969).

Dittmer (1937) and Kramer and Coile (1940) studied root hairs of winter rye and reported that the extension of root per day was sufficient to make available to the plant 1.6 litres of water in sandy soil and 2.9 in heavy clay soil. These amounts could be adequate for normal plant growth. Dittmer found that there was from 700 to 1000 root hairs per millimetre of root. The amount of root hairs varied greatly between species but not between cultivars of cereals (Dittmer, 1949).

Gardner (1960a) considered some water movement concepts which have ready application in dryland cropping practices and related research. He says that not all water in the soil can be used by the plant. Its availability depends on the energy with which it is held by the soil, its rate of movement in the soil and the distance it has to move to reach the root, or on root distribution and ramification. As mentioned above, for water to move into the root and on through the plant a suction or free energy gradient must exist. The energy of the water in the plant is generally called diffusion pressure deficit (DPD). The DPD in the plant must be greater than the soil suction for water to be taken up.

Slatyer (1967) has reviewed wilting. Because of their cell structure, cereal plants do not wilt in the traditional, visible manner but drought stress has the same effect on the plants. Gardner (1960a) says that 10 to 20 bars suction is the range for wilting for most plants. Fifteen bars is often used as the lower limit of available water.

Todd *et al.* (1962) emphasized the importance of measuring moisture tension in the plant rather than in the soil. When transpiration is so high that roots cannot keep up, the tension in the plant can become very high. Oppenheimer (1960) found that resistant wheat cultivars retained more water in the plant under this high stress than non-resistant ones. Kaul (1969) found that cultivars differed significantly in water potential and osmotic pressure. Kaul and Crowle (1974) suggest that pH measurement be taken on slowly stressed plants as a technique for selection for yield. Chinoy (1947) found that Indian cultivars resisted wilting at the beginning of tillering and that stress at this stage increased yield over those not wilted. Chinoy (1962) claimed later that severe stress was not useful in showing differences in resistance of cultivars. Wells and Dubetz (1966) showed that the effect of stress was greatest at anthesis and that moderate stress was useful in classifying drought resistance of cultivars. Wardlaw's (1971) findings agree that anthesis is the critical stage. Stress reduced photosynthesis and root growth and thus reduced final grain weight per ear.

Soil structure has more influence on water holding capacity than texture. Improved aeration is a result of better structure and this results in a healthier more vigorous root system (Gliemeroth, 1952; Gardner, 1960b). Desirable soil structure also leads to great infiltration. Gliemeroth (1952) found that there was a close relationship between the plants ability to take up water and the root system, its density and its spread or network of roots in subsoil layers. Thus drought resistance is due to ability to take up water rather than having an abundant supply of water. He concluded that movement of water to roots from subsoil layers below root zone was not significant and Kramer and Coile (1940) agreed. Conrad and Veihmeyer (1929) say that capillary movement is too slow to be of any effect in California where the water table is far below the surface. Since direct evaporation occurs only in surface layer, plant transpiration must account for all changes in moisture below 8 inches. Conversely, changes indicate the presence of roots. They concluded that if the soil is wet at seeding time to the depth of normal root penetration, subsequent addition of water by rain or irrigation will not affect the extent of the root system developed. Water was removed in successive zones from the surface down. A negative correlation between wetness of soil and the density of roots showed that soil was dried because of the presence of roots. Rennie and Hutcheon (1965) concluded that rate of water use was not affected by fertilization. Water use is a function of plant rather than level of available water in a 4-foot profile. They found no relationship between soil moisture stress and rate of water use. Viets (1972), in a review, showed evidence that whenever fertilizers increased yield, the water use efficiency, that is, dry matter production per unit of water used, was increased. He said that fertilizers play an important role in the efficient use and conservation of water resources.

Cereals have an extensive root system and thus have a lower rate of flow into roots per unit length than most other plants with less extensive roots. Thus deficiencies around a root will build up much more slowly in cereals or in any plant with an extensive root system. Singh (1952) found in his studies that deeper roots were an advantage under moisture stress. He questioned the value of the green-house pots in moisture stress studies.

Gardner (1960b) says that as the soil gets drier and soil suction increases, the suction in the plant root must increase more rapidly than in the soil to maintain transpiration. He found that widely different textures exhibit approximately the same wilting suction because the capillary conductivity is about the same. Burton (1964), on the other hand, says that clay soils hold water more tenaciously than sandy soils. If this is so, plants grown on heavy clays are under greater suction tension than those grown on sand with equal water content.

The more extensive the root system the more water is available to the plant and the lower the rate of water uptake per unit length of root (Gardner, 1960a). A lower rate of uptake requires a smaller difference between DPD in the root and soil suction. This results in a lower stress in the plant for a given rate of transpiration. The average stress on a plant over a given period of time would be less for a large well-developed root system than for a small less extensive root system. Fischer (1973) showed that suction tension measurements taken in the xylem of a plant is a more critical measurement of water stress than tension taken in the leaves. Kramer and Brix (1965) claim that only DPD seems to have the quantitative character required for physiological research. They did not detail where it was best taken.

Water uptake relates closely to root distribution. The rate of water uptake by roots is proportional to the difference between DPD in root and soil suction and the length of root per unit of soil. At first water is taken from the surface layer. As suction increases in upper layer, the gradient is less between lower soil layers and roots in the lower layer, thus a gradual change in pattern of uptake takes place.

According to Gardner (1960a) some workers have found the greatest root development under dry growing conditions while others report better growth under good moisture conditions. Hurd (1964, 1973) found that 'dry' soil boxes had considerably less root than 'wet' boxes. The dryer the dry boxes the greater the difference. Perhaps a decrease in root in moist soils in some reports was due to poor aeration, a factor known to reduce root growth. Wheat plants do not respond to soil water contents greater than half field capacity. 'Dry' soils in these experiments may be about half field capacity and 'more moist' soils may have aeration problem thus reversing the normal trend. Roots do not grow in dry soil and it is presumed that there is a slowing down with the change from moist to dry.

Meige (1938) working in Morroco reported that roots were both hydrotropic and chemotropic. He described the root system as having plasticity, or ability to take advantage of favourable growing conditions. He said that roots were sensitive to environment; respond to friable, fertile, moist, but well-drained soils. There is no conflict here in results rather only in interpretation. Rather than roots growing toward water or fertile soils as suggested by Meige (1938), it seems more likely that they grow more vigorously in such soil and produce a healthier plant. The effects of soil fertility on root growth are discussed later.

Wort (1940) found that root length and branching, as well as the tiller number and plant height, decreased as soil temperature rose from 22 to 42 °C. Low temperature, on the other hand, influences water availability by increasing suction and viscosity of water and thus decreases movement in the soil.

A group of soil researchers in Texas (Ritchie, 1971, 1972; Ritchie & Burnett, 1970; Ritchie et al., 1972a, 1972b; Ritchie & Jordan, 1972) have studied plant water relations in black clay soil. They found that water moved down through cracks, and large pores much faster than in small pores and thus leaves soil moisture quite variable. Evaporation rates become limited by soil water availability at -5 bars tension, however, the figure varied considerably. Water potentials in the soil went down to -13 to -18 bars. Root density was too low to take up water at depths of 100 cm. Evaporation rate was independent of available energy for evaporation and depended on root distribution. All water extracted by the roots moved from soil immediately surrounding the roots. They also conclude that there is a need in growing crops under moisture stress to have deep, dense, root systems.

Plant to Air Water Movement

Water moves from the root to the leaves in the xylem, usually as a result of energy created by transpiration from the leaf surface. Where there is no transpiration, water may still flow and lead to guttation as a result of root pressure. Xylem, formed of end to end empty cells, is a multiple tube-like vessel that maintains columns of water from root to leaf. Some of these columns undoubtedly break under stress but are usually refilled during the night. In the leaf, the xylem bundles break up into many smaller bundles and to single xylem vessels. These lead into parenchyma and thus to the intercellular spaces. Very little difference in water potential is required to move water in the leaf. In the movement of water in plants the vapour phase has the greatest resistance and thus controls water relations in steady state (Dainty, 1969). To complete the chain of events water must overcome stomatal or cuticular resistance as well as the diffusion resistance of the mesophyll cell wall and of the intercellular spaces. The cuticular resistance is usually high, so the only control the plant has is by closing and opening of the stomata.

Vasilicv (1929) found that high soil moisture in south-east Russia would not protect the plant from suffering from atmospheric stress. Excessive transpiration causes the greatest drought losses, especially if severe stress occurs in the early growth stage of the crop. He suggested that moderate daily stresses may harden the crop and thus be an advantage.

Mart'yanova (1960) and others have hardened cultivars by presowing wetting and drying of seed. Whiteside (1941) associated drought and frost hardiness and recommended spring × winter crosses. He said that there was no use testing unhardened cultivars and since uniform hardening was not possible, tests must be conducted over several years under dry field conditions. This agrees with conclusions of Grebner (1963) and Aufhammer et al. (1959).

Ferguson (1965) concluded that evapotranspiration was controlled by meteorological phenomena when moisture is readily available but resistance at the leaf surface controls it when moisture is at an intermediate level and the soil surface is dry. When soil moisture is extremely limited, evapotranspiration is controlled mainly by soil resistance. Mack and Ferguson (1968) reported reductions in yield of wheat of $156 + 40$ kg/ha per cm of water deficit from emergence to harvest and a reduction in yield of 311 kg/ha per cm of deficit from the fifth leaf to the soft dough stage. These results are similar to those obtained by Staple and Lehane (1954).

Some workers (Pohjakas et al., 1967) reported that Kenhi spring wheat (Triticum aestivum L.) used 526 mm of water per season on a 4-year average. Barley and field peas used less. These plants were not under soil water stress as moisture was kept at about 50% of field capacity   Grebner

(1963) stated that the amount of moisture used by cereals from an ample, regular supply has no relevance to water use under stress. He found that drought susceptible cultivars are damaged by drought stress and thus have less ability to utilize water when it became available later, than drought resistant cultivars. This adversely affects yield. With intermittent dry periods, resistant cultivars used less water per gram of grain than susceptible cultivars. This reflects an adaptability in resistant cultivars to reduced water utilization.

Iljin (1957) stated that CO_2 enters some plants through the epidermis (if thin) as well as through thin stomata, so they can grow slowly with their stomata closed. He reported that species differed in ability to withstand desiccation because the time their cells remained alive after being under stress of 50 to 55% relative humidity ranged from two hours to weeks. Cells of such plants have a large proportion of protoplasm and a small vacuole. Iljin also stated that plants exposed to severe drought are not able to re-establish normal functions. Vaadia et al. (1961) said that little is known about intracellular behaviour under stress yet growth itself is an expression of cell enlargement and division. Stomata open slowly and only partially though leaves look normal. Dobrenz et al. (1969) studied grasses and found that there were fewer stomata in drought tolerant clones per unit area than in drought susceptible clones.

Monteith (1965) states that leaves can transpire an amount of water several times their own weight on bright sunny days. For each gram of water that evaporates 585 calories of heat are generated at the surface.

Slatyer (1957) has measured DPD of 40 to 50 atm in days of rapid transpiration. Equilibrium will not be restored during the night so that in a lengthy dry spell plants may not recover for several days. Their ability to survive will depend on their desiccation tolerance. Kaul (1973) has shown that some wheat cultivars are damaged by stresses of about −24 bars and their ability to grow has been irreversibly damaged while others recover from stresses as high as −40 bars. Resistant cultivars retain more water in the plant under desiccation than others (Oppenheimer, 1960). Russell (1959) believed that drought injury was due to mechanical disruption of the protoplasm rather than by loss of water per se. Slatyer (1967) discusses the use of dew and light sprinkle irrigation by plants under stress. Some advantage from reduced evapotranspiration, which allows the plant to reduce water deficit, is substantiated but there is little evidence that water is taken in by leaves.

Kramer (1963) emphasized that plant growth depends directly upon plant water stress and only indirectly on soil water stress. Plant water stress depends on rate of water absorption and water loss. It is not safe to assume that a certain soil water stress will always be associated with an equivalent degree of plant stress.

In order to understand how water stress reduced growth, it is necessary to know how water affects plant processes. Kramer (1963) outlines them as follows:

1. It is a major constituent of physiologically active tissue.
2. It is the reagent in photosynthesis and in hydrolytic processes such as starch digestion.
3. It is the solvent in which salts, sugars and other solutes move from cell to cell and organ to organ.
4. It is essential for maintenance of the turgidity necessary for cell enlargement and growth.

Water stress often increases root/shoot ratio, and leaf area is reduced but thickness increased. It reduces photosynthesis directly by lowering protoplasm capacity and indirectly by less leaf area and closed stomata. Slatyer (1973a) states that photosynthesis is progressively reduced by water stress. It sometimes causes increased respiration. Transpiration rate is controlled by leaf area and structure, extent of stomatal opening, and environmental factors which affect steepness of water vapour pressure gradient such as temperature and vapour pressure of the atmosphere. The rate of absorption is controlled by rate of water loss, extent and efficiency of root systems and environmental factors such as soil aeration, soil temperature, concentration of soil solution and free energy status of soil moisture. Because of differences in factors controlling these two processes they do not always keep in balance. Resistance in the plant, especially in root, causes a lag in water movement. The common daytime loss of water is usually made up overnight. On days of high temperature and low humidity even plants growing on soil at field capacity may suffer from severe water stress and conversely plants growing in dry soil may not suffer stress on cool humid days.

Plant and soil water potential are usually equal at dawn because the internal gradient will have disappeared as the suction takes water in, while little or no evaporation takes place (Slatyer & Gardner 1965). In the absence of rain, water potential of both soil and plant gradually declines day after day. Eventually the wilting point is reached. Of course stomata start to close during the high stress period of the day, long before the plant wilts. This slows the trend of water loss and a new steady state results.

PLANT MODELLING

Many studies of water movement have used formulae derived from detailed measurements of plant parts during growth, especially under moisture stress. From such detailed studies plant models are being developed. While breeders and agronomists are not concerned with the detailed study, they need the information provided by plant modelling. Without the coordination of the work of plant physiologist and soil scientist with that of the breeder and agronomist, applied research is relegated to a trial-and-error approach to solving crop production problems.   Watson (1968) in his review encourages greater use of plant modelling in crop research.

Newton and Martin (1930) classified wheat cultivars as well as grasses, for drought resistance according to bound water.   Kuiper (1967) studied the regulatory effect or surface-active chemicals and found that one chemical increased yield of potatoes by 27%.   Van Bavel *et al.* (1965) developed a method of measuring transpiration resistance of leaves that was useful in predicting losses from plant canopies.

Williams and Robertson (Robertson, 1968, 1973; Williams, 1962, 1969, 1971, 1971/1972; Williams & Robertson 1965) have developed methods of predicting yield of crops from weather data for the large prairie area of western Canada.

Gardner (1960a, 1968) stated that since movement of water is slow in the soil at low water content and conductivity through the vapour phase is as slow or slower than by capillary movement, the value of such water is negligible.   Gardner has developed a method of measuring capillary conductivity and diffusivity of water in soils at high suctions which allow him to evaluate gradients near roots.   He then developed equations describing water movement in unsaturated soils.   This gives a quantitative measure of the role of water movement and its availability to plants.   He concludes that the pattern of water use in the root zone depends upon root distribution, root permeability, and upon water retaining and transmitting properties of the soil.   These can be predicted.

Molz and Remson (1970) also developed a mathematical model describing moisture removal from the soil by roots of transpiring plants. It describes both the removal by the plant and the induced movement in the soil.   In comparing theory and data they show that extraction-term-models are computationally and physically sound. These models give insight into the mechanics of the moisture use process. Slatyer and Gardner (1965) and Gardner (1968) estimate water use by studying one main root and its branches and multiplying that by the number of main roots in the system.   Molz and Remson (1970) consider the mass of soil in which the root is located in their model.

Shawcroft *et al.* (1973) conclude that the water status of a crop must be evaluated to develop crop, soil and water management techniques that can be applied in practical agroclimatological problems.   They have reviewed meteorological tools and considered their combination with plant parameters for arriving at estimates of crop water status.   They used various types of submodels and found reasonable agreement between the main model and the energy balance.

Brouwer and DeWit (1969) have created a model for interpolating and extrapolating knowledge from experimental results. Differences between simulated and actual results are useful for showing where the greatest gaps are in our knowledge. They say that this kind of study will show the plant breeder which properties are worth considering and which are not.

Many plant scientists are developing models for various aspects of plant growth and are struggling to fill the gaps in present knowledge so as to make those models reliable measures of plant interaction with environment. Their work will greatly assist in reaching maximum potential yield.

Nutrient Uptake by Roots

SOURCE AND AVAILABILITY OF NUTRIENTS

Higher plants extend their roots into soil to obtain a supply of water and minerals for vegetative growth and ultimate reproduction. Many chemical, physical and biological processes are involved in nutrient uptake. Fried and Broeshart (1967) describe the dynamics of inorganic plant nutrition using the equation: $M(solid) = M(solution) = M(plant\ root) = M(plant\ top)$ where M is a nutrient which continually moves through the soil plant system. By using an equation they illustrate that there are many physicochemical processes involved, each with rate constants that have the potential to be regulated by various factors. For the system to be functional energy must be available. In higher plants, energy comes from the absorption of light during the process of photosynthesis. Many books and reviews have been written on this subject, including McElroy (1961), Kok (1969) and Stoy (1969).

Comments in this review will be restricted mainly to one aspect of the above equation, namely the absorption of nutrients by roots. To fully understand the dynamics of nutrient uptake one also needs a knowledge of soil solid : soil solution equilibria (soil chemistry) and ion translocation in plants (plant physiology). General statements on these subjects will be made here and details can be obtained from reviews in soil chemistry and biochemistry including Bear (1964), Kononova (1966), McClaren and Peterson (1967) and from reviews on the physiological aspects of nutrient translocation including Crafts (1961), Zimmerman (1969), Moorby (1974) and Leggett and Egli (1974). Books on soil-plant relationships bring all related subjects into perspective (Fried & Broeshart 1967; Black 1968).

The source and availability of nutrients depends on the composition of the soil. The proportions of various primary minerals, such as feldspar, hornblendes, quartz-mica, hematite, magnetite, apatite and calcite determine to a large extent the amounts of uncombined oxides and salts (oxides, carbonates, sulphates, etc.) and influence the supply of Ca, Mg, S and Fe. The organic matter content of soil and its rate of decomposition influences the release of nearly all nutrients since the organic matter originated from plants which contained all mineral nutrients. The secondary minerals, including clays such as kaolinite, montmorillonite and illites are responsible for many of the physicochemical properties of the soil that affect nutrient availability. Finely divided organic matter and clay provide a reactive surface which absorbs cations in exchangeable positions. The intensity of the net negative charge, usually called the cation exchange capacity, and its effect on nutrient availability is dependent on the colloidal composition of the soil and the extent of weathering as influenced by the soil climate (humid, arid, etc.).

The physical-chemical properties of the soil will affect the composition of the soil solution, which is the major source of plant nutrients. As the water content of the soil increases the concentrations of nutrients decrease due to dilution. For anions such as NO_3, SO_4 and Cl there is almost an inverse relationship between water in the soil and concentration since the whole stock of these ions is in the solution. For phosphate and cations like K, Na, Ca and Mg, the situation becomes complicated. Phosphate is readily 'bound' in soils and an equilibrium exists between 'bound' and 'solution' phosphate which is affected by various physical, chemical and biological factors. The concentration of cations in solution and their dilution by increased water varies with the ion species and their valency. With more water there would be a relative increase of the monovalent K and Na ions in the soil solution as compared to the divalent Ca and Mg ions. Moss (1964) showed that the proportion of K ions to Ca plus Mg ions in the soil solution decreased from 0.20 to 0.13 as the pF values rose from 0 to 3. Oliver and Barber (1966) suggest that increasing the water content of the soil will decrease B concentration but increase the amounts of Fe, Zn and Al. The complexities of micronutrient equilibria in soils are explained in reviews by Lindsay (1972) and Stevenson and Ardakani (1972).

The soil solution is generally not a reservoir for a significant amount of the soil's nutrient ions but acts as an instantaneous supply to roots. As water and nutrients are removed from the solution they are replenished from the soil solids and organic matter through chemical and biological processes.

Nutrients are absorbed by the roots along with water as a result of the demand of the growing plant. The rate of physiological development, the demand for nutrient storage, and the rate of water use (transpiration) as influenced by the environment, affect the demand for soil water and nutrients. Cowan (1965) has related the flow of water through plants to the evaporative power of the atmosphere. Nye (1966, 1968) suggests that research should be done to relate nutrient demand to plant growth rates and expected yields which are likewise controlled by meteorological factors.

Baldwin *et al.* (1972) discussed the theoretical effect of rooting density and pattern on uptake of nutrients. Brewster and Tinker (1972) studied the rate of nutrient flow into roots of plants. The work of these researchers support the work of Nye.

ABSORPTION MECHANISMS

Contact exchange and root interception: Jenny and Overstreet (1939) showed that plant roots could absorb nutrients directly from soil solids by a process they called 'contact exchange' and surface migration. However, it was known that most nutrients existed in soil solutions so this method of uptake seemed insignificant. Wiersum (1961) and Barber *et al.* (1963) both estimated that plants grow to and actually contact about 3% of the total volume of soil exploited by the root mass. The actual percentage of the total nutrition derived from root interception is even less (Barber *et al.*, 1963). Most nutrients have to migrate to the root surface to be absorbed.

Mass flow or convection: Bray (1954) described nutrient mobility in soils in terms of those ions which could move over relatively large distances (mobile nutrients) and those which could only move a few millimetres (immobile nutrients). Those nutrients which are not adsorbed by the soil colloids and exist primarily in the soil solution such as NO_3, Cl and SO_4, move with the soil water and are absorbed by the root when water is absorbed. Ideal soil moisture conditions would be favourable for this mode of supply. When soil water is not moving towards the roots, nutrients are absorbed by diffusion. The amounts of nutrient taken up by mass flow is directly related to the amount of water used by the plant (transpiration). Those ions which are adsorbed by the soil and which are in equilibrium with the soil solution do not move as readily with water when it is absorbed by the roots. These include all nutrients in the cationic form and most anions other than nitrates, chlorides and sulphates (e.g., phosphates, borates, zincates and molybdates). Barber (1962) and Barber *et al.* (1963) demonstrated large differences in the amounts of the various ions transported by mass flow. Mass flow may supply the root with much of the plant's need for nitrogen, calcium, magnesium, especially when in high concentrations, but seldom supplies the full requirement of phosphorus or potassium in most soils.

Diffusion: The process of thermodynamic movement of ions in a medium from a point of higher concentration to one of lower concentration is known as diffusion. Diffusion movement of ions in water means movement within the water with no movement of water. The amount of ion migration by this means in soil depends on the concentration gradient and on the pathways of transport. Variations in soil water content have a large influence on both.

Barber *et al.* (1963) stated that most of the supply of phosphorus and potassium reaches the root by diffusion. Oliver and Barber (1966) found that 87 to 96% of the potassium absorbed by soybeans from a silt loam was supplied by diffusion. However, Fried and Broeshart (1967) and Wilkinson (1972) explain how all nutrient ions are taken up by diffusion. If water is able to move in the soil, mass flow supplements the supply of most nutrients to the roots. It is not quite valid to suggest, as does Barber (1962), that ions not associated with the soil particles move in the mass flow of water, whereas those associated with the soil particles move by diffusion. Movement of ions in the soil are influenced by both diffusion and mass flow.

There is a certain volume of soil adjacent to plant roots which is continually supplied with nutrients capable of being delivered to the roots by diffusion. This diffusion volume, as it is sometimes called, is dependent on the diffusion coefficient of the ion in the soil system and the concentration gradients between the soil solution and the plant root. The diffusion volume must take into account the capacity of the soil to maintain a certain concentration of the ions in the soil solution, e.g., the rate of exchange from solid to liquid phase (Olsen *et al.*, 1962). The diffusion volume is dependent on the requirements of the plant for the nutrient; if the nutrient requirement is low, more time is available for diffusion, and ions can thus diffuse for greater distances and still meet the plant's need. The diffusion volume can be supplied with fresh ions by means of mass flow of water. The water containing these ions may not be taken up by the roots but the ions can be absorbed by diffusion.

When ions reach the plant in amounts too high to be utilized by the plant, the diffusion and mass flow processes are effective in reverse.

MINERAL NUTRITION OF ROOTS

Roots, like plants on the whole, need proper nutrition or their growth will be restricted. Hackett (1969a) states that the major effect of nutrient deficiency on cereals is to decrease the length of root and the branching of the primary laterals. With barley he found that K deficiency reduced the mean length of the primary laterals by 33 to 67% and completely inhibited the formation of secondary laterals. P deficiency reduced the length of primary laterals by 33% but did not prevent the formation of secondary laterals. Top growth depends on root activity. Watson (1968) said that the number of leaves per unit area of a crop, their size and persistence, depend on the supply of nutrients and water from the soil. He says that under intensive agricultural production water and nutrients are usually plentiful in the surface soil so that the extent of the root system may not have much influence. He may be referring to humid region agriculture but Danielson (1967) suggests that maximum root growth is needed for efficient production under irrigation. Wiersum (1967a) suggests that there are many circumstances in agriculture where it is deemed desirable for plants to have deep penetrating roots. He showed that the uptake of N, P and K per unit of roots in contact with the soil was highest in the subsoil. Wheat and *Brassica napus* roots actively absorbed nutrients at a depth of 80 cm. Wiersum (1967c) found that oxygen supplies at this depth were adequate for nutrient uptake, with nutrient uptake activity and root growth having about the same oxygen requirement. Bergmann (1954) suggested that excessive CO_2 and not lack of O_2 is one of the most common factors to limit root growth in subsoil.

Epstein (1973) explains how 24 elements of the earth crust play a functional part in living organisms and states that most of these elements come from the soil. The elements most likely to be deficient are N, P, K, S and a few of the micronutrients and much research has been reported on their effect on plant roots.

Nitrogen: In general, deficiencies in soil nitrogen seem to limit foliage growth more than root growth; too high a concentration of N in the soil can restrict root growth. Troughton (1957), in a review, reports research that shows that root production can be increased by fertilizer N when soil N is limited and mentions other work that shows a decline in root growth as N supplies become overabundant. Excess nitrate taken up by the plant may be chemically reduced and combined with free carbohydrates to form amino compounds in the shoots, consequently the roots may be restricted in growth due to lack of carbohydrate translocation from the shoots (Murata, 1969).

At low levels of nitrogen supply, roots are stimulated to grow more than shoots which increases the translocation of carbohydrates to the root. Thus, nitrogen influences the distribution of metabolites among different organs (Murata, 1969). Roots take up nitrate readily at any stage of growth and excess nitrate can accumulate within plants any time during vegetative growth. Langer (1966) reports that the maximum N content of roots, shoots and leaves of wheat occurs just after ear emergence if there is adequate mineral nitrogen available in the soil, and that most of the nitrogen needed for grain filling is translocated from the rest of the plant. Hence, early uptake of nitrogen is important for maximum plant growth. However, Bergmann (1954) found that a continuous supply of nitrogen (split fertilizer applications) gave the best yields and the most roots. Too much nitrogen applied early decreased longitudinal growth of roots. Similarly, Bosemark (1954) found that increasing nitrogen in the soil increased the root growth near the surface of the soil at the expense of depth of penetration and root elongation. On the other hand, Holt and Fisher (1960) report that nitrogen caused Bermuda grass (*Cynodon dactylon*) roots to penetrate deeply into soil. Danielson (1967) reports other research with various perennial grasses which shows that additional nitrogen increases root penetration.

Phosphorus: Soil phosphorus deficiencies will reduce both root and shoot growth. Early workers such as Brenchley and Jackson (1921) and Lees (1924) showed that increasing soil phosphorus increased cereal yields and increased the growth of roots more than of shoots. Brenchley and Jackson (1921) found that phosphorus affected wheat more than barley. Lees (1924) found that adding phosphorus encouraged greater root penetration and speeded rate of growth of roots. However, Troughton (1957), in a review, cites examples of negative, positive and neutral effects of phosphorus on root growth. He discredits the old opinion that phosphorus has some special benefit to root growth. Bergmann (1954) found that phosphorus had the same effect as nitrogen in that it decreased longitudinal growth but increased branching in a moist soil. Nitrogen addition often enhanced the effectiveness of phosphorus (Rennie & Soper, 1958; Duncan & Ohlrogge, 1958).

Potassium: Plants low in potassium are frequently high in nitrogen and low in carbohydrates which limits the production of roots. Liebhardt and Murdock (1965) report the breakage of brace roots of maize when potassium was not supplied. In their experiments, nitrogen induced brace root breakage and lodging; phosphorus increased this tendency and potassium alleviated the problem. Bergmann (1954) found that excessive potassium inhibited longitudinal root growth but stimulated secondary growth. Potassium is essential for carbohydrate production and is therefore very important for the growth of tubers and tap roots. However, cereals and grasses use less potassium and take up most of their needs during early vegetative growth. Haas (1958) showed that root production of grasses was seldom affected by potassium fertilization. In most studies potassium has been evaluated in combination with other fertilizer elements. Invariably, root development has been favoured by adding mixed fertilizer or other soil amendments which improve the general fertility of the soil.

Micronutrients: The importance of micronutrients in root physiology and growth should not be underestimated. Boron and zinc have been shown to be important for root meristem activity and growth (Carlton, 1954; Price *et al.*, 1972). In reviews, Price *et al.* (1972) and Olsen (1972) mention the influence of several micronutrients and nutrient interactions on root and shoot growth. They point to the need for more research to sort out the complexities of micronutrient use by plants.

The implications of mineral nutrition of roots will be discussed in the latter section on soil and crop management practices.

Effects of Limited Soil Moisture on Root Growth and Nutrient Uptake

Earlier sections discussed the importance of soil moisture for plant growth and the role of water in nutrient uptake. A flow of water towards the root can carry mobile nutrients to the roots and a good supply of capillary water enhances diffusion of less mobile ions. As the soil becomes progressively drier the water films around the soil particles becomes thinner thereby decreasing the rate of diffusion of certain elements to the plant root.

Roots grow best when the soil water tension is low but growth can occur up to the wilting point (Fig. 3.1). Root growth is limited by excessive water and they will not penetrate beyond the capillary fringe above a water table (Wiersum, 1967b). Ideal moisture in a soil with no other physical limitations, increases both the mass and distribution of roots in the soil profile and thus more nutrients are taken up by exploring a greater volume of soil. To obtain a steady supply of certain nutrients roots have to continuously grow into fresh zones of soil. If there are nutrient deficiencies which limit root growth, the uptake of nutrients and water will be limited especially if there is severe water stress (Wiersum, 1969). Cornforth (1968) found that the gross volume of soil exploited by roots influenced the uptake

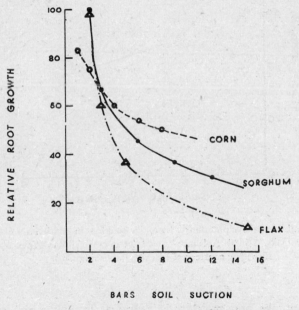

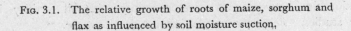

(from Wiersum, 1969)

Fig. 3.1. The relative growth of roots of maize, sorghum and flax as influenced by soil moisture suction.

of nitrogen but the intensity of root growth (mass per unit volume) was more important for phosphate uptake. Brouwer (1966) explains growth and extension rates of roots under different environmental conditions. Barley (1970) also wrote a review on this subject.

Nutrient uptake and moisture use are definitely related. Brown *et al.* (1960) observed that cotton and soybeans increased their absorption of N, P, K and Ca linearly in response to increases in soil moisture levels from the wilting point to field capacity. Watanabe *et al.* (1960) obtained similar results with maize (Fig. 3.2). There are possibilities for interactions between form of nutrient absorbed and soil moisture conditions as found by Spratt and Gasser (1970). They found that wheat, with adequate water, used nitrate-N best but when water was limited, wheat used ammonium-N just as effectively.

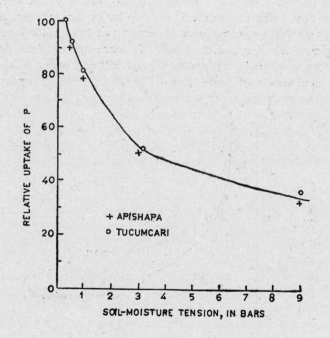

FIG. 3.2. Relative uptake of phosphorus by maize seedlings in relation to soil moisture tension for two soils, named 'Apishapa' and 'Tucumcari' (after Watanabe *et al.*, 1960) (by courtesy of Elsevier Publishing Co.).

Nutrient uptake and moisture withdrawal from the soil profile are related to rooting depths (Rennie & Clayton, 1967). Most research on the relationships between yield, water supply and soil fertility involve fertilizer studies. Fertilizer use is discussed elsewhere.

Effects of Physical Factors and Root Environment on Root Growth and Nutrient Uptake

Soil texture and structure: Pore size, distribution, soil strength, soil air, soil water and soil temperature are all affected by texture, which in turn affects soil structure. The amounts of clay and organic matter affect both soil structure and soil fertility.

De Jong and Rennie (1967) reviewed root penetration as related to bulk density and pore size. Several studies showed that penetration was prohibited when the bulk density was over 1.9 g/cm³ and in clay soils root growth was limited with densities of 1.6 to 1.7 g/cm³. Some studies showed that soil strength and pore size, rather than bulk density, controlled root penetration. Roots penetrated only the pores which were larger than the root diameter unless the roots were able to enlarge the diameter of the pores (Wiersum, 1957). Wheat roots have diameters in the order of 300 μ. The ability of roots to penetrate dense layers of soil depends on the pressure roots can exert and the anchorage of the roots. Root pressure varies with species and root vigour. Barley and Greacen (1967) report work done by Pfeffer in Germany with beans (*Vicia faba*) and maize (*Zea mays*) which shows that the axial pressure (longitudinally) ranged from 11.2 to 70 bars and the transverse pressure (radially) ranged from 4.3 to 6.1 bars. Maize exerted more root pressure than beans. Pressure exerted by roots will depend on growth activity which is dependent on oxygen concentrations in the soil, water supply, available nutrients, temperatures and other growth factors. Deep tillage can often improve root penetration by loosening hard pans and increasing water infiltration (De Roo, 1961).

The effect of root hairs, root exudate, microbial stimulation and root environment on nutrient uptake: Root hairs have been shown to greatly increase the surface area of roots (Dittmer, 1937) and therefore they are generally believed to aid ion uptake by roots, especially the immobile ions such as phosphate and potassium. Drew and Nye (1970), using diffusion equations, showed that root hairs could beneficially affect the absorption efficiency of roots. Lewis and Quirk (1967) published autoradiographs which showed that the zone of phosphorus depletion corresponded to the zone of root hair development. However, the autoradiograph method cannot explain the reasons for phosphorus depletion. It may have been due to enhanced phosphorus diffusion in the root hair zone due to the presence of root exudates or rhizosphere microorganisms. Bole (1973), using wheat cultivars with and without root hairs, found that root hairs had no significant effect on the uptake of soil phosphorus. He found that rape (*Brassica napus* L.) and flax (*Linum usitatissimum* L.), which have roots virtually devoid of root hairs, took up from two to six times as much phosphorus per unit length as the wheat roots with root hairs. Strong and Soper (1973) found that rape and buckwheat roots proliferated in the zone of fertilizer application and consequently took up more fertilizer phosphorus than wheat or flax. Thus, efficiency of plant roots varies amongst species independent of root hairs.

Some of the processes in the root environment have been reviewed by Nye (1968) and Wilkinson (1972). Root exudates and microbial stimulation may change the pH near the soil root and may create a wide range of organic compounds. At least 10 sugars have been identified, with glucose and fructose being the most abundant. Alanine, glutamic acid and aspartic acid are the most common amino acids among the 23 which have been isolated from 15 plant species (Wilkinson, 1972). Organic acids, vitamins and enzymes have been identified in root exudates. Their effect on nutrient uptake should be studied but are expected to be complex.

In respiration roots use oxygen and release carbon dioxide. In an isolated system of H_2O-CO_2-H_2CO_3 with a partial pressure of 0.2% CO_2, the pH would approach 5.3. Also, if plants take up more cations than anions and it is assumed that H^+ ions are excreted to maintain electrical neutrality at the root surface, the pH would also be lowered. In these two cases the lowered pH at the root surface should make nutrient elements more available. However, Cunningham (1964) found that most plants released HCO_3, since they took up more anions (like NO_3) than cations, thus raising the pH of the root surface. In a well-buffered soil (with clay and organic matter) the changes in pH would not greatly affect the local concentration of phosphate or micronutrients.

Researchers have assembled much knowledge about the way most cations and anions move through the soil in a root zone. Models can be made (Nye, 1968). However, the influence of various processes in the root environment on these models still need to be studied; for example, look at the influence of root hairs, hydrogen and bicarbonate ion concentrations, bacterial competition, organic exudates including root growth hormones, and other biochemical compounds. Parr (1967) has reviewed the effects of some of these compounds on nitrogen metabolism.

Root Patterns and Drought Resistance

PHYSIOLOGY AND FUNCTION OF ROOT SYSTEMS

Roots of only a very few plants of themselves have economic value and cereals, oilseeds or grasses are not among them. Because a great preponderance of the acreage of these crops is grown in semiarid areas of the world and under rain-fed conditions, roots which are so necessary in the uptake of water, are very important for efficient production. Most root researchers have stated that there is gross ignorance of the root patterns of crops and their relationship to production and environment. In recent years a substantial number of scientists have undertaken root research and numerous specific studies have been reported, but these studies are unrelated and often of little value to the plant breeder or agronomist. Troughton (1962) summarized the state of knowledge of roots of cereal crops. He referred to his work as a "review of various scattered pieces of information", not as a "resume of the work and life of cereal roots." He said that knowledge of the latter would be invaluable to the farmer and agricultural scientist, but it was not available.

Percival (1921) described roots of the wheat plant as having primary, seminal and nodal roots according to the place of origin on the seedling. The number varies with genetic and environmental control. Most researchers refer to only two kinds of roots on a wheat plant; seminal and crown (nodal or adventitious) (MacKey, 1973). Seminal roots are usually about five in number and are seldom more than eight (Weaver, 1926). Under dry surface conditions crown roots may not form and the plant is limited to seminal roots only (Cravzov, 1928; Engledow & Wardlaw, 1923). This has been observed by the authors in western Canada. Crown roots develop from the nodes, and under favourable growing conditions, can reach a large number. Crown roots anchor the plant by running out laterally and then going down, while seminal roots tend to go down and often penetrate deeper than crown roots. Pavlychenko (1937) and Pavlychenko and Harrington (1934, 1935) found that seminal roots were relatively more important than crown roots in thick stands, especially under water stress. Engledow and Wardlaw (1923) found that seminal roots were important in England with little water stress. They showed consistent differences in pattern of seminal and crown roots between two barley cultivars. De Roo (1969) stated that even under irrigation, plants that did not have a large branching root system are often subject to moisture stress and less than optimum growth. He said that root growth is genetically determined but the pattern is easily changed by chemical, or physical influences and by competition. Chinoy (1962) concluded that apparent differences in resistance to drought of cultivars are due to differences in environmental stage of growth condition and not due to genetic differences. Hoshikawa (1969) studied underground organs of seedlings in 219 species and 88 genera of Gramineae and classified them according to the morphology of their underground parts. Singh (1922) studied root systems of wheat in different soils and at different water levels.

Rawitscher (1937) and Pittman (1964) have found that magnetotropism caused roots to orient in a north-south direction. Dittmer (1937, 1949) and Dittmer and Reinhart (1948) studied root hairs and found that there is great variability, apparently controlled by environment and genetics. Knowledge of their relationship to water uptake and growth is vague. Root hairs act to increase root surface and so are thought to facilitate water uptake under stress.

Troughton (1962) reviewed the studies on the anatomy of different roots, root exudates and mineral nutrition. MacKey (1973), in bringing together some information on the wheat root referred to the importance of a balance between the amount of root that was needed and an excess that might use photosynthate which should go to fill the head. Considerable evidence is available showing that roots of cereals slow down or stop growing at inflorescence, especially under stress (Hurd, 1968). An excessive root, to the point of being a liability to the plant, seems unlikely. Hurd (1968) found that some growth of roots occurred after initial inflorescence in favourable growing conditions and in cultivars with late tillers not yet headed. He found that roots of these cultivars stopped growing at inflorescence under drought stress.

The classic work of Pavlychenko (1937) involved the tedious washing of the roots of weeds and crops from the soil where they were growing in competition with weeds. He recovered them intact and showed the original distribution pattern. While the work was time-consuming, no one has been able to duplicate his work in accuracy or detail by any simpler method. Pavlychenko estimated that one wheat plant had three million first and second order branches as well as unestimated third and fourth order branches. The length of a root of a Marquis (*Triticum aestivum*) wheat plant grown in a solid stand with 15 cm drill widths was near 900 m compared to about 72,000 m for a spaced plant.

Eavis (1972) studied mechanical impedance, aeration and moisture availability as influenced by bulk density and moisture levels in sandy loam soils. As impedance increases, pea roots were shorter and thicker except when aeration was poor. Restricted water availability of over −3.5 bars caused roots to be shorter and thinner. Denser soils had less air and a deficit of air acted in combination with density to retard growth. Warnaar and Eavis (1972) found that soil physical conditions affected seedling root growth. Mechanical impedance, aeration and moisture availability were influenced by the grain-size distribution and moisture content in silica sands. Coarser sand caused greater root impedance and this mechanical resistance increased with reduced aeration. Livingston (1906) stated that in water and in dry soil, roots were thinner and longer with fewer branches and fewer root hairs. He found more extensive branching and in general, more vigorous growth of roots occurring in soil with manure added than in poor or dry soil. Pinthus (1969) found that roots developed from each tiller as well as from the main shoot and that the highest rate of root formation occurred between spike initiation and heading. Thus, the length of this period affects root production. Root production of the main shoot and of the first one or two tillers terminated at heading time. Under favourable environmental conditions early varieties were able to produce additional roots after heading due to renewed growth of late tillers or the initiation of new tillers. Pinthus also found that durum wheat (*T. durum* L.) has greater capacity to produce roots on its main tillers than common wheat (*T. aestivum* L.).

Fujii (1959) found a correlation between growth of primary roots and development of leaves at successive nodes on the main stem. He found that secondary roots began to branch regularly from base to tip with elongation of primary roots. If the top growth was reduced for some reason a similar reduction occurred in root growth.

Cravzov (1928) used spiked boxes to keep roots in place during washing. He found that the primary root system of spring wheat remained fully operational until the plant was mature. Roots penetrated to 100 cm. In instances of dry soil on the surface the primary root carried the plant to maturity because the secondary root system could not become established. He reported that the secondary root system branched in the upper layers (30-35 cm) and could take advantage of summer rains. He concluded that selection for superior root system must be given priority in varieties for dry areas. Lundegårdh (1942) developed a theory that growth of roots is regulated by the ion equilibrium and the electrical charge of the surface of the root. He based his theory on the thesis that the growth promoting quality of the auxin is linked with its ionic activity in the cellulose membrane. Soil temperature affects root and total plant growth (Nielsen & Humphries, 1966).

Aufhammer et al. (1959) showed that an adequate root space was the most important requisite in drought resistance tests for cereals. Pot experiments gave the same results as obtained in the field if the pots were not too small. The cultivarial order was the same for long-term drought as for short periodic dryness. The most reliable criterion of drought resistance of a cereal is its average grain yield under drought in relation to normal yield capacity. Two types of resistance were differentiated: (a) production of a large number of grains though shrivelled, and (b) production of fewer, but well-developed grains. No useful relationship was found between shoot or root growth in young plants. They concluded that in testing drought tolerance, there was no substitute for yield tests under drought conditions. Belyakov (1968) studied the growth and development of primary roots of ten wheat and five barley cultivars. Davilchuk et al. (1971) studied root development of winter wheat cultivars which belong to different ecological groups and differed in productivity and drought resistance. These Russian workers associate root characters with ability to produce grain and discuss application of the data to breeding. Mack (1973) found that under all moisture and temperature conditions, Pitic 62 gave a much heavier root weight and a more fibrous root system than either Manitou or QK3-13 (all *T. aestivum* L.). He found that high temperature depressed the yield of the Mexican cultivars, Pitic 62 and QK3-13, more than of Manitou. Manitou tended to have more tolerance for the wide range of temperature. The relationship of root pattern and drought tolerance of Manitou (Thatcher backcross) and Pitic 62 will be discussed later.

Pinthus and Eshell (1962) studied roots of two durums and two bread wheats and found large differences between cultivars in total length of seminal roots from the seventh to the thirty-fifth day. Adventitious roots started to grow in the second week and even after five weeks showed no significant differences between cultivars. They found differences in adventitious roots at maturity and while there was an association with number of tillers they concluded that there was no additional cultivarial differences. They observed marked differences in the pattern of roots in the surface 25 cm, which was the only layer studied. Spacing altered tillering and thus altered adventitious root patterns, but may not have altered the root/shoot or root/head ratio.

Several researchers (Slucker & Frey, 1960; Katyal & Subbiah, 1971; Pinthus & Eshell, 1962) have studied the root in surface layers and up to about 60 cm. In studying root systems under drought the most important zone seems to be below 60 cm (Weaver, 1926; Russell, 1957; Hurd, 1973). The majority of roots are in the surface to 60 cm layer, but in semiarid climates often all moisture is used up by the grain filling time and it is the root in the lower layers that keeps the plant alive and facilitates filling of the head. Troughton and Whittington (1969) state that drought resistance appears related to root distribution so that maximum quantity occurs in the wettest soil.

Russell (1959) stated that perennial crops develop a well-branched root system that permeates the soil to depths characteristic of the plant. Below that level, root density is less. Roots of some plants grow and branch rapidly and explore more moist soil as the surface becomes dry, so that they do not suffer. Others send only widely dispersed roots into lower layers and leave areas of moist soil between roots. When this happens, moisture determinations from core samples can be misleading and quite variable. Gliemeroth (1952) also found that under long drought periods moisture depletion was not uniform.

Goedewaagen and Schuurman (1956) stated that the percentage of roots of grasses in the deeper layers was considerably less than that of cereals, but grasses usually have a much more dense root system in the surface 20 cm. Schuurman (1959) could not detect any water uptake from below 50 cm though there were roots in that soil zone. As long as the water supply is plentiful nearer to the surface, roots do not seem to take moisture from farther down.

Troughton and Whittington (1969) discussed genetic variation in root systems. They were pessimistic about the value of such knowledge to the plant breeder. They referred to a Ph.D. thesis report of Monyo in which chromosome substantiation was used in the study. Both root and shoot systems, when measured at ear emergence, were controlled by additive genetic systems with little dominance, but with more dominance in the shoot than in the root system. Monyo found segregation for shoot/root ratio in wheat crosses. When water was restricted and drying out occurred from the surface layer down, lines with more roots at lower depths yielded less grain than those with less root. Those with less root had less top growth and probably used the water more efficiently.

Lehane and Staple (1962) found that grain yields were not much influenced by moisture stored above 30 cm but moisture stored below 30 cm had a marked effect on yield. They concluded from their research that under drought, plants growing on clay soils were most efficient in early stages of growth. Plants were smaller and used less water, thus leaving it available for filling grain in the head. Troughton and Whittington (1969) emphasize the necessity of knowing the relationship between root patterns and crop yield. Doss et al. (1960) found that depth of rooting decreased as soil moisture increased. In surface layers the driest moisture regime had the most roots. At 90 cm the middle moisture level gave the greatest root but below that level to 130 cm the most moist soil had the greatest root growth. Miller (1916) found that sorghum had twice the amount of root to that of corn and half the leaf area. Cultivars of both corn and sorghum reached a depth of six feet. Kmoch et al. (1957) reported winter wheat penetrating to 400 cm (13 feet) but more commonly roots reach 120 to 240 cm (Weaver, 1926; Pavlychenko, 1937).

Water cultures were used by Hackett in barley research (Hackett, 1968, 1969a, 1969b, 1971; Hackett & Bartlett, 1970). In Hackett's paper (1968) and the discussion that followed, reference was made to differential response in water and soil media, i.e., different pattern in branching. Hackett thought that water culture as a method was of use but cautioned extrapolation to field response.

Bowen and Ravira (1969) and Neal et al. (1970) showed effects of rhizosphere microflora on root growth. Bowen and Ravira (1969) emphasize that "any consideration of growth and activity of roots must take into account that it is the normal state of the roots to be colonized by bacteria and fungi". Root studies in water culture have advantages, but discoveries thus made must be confirmed in field studies to be useful. Katznelson et al. (1956, 1962) and Chan et al. (1963) studied root exudates and showed that they influence soil mycorrhiza. Griveva (1964) studied alcohol formation and excretion by plant roots under anaerobic conditions and found that even as short a time as a six-hour term of anaerobic conditions adversely affected plant activity.   Anaerobiosis disrupts biochemical transformations and fosters accumulation of excretion of toxic products.

Worzella (1932) found that in non-hardy varieties, many of the seminal roots developed almost horizontally in the early stages of growth, then turned downward, while other roots run obliquely outward. In general, in hardy cultivars studied, most of the seminal roots run obliquely or downward. Non-hardy cultivars showed a greater top growth in the fall and early winter than hardy ones. Oppenheimer (1960) says that it is a well-established fact that under dry conditions plants develop high root/shoot ratios. He calls this an evolutionary adaptation. In the Great Plains the top/root ratio of resistant grasses ranges from 1:3.5 to 1:6 compared with 1:3 in less resistant grasses. Troughton (1955, 1956, 1958, 1960a, 1960b, 1961a, 1961b, 1961c, 1963a, 1963b) studied root/shoot relations in grass swards, but drought was not a serious factor. His ratios were about 1:2.5.

Derera *et al.* (1969) studied the root pattern and drought tolerance of 15 cultivars. They concluded that the extent of root during jointing and flowering was the major determining factor in drought tolerance. In experiments by Derera *et al.* (1969) the diameter of the tubes appear from the diagram to be narrow, thus restricting spread of roots. The amount of soil and water available per plant is small and so all cultivars probably used all of the water regardless of root pattern. Roots were probably much denser than in normal field conditions because of the restrictions in space. The earlier smaller plants were more efficient in their use of water than later ones which had not started to produce seed when the water ran out. In the driest areas of western Canada there is almost always unused water in the lower parts of the potential root zone (Hurd, 1973). A later maturing plant with a deeper penetrating or more dense root system in lower layers of soil, where water remains, could demonstrate good tolerance (e.g., Pelissier durum), but would do poorly in tubes (Derera *et al.*, 1969) while 40 to 90% of the variation in their experiments appeared to be due to earliness, the true drought tolerance of the 15 cultivars tested is likely quite different and earliness only one of many factors to be evaluated.

Deep rooting is an advantage in crop plants if supply of water becomes limiting (Wiersum, 1967c; Gliemeroth, 1952; Hurd, 1973). Roots at all depths can take up nutrients. DE Roo and Wiersum (1963) reported on their ability to train roots in plastic tubes to grow deeper than normal. Nye (1968) said that roots are cylinders with a concentration of soil solutions around them, but we are "extraordinarily ignorant" about the effect of variation in root soil relations, age of root, size of root or demands of the top of the plant.

Hunter and Kelly (1964) set up experiments to check the ability of roots to grow in dry soil and take up nutrients. They found that corn roots did penetrate dry soil below permanent wilting point, and increased the moisture content of the dry soil, but no nutrients were absorbed in dry soil. Slatyer (1960) states that root growth ceases at a water potential value slightly higher than that necessary to cause permanent wilting. This is to be expected because of the effect of wilting on photosynthesis. Goedewaagen (1955) found that drying out of the soil of upper layers increased growth of roots and uptake of water from below the dry soil layer. Salim et al. (1965), and Salim and Todd (1968) found that the extent of root growth correlated with soil moisture. The more drought-hardy cultivars and species had longer seminal roots and usually more of them. They said that little or no root growth took place at or below the permanent wilting point, but leaf growth continues especially in susceptible cultivars. Teare et al. (1973) studied water use efficiency in relation to several plant characters including root distribution. Taylor (1973) studied growth and absorption with parts of roots at different water potentials. Salim et al. (1969) evaluated techniques for measuring drought avoidance in cereal seedlings. Slucker and Frey (1960) studied root weights of oat varieties to a depth of 24 inches. Some varieties had a higher percentage of their roots in the top four inches than others, but the mean dry weight was not significantly different at the root stage. No change in total root weight occurred by harvest time.

Street (1969) outlined factors influencing meristem activity in roots and reported that there is an autonomy of the root system in controlling the distribution pattern of growth regulators and metabolic substrates. The root depends on the plant for metabolic materials used in growth, but appears to control whatever root auxins, cytokinins, and gibberellins that are present in roots. Williams (1960) studied growth of wheat in early stages of germination and found that the root primordium grows faster than leaf primordium up to five days, but then a rapid increase in leaf growth rate is paralleled by a decline in root growth rate. Hackett and Stewart (1969) developed a method of studying primordia in axes of roots without sectioning. Lukeena and Slooshnaya (1971) studied the physiological characters of winter wheat with different strengths of root systems. They found that stronger root systems were associated with greater water content at heading stage than ordinary root systems. They also found that the RNA content was higher and the protoplasm permeability was slightly lower in strong rooted plants over ordinary ones. Kirichenko and Oorazaleiv (1970) studied the degree of inheritance of strength in root system and the plant mass in interspecific hybrids of wheat. The dry matter weight and maximum length of the tops and of the roots were greater in spring × durum hybrids than in either parent in F_1, F_2 and F_3 generations. However, the average F_1 showed a marked increase over parents and over the F_2 average and the F_3 was even slightly less than F_2. This showed the extent of hybrid vigour in such crosses. T. aestivum had a stronger root system than T. durum as well as more top growth.

Methods of Studying Roots

Weaver (1926) studied roots *in situ* by digging a trench along side of the plant and then, by removing soil with a sharp knife, he was able to recover the root. Williams and Baker (1957) reported on their technique in trench method study which they used in herbage root investigation. Many have used modifications such as boring holes through the root zone and observing the appearance of the root and its rate of penetration. Weaver's method was further modified to the use of water to wash away the soil on site. Miller (1916) put a wire mesh cage around the soil block and attached wires through the block so that the roots remained in place when the soil had been washed away. Pinthus and Eshell (1962) used a board with spikes in it which they pushed into the side of the trench. As the soil was removed from other sides, to leave a block of soil and roots, other boards were nailed to the spike board to make a box for transport. Long (1959) used trenches and heavy steel boxes which were forced into the side of the trench. The steel boxes each with a portion of the soil profile were taken to a washing site. This technique was suitable for fertilizer-response studies as he concluded that the application of phosphate fertilizer increased top growth, root and grain yield in wheat. Goedewaagen (1955) used a method of preserving soil profiles in a monolith. The monolith method can provide all of the information researchers might desire. Its only drawback is the time and work involved.

Many researchers have used soil cores as a practical substitute for washing soil-root monoliths (Bloodworth, 1958; Fehrenbacker & Alexander, 1955; Kelley *et al.*, 1947). A steel shaft is thrust into the soil and the soil-root cores that are recovered are washed and the roots recovered by layers. Williams and Baker (1957) reported that the Grassland Research Institute split the tube to allow for easy removal of the core. Wooden and iron hammers used to drive the tube into the soil have been replaced by hydraulic presses. Perhaps the quickest washing method of such cores is to place a section of the core in a 60-mesh sieve and wash with a strong jet of water (Williams & Baker, 1957). Soaking in a solution of sodium pyrophosphate helps to break down the soil particles and leaves the roots suspended in the water. Williams and Baker found that the strong jet of water did not damage the root or cause appreciable losses of even root hairs. Fehrenbacker and Alexander (1955) described a method for studying root distribution using a soil-core machine and shaker-type washer.

In heavy clay soils separation of roots from soil particles is slow, so the Grassland Research Institute built a root washing machine. It has four 30-cm diameter funnels with a 60-mesh screen in each. Perforated brass cylinders, 15 cm in diameter, are put into the funnels and samples are placed in them. The whole apparatus is agitated continuously. The coarse mesh cylinder prevents the screen from getting clogged with larger particles of soil and stones or organic matter. Using this machine, 40 to 80, 30-cm long cores can be washed per day with two men.

Weaver and Darland (1949) modified the method to study roots in solid stands of the crop in the field. Weaver and Voigt (1950) studied the effect of soil type on root pattern using monoliths (6 cm wide × 8 to 15 cm deep × 7 cm thick) taken to the laboratory and washed to recover roots from each 15-cm layer. They found that clays which tend to compact, retarded penetration and branching, but roots that did penetrate such a layer grow more vigorously at lower depths if they encountered a loose moist soil.

Newman (1966) developed a method of estimating the total length of root in a sample. Measurement of root length is tedious because of the great length involved (Marquis wheat—about 300 m) (Pavlychenko, 1937), but length is considered more closely associated with surface than root weight. Newman's technique called "line intersection method" places the recovered roots on a grid and counts the number of intersections with cross wires. This method was compared to actual measurement and shown to be a reliable estimate of actual length. Carly and Watson (1966) used a gravimetric method of estimating root surface area and Purkas et al. (1964) described a method of measuring volume of roots.

Upchurch (1951) developed the soil-elution method and found that it compared well with the trench-wash method. In the soil-elution method 6-inch layers of soil placed in cotton bags by shovel were later transferred to drums with a mesh covered opening. Water was forced into the drum and the soil was floated out leaving the roots behind. This method takes more water and individual plant characters may be lost, but water does not have to be taken to the field and the soil-elution method is faster.

Read et al. (1962) developed a self-irrigating device for green-house pots which within limits could control the moisture level depending on the elevation of a water supply connected by a continuous column of water to a filter cylinder in the soil. Hurd (1968) uses a similar device to control water in glass-faced root boxes.

In the late 1950s, researchers began to use glass-faced root boxes of various dimensions to study the progressive growth of roots, the effect of herbicides and the relationship of roots to soil cracking (Lavin, 1961; Muzik & Whitworth, 1962; Minshall, 1957; Hurd, 1964; Ozanne et al., 1965; Pearson et al., 1970). The method used by the senior author has been described (Hurd, 1964, 1968, 1973). Root growth boxes (Figs. 3.3 & 3.4) were used to study individual plants in the absence of competition. The boxes were filled with a reconstituted profile. This is thought to be important because in a comparison made between reconstituted profile

Fig. 3.3. Root boxes with a sloping glass face covered with a slide: watering is by continuous column of water connected to a porous filter candle installed in the soil. A 75 cm rise in water level from source to candle keeps moisture levels at just below field capacity and a mercury column on the lower candles is adjusted to maintain the same moisture tension. "Dry boxes" are watered to this same moisture tension at planting time and then disconnected from the source so that no more water is added until maturity.

and topsoil at all levels, there was a considerable difference in root pattern (Hurd, 1964). In these boxes there is no impediment to the development of the plants' full potential root pattern except drought, which is the factor under study. Edwards *et al.* (1964) reported that root densities which limit root entrance to the soil layer, 1.80 g per cm^3, was within ten per cent of that found in reconstituted or disturbed soil. Three or four-day old seedlings are transplanted into the boxes so that each box has a plant at the same stage. The root pattern is traced weekly on a transparent foil covering the glass. A different coloured pencil is used each week so as to allow for measuring growth at each level at each stage. Figure 3.6 shows tracing of the roots showing on the glass in "wet" and "dry" boxes at maturity. "Wet" boxes are maintained at just below field capacity throughout the life of the plant by use of porous filter candles connected to a source of water by a continuous column of water (Fig. 3.4). "Dry" boxes are wet in the same manner as wet ones at time of planting, but the filter candles are cut off from the water supply at seeding time, and no water is

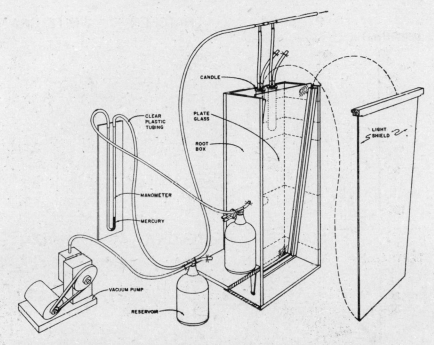

FIG. 3.4. Diagram of boxes illustrated in Fig. 3.3 showing details of construction and operation.

FIG. 3.5. Soil is washed away and roots recovered layer by layer. Roots that break off during washing float on the water and are caught in fine screens.

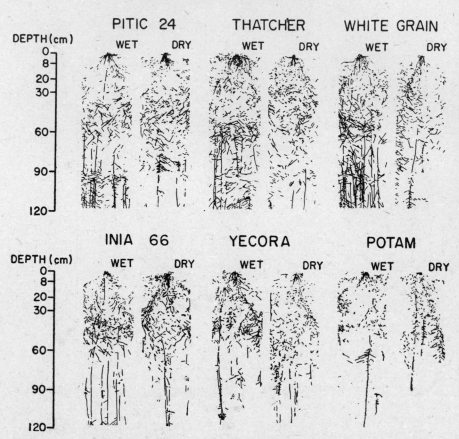

FIG. 3.6.   Photograph of tracings of roots visible on the glass facing at maturity showing differences in response to two levels of moisture.

added. This is not an abnormal condition during the life of roots of cereals grown in western Canada. On the semiarid prairies moisture is usually fairly plentiful in the spring from summer fallow storage and the melting of snow in spring. Stored moisture is augmented in June when the growth rate and water use are high by three or four inches of rain. Heading takes place and root growth usually stops early in July coincidental with the drying out of the soil especially in the surface 60 cm.

At maturity roots are recovered from the boxes (Fig. 3.5) by washing out each layer and weighing the roots. Fig. 3.7 illustrates graphically the weight of roots recovered from the boxes. The same cultivars are grown in the field and soil coring is used to give a similar graphic picture of roots in solid stands in the field (Fig. 3.8). Cores are taken between rows in the field so that the crown is not included as it is in the root boxes.

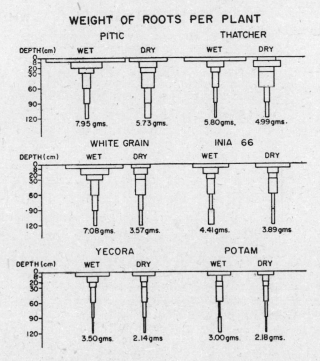

FIG. 3.7. Weight of roots of cultivars shown in Fig. 3.6, illustrated by width of the bar at each depth.

Other than having less weight of root recovered from the field in the surface layer, similar patterns have been obtained. Root boxes give much more information on rate of penetration, time of branching and other specifics of root pattern (Fig. 3.9).

One substantial improvement in this method of study would be the installation of such boxes in a rootatron where the root would be growing in a basement room where cool temperatures could be maintained. The above-ground parts would be in the room above (green-house or growth cabinet) where high temperatures, wind and a dry atmosphere, similar to field conditions, could be maintained. In the above system temperatures are kept at 15 ± 2 °C.

In addition, the boxes should be five or six feet deep as some cultivars do penetrate to such depths and moisture is available but not being used by presently grown cultivars. Ellern (1968) designed a reusable container for the study of roots which combines convenience of use with flexibility. He uses irrigation clay pipes cut longitudinally and clamped together for use and opened for washing. The height and diameter can be chosen to

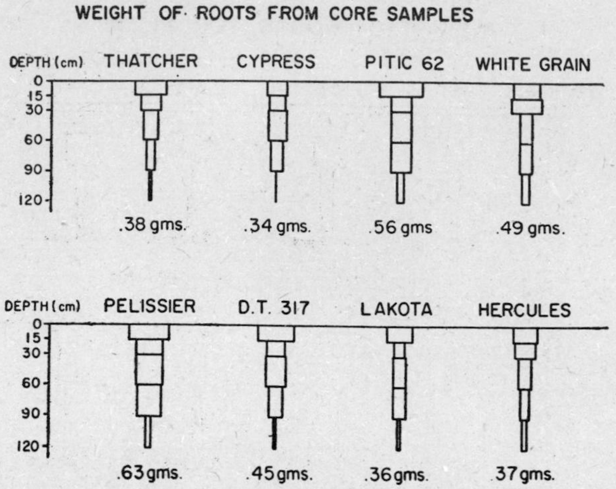

WEIGHT OF ROOTS FROM CORE SAMPLES

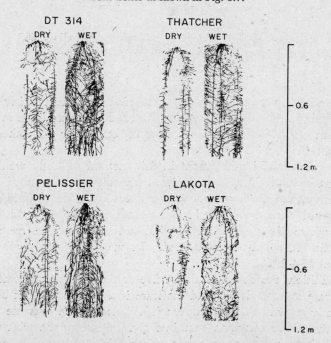

FIG. 3.8. Weight of roots recovered from cores taken in the field of some of the cultivars shown in Figs. 3.6 & 3.9. Cores are 6.5 cm in diameter taken at the midpoint between 22.5 cm spaced rows. This positioning of cores avoids the crown, and the multiplicity of roots near the crown, and thus gives a smaller amount of root in the surface layer related to the total single plant root recovered from boxes as shown in Fig. 3.7.

FIG. 3.9. Photograph of tracings of roots visible on the glass facing at maturity showing differences in response to two levels of moisture.

suit the crop. The container sits in an attached saucer base. Handles allow for carrying and weighing in moisture controlled studies (Fig. 3.10).

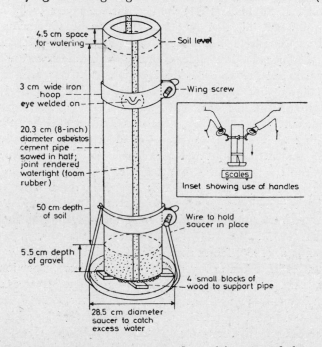

4.5 cm space for watering
— Soil level

3 cm wide iron hoop eye welded on

Wing screw

20.3 cm (8-inch) diameter asbestos cement pipe sawed in half; joint rendered watertight (foam rubber)

scales
Inset showing use of handles

50 cm depth of soil

Wire to hold saucer in place

5.5 cm depth of gravel

4 small blocks of wood to support pipe

28.5 cm diameter saucer to catch excess water

FIG. 3.10. A flexible type of container for studying roots of plants used by S. J. Ellern (by the courtesy of Israel J. agric. Res.).

Rogers (1969) described the East Malling Root Observation Laboratories' underground root facilities. Detailed studies of root environment interaction were possible. The method overcomes the soil temperature question associated with green-house root boxes. Their facilities are much more elaborate than those available elsewhere, but there is no simple cheap way to study root patterns.

Racz et al. (1964) developed an injection method of using ^{32}P in root studies. This was a modification of putting radioactive P in the soil at different levels and measuring the uptake to determine root presence in various parts of the soil. Racz et al. (1964) allowed five days for ^{32}P to equilibrate throughout the root system; then sampled. The soil-root cores were ashed and activity measured. The results were compared to root washing data. When correlations were made for sampling, they said that they had close agreement, though soil-root core activity did not correlate closely with quantitative root measurements. They reported that P fertilization, soil type, soil moisture stress, and an increase in osmotic pressure in the soil solution are expected to influence root development. This method is quick, but limited to non-quantitative studies, i.e., spread, depth and rate of growth.

Katyal and Subbiah (1971) studied surface layers to 32 cm in nine cultivars using ^{32}P injection method. They made statements as to the relative drought resistance of cultivars based on small differences in root patterns. Performance data under even one environment were not produced.

Vijayalakshmi (1971) used the injection technique and, by studying linear relationships of plant growth, activity and ^{32}P movement, was able to make quantitative measurements on wheat, mung and cowpeas. She pointed out that this method is not only easier, but may be more accurate than washing as it does not measure dead or decaying roots. Subbiah et al. (1968) stated that dead and decaying material can only be separated from active roots by the use of ^{32}P or other injection-type procedure. Knievel (1973) suggested a method to identify live from dead roots. Perhaps a combination of injection and commonly used washing techniques will give as accurate a result as the tedious recovery and washing method used by Pavlychenko (1937).

Kafkafi et al. (1965) found that ^{32}P uptake did not reflect water uptake. The amount of ^{32}P taken up by plants was much less proportionately than the water taken up from layers below 90 cm. The ^{32}P uptake reflected the P requirement of the plant which falls off very sharply even before roots have penetrated past 60 cm. They suggest ^{32}P be misleading as a measure of root quantity or water uptake.

Halstead and Rennie (1965) in using the ^{32}P injection technique, showed that the ^{32}P moved into new root growth much more quickly than in older roots. Soil moisture stress seemed to increase activity of roots.

Russell and Ellis (1968) injected ^{86}Rb instead of ^{32}P and found it an improvement. The gamma radiation of rubidium has greater energy than the beta radiation of ^{32}P. It is transferred more rapidly and can be detected well below the toxic level.

Spinks et al. (1951) and Belcher et al. (1950) independently reported on the use of neutron scattering to measure soil moisture. Stone et al. (1954) made operational improvements. Pierpoint (1965) added a surface shield which increased accuracy near the surface especially in low moisture soils. Rennie and Clayton (1967), using a neutron probe, associated moisture withdrawal from the profile with root growth.

In Sweden, root studies have been conducted in water culture (MacKey, 1973) a method with many advantages but eventually results of such studies should not be compared with soil studies as was pointed out by Hackett (1969a) and Bowen and Ravira (1969). MacKey (1973) created stresses and studied their effect on the root system in water cultures. Andrew (1966) compared root volume of plants growing in nutrient solution with root weight of plants growing in the field and obtained a .991 correlation. Neither plant was under water stress. Asher *et al.* (1965) developed a mechanism for using nutrient cultures under a controlled root environment.

A summary of what is known about roots of crop plants (mostly cereals) as gleaned from research:

1. An extensively branched, deeply penetrating root system is an advantage to a plant especially in times of water shortage and also on irrigated land.

2. When drought is severe the ramification of roots below 60 cm is important for survival and crop production.

3. Root patterns are genetically controlled but are sensitive to the soil environment.

4. Selection in segregating populations for plants with an advantageous root pattern (of one parent) can be successful if done in the field under conditions where that pattern is desired (i.e., selection for extensive, deep rooting pattern by growing yield trials under moisture stress and choosing highest yielders).

5. Crown roots seem to dominate under conditions of adequate moisture but seminal roots are deeper penetrating and are more important to the plant when moisture is in short supply. Several researchers have observed plants with no crown roots because of dry surface layer.

6. Most researchers agree that roots do not grow in dry soil.

7. Roots of cereals usually penetrate the soil to a depth of 120 to 240 cm but under extreme drought they may not reach more than 60 cm.

8. Roots of grasses are usually much denser in surface layers than those of cereals, but do not penetrate as deeply in the soil.

9. Roots of cereals grow well in moisture levels of half field capacity. Too much water causes anaerobic conditions to which roots are very sensitive. Most reports of increased root growth in less moist soil were of research conducted under mild drought and thus the "drier" condition may have been nearer optimum than the "wet".

CANADIAN CULTIVARS AND PARENTAL MATERIAL

A greater understanding of root patterns of specific cultivars as affected by moisture stress and the application of that knowledge to agronomy and breeding, could make a substantial contribution to greater production under drought. Any method that could be used to obtain more complete occupancy of the soil by roots, particularly in subsoil, would be of great value (Long, 1959). Others agree that deeper penetration and greater ramification would result in more effective water use (Hurd, 1964, 1968, 1973; Russell, 1957; Weaver, 1926).

Roots of Marquis wheat (*T. aestivum* L.) were studied in Nebraska

(Weaver, 1926) and in Saskatchewan (Pavlychenko, 1937; Simmonds & Sallans, 1933). Marquis roots spread 60 cm horizontally and reached depths of 120 to 150 cm. In very dry fields they penetrated only 65 to 90 cm. Hurd (1964) studied three varieties and found three different patterns of root growth under stress. The cultivar Pelissier (*T. durum* L.) was found to have a very extensive root system but with a relatively small amount of that root in the surface 10 to 15-cm layer. As a consequence Pelissier was only slightly affected by loss of effective root as the soil dried out to four and later six inches from the surface. Pelissier in later experiments showed a proportionately greater amount of root in the 60 to 120-cm layer than other cultivars. Pelissier had more root in non-watered soil than in watered up to six weeks. Thatcher (*T. aestivum* L.) grew faster in the first five weeks and penetrated the soil to the 120-cm layer (bottom of box) faster than the other two cultivars. Cypress (*T. aestivum* L.) branched more quickly behind the growing tip. This research showed that differences in cultivars as to root pattern are considerable and when breeding for drought resistance, roots should not be ignored as they usually have been in the past. The extensive rooting system of Pelissier has been transferred to cultivars now grown in Canada (Hurd *et al.* 1972a, 1972b, 1973). This will be discussed later.

In another study of seven cultivars, Hurd (1968) found that the roots of Thatcher wheat penetrated more quickly in drying than in wet soil and more quickly than the six other cultivars. When soil dried out in surface layers roots of Thatcher increased in moist layers immediately below those drying out. Other cultivars did not show this response. Cultivars Nainari 60, Lemhi 53, and especially Koga II produced more root at high levels of moisture than Thatcher but suffered more under moisture stress. Thatcher appeared to escape drought by its rapid growth in the first seven weeks of growth. This has been confirmed by Kaul (1973) who claims that Thatcher stores photosynthate in roots and stems which it uses to fill the grain when severe drought greatly reduces or stops growth. Steadily declining water potentials are a common occurrence as crops go into the filling period in the Canadian prairies (Kaul, 1969; Kaul & Crowle, 1971). For the past 35 years Thatcher and its backcross derivatives have occupied 60 to 90% of the spring wheat acreage of western Canada. Its rapid spring growth provides these cultivars with a drought escaping mechanism.

Hurd (1973) discusses Kaul's classification of Canadian grown cultivars into three groups according to their ability to survive severe moisture stress. One class has a high assimilation rate in initial stages of growth but plant growth rapidly declines as stress builds up to —24 atm or higher (e.g., Thatcher). The second type is slower growing initially but continues to grow at a relatively high rate under drought stress (e.g., Pitic 62) and the third classification has cultivars that are slow growing in initial stages but do not have the drought tolerance of Pitic (e.g., Selkirk). The stomata of class two may be more sensitive to stress by closing more quickly than other cultivars tested. Such a cultivar would suffer less desiccation than others and may open its stomata and commence growth more quickly when the temperature and wind are reduced. This theory suggests that they do not reach so low a water potential as other wheats which may take all night to regain water balance. Some may not reach this level of water potential for several days during a drought period while others like Pitic may grow a little every afternoon or morning.

Kaul and Crowle (1971, 1974) failed to measure differences in water potential in cultivars under stress and concluded that there were other parameters of greater significance. They showed that there were differences between cultivars in their decline in photosynthetic potential under moisture stress. They showed that cultivars differ in photosynthetic desiccation tolerance. Stomatal impairment differences occurred but there is no known way to measure its effect on yield. They also suspect that light interception, both early and late, in the growth cycle may play a part in productivity under drought. When water is not limiting, weight production is the product of light interception and net photosynthetic rate. On the Canadian prairies where water is the overriding limiting factor it is only in the early stage of growth when light interception is important (Kaul & Crowle, 1974).

The environment interacts with plant type to produce the crop. What has been learnt about the root system of Pitic, Thatcher and other cultivars is useful in interpreting the apparent relationship of other characters with ability to produce with limited moisture supply.

SEMIDWARFS

Roots of five Norin 10 semidwarfs were studied in root boxes and a preliminary report published (Hurd, 1973). Suggestions have been made that semidwarfs have less root than normal height cultivars, and that this accounts for the disappointing results in temperate rain-fed conditions (Briggle & Vogel, 1968). Pitic 62, a cultivar with a high yield potential, seems to be the exception as it yields well on the Canadian prairies in the driest years. In root studies in 1968-69, White grain and Penjamo, as well as Thatcher had more root than Pitic in watered boxes. Sonora 64 was about equal. In non-watered boxes Pitic had more root than all other cultivars tested.

In more extensive studies in 1972-73 (Figs. 3.6 & 3.7) Pitic had more root in non-watered boxes by weight and as shown on the glass than cultivars Thatcher, White grain, Inia 66, Yecora and Potam (Table 3.1). White grain had almost the same amount showing on the glass, but much less by weight. Weight of root of Thatcher was close to that of Pitic but the semi-

Table 3.1. Root, yield, maturity and water use data from root study boxes

Cultivar and moisture level		Weight of root/plant at maturity (g)	Root length/plant showing at maturity (cm)	Time for roots to reach 4 ft (days)	Yield of grain/plant (g)	Water used per plant** (litres)	No. of heads/plant with seed	No. of days to head	No. of days to ripen
Pitic	wet	3.10	1216	37	35.5	27.0	8.0	71	116
	dry	2.87	1114	37	6.5		6.3	68	102
Thatcher	wet	2.22***	1738	35	14.2	30.2	12.0	59	98
	dry	2.60	1060	35	5.2		8.0	55	91
White grain	wet	2.88	1456	35	15.8	27.5	6.0	64	107
	dry	1.92	1108	39*	6.5		4.0	54	100
Inia	wet	1.90	1070	44	14.0	28.9	8.0	53	106
	dry	1.59	1096	43*	5.9		3.6	55	95
Yecora	wet	1.42	1019	40	14.8	18.9	7.0	57	107
	dry	1.33	838	35	5.6		5.0	49	95
Potam	wet	1.36	559	42	9.7	22.2	4.3	51	104
	dry	1.04	670	42*	4.7		3.6	48	95

* Roots did not reach the bottom of the box in all replicates.

** Water added to keep supply to wet boxes at original level. Dry boxes all started near field capacity but no water was added.

*** No reasonable explanation can be made for the low reading for Thatcher wet. We suspect a mistake in recording.

dwarfs ranged from one-third to two-thirds of Pitic. Potam, Yecora and Inia had only slightly more root in watered boxes than in dry ones while White grain had nearly as much root in watered boxes as Pitic. Pitic, Thatcher and Inia had more root in non-watered boxes up to shot blade (flag leaf) stage than in watered boxes as shown by root exposed on glass. This supports conclusions reached earlier that optimum growth of roots is substantially below field capacity. Hurd concluded that differences in root pattern and response to moisture stress are substantial. For some reason (to be discussed later) most of the semidwarfs did not grow as would be expected under the conditions of the green-house box environment.

In 1963 to 1965 two semidwarfs, Nainari 60 and Narino 59, were studied along with normal height cultivars. Nainari produced more root and yielded more in watered boxes than Thatcher and had more root but yielded less in non-watered boxes. Narino headed very early at both moisture levels and had few tillers as well as a sparse root system. As a result of this growth pattern its yields were low relative to Thatcher.

Sage (1973) and his colleagues at Cambridge suggest that most of the Mexican produced Norin 10 semidwarfs are not suited to the long days of the northern Hemisphere. With the exception of Pitic, White grain and Nainari, the Saskatchewan work confirms these findings (Hurd, 1968, 1973). The lack of vigour as expressed by the production of few tillers and few roots supports this. The poor root system is only a reflection of their less vigorous plant growth. Some of the semidwarfs may contribute drought resistance characters if not influenced by sensitivity to long days. Breeders at Cambridge have transferred dwarf genes into long-day adapted cultivars (Sage, 1973). They found that some semidwarfs had more root at lower levels in the soil than normal height plants, but in drought tests semidwarfs suffered more (Cannell & Drew, 1973). Since roots are only one aspect of drought resistance and selections were not made under moisture stress, interaction of factors may mask root effects.

At time of writing, field core samples which had been taken to compare with root box data, had not been washed out and weighed, so no comparison can be made between roots in root boxes and in the field. Root cores taken in the field have given similar patterns of roots to those studied in root boxes (Hurd, 1973).

BREEDING FOR IMPROVED ROOTING SYSTEMS

Few crosses have been made to study the inheritance of rooting characters and a much smaller number still has been made with the objective of transferring a particular root character from one parent into a new cultivar. Troughton and Whittington (1969) in a review of genetic variation in root systems refer to several root characters that have been shown to be controlled by single genes. The number of characters of the root is very large covering many aspects of growth, form and metabolism. Root weights have been most frequently studied but volume, length, diameter, depth of penetration, distribution in the soil, degree of branching, number of root hairs are all aspects of form (Troughton & Whittington, 1969). Ashton (1948) reviewed techniques of breeding for drought resistance but did not attempt to summarize or evaluate various methods.

Raper and Barber (1970a, b) isolated two soybean cultivars (*Glycine max* L.) with different root systems from a study of 26 cultivars. One cultivar, Harosoy 63, had about twice the root surface of the other, Aoda, though their top growths were similar. Their method of study was soil cores and monolith in spaced and rowed plants in the field. Nutrient solutions were used to determine the rate of uptake of potassium. The weak-rooted Aoda, showed twice the K uptake per unit of root in the seedling stage to that of Harosoy 63 at high levels of K. They had similar uptake ratios when K was at a low level in the solution. Roots of plants appear to vary greatly in their uptake rates, but the extent of the root would likely override such differences under moisture stress much as it did when K was in short supply in the soybean studies.

Engledow and Wardlaw (1923) studied two barley cultivars and showed distinct cultivarial differences in pattern of root, one being deeper rooted than the other. Miller (1916) associated drought resistance with extensive root system. He found that sorghum had twice the root of corn. As previously shown, roots vary genetically in their rate of uptake of ions. Pohjakallio (1945) crossed two oat cultivars—one, Klock III, a deep-rooted cultivar and the other Golden Rain, possessing physiological drought resistance (required less water). Promising high yielding selections were obtained. Todd and Webster (1965) used successive cycles of drought to test drought hardiness of wheat and oat cultivars. Plants were grown in flats in a closed system in which per cent turgidity and per cent photosynthesis were recorded. All plants were able to carry on photosynthesis at low turgor after a single drought period. Variations in rate of photosynthesis occurred, but were not large. Survival studies on nine wheats subjected to eight weekly cycles of drought followed by rewatering sorted the varieties into known drought hardiness classes. In three cultivars thus tested turgidity values dropped much lower than in six other cultivars. Two of the three seemed to withstand the low turgor while the other did not. All plants were assumed to be subjected to the same moisture stress. Thus cultivars vary in their ability to maintain turgor under stress and in their ability to survive severe plant drought stress.

The survival test is a modification of Platt and Darroch's test (1942). Chinoy (1961) evaluated drought resistance in eight cultivars of wheat on the basis of growth analysis. Plants were grown in boxes subjected to desiccation to wilting and then watered. Because of the small amount of soil in the boxes this treatment is quite severe whereas field drought usually occurs gradually giving the plant opportunity to adjust. For this reason the application of his findings to field experience is of limited value. Roma (1962) studied the heritability of root systems in 14 cultivars of wheat and found that parental systems were passed on in crosses. Hubbard (1938) found differences in diameter and weight of roots per unit length in four cultivars of spring wheat, but was unable to associate these differences with yield or drought resistance. Vijayalakshmi (1971) suggests that coarseness of roots in nutrient solution is of little importance. Syme (1970, 1972) studied the relationship of plant characters and yield in semi-dwarfs under favourable growing conditions. Derera et al. (1969) reported genetic difference under moist conditions, but did not measure drought effects on the root system. In the majority of reports of root research, little or no use is apparently made of the knowledge in developing improved varieties. Levitt et al. (1960) pointed out the difficulties in assessing drought resistance in field experiments because it is not possible to separate it from avoidance. Their results do not give encouragement to the possibility of significant hardening of plants. They suggest that the first step must be to demonstrate that a cultivar has drought resistance as differentiated from superior yielding ability. Then separate the two components drought avoidance from drought tolerance. If avoidance is responsible, determine which action(s) is (are) responsible, transpiration, absorption or translocation of water. If tolerance is responsible for resistance, determine which action(s) is (are) responsible, cell sap concentration, bound water, etc. In the "etc." part of Levitt's statement tolerance to desiccation should be added (Kaul, 1966, 1973). The methods of testing for the above may not be worked out but if the physiologist can identify even a portion of the action responsible for drought avoidance or tolerance and can provide a quick method of measuring the difference in action between cultivars then he has provided the plant breeder and/or the agronomist with a tool that is useful in advancing yield under drought stress. Levitt et al. (1960) designed a plexiglass drought chamber to evaluate a plant's ability to resist water loss and tolerance to decrease in water. They used shoots with root removed. Their machine does not measure the plants ability to take up water, so ignores the root-plant relationship which seems at least as important as water use efficiency. Care needs to be taken in interpreting results of genetic research on roots because they are very sensitive to changes in environment but the majority of workers have tested root response in only one environment. Genetic control of resistance to root diseases or insects which attack roots is one kind of information of immediate use by the plant breeder. Troughton and Whittington (1969) suggest that to select for a root pattern in segregating populations one would require vegetative propagation since most methods of study require plant destruction. Otherwise the breeder will have to wait to test material until it is near homozygosity. The development of creeping-rooted alfalfa (Heinrichs, 1963) is one of few examples of breeding for a root characteristic. More recently reports from the same institution describe a successful programme of breeding for a desirable root pattern in *Triticum durum* L. Hurd *et al.* (1972a, b, 1973) have transferred the Pelissier root pattern into Wascana and Wakooma, which are high quality cultivars with a 15 to 20% increase in yield over cultivars previously grown in the fairly arid durum growing area of Saskatchewan. Pelissier has been grown for many years in spite of being downgraded and not recommended. The reason of its persistence is that Pelissier under severe drought, has always given an economic return. Wascana and Wakooma, and a third cultivar in the series to be released in 1974, withstand severe drought, as well as Pelissier. Pelissier has been studied by Kaul and Crowle (1971) and not found to have any particular ability to withstand severe desiccation or to escape drought by rapid early growth. Pelissier has a root pattern that allows it to escape drought and to utilize moisture stored deep in the soil. It may have other characteristics which have not been isolated in previous studies. Pelissier has few roots in the surface layer so drying out of the soil to a depth of 8 or 10 cm does not appear to reduce root effectiveness as it probably does with most cultivars. Pelissier has a massive root system at lower depths, especially at the 60 to 120-cm levels relative to other wheat cultivars studied (Aamodt & Johnston, 1936; Hurd, 1964). Read (1973) has shown that there is nearly always moisture left in the soil at harvest time in these lower depths even on the dry prairies. Pelissier appears to take advantage of this reserve.

In a study by the senior author, Pelissier was crossed and backcrossed to Lakota, a good quality disease resistant durum cultivar. About 1500 lines from the backcross (P/*2L) were yield tested in F_4 and again in F_6 generations. Selection was made for yield on the dry prairie (Hurd *et al.*, 1972a, b). Figures 3.8 and 3.9 show the respective root pattern of the parents and one of the high yielding lines from the cross. The developers of these new durum cultivars conclude that root patterns are hereditary, that extensive root systems are an advantage to plants grown under moisture stress and that selection for yield in large populations grown under droughty conditions will result in the choice of lines that possess the extensive root system.

Simple techniques for screening out highly susceptible material early in the breeding programme are needed. Hurd (1964) reported that some cultivars of wheat produce more root in the seedling stage than other cultivars and that these also had more at maturity by weight. Seedling tests were conducted to see if there was a relationship between rate of early growth and total length of root at maturity. If there was a positive relationship, seedling tests could be used to screen populations for extent of mature plant root systems. Townley-Smith and McBean, colleagues at Swift Current, screened commonly grown cultivars, some of which had been studied in the root boxes. Sorting, according to length of root at five or six days, consistently placed cultivars in a known order of total root length and yield under moisture stress (Table 3.2). An experiment to verify the heritability of this relationship in a segregating population is underway at present along with germination in mannitol tests. Kaul (1973) found that in a 20 atm mannitol solution Pitic germinated 49% compared to 27% for Manitou and as low as 3% and 5% for other cultivars which are known to be drought susceptible.

Table 3.2. Number and length of primary roots of
durum cultivars at seven days

Cultivar		Number of roots	Total root* length (cm)
Hercules	..	4.0	35.3a
Kakota	..	4.3a	36.8a
Stewart 63	..	4.4a	39.4ab
Pelissier	..	4.8b	46.2bc
Wascana	..	4.9b	49.3c

* Cultivars with the same letter were not shown to be significantly different.

In a search for parents, Ivanov working in Russia in 1939, suggests a pattern of root growth worth looking for (reported by Ashton, 1948). He found that a cultivar Graecum 0289 (*T. aestivum*) had a small growth of foliage and low number of secondary roots in early stages of development and during tillering and ear emergence. This cultivar had the least root of all cultivars studied. But after ear emergence the root system grew vigorously while the foliage grew slowly. This cultivar had poor productivity generally but had drought resistance.

Troughton and Whittington (1969) discuss work done by Monyo who showed that substitution lines could have the same top growth but differ in single plant root weights by 7.4 to 4.2 g. They suggest that if these differences are associated with different patterns such as feeding levels, there may be potential for increasing yield by mixing a number of lines to make a composite.

Russell (1959) found that plants varied genetically in rooting characteristics. Plants show large differences in drought tolerance. These reflect the ability of the plant, first, to avoid internal water stress by effectively balancing water intake and water loss or, second, to adapt physiologically to such stress. Drought injury is thought by Russell to be caused by mechanical disruption of the protoplasm rather than by loss of water *per se*. Iljin (1957) reports that plants differ in respect to the duration and degree of the dry period which they can withstand.   Cells having a large proportion of protoplasm and a small vacuole are least disturbed by desiccation.   Kaul (1973) believes that a major factor in drought resistance is desiccation toler- ance and he has found large differences between wheat cultivars in this character.   Haise *et al.* (1966) studied the relationships of soils at 15 and 26 atm.   Watson (1947) determined net assimilation rate (NAR) and leaf area throughout the growth of five field crops.   The NAR increased from wheat to barley, potatoes, mangolds and sugar beets, with sugar beets doubling the NAR of wheat.   Significant cultivarial differences were measured for all crops except wheat.   Leaf area varied much more from year to year than NAR and leaf area was much more important in determin- ing yield than NAR.   Russell (1959) believes that water use efficiency can be improved by breeding.   Cultivars having extensive root systems are more effective in meeting water needs.   Since water use efficiency is reflected in yield, selection for higher yield under drought stress should be effective.

Breeding for morphological or physiological traits depends on first establishing their significance and their inheritance characteristics.   So far, there is very little established relationship of this kind and even where correlations have been found there is the cause-effect problem to solve. Milthorpe (1960) in studying the loss of water from the reservoir, root zone, concluded that principles are well-established but the urgent task of the ecologist and soil physicist is to replace vague guesses by quantitative estimates.   Frankel (1947) and Bell (1963) have said that increasing yield, up to that time, had come from overcoming limiting factors rather than assembling productivity genes.   Bell also said that there is need for more fundamental physiological knowledge in barley to enable the breeder to produce higher yielding cultivars.   Burton (1964) has said that geneticists have not made progress in selecting for drought resistance using physical characters (water requirement and transpiration rate) though these are agreed to be important.   Klages (1960) claimed that little can be done to reduce transpiration losses.   Todd *et al.* (1962) found that cultivars differ in their ability to utilize available moisture.   As has been noted here, cultivars differ in many characters related to drought, especially in rooting systems. Perhaps researchers have expected too simple a solution to drought resistance. Drought resistance is really, yield in a specific environment.   Burton (1964) and Hurd (1968) have shown that cultivars that yield the highest under favourable growing conditions may be low under drought.

Hurd (1969, 1971) outlines a successful method of breeding for yield in a droughty environment.   Because genetic balance is so important in plant-environment interaction, methods of breeding must be designed to allow and encourage the superior types to be present in segregating populations and to be identified. The South Saskatchewan Wheat Programme places its first emphasis on careful study of potential parents and judicious selection of a few three-way or double crosses. Once a parent with a superior character for avoiding or tolerating drought is identified (i.e., Pelissier with its root character) complementary well-adapted parents are chosen to combine with it. A F_2 of 20,000 or more are space planted and about 1000 F_3 are raised in a winter nursery. A small percentage of high yielding lines is identified in replicated F_4 yield trials grown at two locations. Selections are made in these lines and the cycle is repeated. Yield tests are grown in normal droughty conditions. Aufhammer *et al.* (1959) said that the most reliable criterion of drought resistance in cereals is its average grain yield under drought in relation to normal yield capacity. Only in this way can the rare genotypes that have the balance with the environment be present. With droughty weather conditions and careful testing, high yielding, well-adapted cultivars are being produced (Hurd, 1969; Hurd *et al.*, 1972a, 1973).

Perhaps the greatest progress in crop production to be made in the next two decades in the semiarid areas of the world is through root and other drought investigation and in the use of the resultant expanded knowledge in the breeding of improved varieties. The difficulties in this kind of research have discouraged plant scientists heretofore, but the urgency to increase food production and the pressure to utilize marginal land is encouraging researchers to accept the challenge. Two blades of grass will grow where one grew before.

Cultural Practices Affecting Root Growth

Growth of roots, like that of shoots, is favoured by moist fertile soil. Therefore, management practices such as crop rotations, fertilizer use and moisture conservation which tend to improve the growing conditions of the soil will favour root growth and crop production.

CROP ROTATIONS

Work such as those reported by Haas (1958) and Spratt (1966) show that crop rotations can affect the chemical, physical and biological properties of soil and thus enhance yield potential. Deep-rooted legumes have a particularly beneficial effect on subsequent crops as they did in the experiment described by Spratt and McCurdy (1966). In India, crops following pigeon pea (*Cajanus cajan*), a deep-rooted vigorous legume, are often better for two reasons: (1) due to root residue and fixed nitrogen, and (2) due to loosened subsoil for better infiltration of moisture. Their roots can penetrate through a rigid textural murrum found in red and lateritic soils whereas cereal crops cannot. Post-harvest rains can then penetrate deep into the soil. However, the moisture withdrawn from depth during growth must be replaced before subsequent crops can be grown to their full potential. In the U.S.A., Fehrenbacker *et al.* (1960) showed that root development in a Cisne silt loam soil with a clay pan plough sole could be increased with adequate fertilization and a proper cropping system which included legumes. With optimum lime, phosphorus and potassium applications, the root systems of corn showed intensive development to five feet; whereas development was only to three feet where no fertilizer or lime was applied.

Monyo in a Ph.D. thesis study found considerable variation in root distribution in substitution lines at heading time (Troughton & Whittington, 1969). Monyo added no water to his plants after heading (grown in compost in drainpipe containers). The upper layer dried out first and thus, in later flowering lines, there was a significant correlation between the proportion of root system in bottom zone of the container and the degree of reduction in yield on control.

By greater study of root systems of crops it may be possible to increase production per unit area by choosing cultivars that feed at different levels, i.e., extensive early surface feeder and a deep penetrating later feeder with extensively branched system below 40 cm. The one would grow fast and build up a reserve of photosynthate in seedling to shot blade (flag leaf) stage while the other would grow more slowly but would continue growing and producing because it would feed at lower depths where moisture is still plentiful. One cultivar would be filling the head from stored photosynthate while the other would fill the head from currently produced photosynthate. In this respect the mixed cropping system of *Cajanus* and sorghum have been successful in India.

Effect of Fertilizers on Root Growth

As mentioned earlier, proper nutrition of roots is needed for maximum plant growth and yields. The most extensive plant roots are usually found where nutrients are most abundant. Wilkinson and Ohlrogge (1962) show how roots of soybeans concentrate in fertilizer zones. The proliferation of roots in the fertilizer band is related to the build up of high nitrogen and phosphorus in the root cells which hastens cell division and elongation. It may also increase growth regulator auxins and thus increase branching.

Rennie and Clayton (1967) showed that the level of phosphorus in the surface soil influenced the intensity of rooting of wheat but phosphate fertilizers also increased water use efficiency which in turn was related to depth of moisture withdrawal (or rooting depth). Continual use of phosphate fertilizers will increase the levels of available phosphorus in the surface and crop growth.

Various species absorb fertilizer and soil nutrients with different degrees of intensity. Bole (1973) showed that rapeseed (*Brassica napus*) roots took up phosphorus six times faster than wheat roots. Also, Strong and Soper (1973) showed that rape and buckwheat took up more phosphate from a fertilizer band than wheat and flax, due to their intensive root systems near the concentrated fertilizer source. Flax was more efficient in absorbing soil phosphorus. Some varieties within species may also vary in this ability to absorb nutrients since their rooting patterns and potential for water uptake varies (as shown elsewhere in this review). This could lead to variety X fertilizer interactions. However, few of these types of interactions have been shown to be of practical significance (Worzella, 1943; Sen & Pal, 1953; Pendleton et al., 1953; Knott, 1974). The relationship between root growth and these interactions has not been studied. The effects of fertilizer use on physiological aspects of plant growth have been discussed in Chapter 1 of this book.

EFFECT OF TILLAGE PRACTICES ON ROOT GROWTH

Burton (1964) emphasized the importance of cultural practices to increase the root system. Soil treatments, both physical and chemical, that will increase rooting volume of the soil, will make for better crop yields and more efficient water use. Bergmann (1954) stresses the importance of maintaining optimum aeration and fertility to encourage root growth. Mirreh and Ketcheson (1972) reported that soil moisture tension may have a double effect on root growth: (1) increase resistance to root growth, and (2) decrease the roots' penetrating ability.

McCartney (1969) showed that a change in cultural practice from ploughing to surface tillage increased root penetration and branching at lower levels in the soil and gave substantially higher yields. He attempted to break up the hardpan by deep cultivation to a depth of 60 cm, but there was no advantage from such an operation. The hardpan disappeared probably by water movement, insects and root growth. Hardpans and excessive compaction are often caused by ploughing which usually takes a narrow cut and thus many trips across the field. Ploughing has to be followed by subsequent cultivations to prepare a level seed-bed. Surface tillage cultivates five to six times the area per trip with similar power and leaves the soil level for seeding or does the seeding in one operation. Surface tillage in addition to reducing soil compaction is much less expensive. Unfortunately, it is not always sufficient to control weed growth. Surface tillage only works well when the soil surface is dry and remains dry for several days following cultivation. Chemical fallow avoids excessive travel over the land and may be used in conjunction with shallow tillage to encourage greater root growth below 20 or 30 cm. By keeping the soil free of weeds for six months with surface tillage in Kenya, yields from this practice were about three times those of the traditional ploughing because of increased stored moisture and presumably a better root system due to absence of hardpan (Paulsen, 1973). Allmaras *et al.* (1973) agree that surface tillage results in yields that are at best equal to ploughing when moisture is limiting. They report, however, that when moisture is plentiful the use of surface tillage may decrease yield over ploughing. This may be due to a shortage of N on cooler soils under stubble mulch. Papendick *et al.* (1973) showed that the use of the Rod-weeder conserved more water than other implements that left the surface cloddy (plough leaves a very rough cloddy surface) because of less evaporation. Rod-weeding also keeps moisture near the surface and thus ensures better germination and early growth especially with small seeded crops. Anderson and Russell (1964) point out advantages for a straw mulch.

Taylor and colleagues (Taylor, 1967, 1973; Taylor & Gardner, 1960; Taylor & Bruce, 1967; Taylor & Ratliff, 1969) studied root growth as influenced by soil strength or density as measured with a penetrometer. High strength soil pans reduced crop rate growth and yield especially under water or nutrient stress. Both worm holes and cracks in clay soils make root penetration easier. Meige (1938) showed that roots have a plasticity allowing greater adaptation to their environment than above-ground parts according to the author. He stressed the importance of providing a friable soil accomplished by manuring, crop rotation, good drainage and good aeration. Deep tillage and subsoiling should be practised when necessary. Bowser and Cairns (1967) found that ploughing solonetz soil to a depth of 56 cm compared to 10 cm reduced salts to 150 cm depth and gave equal cereal yields but increased alfalfa-brome yields and rooting in ploughed soil.

One advantage of surface tillage is the maintenance of a mulch on the surface which decreases evaporation from surface layers and keeps the soil cooler (Anderson & Russell, 1964). In northern areas where the soil is too cool for optimum growth this may tend to decrease root growth but in warmer climates it may encourage root growth.

Eavis and Payne (1969) discussed the soil physical conditions as they affected root growth. They emphasize the importance of soil moisture as it has an overriding effect on oxygen in the soil, soil density and pore space, and soil temperature. Soil physical condition limits root growth in spite of genetic factors. De Roo (1969) says that there is little doubt that increased bulk density or decreased porosity decreases root growth. Cover crops or the turning in of residue provides a 'cushion' so that the traffic of implements does not cause excessive compaction. He says that the plough-pan formation can be a serious problem. Deep tillage may be necessary to allow roots to express their root growth potential. De Roo suggests, where ploughing is necessary, that altering the depth of cut or shattering of the hardpan just below plough depth in the same operation are useful in increasing root penetration. Subsoiling as a separate operation may occasionally be necessary to reduce compaction. Reduced compaction also results in greater penetration of the soil by moisture. Russell (1959) suggests that tillage encourages penetration of moisture and results in storage of that moisture where it is safe from evaporation losses. Warder *et al.* (1962) reported that fertilized crops used more moisture than unfertilized crops between germination and heading stages, but when increased yields were produced by fertilizers, the fertilized crop used moisture more efficiently. Water stress at any stage will decrease yield but Day and Intalap (1970) found that the most critical time for stress was the jointing stage. Dubetz and Bole (1973), also studying wheat, reported that flowering time was the most critical. Time of planting in some areas can be adjusted so that the critical stage of growth will coincide with or just follow the heaviest rain.

REFERENCES

AAMODT, O. S. and W. H. JOHNSTON, 1936. Studies on drought resistance in spring wheat. Can. J. Res. 14: 122-52.

ALLMARAS, R. R.; A. L. BLACK and R. W. RICHMAN, 1973. Tillage, soil environment, and root growth. *In:* Conservation Tillage, Proc. Nat. Conf. Soil Cons. Soc. Am. Ankeny, Iowa, pp. 62-86.

ANDERSON, D. T. and G. C. RUSSELL, 1964. Effects of various quantities of straw mulch on the growth and yield of spring and winter wheat. Can. J. Soil Sci. 44: 109-18.

ANDREW, R. H. 1966. A technique for measuring root volume *in vivo*. Crop Sci. 6: 384-6.

ASHER, C. J.; P. G. OZANNE and J. F. LONGERAGAN, 1965. A method for controlling the ionic environment of plant roots. Soil Sci. 100: 149-56.

ASHTON, T. 1948. Techniques of breeding for drought resistance in crops. Tech. Com. No. 14, Com. Bur. Pl. Breed. Genet., p. 34.

AUFHAMMER, G.; G. FISCHBECK and H. GREBNER, 1959. Testing drought resistance in spring cereals. Zeitschrift fuer acher und Pflanzenban 110: 117-34.

BALDWIN, J. P.; P. B. H. TINKER and P. H. NYE, 1972. Uptake of solutes by multiple root systems from soil. II. The theoretical effects of rooting density and pattern on uptake of nutrients from soil. Plant & Soil 36: 693-708.

BARBER, S. A. 1962. A diffusion and mass-flow concept of soil nutrient availability. Soil Sci. 93: 39-49.

BARBER, S. A. 1969. On the mechanisms governing nutrient supply to plant roots growing in soil. J. Paper No. 3132, Purdue Univ., Agr. Exp. Sta., Lafayette, Indiana.

BARBER, S. A.; J. M. WALKER and E. H. VASEY, 1963. Mechanisms for the movement of plant nutrients from the soil and fertilizer to the plant root. J. Agr. Food Chem. 11: 204-7.

BARLEY, K. P. 1970. The configuration of the root system in relation to nutrient uptake. Adv. Agron. 22: 159-201.

BARLEY, K. P. and E. L. GREACEN, 1967. Mechanical resistance as a soil factor influencing the growth of roots and underground shoots. Adv. Agron. 19: 1-43.

BEAR, R. E. 1964. Chemistry of the Soil. 2nd ed. ACS Mimeo. No. 160, Reinhold, New York.

BELCHER, D. J.; T. R. CUYKENDALL and H. S. SACK, 1950. The measurement of soil moisture and density by neutron and gamma ray scattering. Civil Aeron. Admin. Tech. Devel. Rep. 127.

BELL, G. P. H. 1963. Breeding techniques—general techniques. Barley genetics I. Centre for Agr. Pub. and Doc., Wageningen, pp. 285-302.

BELYAKOV, I. 1968. The growth and development of wheat and barley roots in the semi-desert zone. Nestnik. sels' skokh nauki 13: 31-3.

BERGMANN, W. 1954. Wurzelwachstum und Ernteertrag (Root growth and harvest yield). Z. Acker—u. PflBau 97: 336-68. Field Crop Abstr. 7: 1042.

BLACK, C. A. 1968. Soil Plant Relationships. 2nd ed. John Wiley and Sons, Inc., New York.

BLOODWORTH, M. E. 1958. Root distribution of some irrigated crops using undisturbed soil cores. Agron. J. 50: 317-20.

BOLE, J. B. 1973. Influence of root hairs in supplying soil phosphorus to wheat. Can. J. Soil Sci. 53: 169-75.

BOSEMARK, N. O. 1954. The influence of nitrogen on root development. Pl. Physiol. 7: 497-502.

BOWEN, G. D. and A. D. RAVIRA, 1969. The influence of microorganisms on growth and metabolism of plant roots in root growth. In: Root Growth, pp. 170-201, Whittington, W. J. (ed), Butterworths, London.

BOWSER, W. E. and R. R. CAIRNS, 1967. Some effects of strip ploughing a solonetz soil. Can. J. Soil Sci. 47: 239-44.

BRAY, R. N. 1954. A nutrient mobility concept of soil-plant relationships. Soil Sci. 78: 9-22.

BRENCHLEY, W. E. and V. G. JACKSON, 1921. Root development in barley and wheat under different conditions of growth. Ann. Bot. 35: 533-56.

BREWSTER, J. L. and P. B. H. TINKER, 1972. Nutrient flow rates into roots. Soils & Fertil. 35: 355-9.

BRIGGLE, L. W. and O. A. VOGEL, 1968. Breeding short-stature, disease resistant wheats in the United States. Euphytica 17: 107-30.

BROUWER, R. 1966. Root growth of cereals and grasses. *In*: Growth of Cereals and Grasses. Milthorpe, F. L. and J. D. Ivins (eds), Butterworths, London.

BROUWER, R. and C. T. DEWIT, 1969. A similation model of plant growth with special attention to root growth and its consequences in root growth. *In:* Root Growth, pp. 224-44, Whittington, W. J. (ed), Butterworths, London.

BROWN, D. A.; C. A. PLACE and J. V. PETTIET, 1960. The effect of soil moisture upon cation exchange in soils and nutrient uptake by plants. Trans. 7th Int. Congr. Soil Sci. 3: 433-9.

BURTON, G. W. 1964. The geneticists role in improving water use efficiency by crops. Research on Water, ASA Special Publication, Series 4.

CANNELL, R. Q. and M. C. DREW, 1973. Plant root systems and crop growth. Span 16: 38-40.

CARLTON, W. M. 1954. Some effects of zinc deficiency on the anatomy of the tomato. Bot. Gaz. 116: 52-64.

CARLY, H. E. and R. D. WATSON, 1966. A new gravimetric method for estimating root-surface areas. Soil Sci. 102: 289-91.

CHAN, E. C. S.; H. KATZNELSON and J. W. ROUATT, 1963. The influence of soil and root extracts on the associative growth of selected soil bacteria, Can. J. Microbiol. 9: 187-97.

CHANDLER, W. V. 1958. Effect of long time surface fertilization on rooting depth and habit of oats. Agron. J. 50: 286.

CHINOY, J. J. 1947. How drought affects Indian wheats. Indian Fmg. 8: 72-4.

CHINOY, J. J. 1961. Physiology of drought resistance in wheat. II. Evaluation of drought resistance in eight varieties of wheat on the basis of growth analysis. Int. exp. Bot. 16: 131-39.

CHINOY, J. J. 1962. Physiology of drought resistance in wheat. IV. Effect of wilting at different growth and developmental stages on characters determining yield of grain in eight varieties of wheat. Phyton 19: 5-10.

CONRAD, J. O. and F. J. VEIHMEYER, 1929. Root development and soil moisture. Hilgardia 4: 113-24.

CORNFORTH, I. S. 1968. Relationship between soil volume used by roots and nutrient accessibility. J. Soil Sci. 19: 291-301.

COWAN, I. R. 1965. Transport of water in soil plant atmosphere system. J. appl. Ecol. 2: 221-39.

CRAFTS, A. S. 1961. Translocation in plants. Holt, Rinehart and Winston, New York.

CRAVZOV, M. N. 1928. Studies on the root system of spring wheat. J. Lander Wiss. Mosk. 5: 80-93.

CUNNINGHAM, R. K. 1964. Cation-anion relationships in crop nutrition.

III. Relationships between the ratios of some of the cations : sum of the anions and nitrogen concentrations in several plant species. J. agr. Sci. 63: 109-11.

DAINTY, J. 1969. The water relations in plants. *In:* Physiology of Plant Growth and Development, Wilkins, M. B. (ed), McGraw-Hill Book Co., pp. 420-52.

DANIELSON, R. E. 1967. Root systems in relation to irrigation. Agron. J. 11: 390-424.

DAVILCHUK, P.; G. YALSENKO and V. SHLIFASOVSKY, 1971. The development of roots and ground mass in winter wheat. Vestnik sels' skokh nauki 10: 50-5.

DAY, A. D. and S. INTALAP, 1970. Some effects of soil moisture stress on the growth of wheat. Agron. J. 62: 27-9.

DE JONG, E. and D. A. RENNIE, 1967. Physical soil factors influencing the growth of wheat. *In:* Canadian Centennial Wheat Symposium, Nielsen, K. F. (ed), Modern Press, Saskatoon.

DERERA, N. F.; D. R. MARSHALL and L. M. BALAAM, 1969. Genetic variability in root development in relation to drought tolerance in spring wheats. Exp. Agr. 5: 327-38.

DE ROO, H. C. 1961. Deep tillage and root growth. Bull. 644, Conn. Agr. Exp. Sta., New Haven, U.S.A.

DE ROO, H. C. 1969. Tillage and root growth. *In:* Root Growth, pp. 339-58, Whittington, W. J. (ed), Butterworths, London.

DE ROO, H. C. and L. K. WIERSUM, 1963. Root training by plastic tubes. Agron. J. 55: 402-5.

DITTMER, H. J. 1937. A quantitative study of the root hair of a winter rye plant (Secale cereals). Am. J. Bot. 24: 417-20.

DITTMER, H. J. 1949. Root hair variation in plant species. Am. J. Bot. 36: 152-5.

DITTMER, H. J. and J. REINHART, 1948. Root hair development on gymnosperm seedlings. Am. J. Bot. 35: 791.

DOBRENZ, A. K.; L. NEAL WRIGHT; A. B. HUMPHREY; M. A. MASSENGALE and W. R. KNEEBONE, 1969. Stomata density and its relationship to water use efficiency of blue panic grass (*Panicum antidotale* Retz.). Crop Sci. 9: 354-7.

DOSS, B. D.; D. A. ASHLEY and O. L. BENNETT, 1960. Effect of moisture regime on root distribution of warm season forage species. Agron. J. 52: 569-72.

DREW, M. C. and P. H. NYE, 1970. The supply of nutrient ions by diffusion to plant roots in soil. III. Uptake of phosphate by roots of onion, leek and rye grass. Plant & Soil 33: 545-63.

DUBETZ, S. and J. B. BOLE, 1973. Effects of moisture stress at early heading and of nitrogen fertilizer on three spring wheat cultivars. Can. J.

Pl. Sci. 53: 1-5.

DUNCAN, W. G. and A. J. OHLROGGE, 1958. Principles of nutrient uptake from fertilizer bands. II. Root development in the band. Agron. J. 50: 605-8.

EAVIS, B. W. 1972. Soil physical conditions affecting seedling root growth. I. Mechanical impedance, aeration and moisture availability as influenced by bulk density and moisture levels in a sandy loam soil. Plant & Soil 36: 613-22.

EAVIS, B. W. and D. PAYNE, 1969. Soil physical conditions and root growth. In: Root Growth, pp. 315-35, Whittington, W. J. (ed), Butterworths, London.

EDWARDS, W. M.; J. B. FEHRENBACKER and J. P. VANRA, 1964. The effect of discrete fed density on corn root penetration in planosol. Soil Sci. Soc. Am. Proc. 28: 560-4.

ELLERN, S. J. 1968. A reusable experimental container for root studies. Israel J. agr. Res. 18: 135-6.

ENGLEDOW, F. L. and S. WARDLAW, 1923. Investigation on yield in cereals. J. agr. Sci. 13: 390-439.

EPSTEIN, E. 1973. Roots. Sci. Am. 228: 48-58.

FEDDES, R. A. and P. E. RIJTEMA, 1972. Water withdrawal by plant roots. J. Hydrol. 17: 33-59.

FEHRENBACKER, J. B. and J. D. ALEXANDER, 1955. A method for studying corn root distribution using a soil-core sampler machine and a shaker-type washer. Agron. J. 47: 408-72.

FEHRENBACKER, J. B.; P. R. JOHNSON; R. T. ODELL and P. E. JOHNSON, 1960. Root penetration and development of some farm crops as related to soil physical and chemical properties. Trans. 7th Int. Congr. Soil Sci. 3: 243-52.

FERGUSON, W. S. 1965. Relationship between evapotranspiration by wheat and the stage of crop development, Bellani-plate evaporation, and soil moisture content. Can. J. Soil Sci. 45: 33-8.

FINNEY, J. R. and B. A. G. KNIGHT, 1973. The effect of soil physical condition produced by various cultivation systems on the root development of winter wheat. J. agr. Sci. 80: 435-42.

FISCHER, R. A. 1973. The effect of water stress at various stages of development on yield processes in wheat. In: Plant Response to Climatic Factors, pp. 233-41, Proc. Uppsala Symp. UNESCO.

FOGG, G. E. 1965. The state and movement of water in living organisms. Symp. Soc. exp. Biol. Cambridge University Press.

FRANKEL, O. H. 1947. The theory of plant breeding for yield. Heredity 1: 109-20.

FRIED, M. and H. BROESHART, 1967. The soil-plant system in relation to inorganic nutrition. Academic Press, New York & London.

FUJII, Y. 1959. On the correlation between development of branch roots and emergence of the leaves at the successive nodes of the main stem of wheat plants. Proc. Crop Sci. Soc., Japan 27: 232-4.

GARDNER, W. R. 1960a. Soil-Water Relationships in Arid and Semiarid Conditions. UNESCO Pub. Bucher, Lucerne, Switzerland.

GARDNER, W. R. 1960b. Dynamic aspects of water availability to plants. Soil Sci. 89: 63-73.

GARDNER, W. R. 1965. Dynamic aspects of soil water availability to plants. Ann. Rev. Pl. Physiol. 16: 323-42.

GARDNER, W. R. 1968. Availability and measurement of soil water. *In:* Water Deficits and Plant Growth. Vol. I., Kozlowski, T. T. (ed), pp. 107-35.

GLIEMEROTH, G. 1952. Water content of the soil in relation to the root development of some cultivated plants. Zutschruft fur Acher und Pflangenban 95: 21-46.

GOEDEWAAGEN, M. A. J. 1955. The ecology of the root system of crops. De plantenwortel in de landbouw 31-68's—Gravenhage. Versl. land-bouwk. Onterz. 61. 7. p. 137.

GOEDEWAAGEN, M. A. J. and J. J. SCHUURMAN, 1956. Root development of grassland with special reference to water conditions of the soil. Proc. 7th Int. Grassland Cong., New Zealand, pp. 45-55.

GREBNER, H. 1963. Untersuchungen uber den Wasserbaushalt verschieden durreresist enter Sommergetreidesorten (The water economy of various drought resistant spring cereal varieties). Yeitschrift fur Acher und Pflangenbau 119: 138-48.

GRIVEVA, C. M. 1964. Alcohol formation and excretion by plant roots under anaerobic conditions. Soviet Pl. Physiol. 10: 331-426.

HAAS, H. J. 1958. Effects of fertilization age of stand, and decomposition on weight of grass roots and of grass and alfalfa on soil nitrogen and carbon. Agron. J. 50: 5-9.

HACKETT, C. 1968. A study of the root system of barley. I. Effects of nutrition on two varieties. New Phytol. 67: 287-300.

HACKETT, C. 1969a. Quantitative aspects of the growth of cereal root systems. *In:* Root Growth, pp. 134-47, Whittington, W. J. (ed), Butterworths, London.

HACKETT, C. 1969b. A study of the root system of barley. II. Relationships between root dimensions and nutrient uptake. New Phytol. 68: 1023-30.

HACKETT, C. 1971. Relations between the dimensions of the barley root system: Effects of mutilating the root axes. Aust. J. biol. Sci. 24: 1057-74.

HACKETT, C. and B. O. BARTLETT, 1970. A study of the root system of barley. III. Branching pattern. New Phytol. 70: 409-13.

HACKETT, C. and H. E. STEWART, 1969. A method for determining the position and size of lateral primordia in the axes of roots without sectioning. Ann. Bot. 32: 679-82.

HAISE, H. R.; H. J. HAAS and L. R. JENSEN, 1966. Soil moisture studies of some Great Plains soils. II. Field capacity as related to 1/3 atmosphere percentage, and 'minimum point' as related to 15- and 26-atmospheres. Soil Sci. Soc. Am. Proc. 19: 20-5.

HALSTEAD, E. H. and D. A. RENNIE, 1965. The movement of injected ^{32}P through the wheat plant. Can. J. Bot. 43: 1359-66.

HEINRICHS, D. H. 1963. Creeping alfalfas. Adv. Agron. 15: 317-37.

HOLT, E. C. and F. L. FISHER, 1960. Root development of coastal Bermuda grass with high nitrogen fertilization. Agron. J. 52: 593-6.

HOSHIKAWA, K. 1969. Underground organs of the seedlings and the systematics of gramineae. Bot. Gaz. 130: 192-203.

HUBBARD, V. C. 1938. Root studies on four varieties of spring wheat. J. Am. Soc. Agron. 30: 62.

HUNTER, A. S. and D. J. KELLY, 1964. The extension of plant roots into dry soil. Pl. Physiol. 21: 445-51.

HURD, E. A. 1964. Root study of three wheat varieties and their resistance to drought and damage by soil cracking. Can. J. Pl. Sci. 44: 240-8.

HURD, E. A. 1968. Growth of roots of seven varieties of spring wheat at high and low moisture levels. Agron. J. 60: 201-5.

HURD, E. A. 1969. A method of breeding for yield of wheat in semiarid climates. Euphytica 18: 217-26.

HURD, E. A. 1971. Can we breed for drought resistance? In: Drought Injury and Resistance in Crops, Larson, K. L. (ed), Crop Sci. Soc. Pub. No. 2, pp. 77-88.

HURD, E. A. 1973. Phenotype and drought tolerance in wheat. In: Plant Modification for More Effective Water Use. A Symp. (in press).

HURD, E. A.; T. F. TOWNLEY-SMITH; L. A. PATTERSON and C. H. OWEN, 1972a. Wascana, a new durum wheat. Can. J. Pl. Sci. 52: 687-8.

HURD, E. A.; T. F. TOWNLEY-SMITH; L. A. PATTERSON and C. H. OWEN, 1972b. Techniques used in producing Wascana wheat. Can. J. Pl. Sci. 52: 689-91.

HURD, E. A.; T. F. TOWNLEY-SMITH; D. MALLOUGH and L. A. PATTERSON, 1973. Wakooma durum wheat. Can. J. Pl. Sci. 53: 261-2.

ILJIN, W. C. 1957. Drought resistance in plants and physiological processes. Ann. Rev. Pl. Physiol. 8: 257-74.

JENNY, H. and R. OVERSTREET, 1939. Surface migration of ions and contact exchange. J. Phys. Chem. 43: 1185-96.

KAFKAFI, U.; Z. KAKRI; N. ALBASAL and J. ROOEICK, 1965. Root activity of dryland sorghum as measured by radioactive phosphorus uptake and water consumption. In: Proc. Symp. Use of Isotopes and

Irradiation in Soil-Plant Nutrition Studies. Int. At. Energy Agency, Turkey, pp. 481-8.

KATYAL, J. C. and B. V. SUBBIAH, 1971. Root distribution pattern of some wheat varieties. Indian J. agr. Sci. 41: 786-90.

KATZNELSON, H.; E. A. PETERSON and J. W. ROUATT, 1962. Phosphate-dissolving microorganisms on seed and in the root zone of plants. Can. J. Bot. 40: 1181-96.

KATZNELSON, H.; J. W. ROUATT and T. M. B. PAYNE, 1956. The liberation of amino acids and reducing compounds by plant roots. Plant & Soil 7: 35-48.

KAUL, R. 1966. Effect of water stress on respiration of wheat. Can. J. Bot. 44: 623-32.

KAUL, R. 1967. A survey of water suction forces in some prairie wheat varieties. Can. J. Pl. Sci. 47: 323-6.

KAUL, R. 1969. Relations between water status and yield of some wheat varieties. Z. Pflanyenzuchtg 62: 145-54.

KAUL, R. 1973. Personal communication.

KAUL, R. and W. L. CROWLE, 1971. Relation between water status, leaf temperature, stomatal aperture and productivity of some wheat varieties. Z. Pflanyenzuchtg 65: 233-43.

KAUL, R. and W. L., CROWLE, 1974. An index derived from photosynthetic parameters for predicting grain yields of drought stressed wheat cultivars. Z. Pflanyenzuchtg (in press).

KELLEY, O. J.; J. A. HARDMAN and D. S. JENNINGS, 1947. A soil sampling machine for obtaining two-, three- and four-inch diameter cores of undisturbed soil to a depth of six feet. Soil Sci. Soc. Am. Proc. 12: 85-6.

KIRICHENKO, F. G. and R. A. OORAZALEIV, 1970. Degree of inheritance of strength of root system and the plant mass in interspecies hybrids of wheat. Ref. V. I. Lenin All-Un. Acad. Sci. 4: 9-13.

KLAGES, K. H. W. 1960. Crop adaptation in relation to the economic use of water. Agr. Exp. Sta. Bull. Syomping, pp. 11-23.

KMOCH, H. G.; R. E. RAMIG and F. F. KOEHLER, 1957. Root development of winter wheat as influenced by soil moisture and nitrogen fertilization. Agron. J. 49: 20-5.

KNIEVEL, D. P. 1973. Procedure for estimating ratio of live to dead dry matter in root core samples. Crop Sci. 13: 124-6.

KNOTT, D. R. 1974. Effect of nitrogen fertilizer on yield and protein content of five spring wheats. Can. J. Pl. Sci. 54: 1-7.

KOK, B. 1969. Photosynthesis. In: Physiology of Plant Growth and Development, Wilkins, M. B. (ed), McGraw-Hill Book Co., Maidenhead, England.

KONONOVA, M. M. 1966. Soil Organic Matter. Pergamon Press, Inc., New York.

KRAMER, P. J. 1963. Water stress and plant growth. Agron. J. 55: 31-5.

KRAMER, P. J. and H. BRIX, 1965. Measurement of water stress in plants. Methodology of plant eco-physiology. UNESCO Arid Zone Research, p. 343.

KRAMER, P. J. and T. S. COILE, 1940. An estimation of the volume of water made available by root extension. Pl. Physiol. 15: 743-7.

KUIPER, P. J. C. 1967. Surface-active chemicals as regulators of plant growth, membrane permeability and resistance to freezing. Laboratory of plant physiological research, Agricultural University, Wageningen, The Netherlands, 253rd Communication 67-3.

LANGER, R. H. M. 1966. Mineral nutrition of grasses and cereals. *In:* Growth of Cereals and Grasses, Milthorpe, F. L. and J. D. Ivins (eds), Butterworths, London, pp. 213-26.

LAVIN, F. 1961. A glass faced planter box for field observation on roots. Agron. J. 53: 265-8.

LEES, R. D. 1924. Root development in wheat. Agr. Gaz., of N. S. Wales 35: 609-12.

LEGGETT, J. E. and D. EGLI, 1974. Ion accumulation by crop plants. *In:* Physiological Aspects of Crop Nutrition and Resistance, Gupta, U. S. (ed), Haryana Agric. Univ., Hissar, India.

LEHANE, J. J. and W. J. STAPLE, 1962. Effects of soil moisture tension on growth of wheat. Can. J. Soil Sci. 42: 180-88.

LEVITT, J.; C. Y. SULLIVAN and E. KRULL, 1960. Some problems in drought resistance. Bull. Res. Council, Israel 80: 173-80.

LEWIS, D. G. and J. P. QUIRK, 1967. Phosphate diffusion in soil and uptake by plants. III. ^{31}P, movement and uptake by plants as indicated by ^{32}P autoradiography. Plant & Soil 26: 445-53.

LIEBHARDT, W. C. and J. T. MURDOCK, 1965. Effect of potassium on morphology and lodging of corn. Agron. J. 57: 325-8.

LINDSAY, W. L. 1972. Inorganic phase equilibria of micronutrients in soils. *In:* Micronutrients in Agriculture, Dinauer, R. C. (ed), Soil Sci. Soc. Am., Madison, Wisconsin.

LIVINGSTON, B. E. 1906. Note on the relation between growth of roots and of tops of wheat. Bot. Gaz. 41: 139-43.

LONG, O. H. 1959. Root studies on some farm crops in Tennessee. Univ. Tennessee Agr. Exp. Sta. Bull. 301, pp. 1-41.

LUKEENA, L. F. and N. P. SLOOSHNAYA, 1971. Physiological characteristics of winter wheat which have different strengths of root systems. Ref. V. I. Lenin All-Un. Acad. Agr. Sci. 9: 8-10.

LUNDEGÅRDH, H. 1942. The growth of roots as influenced by pH and salt content of the medium. K. Lantler Hogsk. Ann. 10: 31-55.

MACK, A. R. 1973. Influence of soil moisture and moisture condition on growth and protein production of Manitou and two dwarf Mexican spring wheats. Can. J. Pl. Sci. 53: 721-36.

MACK, A. R. and W. S. FERGUSON, 1968. A moisture stress index for wheat by means of a modulated soil moisture budget. Can. J. Pl. Sci. 48: 535-43.

MACKEY, J. 1973. The wheat root. The 4th World Wheat Genetics Symposium, Missouri (in press).

MART'YANOVA, K. L. 1960. Result of field experiments with barley seed which had undergone a presowing hardening to drought. Translated from Fiziologiya Rastenii 7: 363-5.

McCARTNEY, 1969. Personal communication (work toward Ph.D. thesis, Univ. of East Africa).

McCLAREN, A. D. and G. H. PETERSON (eds), 1967. Soil Biochemistry. Marcel Dekker, New York.

McELROY, W. D. (ed) 1961. A symposium on Light and Life. The John Hopkins Press, Baltimore, Md.

MEIGE, F. 1938. Study of the development of the root system of wheat. Rev. Bot. Appl. 18: 233-59.

MILLER, E. C. 1916. Comparative study of the root systems and leaf areas of corn and the sorghums. J. agr. Res. 6: 311-32.

MILTHORPE, F. L. 1960. The income and loss of water in arid and semiarid zones. In: Plant Water Relationships in Arid and Semiarid Conditions. UNESCO, pp. 9-36.

MINSHALL, W. H. 1957. Primary place of action and symptoms indicated in plants by 3-(4-chlorophenyl)-1, 1-dimethylurea. Can. J. Pl. Sci. 37: 157-66.

MIRREH, H. F. and J. W. KETCHESON, 1972. Influence of soil bulk density and matric pressure on soil resistance to penetration. Can. J. Soil Sci. 52: 477-83.

MIRREH, H. F. and J. W. KETCHESON, 1973. Influence of soil matric pressure and resistance to penetration on corn root elongation. Can. J. Soil Sci. 53: 383-8.

MOLZ, F. J. and I. REMSON, 1970. Extraction term models of soil moisture use by transpiring plants. Water Resour. Res. 6: 1346-56.

MONTEITH, J. L. 1965. Evaporation and environment. The state and movement of water in living organisms. Symp. Soc. exp. Biol. 19: 205-34.

MOORBY, J. 1974. Ion transport and crop growth. In: Physiological Aspects of Crop Nutrition and Resistance, Gupta, U. S. (ed), Haryana Agric. Univ., Hissar, India.

MOSS, P. 1964. Some aspects of the cation status of soil moisture. V. The effect of soil moisture tension on growth and cation uptake by plants. Plant & Soil 20: 271-86.

MURATA, Y. 1969. Physiological responses to nitrogen in plants. In:

Physiological Aspects of Crop Yield, Dinauer, R. C. (ed), Am. Soc. Agron., Madison, Wisconsin.

MUZIK, T. J. and J. W. WHITWORTH, 1962. A technique for periodic observation of root systems *in situ.* Agron. J. 54: 56.

NEAL, J. L. JR.; T. G. ATKINSON and R. I. LARSON, 1970. Changes in the rhizosphere microflora of spring wheat reduced by disomic substation of a chromosome. Can. J. Microbiol. 16: 153-8.

NEWMAN, E. I. 1966. A method of estimating total length of root in a sample. J. appl. Ecology 3: 139-45.

NEWTON, R. and W. M. MARTIN, 1930. Physicochemical studies on the nature of drought resistance in crop plants. Can. J. Res. 3: 385-427.

NIELSEN, K. F. and E. C. HUMPHRIES, 1966. Effects of root temperature on plant growth. Soils & Fertil. 29: 1-7.

NYE, P. H. 1966. The effect of the nutrient intensity and buffering power of a soil and the absorbing power, size and root hairs of a root on nutrient absorption by diffusion. Plant & Soil 25: 81-105.

NYE, P. H. 1968. Processes in the root environment. J. Soil Sci. 19: 205-15.

OLIVER, S. and S. A. BARBER, 1966. An evaluation of the mechanisms governing the supply of Ca, Mg, K and Na to soybean roots. Soil Sci. Soc. Am. Proc. 30: 82-6.

OLSEN, S. R. 1972. Micronutrient interactions. *In:* Micronutrients in Agriculture, Dinauer, R. C. (ed), Soil Sci. Soc. Am. Inc., Madison, Winconsin.

OLSEN, S. R.; W. D. KEMPER and R. D. JACKSON, 1962. Phosphate diffusion to plant roots. Soil Sci. Soc. Am. Proc. 26: 222-7.

OPPENHEIMER, H. R. 1960. Adaptation to drought. Zerophytism in plant-water relationships in arid and semiarid conditions. UNESCO.

OZANNE, P. G.; C. J. ASHEN and D. J. KIRTON, 1965. Root distribution in a deep sand and its relationship to the uptake of added potassium by pasture plants. Aust. J. agr. Res. 16: 785-800.

PAPENDICK, R. I.; M. J. LINDSTORM and V. L. COCHRAN, 1973. Soil mulch effects on seed-bed temperature and water during fallow in eastern Washington. Soil Sci. Soc. Am. Proc. 37: 307-14.

PARR, J F. 1967. Biochemical considerations for increasing the efficiency of nitrogen fertilizers. Soil & Fertil. 30: 207-13.

PAULSEN, K. 1973. Personal communication.

PAVLYCHENKO, T. K. 1937. Quantitative studies of the entire root systems of weed and crop plants under field conditions. Ecology 18: 62-79.

PAVLYCHENKO, T. K. and J. B. HARRINGTON, 1934. Competitive efficiency of weed and cereal crops. Can. J. Res. 10: 77-94.

PAVLYCHENKO, T. K. and J. B. HARRINGTON, 1935. Root development of weeds and crops in competition under dryfarming. Sci. Agr. 16: 151-90.

228 E. A. HURD & E. D. SPRATT

PEARSON, R. W.; L. F. RATLIFF and H. M. TAYLOR, 1970. Effect of soil temperature, strength and pH on cotton seedling root elongation. Agron. J. 62: 243-6.

PENDLETON, J. W.; A. L. LANG and G. H. DUNGAN, 1953. Response of spring barley varieties to different fertilizer treatments and seasonal growing conditions. Agron. J. 45: 529-32.

PERCIVAL, J. 1921. The Wheat Plant. A Monograph. Duchworth and Co. pp. 1-463.

PIERPOINT, G. 1965. Measuring surface soil moisture with the neutron depth probe and a surface shield. Soil Sci. 10: 189-92.

PINTHUS, M. J. 1969. Tillering and coronal root formation in some common and durum wheat varieties. Crop Sci. 9: 267-72.

PINTHUS, M. J. and Y. ESHELL, 1962. Observations on the development of the root system of some wheat varieties. Israel J. agr. Res. 12: 13-20.

PITTMAN, U. J. 1964. Magnetism and plant growth. II. Effect on root growth of cereals. Can. J. Pl. Sci. 44: 283-7.

PLATT, A. W. and J. G. DARROCH, 1942. The seedling resistance of wheat varieties to artificial drought in relation to grain yield. Sci. Agr. 22: 521-7.

POHJAKALLIO, O. 1945. The question of the resistance of plants to drought periods in Finland. Nord. Jordbr. Forskn. 5-6: 206-26.

POHJAKAS, K.; D. W. L. READ and H. C. KORVEN, 1967. Consumptive use of water by crops at Swift Current, Saskatchewan. Can. J. Soil. Sci. 47: 131-8.

PRICE, C. A.; H. E. CLARK and E. A. FUNKHOUSER, 1972. Functions of micronutrients in plants. In: Micronutrients in Agriculture, Dinauer, R. C. (ed), Soil. Soc. Am., Madison, Wisconsin.

PURKAS, L.; M. R. TEEL and D. SWATYENDRUBER, 1964. A method of measuring the volume of small root systems. Agron. J. 59: 90-91.

RACZ, C. J.; D. A. RENNIE and W. L. HUTCHEON, 1964. The ^{32}P injection method for studying the root system of wheat. Can. J. Soil Sci. 44: 100-8.

RAPER, C. D. and S. A. BARBER, 1970a. Rooting systems of soybeans. I. Differences in root morphology among varieties. Agron. J. 62: 581-4.

RAPER, C. D. and S. A. BARBER, 1970b. Rooting systems of soybeans. II. Physiological effectiveness of nutrient absorption surfaces. Agron. J. 62: 585-8.

RAWITSCHER, F. 1937. Tropism in roots. Bot. Rev. 3: 175.

READ, D. W. L. 1958. Horizontal movement of water in soil. Can. J. Soil. Sci. 39: 27-31.

READ, D. W. L. 1973. Personal communication.

READ, D. W. L.; S. V. FLECK and W. L. PELTON, 1962. Self-irrigating green-house pots. Agron. J. 54: 467-8.

RENNIE, D. A. and J. S. CLAYTON, 1967. An evaluation of techniques used to characterize the comparative productivity of soil profile types in Saskatchewan. *In:* Soil Chemistry and Fertility, Jacks, G. V. (ed), Int. Soc. Soil Sci., Aberdeen, Scotland, pp. 365-76.

RENNIE, D. A. and W. L. HUTCHEON, 1965. Soil plant nutrient research report. Dep. Soil Sci., Univ. of Sask., Saskatoon, Sask.

RENNIE, D. A. and R. J. SOPER, 1958. The effect of nitrogen additions on fertilizer-phosphorus availability. II. J. Soil Sci. 9: 155-67.

RITCHIE, J. T. 1971. Dryland evaporative flux in a subhumid climate. I. Micrometeorological influences. Agron. J. 63: 51-62.

RITCHIE, J. T. 1972. Model for predicting evaporation from a row crop with incomplete cover. Water Resour. Res. 8: 1204-13.

RITCHIE, J. T. and E. BURNETT, 1970. Dryland evaporative flux in a subhumid climate. II. Plant influences. Agron. J. 62: 51-62.

RITCHIE, J. T.; D. E. KISSEL and E. BURNETT, 1972a. Water movement in undisturbed swelling clay soil. Soil Sci. Soc. Am. Proc. 36: 974-9.

RITCHIE, J. T.; E. BURNETT and R. C. HENDERSON, 1972b. Dryland evaporative flux in a subhumid climate. III. Soil water influence. Agron. J. 64: 168-73.

RITCHIE, J. T. and W. R. JORDAN, 1972. Dryland evaporative flux in a subhumid climate. IV. Relation to plant water status. Agron. J. 64: 173-6.

ROBERTSON, G. W. 1968. A biometeorological time scale for a cereal crop involving day and night temperatures and photoperiod. Int. J. Biometeor. 12: 191-223.

ROBERTSON, G. W. 1973. Development of simplified agroclimatic procedures for assessing temperature effect on crop development. *In:* Plant Response to Climatic Factors, Proc. Uppsala Symp., pp. 327-40.

ROGERS, W. S. 1969. The East Malling Root-Observation Laboratories. *In:* Root Growth, pp. 361-76, Whittington, W. J. (ed), Butterworths, London.

ROMA, A. 1962. Heritability in the root system characters of wheat in correlation with lodging resistance. Lucrari Stuntifice (Clij) 18: 81-90.

RUSSELL, M. B. 1957. (Coordinator) water and its relation to soils and crops. Dep. Agron., Univ. of Illinois, Urbana, Illinois.

RUSSELL, M. B. 1959. Water and its relation to soils and crops. Adv. Agron. 11: 1-124.

RUSSELL, R. S. and F. B. ELLIS, 1968. Estimation of the distribution of plant roots on soil. Nature 217: 582-3.

SAGE, G. C. M. 1973. Personal communication.

SALIM, M. H. and G. W. TODD, 1968. Seed soaking as a presowing, drought-hardening treatment in wheat and barley seedlings. Agron. J. 60: 179-82.

SALIM, M. H.; G. W. TODD and A. M. SCHLCHUBER, 1965. Root development of wheat, oats and barley under conditions of soil moisture stress. Agron. J. 57: 603-7.

SALIM, M. H.; G. W. TODD and C. A. STUTTE, 1969. Evaluation of techniques for measuring drought avoidance in cereal seedlings. Agron. J. 61: 182-6.

SCHUURMAN, J. J. 1959. Root development, water uptake and growth of spring wheat and perennial ryegrass on three profiles. Rep. Conf. Suppl. Irr. Comm. 6th Int. Soil Sci., pp. 71-88.

SEN, S. and B. P. PAL, 1953. Response of certain varieties of wheat to different fertility levels. Indian J. agr. Sci. 23: 1-26.

SHAWCROFT, W. W.; E. R. LEMON and D. W. STEWART, 1973. Estimation of internal crop water status from meteorological and plant parameters in plant response to climatic factors. Proc. Uppsala Symp., UNESCO, pp. 449-59.

SIMMONDS, P. M. and B. J. SALLANS, 1933. Some observations on the growth of Marquis wheat with special reference to root development. Proc. World Grain Exhib. and Conf. 2: 163-77.

SINGH, K. 1922. Development of root system of wheat in different kinds of soil and with different methods of watering. Ann. Bot. 36: 353-60.

SINGH, K. 1952. Effect of soil cultivation on the growth and yield of winter wheat. IV. Effect of cultivation on root development. V. Sci. Food Agr. 3: 514-25.

SLATYER, R. O. 1957. The significance of the permanent wilting percentage in studies of plant and soil water relations. Bot. Rev. 23: 586-636.

SLATYER, R. O. 1960. Absorption of water by plants. Bot. Rev. 26: 331-92.

SLATYER, R. O. 1967. Plant-Water Relationships. Academic Press, New York, pp. 1-366.

SLATYER, R. O. 1973a. The effect of internal water status on plant growth, development and yield. In: Plant Response to Climatic Factors. Proc. Uppsala Symp. UNESCO pp. 177-91.

SLATYER, R. O. 1973b. Plant response to climatic factors. Proc. Uppsala Symp. UNESCO, Paris, pp. 1-574.

SLATYER, R. O. and W. R. GARDNER, 1965. Overall aspects of water movement in plants and soils. The state and movement of water in living organisms. Symp. Soc. exp. Biol. 19: 313-50.

SLUCKER, R. and K. J. FREY, 1960. The root-system distribution patterns for five oat varieties. Proc. Iowa Acad. Sci. 67: 98-102.

SPINKS, J. W. T.; D. A. LANE and B. B. TORCHINSKY, 1951. A new method for moisture determination in soil. Can. J. Tech. 29: 371-4.

SPRATT, E. D. 1966. Fertility of a chernozemic clay soil after 50 years of cropping with and without forage crops in rotation. Can. J. Soil Sci. 46: 207-12.

SPRATT, E. D. and J. K. R. GASSER, 1970. Effect of ammonium and nitrate forms of nitrogen and restricted water supply on growth and nitrogen uptake of wheat. Can. J. Soil Sci. 50: 263-73.

SPRATT, E. D. and E. V. McCURDY, 1966. The effect of various long-term soil fertility treatments on the phosphorus status of a clay chernozem. Can. J. Soil Sci. 46: 29-36.

STAPLE, W. J. and J. J. LEHANE, 1954. Weather conditions influencing wheat yields in tanks and field plots. Can. J. agr. Sci. 34: 553-64.

STEVENSON, F. J. and M. S. ARDAKANI, 1972. Organic matter reactions involving micronutrients in soil. In: Micronutrients in Agriculture, Dinauer, R. C. (ed), Soil Sci. Soc. Am., Madison, Wisconsin.

STONE, J. F.; D. KIRKHAM and A. A. READ, 1954. Soil moisture determination by a portable neutron scattering moisture-meter. Soil Sci. Soc. Am. Proc. 19: 419-23.

STOY, V. 1969. Interrelationships among phytosynthesis, respiration and movement of carbon in developing crops. In: Physiological Aspects of Crop Yield, Dinauer, R. C. (ed), Am. Soc. Agron., Madison, Wisconsin.

STREET, H. E. 1969. Factors influencing the initiation and activity of meristems in roots. In: Root Growth, pp. 20-41, Whittington, W. J.(ed), Butterworths, London.

STRONG, W. M. and R. J. SOPER, 1973. Utilization of pelleted phosphorus by flax, wheat, rape and buckwheat from a calcareous soil. Agron. J. 65: 18-21.

SUBBIAH, B. V.; J. C. KATYAL; R. L. NARASIMHON and C. DAKSHINAMURTI, 1968. Preliminary investigation and root distribution of high yielding wheat varieties. Proc. Int. J. appl. Rad. Isotope 19: 385-90.

SYME, J. R. 1970. A high-yielding Mexican semidwarf wheat and the relationship of yield to harvest index and other varietal characteristics. Aust. J. exp. Agr. An. Husb. 10: 350-5.

SYME, J. R. 1972. Single-plant characters as a measure of field plot performance of wheat cultivars. Aust. J. agr. Res. 23: 753-60.

TAYLOR, D. W. 1973. Growth and water absorption of wheat with parts of roots at different water potentials. New Phytol. 72: 297-305.

TAYLOR, H. M. 1967. Effects of tillage induced soil environmental changes on root growth. Tillage for greater crop production (Conference Proc.). Am. Soc. Eng., St. Joseph, Michigan, pp. 15-18, 25.

TAYLOR, H. M. and R. R. BRUCE, 1967. Effects of soil strength on root growth and crop yield in the southern United States. 9th Int. Cong. Soil Sci. Trans. 1: 803-11.

TAYLOR, H. M. and H. R. GARDNER, 1960. Relative penetrating ability of different roots. Agron. J. 52: 579-81.

TAYLOR, H. M. and L. F. RATLIFF, 1969.   Root elongation rates of cotton and peanuts as a function of soil strength and soil water content.   Soil Sci. 108: 113-19.

TEARE, I. D.; E. T. KANEMASU; W. L. POWERS and H. S. JACOBS, 1973. Water use efficiency and its relation to crop canopy area, stomatal regulation and root distribution.   Agron. J. 65: 207-11.

TODD, G. W.; F. W. INGHAM and C. A. STUTTE, 1962.   Relative turgidity as an indication of drouth stress on cereal plants.   Biol. Sci. Proc. Okla. Acad, Sci. 42: 55-60.

TODD, G. W. and D. L. WEBSTER, 1965.   Effects of repeated drought periods on photosynthesis and survival of cereal seedlings.   Agron. J. 57: 399-404.

TROUGHTON, A. 1955.   The application of the allometric formula to the study of the relationship between the roots and shoots of young grass plants. Agr. Progress 30: 1-7.

TROUGHTON, A. 1956.   Studies on the growth of young grass plants with special reference to the relationship between the shoot and root systems. J. Brit. Grassland Soc. 2: 56-65.

TROUGHTON, A. 1957.   The underground organs of herbage grasses.   Commonwealth Bur. Pastures Field Crops Bull. 44.

TROUGHTON, A. 1958.   The roots of grasses.   II. In relation to the soil. Worcestershire Agr. Chron. 27: 2-8.

TROUGHTON, A. 1960a.   Uptake of phosphorus 32 by the roots of *Lolium perenne*. Nature 188: 593.

TROUGHTON, A. 1960b.   Growth correlations between the roots and shoots of grass plants.   Proc. of VIII Int. Grassland Cong. pp. 280-83.

TROUGHTON, A. 1961a.   Studies on the roots of leys and the organic matter and structure of the soil.   Empire J. exp. Agr. 29: 165-75.

TROUGHTON, A. 1961b.   The effect of photoperiod and temperature on the relationship between the root and shoot systems of *Lolium perenne*. J. Brit. Grassland Soc. 16: 291-95.

TROUGHTON, A. 1961c.   The effect on the components and management of a ley.   J. Brit. Grassland Soc. 16: 1-5.

TROUGHTON, A. 1962.   The roots of temperate cereals (wheat, barley, oats and rye).   Mimeo Publ. No. 2. Com. Bur. Pastures and Field Crops.

TROUGHTON, A. 1963a.   The root weight under swards of equal age in successive years.   Empire J. exp. Agr. 31: 274-81.

TROUGHTON, A. 1963b.   A comparison of five varieties of *Lolium perenne* with special reference to the relationship between the root and shoot systems.   Euphytica 12: 49-56.

TROUGHTON, A. and W. J. WHITTINGTON, 1969.   The significance of genetic variation in root systems.   *In:* Root Growth, pp. 296-314,

Whittington, W. J. (ed), Butterworths, London.

UPCHURCH, R. P. 1951. The use of the trench-wash and soil-elution method for studying alfalfa roots. Agron. J. 43: 552-5.

VAADIA, Y.; F. C. RANEY and R. M. HAGAN, 1961. Plant water deficit and physiological processes. Ann. Rev. Pl. Physiol. 12: 265-92.

VAN BAVEL, C. H. M.; F. S. NAKAYAMA and W. L. EHRLER, 1965. Measuring transpiration resistance of leaves. Pl. Physiol. 40: 535-40.

VASILIEV, J. 1929. The investigations of drought resistance in wheat. Bull. Physiol. Bot. Genet. & Plant Breed. 22: 147-219.

VIETS, F. G. 1972. Water deficit and nutrient availability. In: Water Deficits and Plant Growth. Vol. III. pp. 217-39, Kozlowski, T. T. (ed), Academic Press, New York.

VIJAYALAKSHMI, K. 1971. Root growth studies of wheat and pulse crops using radioisotope injection techniques. Ph.D. thesis submitted to Division of Agr. Physics, Indian Agr. Res. Inst., New Delhi.

WARDER, F. G.; J. J. LEHANE; W. C. HINMAN and W. J. STAPLE, 1962. The effect of fertilizer on growth, nutrient uptake and moisture use of wheat on two soils in south-western Saskatchewan. Can. J. Soil Sci. 43: 107-16.

WARDLAW, I. F. 1971. The early stages of grain development in wheat: response to water stress in a single variety. Aust. J. biol. Sci. 24: 1047-55.

WARNAAR, B. C. and B. W. EAVIS, 1972. Soil physical conditions affecting seedling root growth. II. Mechanical impedance, aeration and moisture availability as influenced by grain size distribution and moisture content in silica sands. Plant & Soil 36: 623-34.

WATANABE, F. S.; S. R. OLSEN and R. E. DANIELSON, 1960. Phosphorus availability as related to soil moisture. Trans. 7th Int. Congr. Soil Sci. 3: 450-56.

WATSON, D. J. 1947. Comparative physiological studies on the growth of field crops. I. Variation in net assimilation rate and leaf area between species and varieties, and within and between years. Ann. Bot. 11: 41-76.

WATSON, D. J. 1968. A prospect of crop physiology. Ann. appl. Biol. 62: 1-9.

WEAVER, J. E. 1926. Root habits of wheat. In: Root Development of Field Crops, pp. 133-61, McGraw-Hill Book Co., New York.

WEAVER, J. E. and R. W. DARLAND, 1949. Soil-root relationship of certain native grasses in various soil types. Ecol. Mong. 19: 303-38.

WEAVER, J. E. and J. W. VOIGT, 1950. Monolith method of root-sampling in studies on succession and degeneration. Bot. Gaz. 3: 286-99.

WELLS, S. A. and S. DUBETZ, 1966. Reaction of barley varieties to soil water stress. Can J. Pl. Sci. 46: 507-12.

WHITESIDE, A. G. O. 1941.   Effect of soil drought on wheat plants.   Sci.
    Agr. 21: 320-34.

WHITTINGTON, W. J. (ed) 1969.   "Root growth" Proc. Easter School in Agr.
    Sci., Univ. of Nottingham, p. 400, Butterworths, London.

WIERSUM, L. K. 1957.   The relationship of the size and structural rigidity
    of pores to their penetration of roots.   Plant & Soil 9: 75-85.

WIERSUM, L. K. 1961.   Utilization of soil by the plant root system.   Plant
    & Soil 15: 189-92.

WIERSUM, L. K. 1967a.   In: Soil Moisture and Irrigation Studies.   Proc.
    Vienna. 14-18, March 1966, Vienna I. A. E. A. 83.

WIERSUM, L. K. 1967b.   The mass-flow theory of phloem transport; a sup-
    porting calculation.   J. exp. Bot. 18: 160-62.

WIERSUM, L. K. 1967c.   Potential subsoil utilization by roots.   Plant &
    Soil 27: 383-401.

WIERSUM, L. K. 1969.   Soil water content in relation to nutrient uptake by
    the plant.   Comm. Hydrol. Onderzock-TNO. Verslag. Medeol.
    15: 74-89.

WILKINSON, H. F. 1972.   Movement of micronutrients to plant roots.   In:
    Micronutrients in Agriculture, Dinauer, R. C. (ed), Soil Sci. Soc. Am.
    Inc., Madison, Wisconsin.

WILKINSON, S. R. and A. J. OHLROGGE, 1962.   Principles of nutrient uptake
    from fertilizer bands.   V. Mechanisms responsible for intensive root
    development in fertilized zones.   Agron. J. 54: 288-91.

WILLIAMS, G. D. V. 1962.   Prairie droughts: "the sixties compared with
    thirties."   Agr. Inst. Rev. 17: 16-8.

WILLIAMS, G. D. V. 1969.   Weather and prairie wheat production.   Can.
    J. agr. Econ. 17: 99-109.

WILLIAMS, G. D. V. 1971.   Wheat phenology in relation to latitude, longi-
    tude and elevation on the Canadian Great Plains.   Can. J. Pl.
    Sci. 51: 1-12.

WILLIAMS, G. D. V. 1971/1972.   Geographical variations in yield-weather
    relationships over a large wheat growing region.   Agr. Meteorol.
    9: 265-83.

WILLIAMS, G. D. V. and G. W. Robertson, 1965.   Estimating most probable
    prairie wheat production from precipitation data.   Can. J. Pl.
    Sci. 45: 34-47.

WILLIAMS, R. F. 1960.   The physiology of growth in the wheat plant.   I.
    Seedling growth and the pattern of growth at the shoot apex.   Aust.
    J. biol. Sci. 13: 401-31.

WILLIAMS, T. F. and H. M. BAKER, 1957.   Studies of the root development of
    herbage root investigation.   Brit. Grassland Soc. 12: 49-55.

WILLIAMS, T. V.; R. S. SNELL and J. F. ELLIS, 1967.   Methods of measuring
    drought tolerance in corn.   Crop Sci. 7: 179-82.

WORT, D. J. 1940. Soil temperature and growth of Marquis wheat. Pl. Physiol. 15: 335-42.

WORZELLA, W. W. 1932.   Root development in hardy and non-hardy winter wheat varieties. J. Am. Soc. Agron. 24: 626-37.

WORZELLA, W. W. 1943.   Response of wheat varieties to different levels of soil productivity. I. Grain yield and total weight. J. Am. Soc. Agron. 35: 114-42.

ZIMMERMAN, M. 1969. Translocation of nutrients. *In:* Physiology of Plant Growth and Development, Wilkins, M. B. (ed), McGraw-Hill Book Co., Maidenhead, England.

Dr. Paul W. Unger

Dr. Unger is a Soil Scientist for the Agricultural Research Service, United States Department of Agriculture, and is stationed at the USDA South-western Great Plains Research Centre, Bushland, Texas. Much of Dr. Unger's research concerns the effects of tillage and cropping systems and residue management practices on physical conditions and water relations of soils.

Dr. Unger is a native of the State of Texas (USA) and was born in 1931. He received the B.S. degree from Texas A & M University in Agricultural Education in 1961 and the M.S. and Ph.D. degrees from Colorado State University in Soil Science in 1963 and 1966, respectively.

4. ROLE OF MULCHES IN DRYLAND AGRICULTURE[1]

PAUL W. UNGER
*USDA South-western Great
Plains Research Centre
Bushland, Texas*

Introduction

The practice of applying mulches to soil is possibly as old as agriculture itself (Jacks *et al.*, 1955). Ancient Romans placed stones on the soil surface to conserve water and the Chinese used pebbles from streambeds for similar purposes. These practices were suitable to areas where hand labour was readily available, but became impractical when mechanized agriculture was introduced. The current trend under mechanized agriculture is to utilize crop residues as mulches on the area where grown or to use transported and manufactured materials as mulches for some high-value crops.

REASONS FOR USING MULCHES

Mulches are used for various reasons, but water conservation and erosion

[1] Contribution from the Soil, Water, and Air Sciences, Southern Region, Agricultural Research Service, USDA, in cooperation with the Texas Agricultural Experiment Station, Texas A & M University.

control are undoubtedly the most important for agriculture in dry regions. While the effectiveness of mulches for water conservation is highly variable, mulches when properly managed definitely aid wind and water erosion control. Other reasons for mulching include soil temperature moderation, soil nutrient effects, soil salinity control, soil structure improvement, crop quality control, and weed control.

DEFINITIONS

For this review article, a *mulch* is any material at the soil surface that was grown and maintained in place; any material grown, but modified before placement; and any material processed or manufactured and transported before placement. Some examples of the materials included are crop residues, leaves, clippings, bark, manure, paper, plastic films, petroleum products and gravel.

In a broad sense, *dryland* agriculture implies agriculture without irrigation. This could occur in almost any geographic area. For this article, dryland agriculture is defined as agriculture in areas where potential evaporation and transpiration are greater than the amount of water supplied by precipitation. This definition applies to the dry areas of the 17 western states of the United States and to similar areas of other countries where the precipitation effectiveness index (P-E index) is less than 50 (Thornthwaite, 1931). Considerable research on the use of mulches has been conducted in these areas. This research forms the basis for this article, but where pertinent, research from other regions is cited.

Webster defines *agriculture* as "the work of cultivating the soil, producing crops, and raising livestock." In its broad sense, this definition includes field, range, horticultural, floricultural and silvicultural crops. A more restrictive meaning, namely the production of any crop under cultivated conditions, is adhered to in this article. Although the emphasis is on crop production without irrigation, some studies involving irrigated crops are mentioned.

PREVIOUS REVIEWS

Extensive reviews and summaries pertaining to mulches and specialized mulching systems have been published by Jacks *et al.* (1955), Johnson and Davis (1972), McCalla and Army (1961), and Zingg and Whitfield (1957). While reference is made to some work covered in these reports, the emphasis is on recent studies concerning the use of mulches for crop production, generally under field or simulated field conditions.

Effects of Mulches on Some Soil Properties and Conditions

Numerous soil properties and conditions are affected by mulches, either directly or indirectly. Among those affected are soil water through runoff control, increased infiltration, decreased evaporation, and weed control; soil temperature through radiation shielding, heat conduction and trapping, and evaporative cooling; soil nutrients through organic matter additions, differential nitrification, and mineral solubility; soil structure; soil biological regime through organic matter additions, microbial and soil fauna populations, and plant root distributions; soil erodibility; and soil salinity through leaching and evaporation control. Probably of greatest importance, however, for agriculture in dry regions are soil water, temperature, structure and salinity. The effects of mulches on these properties and conditions are discussed in the following sections.

Soil Water

By their very nature, dry regions generally receive inadequate precipitation for good crop production. Furthermore, much of the precipitation that is received is lost by runoff and evaporation. Also, some water that enters the soil may evaporate before a crop is planted. For the interval between crops, precipitation storage efficiencies ranging from 15 to 25 per cent are common in the Great Plains of the United States (Mathews & Army, 1960; Unger, 1972).

While precipitation is limited and erratic and the evaporation potential is high, good yields could be obtained if most precipitation that occurs in dry regions would be effectively conserved and used for crop production. For example, grain sorghum (*Sorghum vulgare* Pers.) in Oklahoma (U.S.A.) produced 6270 kg grain per hectare with only 17.8 cm of water use from the soil (Griffin *et al.*, 1966). The soil surface was covered with a white polyethylene film to prevent evaporation and precipitation infiltration during the growing season. In a more northern region, corn (*Zea mays* L.) produced 4330 kg grain per hectare with 37.8 cm of water use in 1960 and 3930 kg grain per hectare with 19.8 cm of water use in 1961 (Willis *et al.*, 1963). The soil surface was ridged and 90 per cent covered with a black polyethylene film. Corn grain production at relatively high levels with similar amounts of water use was reported by Harrold *et al.* (1959) and Peters (1960) for a more humid climate. The amounts of water used were well below the average annual precipitation received in many dry regions. Thus precipitation generally is adequate, but it is not efficiently used for crop production.

Numerous studies have been conducted to determine the influence of mulches on soil water storage, content and evaporation. Many different materials have been used, but one of the more widely researched has been plastic film (included are polyethylene, polyvinyl chloride, and similar films, but the term "plastic" will be used hereafter). In Europe, Linden (1963), Manescu and Ciofu (1970), and Pusztai (1963) reported increased soil water contents due to plastic films, with increases ranging up to 32 per cent (Manescu & Ciofu, 1970). In North America, plastic films resulted in higher water contents than bare soil in most cases (Army & Hudspeth, 1960; Lippert et al., 1964; Liptay & Tiessen, 1970; Willis et al., 1963), but Schales (1964) reported a lower water content, apparently due to the film preventing infiltration. Other increases in soil water due to plastic films were reported by Bansal et al. (1971) and Baumer (1964). The higher water contents resulted from reduced evaporation, induced infiltration, reduced transpiration by weeds, or a combination of these factors (Austin, 1964; Hanks, et al., 1961; Linden, 1963; Lippert et al., 1964; Liptay & Tiessen, 1970; Willis, 1962; Willis et al., 1963). The effectiveness of plastic films depended upon the amount of surface covered (Austin, 1964; Lippert et al., 1964; Willis, 1962; Willis et al., 1963).

Although plastic films generally resulted in higher water contents and reduced evaporation as compared with bare soil, they are relatively expensive and difficult to manage, especially under large scale field conditions for low value crops. Consequently, less expensive and more readily applicable materials have been sought. Petroleum and asphalt sprays and resins have received considerable attention (Baroccio & Morani, 1965; Kowsar et al., 1969; Lippert et al., 1964; Nerpin & Pakshina, 1965; Sale, 1966a; Takatori et al., 1971; Wendt, 1971). These materials affected soil water in a manner similar to plastic films. Their effectiveness depended upon the amount of surface covered (Lippert et al., 1964).

The greatest amount of research with mulches concerned crop residues and other plant waste products (straw, stover, leaves, corn cobs, sawdust, woodchips, etc.). These materials are cheap and often readily available, and they permit water to enter the soil readily. When maintained at adequate levels, these materials resulted in increased water contents and reduced evaporation (Adams, 1966; Bansal et al., 1971; Hanks & Woodruff, 1958; Mannering & Meyer, 1963; Moody et al., 1963; Prihar et al., 1968; Wiegand et al., 1968). However, residue production in dry regions often is inadequate to result in substantial water conservation. Even where most or all residues from dryland crops were maintained on the soil surface through stubble-mulch tillage and chemical fallow, rather dismal water storage often occurred (Black & Power, 1965; Harris, 1963; Johnson & Davis, 1972; Mathews & Army, 1960; McCalla & Army, 1961; Unger, 1972; Wiese et al., 1967; Zingg & Whitfield, 1957). Major reasons for the poor water storage results were the production of inadequate residues to enhance infiltration and to suppress subsequent evaporation, and incomplete weed control with tillage and chemicals.

Greb *et al.* (1967, 1970) conducted field studies with controlled residue levels to determine their influence on soil water storage during fallow in the Great Plains (U.S.A.). The results were:

Residue level (kg/ha)	% precipitation stored
0	16-26
1680	19-28
3360	22-33
6720	28-37

The favourable water storage results obtained from higher residue levels, interest in reduced tillage systems, and the availability of new and improved herbicides caused renewed interest in chemical fallow in the Great Plains. Water storage efficiencies during fallow were 35 and 42 per cent for tillage and chemical treatments, respectively, in a 3-year wheat (*Triticum aestivum* L.) —sorghum (*Sorghum bicolour* Moensch)—fallow rotation (Smika & Wicks, 1968). For a 2-year wheat-fallow rotation, efficiencies during fallow were 25 and 44 per cent for the tillage and chemical treatments, respectively. Efficiencies for treatments involving both tillage and chemicals fell between those for tillage or chemicals only. In 1973, Wicks and Smika reported similar water storage efficiencies for the study when data for more years were evaluated. The good results obtained with chemicals were attributed to nearly complete weed control and better residue preservation.

Significant increases in water storage resulted from the application of a cotton (*Gossypium hirsutum* L.) bur mulch to a loam soil (Koshi & Fryrear, 1971). Each higher mulch level (5.6, 11.2 or 22.4 tons/ha) resulted in increased water storage over the no mulch treatment. Storage efficiencies ranged from 36 to 46 per cent with no mulch to 66 to 80 per cent with 22.4 tons mulch per hectare in 1968 and 1969, respectively. The additional stored water significantly increased subsequent cotton lint yields.

Unger *et al.* (1971) used tandem disk, disk plus sweep, and chemical weed control treatments during fallow between wheat harvest in July and grain sorghum seeding the following June. Residues at harvest of the irrigated wheat crop were estimated at 11,000 kg per hectare. Effects of the treatments on subsequent surface residue levels, weed control, and water storage from 36.1 cm of precipitation during fallow were:

	Disk	Disk + Sweep	Chemicals
Surface residues (kg/ha)	< 200.0	1100.0	4600.0
Weed control (%)	76.0	52.0	100.0
Water storage (cm)	7.9	5.1	14.2

The studies of Bond and Willis (1969, 1970, 1971), although conducted under laboratory conditions with soil columns initially wetted to a given level, suggest that water storage can be increased where residue levels are adequate to reduce initial evaporation and thus permit water from precipitation to penetrate to greater depths.   However, large amounts of surface residues are required to obtain water savings over an extended period.

The effectiveness of various other materials for use as mulches has been investigated.   These materials have favourably influenced soil water content and evaporation in many cases, but their use does not appear practical under large scale conditions.   Materials studied included gravel, stones, desert pavement, bitumen and similar granular materials, and manure (Adams, 1966; Dancer, 1964; Lyford & Qashu, 1969; Mustafaev, 1964; Nerpin & Pakshina, 1965; Qashu & Evans, 1967; Unger, 1971a).

SOIL TEMPERATURE

When surface cover was adequate, mulches generally resulted in greater water contents and lower evaporation than bare soil; however, the effects of soil temperatures were highly variable.   Although variable, results from numerous studies where temperatures were measured indicate that the effects are predictable.

Colour of plastic mulches greatly affected soil temperature.   White or reflective plastic decreased temperatures (Pusztai, 1963) or had no effect (Schales, 1964), while clear plastic consistently resulted in higher temperatures than bare soil (Adams, 1970; Schales, 1964; Takatori et al., 1964; Zakharov & Semikina, 1964).   With black plastic, the results were variable. Linden (1963), Pusztai (1963) and Schales (1964) reported increased temperatures, Austin (1964) reported little effect, and Zakharov and Semikina (1964) reported generally lower temperatures with black plastic. For plastics in general, Adams (1962) stated that clear plastics result in higher temperatures because the soil directly absorbs most of the energy from incoming solar radiation.   With black plastic, the soil received only a portion of the incoming energy absorbed by the film.   Apparently, degree of contact between soil and black plastic influences the extent of temperature increase under a black plastic.   White and reflective plastics resulted in cooler temperatures because they did not absorb the incoming radiation.

Petroleum spray and resin mulches consistently resulted in higher temperatures than bare soil (Adams, 1970; Baroccio & Morani, 1965; Kowsar et al., 1969; Sale, 1966a; Schales, 1964; Takatori et al., 1964, 1971).   The maximum difference usually occurred during the hottest part of the day. At night, the mulches had slight or no effect on soil temperatures (Takatori et al., 1964, 1971).   The effects of asphalt and related substances on temperatures were similar to those of petroleum sprays and resins (MacMillan & Millette, 1971; Miller, 1968; Wann, 1969). These materials (petroleum, asphalt, etc.) absorbed the incoming solar radiation and, because of their close contact with the soil, readily conducted heat to the soil. Hence, the consistently higher temperatures with these mulches as compared with the variable influence of black plastic.

Mulches of plant materials (straw, stover, leaves, etc.) reduced soil temperatures (Adams, 1965; Allmaras et al., 1964; Anderson & Russell, 1964; Bansal et al., 1971; Bond & Willis, 1971; Brengle & Whitfield, 1969; Burrows & Larson, 1962; Dhesi et al., 1964; Evenson & Rumbaugh, 1972; Kohnke & Werkhoven, 1963; Schales, 1964). However, there were seasonal differences. Kohnke and Werkhoven (1963) and Onchev (1960) reported lower summer and higher winter temperatures, and Lehne (1961) reported lower spring and higher fall temperatures due to straw mulches as compared with bare soil. The combined effects of radiation interception and evaporative cooling were responsible for the lower temperatures under this type of mulch. However, the finding that each 2.2 tons of mulch in the 0 to 9-ton per hectare range reduced soil temperature at a 10-cm depth by 0.39°C (Burrows & Larson, 1962) suggests that evaporative cooling was less important in reducing temperatures than was radiation interception by the mulch. The thicker mulches reduce evaporation more than thinner mulches (Bond & Willis, 1969; Greb et al., 1967; Nerpin & Pakshina, 1965); hence, evaporative cooling would be less with thick mulches.

A group of miscellaneous mulching materials variously and somewhat unpredictably influenced soil temperatures. Black granular materials (coke, bitumen, etc.) increased temperatures (Jordan & Sampson, 1967; Qashu & Evans, 1967), whereas gravel (lighter coloured than above materials) reduced temperatures as compared with bare soil (Adams, 1965). The dark materials absorbed more radiation than the lighter coloured gravel; hence, the higher temperatures with the black materials. A colour effect was also reported by Cohen et al. (1965). A black rubber mulch resulted in higher temperatures than a brown rubber mulch. The response was similar to that of plastic mulches. Wood shavings and strawy manure reduced temperatures (Dancer, 1964; Lavee, 1963). The response was similar to that caused by plant materials. Glass and water mulches (water in plastic bags) increased temperatures with the water mulches being effective for reducing temperature fluctuations (Bowers, 1968; Miller, 1968).

SOIL STRUCTURE

In dry regions, the precipitation frequently occurs in high-intensity storms. When falling raindrops strike bare soil, soil particles are dispersed and surface sealing may occur, thus reducing infiltration. Consequently, water that could be conserved for plant use is lost by runoff. The dispersed soil at the surface often forms a hard crust when dry, which may adversely affect seedling emergence and plant growth.

Beneficial effects on soil structure due to surface mulches result primarily from the mulches absorbing the energy of falling raindrops, thus reducing dispersion and surface sealing. Infiltration rates generally are maintained and subsequent crusting is reduced. Other benefits possibly result from greater microbe and fauna activity in the soil, greater root proliferation, and the cushioning effect, which reduce compaction due to tractor, implement and animal traffic.

The degree of protection provided at the soil surface is related to surface coverage provided by the mulch. Plastic films prevent raindrops from striking the soil and thus prevent dispersion. However, unless special provisions are made (Willis *et al.*, 1963), they also prevent water infiltration. Less compaction was also ascribed to a plastic mulch (Liptay & Tiessen, 1970).

Petroleum, bitumen, coke and desert pavement mulches reduced surface crusting and soil density (Jordan & Sampson, 1967; Lyford & Qashu, 1969; Qashu & Evans, 1967). Although not reported, the materials except possibly petroleum undoubtedly also resulted in greater water infiltration. Although effective for reducing crusting, these materials do not provide the necessary binding substances for improved soil aggregation. However, if the surface remains adequately covered, stable aggregates at the surface are less important than where the soil is partially or completely exposed.

Crop residues and other similar mulches, when applied at adequate levels, have maintained high infiltration rates (Mannering & Meyer, 1963; Wann, 1969; Williams & Doneen, 1960) and resulted in less soil crusting (Mannering & Meyer, 1963). The high infiltration rates resulted from less surface sealing due to the protection against falling raindrops afforded by the mulches. Decomposition products of the mulches resulted in improved soil aggregation with respect to size, numbers and stability (McCalla, 1943; Siddoway, 1963). Although aggregation was improved, the aggregates were not sufficiently stable to withstand the impact of water drops without a protective cover (McCalla, 1943).

Stubble-mulch tillage, which maintains much of the crop residue on the surface, has given variable results with respect to soil structure. Army *et al.* (1961) reported reduced crusting and Ramig and Mazurak (1964) and Turelle and McCalla (1961) reported larger water stable aggregates and lower bulk densities as a result of stubble-mulch tillage than clean tillage. Unger (1969) reported higher water stable aggregation for a delayed stubble-mulch treatment (tillage delayed until weed growth begins the spring after wheat harvest in June or July) than for clean tillage but no effect when tillage was performed soon after wheat harvest. No effect on aggregation due to stubble-mulch tillage was also reported by McCalla *et al.* (1962). Where improved water stable aggregation occurred, the degree of aggregation was greatest soon after crop harvest and initial tillage, but decreased with time thereafter (Unger, 1972).

SOIL SALINITY

Many dry region soils have a high salt content. Since some of the salts are readily soluble in water, they move with the water. The salts could be removed from the soil by leaching if precipitation were adequate. However, due to limited precipitation, they move only to a limited depth and readily return to the surface as the soil water evaporates. Under such conditions, susceptible plants, especially at the germination and seedling stages, may be severely injured by the salts.

Under irrigated conditions, the salt problem may be aggravated by applying water having a high salt content and by applying insufficient water to move the salts well below the plant root zone. The management of saline soils has been widely investigated (U.S. Salinity Lab Staff, 1954). In this article, only the effects of mulches on salinity control are discussed.

Since salts readily move with soil water, any practice that maintains infiltration rates and reduces subsequent evaporation should moderate the adverse effects due to soil salinity. In previous sections, reference was made to numerous studies for which infiltration rates were maintained and evaporation was reduced. However, the effects of mulches on salinity control were mentioned only in a few cases.

Heilman *et al.* (1968) reported significant reductions in soil electrical conductivity (0 to 61-cm depth) from rainfall due to the application of sand and cotton bur mulches to saline soil. Similar results for a cotton bur mulch were reported by Carter and Fanning (1965) and Fanning and Carter (1963). The mulches, by reducing evaporation, reduced subsequent return of the salts to the leached zone.

Since damage due to salts is most severe at germination and plant seedling stages, any practice that reduces the salt content in the seed zone should be beneficial for plant establishment. While complete soil covers may be too expensive and impractical for extensive areas, strip mulches (plastic films, petroleum sprays, etc.) that maintain a higher water content in and reduce evaporation from the seed zone should reduce the salinity hazard and aid plant establishment. Additional benefits should result if the mulches continue to reduce evaporation, and if the crop yield and quality are improved due to salinity control.

Effects of Mulches on Erosion

Because of low residue production and dry soil surface conditions, dry regions are highly susceptible to wind erosion. Dry regions are also highly susceptible to water erosion because the precipitation frequently occurs during intense storms and the surface is inadequately protected by vegetation to effectively retard runoff. Therefore, to reduce erosion by wind and water is an important reason for using mulches in dry regions.

The ease by which soil particles are moved by wind and water is related to particle size and to wind or water velocity. Although particles greater than 0.84 mm in diameter are generally considered non-erodible by wind, water may cause erosion of almost any sized particles.

As indicated in the last section, decomposition products of some mulching materials may increase soil aggregation, which should reduce the susceptibility of soil to erosion. The chief value of mulches with regard to erosion control, however, is not their effect on soil structure, but upon their moderating the wind and water forces at the soil surface. Additional benefits for water erosion control result from high water infiltration rates and reduced surface runoff due to mulches.

A wind erosion equation has been developed which relates soil loss by wind to the: (1) soil erodibility index measured in terms of soil clods greater than 0.84 mm in diameter; (2) climatic factor measured in terms of wind velocity and surface soil moisture; (3) soil surface roughness; (4) unsheltered field width; and (5) vegetative cover (Woodruff & Siddoway, 1965). Based on the equation and some selected conditions for Kansas (U.S.A.), Woodruff (1972) has shown that 1100, 2200, and 6600 kg/ha standing wheat, flattened wheat, and flattened sorghum residues, respectively, were required to keep wind erosion to a tolerable 11.2 tons of soil loss per hectare annually. These results show the importance of standing stubble for wind erosion control. Also, the residues should be anchored in the soil to prevent them from being blown away by the wind.

The stubble-mulch farming system, widely used in North America, was developed primarily for wind erosion control. The value of stubble-mulch tillage for erosion control is widely recognized (Black & Power, 1965; McCalla & Army, 1961; Wiese et al., 1967; Zingg & Whitfield, 1957). In general, erosion by wind decreased as the amounts of crop residues maintained on the surface were increased by stubble-mulch tillage. Wind erosion was even more effectively controlled where higher amounts of residue were maintained on the surface by chemical fallow (Black & Power, 1965; Wiese et al., 1967).

Fryrear and Armbrust (1969) used a cotton gin trash mulch, a cotton ginning waste product, on a loamy fine sand to determine its effectiveness for wind erosion control. Each additional mulch increment further reduced erosion over the no-mulch treatment, but about 11.2 tons of mulch per hectare were required to reduce erosion to tolerable levels.

Standing stubble was more effective for wind erosion control than flattened stubble, but to shield against the erosive action of moving water, the mulch must oppose water flow at the soil-water interface. Hence, a maximum amount of the material should be in contact with the soil surface.

Numerous studies concerning the effectiveness of mulches for reducing water erosion have been conducted (Mannering & Meyer, 1961, 1963; Meyer et al., 1970; Taylor et al., 1964). In general, erosion was reduced as the amount of mulch was increased. However, if the mulch was not in adequate contact with the soil, erosion could occur under the mulch.

In recent years, no-tillage systems have received considerable attention. Crop residues are maintained on the surface, weeds are controlled with chemicals, and subsequent crops are seeded with no more soil disturbance than that necessary to place the seeds in the soil. Excellent control of erosion by wind and water has been obtained (Fowler, 1972; Harrold & Edwards, 1972; Harrold et al., 1967). For a rain storm having over a 100-year recurrence frequency, Harrold and Edwards (1972) reported the following:

Tillage	Slope (%)	Rain (cm)	Runoff (cm)	Sediment yield (kg/ha)
Ploughed, clean tilled, sloping rows	6.6	14.0	11.2	50,700
Ploughed, clean tilled, contour rows	5.8	14.0	5.8	7,200
No-tillage, contour rows	20.7	12.9	6.4	71

While this occurred in a more humid region (Ohio, U.S.A.), major reductions in erosion should be possible for dry regions where residue density at the soil-water interface is adequate.

Effects of Mulches on Plants

The effects of mulches on plants are operative through the effects of mulches on soil water, temperature, structure, salinity and erosion. Other factors mentioned in the introduction are also affected by mulches and have an effect on plants. However, those discussed are considered most important. Besides, little information is available concerning those factors not discussed as they relate to the effects of mulches on plants.

One of the most critical periods in the life cycle of a plant is the period of germination, emergence and seedling establishment. For germination to occur, viable seeds must be placed in a favourable environment with respect to water supply, temperature and aeration. After germination, the seedlings must emerge and become established. Due to their small size and tenderness, seedlings can easily be adversely affected by an unfavourable environment. Mulches can aid germination, emergence and seedling growth by moderating or improving the soil and aerial environment to which the seeds and seedlings are subjected.

Higher soil water contents and reduced evaporation were major reasons for improved germination, emergence and seedling growth due to mulches (Army *et al.*, 1961; Kowsar *et al.*, 1969; Mustafaev, 1964; Sale, 1966a, b; Takatori *et al.*, 1971; Unger, 1971b; Wann, 1969). Straw, petroleum, gravel, stones and plastic films increased germination and early growth, but the plastic films had to be slit or removed for continued growth.

Higher soil temperatures due to mulches also improved germination, emergence and seedling growth (Adams, 1962; Dhesi *et al.*, 1964; Miller & Bunger, 1963; Mustafaev, 1964; Sale, 1966a, b; Willis *et al.*, 1957). The higher temperatures, either alone or in combination with higher water contents, were also effective for promoting later plant growth and hastening plant maturity (Bowers, 1968; Linden, 1963; Miller, 1968; Miller & Bunger, 1963; Mustafaev, 1964; Sale, 1966a, b; Takatori *et al.*, 1964; Willis *et al.*, 1957). Early seeding of sweet corn, made possible by using a clear plastic mulch, resulted in the corn being ready for harvest 2 weeks before corn seeded in bare soil (Miller & Bunger, 1963).

Surface mats, which maintained a lower, more constant soil temperature than other materials after irrigation, were effective for improving early potato (*Solanum tuberosum* L.) growth (Dhesi *et al.*, 1964). In other cases, lower temperatures due to mulches reduced germination and early plant growth (Allmaras *et al.*, 1964; Burrows & Larson, 1962; Moody *et al.*, 1963; Van Wijk *et al.*, 1959). However, later growth sometimes was better on mulched than on bare soil due to improved water conditions under the mulch (Moody *et al.*, 1963).

A majority of the reports indicated higher yields when crops were grown with rather than without mulches, with most materials being effective for increasing yields (Adams, 1970; Austin, 1964; Bansal *et al.*, 1971; Baroccio & Morani, 1965; Baumer, 1964; Bowers, 1968; Carter & Fanning, 1965; Dixit & Agarwal, 1971; Evenson & Rumbaugh, 1972; Griffin *et al.*, 1966; Harrold *et al.*, 1959; Lehne, 1961; Linden, 1963; MacMillan & Millette, 1971; Moody *et al.*, 1963; Onchev, 1960; Puszta, 1963; Sale, 1966a, b; Taylor *et al.*, 1964; Willis *et al.*, 1963; Zakharov & Semikina, 1964). Although the yield increases generally were moderate, some very substantial increases were reported (Moody *et al.*, 1963; Pusztai, 1963;

Sale, 1966a; Zakharov & Semikina, 1964). These ranged from about 50 to 300 per cent.

Yield response due to mulches, although primarily related to soil water and temperature, was also affected by better plant populations (Sale, 1966a, b; Takatori *et al.*, 1971), reduced root rot (Lavee, 1963), and reduced soil salinity (Carter & Fanning, 1965; Heilman *et al.*, 1968). Undoubtedly, mulch effects on soil structure, nutrients, microbial activity, root distributions, etc., also played an important role in the higher yields.

Reduced crop yields due to mulches have been related to some specific condition, generally soil temperature. Corn apparently is very sensitive to low temperatures under a straw mulch early in the season when temperatures normally limit plant growth (Allmaras *et al.*, 1964; Burrows & Larson, 1962; Moody *et al.*, 1963; Van Wijk *et al.*, 1959). The adverse effects of low temperatures were reflected in lower yields in more northern regions (Allmaras *et al.*, 1964; Burrows & Larson, 1962; Van Wijk *et al.*, 1959), but were largely overcome in the more southern regions (Moody *et al.*, 1963; Van Wijk *et al.*, 1959). For a black tar mulch, corn yields were increased in Quebec (Canada), apparently due to higher soil temperatures (MacMillan & Millette, 1971). A straw mulch in Alberta (Canada), however, delayed maturity and reduced wheat yields due to lower soil temperatures and increased soil shading, and occasionally due to lower nitrate production (Anderson & Russell, 1964).

A gravel mulch in Texas (U.S.A.) reduced grain sorghum yields, but the yield reduction was not due to lower soil water contents or lower temperatures. Water was adequate and a straw mulch resulted in even lower temperatures than the gravel, but yields with straw were higher than with gravel. Plants on the gravel-mulch plots appeared nitrogen deficient, but the soil nitrogen content was not determined. Lower soil nitrate-nitrogen may have been a factor, but the quality and intensity of reflected radiation from the gravel may also have been factors contributing to the reduced yields (Adams, 1965). Apparent nitrogen-deficiency symptoms were also observed by Unger (1971b) for forage sorghum growing on gravel-mulched plots. The symptoms disappeared after ammonium nitrate fertilizer was applied.

Tillage systems that maintain high levels of crop residue on the soil surface have resulted in variable responses with respect to crop yields in the western United States. At drier locations, stubble-mulch tillage generally resulted in higher wheat yields than moldboard ploughing, while the opposite generally occurred at more humid locations. One-way tillage, which incorporated crop residues with soil, resulted in yields between stubble-mulch tillage and moldboard ploughing, regardless of which method resulted in the higher yields (Zingg & Whitfield, 1957). In Texas (U.S.A.), 27-year average grain yields for one-way and stubble-mulch tillage were 585 and 685 kg/ha, respectively, in a continuous wheat system, and 927 and 1055 kg/ha, respectively, in a wheat-fallow system (Johnson & Davis, 1972).

At the drier locations, wheat yield increases due to stubble-mulch tillage resulted from greater soil water contents at seeding (Johnson & Davis, 1972; Zingg & Whitfield, 1957). For a number of Great Plains (U.S.A.) locations, the average contributions to yield of a centimetre of stored water at seeding were 64.6 and 72.5 kg/ha for spring and winter wheat, respectively. These values were based on the assumption that management practices affect yields solely through their effects on soil water (Johnson, 1964). Yield reductions due to stubble-mulch tillage at more humid locations resulted from fertility, weed control and residue management problems (Zingg & Whitfield, 1957).

When weed control chemicals became available, chemical fallow systems were investigated at a number of locations. Although these systems maintained the available crop residues on the surface at higher levels than where tillage was used for weed control, and thus gave better protection against erosion, crop yields generally were not increased and frequently were decreased (Army *et al.*, 1961; Black & Power, 1965; Wiese & Army, 1958; Wiese *et al.*, 1960, 1967). Residue levels at the beginning of fallow apparently were too low to increase infiltration and reduce subsequent evaporation, especially in the southern Great Plains (U.S.A.). Hence, water storage was not increased. Poor water storage coupled with poor weed and volunteer crop plant control were major factors that contributed to the generally poor results with chemical fallow on dryland in the early studies.

With the introduction of suitable seeding equipment and more effective chemicals for weed and volunteer crop plant control, reduced and no-tillage cropping systems are gaining favour in the western United States. In the central Great Plains (U.S.A.), the use of chemical fallow for weed control resulted in greater water storage than where subsurface tillage was used for weed control. Chemical fallow also resulted in wheat and sorghum grain yields that were equal to or higher than those obtained with tillage (Smika & Wicks, 1968; Wicks & Smika, 1973). Residue production in the central to northern Great Plains apparently is adequate to increase infiltration and suppress evaporation. Also, standing wheat stubble is effective for increasing water storage during fallow through snow trapping.

In the southern Great Plains (U.S.A.), residue production by dryland crops often is lower than at more northern locations and water storage during fallow also is lower. However, irrigated crops (wheat and grain sorghum), which are grown on extensive areas of the southern Great Plains, produce large quantities of residues. These residues, when maintained as a mulch on the surface, resulted in increased water storage during fallow when weeds and volunteer crop plants were controlled with herbicides (Musick *et al.*, 1973; Unger *et al.*, 1971; Unger & Parker, 1974). The additional stored water was effective for reducing pre-plant or seasonal irrigations for subsequent irrigated crops (Musick *et al.*, 1973; Unger *et al.*, 1971) or for increasing yields of subsequent dryland crops (Unger & Parker, 1974).

Conclusions

Mulches have been used throughout much of the history of agriculture. Various mulching materials have been used and, where effective soil cover was afforded, substantial yield increases often occurred. The higher yields resulted from improved soil water and temperature regimes: improved soil structure; improved soil salinity and erosion control; and various other soil and plant environmental factors associated with the mulches.

With respect to dryland agriculture, the greatest benefits due to mulches undoubtedly resulted from increased soil water for plant growth. Relatively high crop yields were obtained where plastic films covered wet soil and the crops were grown on stored soil water. The films, however, prevented water entry, were rather expensive, and sometimes difficult to manage. Consequently, their use as mulches was generally restricted to high value crops on limited areas.

Crop residues have been widely used as mulches. These materials have conserved water for greater crop production when present at adequate levels. Under dryland conditions, residue production frequently was inadequate to substantially increase soil water. Hence, the primary reason for their use has been for erosion control. The stubble-mulch tillage systems have been used to maintain a major portion of the available residues on the soil surface.

In recent years, reduced and no-tillage cropping systems have been introduced wherein most or all tillage operations are eliminated and weeds and volunteer crop plants are controlled with chemicals. The residues are maintained on the surface as a mulch. Where residue levels and weed control were adequate, substantial increases in soil water were obtained and yields were often increased. At some locations, residues from irrigated crops have resulted in increased soil water storage, thus reducing irrigation water requirements for subsequent irrigated crops or increasing yields of subsequent dryland crops. The reduced tillage systems have given good protection against wind and water erosion.

252 P. W. UNGER

REFERENCES

ADAMS, J. E. 1962. Effect of soil temperature on grain sorghum growth and yield. Agron. J. 54: 257-61.

ADAMS, J. E. 1965. Effect of mulches on soil temperature and grain sorghum development. Agron. J. 57: 471-4.

ADAMS, J. E. 1966. Influences of mulches on runoff, erosion and soil moisture depletion. Soil Sci. Soc. Am. Proc. 30: 110-14.

ADAMS, J. E. 1970. Effect of mulches and bed configuration. II. Soil temperature and growth and yield responses of grain sorghum and corn. Agron. J. 62: 785-90.

ALLMARAS, R. R.; W. C. BURROWS and W. E. LARSON, 1964. Early growth of corn as affected by soil temperature. Soil Sci. Soc. Am. Proc. 28: 271-5.

ANDERSON, D. T. and G. C. RUSSELL, 1964. Effects of various quantities of straw mulch on the growth and yield of spring and winter wheat. Can. J. Soil Sci. 44: 109-18.

ARMY, T. J. and E. B. HUDSPETH, JR. 1960. Alteration of microclimate of the seed zone. Agron. J. 52: 17-22.

ARMY, T. J.; A. F. WIESE and R. J. HANKS, 1961. Effect of tillage and chemical weed control practices on soil moisture losses during the fallow period. Soil Sci. Soc. Am. Proc. 25: 410-13.

AUSTIN, R. B. 1964. Plastic mulches for outdoor tomato crops and a trial of varieties. Exp. Hort. No. 11, pp. 17-22.

BANSAL, S. P.; P. R. GAJRI and S. S. PRIHAR, 1971. Effect of mulches on water conservation, soil temperature and growth of maize (*Zea mays* L.) and pearl millet [*Pennisetum typhoides* (Burm. f.) Stapf and C. E. Hubb.]. Indian J. agr. Sci. 41: 467-73.

BAROCCIO, A. and V. MORANI, 1965. Trials on covering the soil surface with petroleum resins (black mulch). Ital. Agr. 102: 39-44.

BAUMER, M. 1964. Plastic mulch, nitrogen fixation and root development. Sudan J. Vet. Sci. & An. Husb. 5: 38-9.

BLACK, A. L. and J. F. POWER, 1965. Effect of chemical and mechanical fallow methods on moisture storage, wheat yields and soil erodibility. Soil Sci. Soc. Am. Proc. 29: 465-8.

BOND, J. J. and W. O. WILLIS, 1969. Soil water evaporation: Surface residue rate and placement effects. Soil Sci. Soc. Am. Proc. 33: 445-8.

BOND, J. J. and W. O. WILLIS, 1970. Soil water evaporation: First stage drying as influenced by surface residue and evaporation potential. Soil Sci. Soc. Am. Proc. 34: 924-8.

BOND, J. J. and W. O. WILLIS, 1971. Soil water evaporation: Long-term drying as influenced by surface residue and evaporation potential.

Soil Sci. Soc. Am. Proc. 35: 984-7.

BOWERS, S. A. 1968.   Influence of water mulches on soil temperatures and sweet corn and green bean production.   Soil Sci. 105: 335-45.

BRENGLE, K. G. and C. J. WHITFIELD, 1969.   Effect of soil temperature on the growth of spring wheat with and without wheat straw mulch. Agron. J. 61: 377-9.

BURROWS, W. C. and W. E. LARSON, 1962.   Effect of amount of mulch on soil temperature and early growth of corn.   Agron. J. 54: 19-23.

CARTER, D. L. and C. D. FANNING, 1965.   Cultural practices for grain sorghum production through a cotton bur mulch. J. Soil & Water Conserv. 20: 61-2.

COHEN, O. P.; L. SHANAN and M. EVENARI, 1965.   Effect of synthetic rubber crusts on soil temperatures.   Israel J. agric. Res. 15: 147-8.

DANCER, J. 1964.   The influence of soil moisture and temperature on the growth of apple trees.   I. Some observations on moisture and temperature conditions under grass, arable and mulch.   Hort. Res. 4: 3-13.

DHESI, N. S.; K. J. NANDPURI and A. SINGH, 1964.   Effect of mulching and irrigation on the soil temperature for potato culture.   Indian J. Agron. 9: 277-80.

DIXIT, S. P. and M. C. AGARWAL, 1971.   Effect of rubber solution mulch on moisture regime of soil and growth and yield of maize.   Indian J. agr. Res. 5: 74-8.

EVENSON, P. D. and M. D. RUMBAUGH, 1972.   Influence of mulch on postharvest soil temperatures and subsequent regrowth of alfalfa (*Medicago sativa* L.).   Agron. J. 64: 154-7.

FANNING, C. D. and D. L. CARTER, 1963.   The effectiveness of a cotton bur mulch and a ridge-furrow system in reclaiming saline soils by rainfall. Soil Sci. Soc. Am. Proc. 27: 703-6.

FOWLER, L. 1972.   Experience with no-tillage—Winrock Farms.   Proc. No-tillage Systems Symposium, Columbus, Ohio, pp. 108-12.

FRYREAR, D. W. and D. V. ARMBRUST, 1969.   Cotton gin trash for wind erosion control.   Texas Agr. Exp. Sta. Misc. Pub. No. 928.

GREB, B. W.; D. E. SMIKA and A. L. BLACK, 1967.   Effect of straw-mulch rates on soil water storage during summer fallow in the Great Plains. Soil Sci. Soc. Am. Proc. 31: 556-9.

GREB, B. W.; D. E. SMIKA and A. L. BLACK, 1970.   Water conservation with stubble-mulch fallow.   J. Soil & Water Conserv. 25: 58-62.

GRIFFIN, R. H., II; B. J. OTT and J. F. STONE, 1966.   Effect of water management and surface applied barriers on yields and moisture utilization of grain sorghum in the southern Great Plains.   Agron. J. 58: 449-52.

HANKS, R. J.; S. A. BOWERS and L. D. BARK, 1961.   Influence of soil surface conditions on net radiation, soil temperature and evaporation.

Soil Sci. 91: 233-8.

HANKS, R. J. and N. P. WOODRUFF, 1958. Influence of wind on water vapour transfer through soil, gravel and straw-mulches. Soil Sci. 86: 160-64.

HARRIS, W. W. 1963. Effects of residue management, rotations and nitrogen fertilizer on small grain production in north-western Kansas. Agron. J. 55: 281-4.

HARROLD, L. L. and W. M. Edwards, 1972. A severe rainstorm test of no-tilllage corn. J. Soil & Water Conserv. 27: 30.

HARROLD, L. L.; D. B. PETERS; F. R. DREIBELBIS and J. L. McGUINNES, 1959. Transpiration evaluation of corn grown on a plastic covered lysimeter. Soil Sci. Soc. Am. Proc. 23: 174-8.

HARROLD, L. L.; G. B. TRIPLETT, JR. and R. E. YOUKER, 1967. Watershed test of no-tillage corn. J. Soil & Water Conserv. 22: 98-100.

HEILMAN, M. D.; C. L. WIEGAND and C. L. GONZALEZ, 1968. Sand and cotton bur mulches, Bermuda grass sod and bare soil effects on: II. Salt leaching. Soil Sci. Soc. Am. Proc. 32: 280-83.

JACKS, G. V.; W. D. BRIND and R. SMITH, 1955. Mulching. Commonwealth Bur. Soil Sci. (England) Tech. Comm. No. 49.

JOHNSON, W. C. 1964. Some observations on the contribution of an inch of seeding-time soil moisture to wheat yield in the Great Plains. Agron. J. 53: 29-35.

JOHNSON, W. C. and R. G. DAVIS, 1972. Research on stubble-mulch farming of winter wheat. U.S. Dept. Agr. Conserv. Res. Rpt. No. 16.

JORDAN, D. and A. J. SAMPSON, 1967. Effect of bitumen mulching on soil conditions. J. Sci. Food & Agr. 18: 486-91.

KOHNKE, H. and C. H. WERKHOVEN, 1963. Soil temperature and soil freezing as affected by an organic mulch. Soil Sci. Soc. Am. Proc. 27: 13-7.

KOSHI, P. T. and D. W. FRYREAR, 1971. Effect of seed-bed configuration and cotton bur mulch on lint cotton yield, soil water and water use. Agron. J. 63: 817-22.

KOWSAR, A.; L. BOERSMA and G. D. JARMAN, 1969. Effects of petroleum mulch on soil water content and soil temperature. Soil Sci. Soc. Am. Proc. 33: 783-6.

LAVEE, S. 1963. The effect of mulch on the resistance of E. M. II. Apple stock to *Sclerotium rolfsii* (Sacc.). Proc. Am. Soc. hort. Sci. 82: 25-34.

LEHNE, I. 1961. Mulching of arable soil with organic material. Deutsche Landwirtschaft 12: 525-9.

LINDEN, R. 1963. Soil protection with plastic mulches. Ann. Gembl. 69: 601-8.

LIPPERT, L. F.; F. H. TAKATORI and F. J. WHITING, 1964. Soil moisture under bands of petroleum and polyethylene mulches. Proc. Am. Soc. hort. Sci. 85: 541-6.

LIPTAY, A. M. and H. TIESSEN, 1970. Influences of polyethylene-coated paper mulch on soil environment. J. Am. Soc. hort. Sci. 95: 395-8.

LYFORD, F. P. and H. K. QASHU, 1969. Infiltration rates as affected by desert vegetation. Water Resour. Res. 5: 1373-6.

MACMILLAN, K. A. and J. F. G. MILLETTE, 1971. Influence of mulch on soil temperature and corn yield. Can. J. Soil Sci. 51: 305-7.

MANESCU, B. and R. CIOFU, 1970. The influence of mulching with plastics on the thermal and water conditions of soil. Lucrari Stiintifice Institutul Agronomic N. Balcescu, Seria B, Horticultura 13: 63-72.

MANNERING, J. V. and L. D. MEYER, 1961. The effects of different methods of corn-stalk residue management on runoff and erosion as evaluated by simulated rainfall. Soil Sci. Soc. Am. Proc. 25: 506-10.

MANNERING, J. V. and L. D. MEYER, 1963. The effects of various rates of surface mulch on infiltration and erosion. Soil Sci. Soc. Am. Proc. 27: 84-6.

MATHEWS, O. R. and T. J. ARMY, 1960. Moisture storage on fallowed wheatland in the Great Plains. Soil Sci. Soc. Am. Proc. 24: 414-18.

MCCALLA, T. M. 1943. Influence of biological products on soil structure and infiltration. Soil. Sci. Soc. Am. Proc. 7: 209-14.

MCCALLA, T. M. and T. J. ARMY, 1961. Stubble-mulch farming. Adv. Agron. 13: 125-96.

MCCALLA, T. M.; T. J. ARMY and A. F. WIESE, 1962. Comparison of the effects of chemical and sweep tillage methods of summer fallow on some properties of Pullman silty clay loam. Agron. J. 54: 404-7.

MEYER, L. D.; W. H. WISCHMEIER and G. F. FOSTER, 1970. Mulch rates required for erosion control on steep slopes. Soil Sci. Soc. Am. Proc. 34: 928-31.

MILLER, D. E. 1968. Emergence and development of sweet corn as influenced by various soil mulches. Agron. J. 60: 369-71.

MILLER, D. E. and W. C. BUNGER, 1963. Use of plastic soil covers in sweet corn production. Agron. J. 55: 417-19.

MOODY, J. E.; J. N. JONES, JR. and J. H. LILLARD, 1963. Influence of straw-mulch on soil moisture, soil temperature and the growth of corn. Soil Sci. Soc. Am. Proc. 27: 700-3.

MUSICK, J. T.; A. F. WIESE and D. A. DUSEK, 1973. Evaluation of tillage and herbicides for grain sorghum residue management in an irrigated wheat-sorghum-fallow cropping sequence. Texas Agr. Exp. Sta. Prog. Rpt.

MUSTAFAEV, KH. M. 1964. A stone mulch for tree corps. Vestn. S.-kh. Nauki No. 10, pp. 88-92.

NERPIN, S. V. and S. M. PAKSHINA, 1965. Residues from the distillation of alcohols as effective preparations for decreasing physical evaporation from soil. Dokl. Vses. Akad. Sel.-khos. Nauk No. 10, pp. 4-7.

ONCHEV, N. G. 1960. The effect of mulching on the moisture content and heat regime of soil. Khidrologiya i Meteorologiya No. 4, pp. 43-52.

PETERS, D. B. 1960. Relative magnitude of evaporation and transpiration. Agron. J. 52: 536-8.

PRIHAR, S. S.; B. SINGH and B. S. SANDHU, 1968. Influence of soil and climatic environments on evaporation losses from mulches and unmulched pots. J. Res., Punjab Agr. Univ. 5: 320-8.

PUSZTAI, A. 1963. The effect of plastic mulch on the soil and plant. Agrokem. Talajt. 12: 351-60.

QASHU, H. K. and D. D. EVANS, 1967. Effect of black granular mulch on soil temperature, water content and crusting. Soil Sci. Soc. Am. Proc. 31: 429-35.

RAMIG, R. E. and A. P. MAZURAK, 1964. Wheat stubble management. I. Influence on some physical properties of a chernozem soil. Soil Sci. Soc. Am. Proc. 28: 554-7.

SALE, P. J. M. 1966a. Effect of petroleum mulch on seedling emergence, soil moisture and soil temperature. Exp. Hort. No. 14, pp. 43-52.

SALE, P. J. M. 1966b. Effect of a petroleum mulch on the marketable yields of some vegetable crops. Exp. Hort. No. 14, pp. 53-61.

SCHALES, F. D. 1964. A study of some physical and biological effects of various mulching materials when used with several vegetable crops. Diss. Abstr. 24: 3487.

SIDDOWAY, F. H. 1963. Effects of cropping and tillage methods on dry aggregate soil structure. Soil Sci. Soc. Am. Proc. 27: 452-4.

SMIKA, D. E. and G. A. WICKS, 1968. Soil water storage during fallow in the central Great Plains as influenced by tillage and herbicide treatments. Soil Sci. Soc. Am. Proc. 32: 591-5.

TAKATORI, F. H.; L. F. LIPPERT and J. M. LYONS, 1971. Petroleum mulch studies for row crops in California. Calif. agr. Exp. Sta. Bull. No. 849.

TAKATORI, F. H.; L. F. LIPPERT and F. L. WHITING, 1964. The effect of petroleum mulch and polyethylene films on soil temperature and plant growth. Proc. Am. Soc. hort. Sci. 85: 532-40.

TAYLOR, R. E.; O. E. HAYS; C. E. BAY and R. M. DIXON, 1964. Corn stover mulch for control of runoff and erosion on land planted to corn after corn. Soil Sci. Soc. Am. Proc. 28: 123-5.

THORNTHWAITE, C. W. 1931. The climates of north America according to a new classification. The Geogr. Rev. 21: 633-5.

TURELLE, J. W. and T. M. McCALLA, 1961. Photomicrographic study of soil aggregates and microorganisms as influenced by stubble-mulching and ploughing. Soil Sci. Soc. Am. Proc. 25: 487-90.

UNGER, P. W. 1969. Physical properties of Pullman silty clay loam as affected by dryland wheat management practices. Texas agr. Exp.

Sta. Misc. Pub. No. 933.

UNGER, P. W. 1971a. Soil profile gravel layers. I. Effect on water storage distribution, and evaporation. Soil Sci. Soc. Am. Proc. 35: 631-4.

UNGER, P. W. 1971b. Soil profile gravel layers. II. Effect on growth and water use by a hybrid forage sorghum. Soil Sci. Soc. Am. Proc. 35: 980-83.

UNGER, P. W. 1972. Dryland winter wheat and grain sorghum cropping systems—Northern High Plains of Texas. Texas agr. Exp. Sta. Bull. No. 1126.

UNGER, P. W.; R. R. ALLEN and A. F. WIESE, 1971. Tillage and herbicides for surface residue maintenance, weed control and water conservation. J. Soil & Water Conserv. 26: 147-50.

UNGER, P. W. and J. J. PARKER, 1974. No-tillage dryland grain sorghum after irrigated wheat with intervening fallow. Texas agr. Exp. Sta. Prog. Rpt. (in press).

UNITED STATES SALINITY LABORATORY STAFF, 1954. Diagnosis and improvement of saline and alkali soils. Richards, L. A. (ed), U.S. Dept. Agr. Handbook No. 60.

VAN WIJK, W. R.; W. E. LARSON and W. C. BURROWS, 1959. Soil temperature and the early growth of corn from mulched and unmulched soil. Soil Sci. Soc. Am. Proc. 23: 428-34.

WANN, S. S. 1969. Effect of cover crops and mulching on infiltration rates on sloping land. J. Agr. Ass. China No. 67, pp. 50-57.

WENDT, C. W. 1971. A study of the mechanisms and suppression of evaporation of water from soils. Texas A & M Univ., Water Resources Inst. Tech. Rpt. No. 33.

WICKS, G. A. and D. E. SMIKA, 1973. Chemical fallow in a winter wheat-fallow rotation. Weed Sci. 21: 97-102.

WIEGAND, C. L.; M. D. HEILMAN and W. A. SWANSON, 1968. Sand and cotton bur mulches, Bermuda grass sod and bare soil effects on: I. Evaporation suppression. Soil Sci. Soc. Am. Proc. 32: 276-80.

WIESE, A. F. and T. J. ARMY, 1958. Effect of tillage and chemical weed control practices on soil moisture storage and losses. Agron. J. 50: 465-8.

WIESE, A. F.; J. J. BOND and T. J. ARMY, 1960. Chemical fallow in dryland cropping sequences. Weeds 8: 284-90.

WIESE, A. F.; E. BURNETT and J. E. BOX, JR. 1967. Chemical fallow in dryland cropping sequences. Agron. J. 59: 175-7.

WILLIAMS, W. A. and L. D. DONEEN, 1960. Field infiltration studies with green manures and crop residues on irrigated soils. Soil Sci. Soc. Am. Proc. 24: 58-61.

WILLIS, W. O. 1962. Effect of partial surface covers on evaporation from soil. Soil Sci. Soc. Am. Proc. 26: 598-601.

WILLIS, W. O.; H. J. HAAS and J. S. ROBINS, 1963. Moisture conservation by surface or subsurface barriers and soil configuration under semiarid conditions. Soil Sci. Soc. Am. Proc. 27: 577-80.

WILLIS, W. O.; W. E. LARSON and D. KIRKHAM, 1957. Corn growth as affected by soil temperature and mulch. Agron. J. 49: 323-8.

WOODRUFF, N. P. 1972. Wind erosion as affected by reduced tillage systems. Proc. No-tillage Systems Symposium, Columbus, Ohio, pp. 5-20.

WOODRUFF, N. P. and F. H. SIDDOWAY, 1965. A wind erosion equation. Soil Sci. Soc. Am. Proc. 29: 602-8.

ZAKHAROV, N. G. and G. G. SEMIKINA, 1964. Investigation of the agro-physical effectiveness of mulching soil with a film of polyethylene. Dokl. Akad. S.-kh. Nauk No. 12, pp. 14-6.

ZINGG, A. W. and C. J. WHITFIELD, 1957. A summary of research experience with stubble-mulch farming in the western States. U. S. Dept. Agr. Tech. Bull. No. 1166.

Prof. James W. O'Leary

Prof. James W. O'Leary was born in 1938 in Painesville, Ohio. He received his B.S. and M.S. degrees from Ohio State University, with majors in Horticulture and Plant Physiology, respectively. His Ph.D. was earned at Duke University, where he specialized in plant-water relations under Professor P. J. Kramer. He has been at the University of Arizona since 1963, where he now is Professor of Biological Sciences and Plant Physiologist at the Environmental Research Laboratory. During that period he has spent time as a visiting assistant professor at Bowling Green State University.

Prof. O'Leary has been an invited speaker at international conferences and author of chapters in books on plant water relations, salinity and biophysical ecology. He also has published numerous research articles in journals on these topics as well. His more recent publications and current areas of major research interest are in controlled environment agriculture, especially the effects of humidity and carbon dioxide concentration of the atmosphere.

5. THE EFFECT OF HUMIDITY ON CROP PRODUCTION

JAMES W. O'LEARY
University of Arizona

Introduction

It is well-known how the moisture content of the atmosphere affects traspiration, but comparatively little is known about its effects on overall growth of plants. One of the reasons for this apparent scarcity of information is the difficulty in accurately measuring and controlling atmospheric moisture content in the crop environment. Much of the information relating transpiration and atmospheric moisture content has been obtained through the use of transparent leaf chambers within which the environment can be precisely controlled and monitored. This becomes considerably more difficult to do, however, when one moves from the short term study of a single leaf or plant to a long term study of a crop of plants. Nevertheless, attempts have been made to study the effect of atmospheric moisture content on overall plant growth, and this information will be reviewed before considering the specific ways in which various physiological processes are influenced by the moisture content of the air. Most of these studies have utilized relative humidity (RH) as the indicator of the atmospheric moisture content, and this expression will be maintained for the present purposes.

Another apparent reason for the scarcity of information is that little importance has been attached to the effect of atmospheric moisture content on plant growth. Thirty years ago, after one of the most thorough investigations of plant growth under controlled environmental conditions up to that time, Went (1944) concluded that relative humidity had no effect on growth of tomato plants. Several years later, Went (1957) still felt that, "relative humidity has only a minor effect on the growth of plants which have an adequate water supply." This view undoubtedly influenced other investigators since there was no mention of the effect of humidity on plant growth at the international symposium convened at the dedication of the Australian phytotron a decade ago, in which the main theme was the natural microclimatic environments of plants and the responses of plants to the environment (Evans, 1963). Cotter and Walker (1967) recently reviewed the literature on relative humidity and plant growth and concluded that, "there is, however, a lack of direct experimental information on the effect of relative humidity on the growth of plants." It is surprising to this author that such an attitude of little concern for the role of atmospheric humidity in controlling plant growth has prevailed for so long in view of the large part that plant water relations has played in the development and history of plant physiology.

Survey of Plant Responses to Humidity

Went (1944) compared growth of tomato plants at 45% and 75% RH and found no differences. However, Nightingale and Mitchell (1934) had found that tomato plants grew more rapidly at 95% RH than at 35% RH. Rather than being exceptional, this apparent lack of agreement among the results with tomato plants is characteristic of the experiences of others. For example, Nieman and Poulsen (1967) found vegetative growth of cotton less at 85-100% RH than at 30-40%, while Hoffman et al. (1971) found the growth to be 40% higher at 90% RH than it was at 25, 40, or 65% RH. Nieman and Poulsen (1967) also found that vegetative growth of bean (*Phaseolus vulgaris* L.) was less at 85-100% than at 30-40% RH, while O'Leary and Knecht (1971) found no differences at 30-40%, 70-75% and 95-100% RH. Prisco and O'Leary (1973), however, did find that vegetative growth of beans was enhanced by high humidity. Bean seed yield was found to be reduced at the lower humidities (Hoffman et al., 1971; O'Leary & Knecht, 1971). The quality of beans produced at the lower humidities is also less due to higher fibre content (Kaldy, 1966). McIntyre (1973) found that cotyledonary bud growth was also increased by increases in RH from 30% to 60% to 90%.

Other crops in which vegetative growth seems to be increased with increasing RH include corn (Pareek et al., 1969), beets (Hoffman & Rawlins, 1971), kale and sugar beets (Watson, 1964) and peanut (Fortanier, 1957).

Flowering and fruiting of peanut is also enhanced by higher RH (i.e. 90-95%) (Fortanier, 1957; Lee *et al.*, 1972). Crops in which growth seems to be reduced at higher humidities include sunflower (Winneberger, 1958), cacao (Sale, 1970) and tobacco (Michael *et al.*, 1969). Some crops have not shown a response to humidity, such as wheat (Watson, 1964), even though seed set in wheat is enhanced by low RH at low soil moisture stress levels (Campbell *et al.*, 1969).

There are several possible reasons for the apparent lack of uniformity among the results of such studies. Tromp and Oele (1972), for example, found that shoot growth of apple trees was considerably better at high relative humidity (75% day/100% night) than at low relative humidity (45-55% continuous) as long as nitrogen fertilization was adequate. When the nitrogen level in soil was low, there was no response to relative humidity. This emphasizes an important point in studying the response of plants to any environmental factor. Care must be taken to ensure that some other factor is not limiting growth. Similarly, Brouwer and DeWit (1969) found no difference in growth of *Phaseolus vulgaris* leaves at different relative humidities when root temperature was between 20 and 30 °C. However, when root temperature was either above or below this range, leaf growth was affected by relative humidity of the air. For example, at 15 °C root temperature, leaf growth was almost three times greater at 80% RH than at 65% RH, and at 35 °C root temperature, leaf growth at 80% RH was about double that at 65% RH. Much the same observation has been made by Watts (1972). Leaf extension in corn was about the same at 50% RH as at 100% over the range of root temperature from 15 to 25 °C. However, below this temperature range, leaf extension was better at 100% RH than at 50% RH, and above this temperature range, leaf extension was better at 50% RH. In this case, when root temperature was too low, root resistance to water uptake probably was limiting leaf extension through its effect on water status of the leaves. Therefore, reducing transpirational loss of water by maintaining relative humidity high was beneficial. When the root temperature (and the temperature of the water around the roots) was maintained high, the transport of this warm water to the leaves may have affected leaf cell temperature, and increasing transpirational cooling by maintaining the relative humidity lower may have been the reason for the better growth at 50% RH than at 100% RH.

In addition to effects on dry matter production in plants, there are morphological differences also associated with humidity. Stem length is greater, in general, at higher humidities (Went, 1944; Fortanier, 1957; Hughes, 1966; Sale, 1970). Leaf size also is affected. In cacao, leaves are smaller at higher RH (Sale, 1970), but leaf area increased with increasing RH in bean (O'Leary & Knecht, 1971), wheat, kale and sugar beet (Watson, 1964). The dry weight per unit leaf area increased with increasing RH in cacao, kale and sugar beet but decreased in bean.   In general, relative humidities that produced the best vegetative growth also resulted in most profuse flowering (Fortanier, 1957; Sale, 1970; Lee *et al.*, 1972).

In assessing the responses of plants to RH, especially to extreme high humidities, consideration must be given to differences among species and types of plants.   For example, plants that have evolved in tropical or naturally moist conditions should be expected to react differently to high humidity than plants that originated in drier climates.   This is well illustrated by the observation of Jensen (1972) in evaluating numerous tomato cultivars for use in green-houses where the humidity is maintained near saturation.   He found that those cultivars developed in hot, humid areas grew best in the high humidity green-houses.   Furthermore, the cultivars that did not originate from hot, humid areas exhibited growth anomalies in the high humidity, such as extended flower clusters and adventitious root production along the stem, while those originating in hot, humid areas had no such problems.   The main problem in studies reviewed here, however, may be in the use of relative humidity as the indicator of atmospheric moisture content.   This will be discussed in the following section.

Humidity and Transpiration

Obviously, the influence of atmospheric moisture content on plant growth is going to be exerted through its effect on plant-water relations. This primarily will result from the direct effect on transpiration, as shown in the following relationship,

$$\text{Transpiration} = \frac{e_{\text{leaf}} - e_{\text{air}}}{r_{\text{leaf}} + r_{\text{air}}} \tag{1}$$

where, e_{leaf} is the actual vapour pressure of the intercellular spaces of the leaf, e_{air}—the actual vapour pressure of the bulk air outside the leaf, r_{leaf}—the diffusional resistance of the leaf, and r_{air}—the diffusional resistance of the adjacent boundary layer of air.   The intercellular air space usually is assumed to be saturated, and the vapour pressure therein is taken to be the saturation vapour pressure at that temperature (i.e., the leaf temperature).   The vapour pressure of the bulk air is the *actual* vapour pressure of the air which is a direct indicator of the moisture content of the air. This vapour pressure is related to the saturation vapour pressure (e_s) at the same temperature by the following expression,

$$\text{Relative Humidity} = \frac{e}{e_s} \times 100. \tag{2}$$

Thus, as air temperature changes, the relative humidity changes, even though the actual moisture content of the air remains the same. Relative humidity, therefore, is meaningless in itself in consideration of transpiration. Vapour pressure deficit (VPD) which often is used also as an indicator of atmospheric moisture content likewise is not of much value in itself unless the leaf and air temperatures are identical. VPD is the difference between the saturation vapour pressure and the actual vapour pressure at the same temperature. If leaf and air temperatures are identical, the VPD of the air is the same as ($e_{leaf} - e_{air}$) which is the information really needed for consideration of the transpiration rate.

Under natural conditions, the vapour pressure may not significantly change during the course of a day, but the air temperature will. Thus, the relative humidity and vapour pressure deficit will change concomitant with the temperature change, even though the moisture content of the air remains the same. If leaf temperature increases, the vapour pressure inside the leaf changes (assuming the intercellular air space remains saturated, which probably is true most of the time), and this increases the vapour pressure gradient from leaf to air. The increase in transpiration from morning to afternoon, in other words, is due to the increase in leaf temperature, not the decrease in relative humidity or increase in VPD of the air. It is unfortunate that what little is known about the relationship between plant growth and atmospheric moisture content has been determined under conditions of continuous levels of RH rather than continuous vapour pressure. Comparison of results at similar relative humidities is dangerous unless the air temperatures are the same. Furthermore, the leaf temperatures should also be the same, but this probably rarely has been the case. Unfortunately, leaf temperature usually is not measured by investigators. As an example, consider two investigators studying the response of a plant in the same relative humidity conditions. They even assure that air temperature is the same. For discussion purposes, let the conditions be 25 °C and 80% RH, which corresponds to a vapour pressure of 25.34 millibars (mb). If in one case, the radiation is high and air flow across the leaf surface is low, the leaf temperature may be higher than air temperature, say 30 °C. This corresponds to a vapour pressure in the saturated intercellular air spaces of the leaf of 42.43 mb. However, if in the other case, the radiation is low, as it often is in controlled environment chambers, and air flow across the leaf surfaces is high, then leaf temperature may be several degrees below air temperature. If leaf temperature were 22 °C, for example, the vapour pressure inside the leaf would be 26.43 mb. Thus, in the first case, the vapour pressure gradient from leaf to outside air is 17.09 mb, while in the second case it is only 1.09 mb. The water status of the plants in those two cases could be drastically different even though the air temperature and relative humidity were the same. This emphasizes another important point in studies of effects of some environmental factor on plant growth. Other environmental variables must be carefully controlled, or at least well-monitored.

Transpiration and Leaf Growth

As pointed out in the previous section, humidity probably affects plant growth primarily through its influence on transpiration rate and consequently the water balance of leaves. This is because leaf growth depends not only on synthetic activities resulting from biochemical processes, but also upon the physical process of cell enlargement. The cell enlargement occurs as a result of turgor pressure (TP) developed within the cells. There is a minimum TP required for any cell enlargement to occur (Cleland, 1967; Boyer, 1968, 1970), and the rate of leaf enlargement is a function of the actual TP in the cells (Millar *et al.*, 1971). Thus, it is important that leaf TP be maintained above the critical TP necessary for cell enlargement to occur. This critical TP is different for different plants and it is well above the point where visible wilting is evident. This means that a plant that looks turgid and seems not to be suffering from water stress may in fact not necessarily be actively growing. Water stress, if this means a situation where the water status of a tissue is limiting its growth rate, is not something that can be visibly detected. Furthermore, to obtain high growth rates, the turgor pressure of the leaf cells must be greater than the minimum TP necessary for cell enlargement. Millar *et al.* (1971) found that leaf growth rate was 10 times higher at 3 bars TP than at 1 bar TP for onions. This corresponded to leaf water potential values of −2 and −5 bars, respectively. Chances are most plant leaves would not look much different within this water potential range, yet the growth rates can be so significantly different.

The greatest determinant of the TP value in a leaf probably is the transpiration rate. Even under conditions of high soil water potential, the transpiration rate can be significantly high enough that water absorption and transport to leaves is insufficient to maintain leaf turgor high, and leaf growth is correspondingly lowered (Millar & Gardner, 1972). Thus, it is not surprising that there is good correlation between vapour pressure of the air and leaf water potential (Elfving & Kaufmann, 1972; Elfving *et al.*, 1972) and between atmospheric moisture content and leaf growth. For example, at soil water potential of −10 bars, wheat leaf water potential was −18 bars at 80% RH and −24 bars at 50% RH (Yang & De Jong, 1972), and this difference was consistent over a wide range of soil water potentials. The importance of these relationships between humidity, transpiration, leaf turgor, and plant growth is amplified by the realization that there actually is a relatively narrow range of leaf water potentials (or turgor pressures) within which growth will occur. In soybeans, corn and sunflower, maximal leaf enlargement occurred at leaf water potentials of −1.5 to −2.5 bars and was nearly zero at leaf water potentials of only −4 or −5 bars (Boyer, 1970). These same relationships hold for crop yield also. For example, the range of leaf water potentials that corresponded to the difference between no yield and maximum yield was 13 bars for beets, 6 bars for radish and only 4 bars for onion (Hoffman & Rawlins, 1971). The importance of humidity in determining the leaf water potential and consequent growth response is emphasized by the observation that at a very high soil water potential (−0.4 bars) beet yield was 50% higher at 90% RH than at 45% RH (Hoffman & Rawlins, 1971).

Thus, the moisture content of the air becomes an important growth-limiting environmental parameter under many agricultural situations. When the radiant energy load on the crop is high and air temperature is high, the moisture content of the air can impose a considerable constraint upon the growth rate of the crop. This combination of high light, warm temperatures and low atmospheric moisture content is typical of many irrigated agricultural areas. The warm temperatures and high number of cloudless days in the south-western United States dictates that this must be an intensively cropped area, for example, in spite of the low incidence of rainfall. This means that considerable amounts of water must be used for surface irrigation, and this necessarily raises the cost of crop production. One of the greatest limits to the total productivity probably is the low atmospheric moisture content during a significant part of the growing season. The transpiration rate is so high, much of the time that leaf water potentials, and turgor pressure, are below the critical threshold for leaf growth enough of the time to significantly limit the total crop production. This effect is especially intensified when the cropped areas are interspersed with non-cropped areas, as is typical in many of the irrigated areas of the world. Under such conditions, the movement of hot, dry air from over the barren soil through the cropped area leads to an advective heating of the leaves and thereby increases the amount of heat dissipation that must be done by latent heat transfer or transpiration. The transpiration rate then must be high enough to not only balance the radiation load but also must compensate for the increased heat load due to advection. This is the well-known "oasis effect". Hanks et al. (1971) have observed this effect in wide-row sorghum crops adjacent to non-cropped areas in the Great Plains of the United States, for example. Crop growth in areas such as this is necessarily going to be maintained in spite of the large water consumption. However, productivity must be as high as possible. With the realization that the moisture content of the air in these areas is an important limiting factor to higher productivity, it becomes extremely important to examine ways and develop technology to modify or influence the humidity over and within cropped areas.

Humidity and Stomata

In their excellent review of stomatal physiology, Meidner and Mansfield (1968) categorically state that "although stomatal behaviour is very sensitive to the turgor relations of the plant, it is comparatively unaffected by changes in the relative humidity of the ambient air." In view of what we know about stomatal apertures as related to guard cell turgor pressure and the relationship of turgor pressure to transpiration rate as described above, this does not seem to be a justified conclusion. They apparently based their conclusion on one source of data (Wilson, 1948). However, there are sufficient examples in the literature now to justify negating that conclusion. As might be expected, stomatal aperture, in general, increases with increasing relative humidity of the air (Macklon & Weatherley, 1965; Otto & Daines, 1969; Raschke & Kuhl, 1969; Raschke, 1970; Aubert & Catsky, 1970; Lange *et al.*, 1971). The response of guard cell turgor, and thereby stomatal aperture to change in relative humidity is extremely rapid (e.g., Lange *et al.*, 1971), and the rate of transpiration changes correspondingly (Macklon & Weatherley, 1965; Aubert & Catsky, 1970). The advantage to the plant of having such a tight coupling between stomatal aperture and atmospheric moisture content is great. For example, Hoffman *et al.* (1971) found that transpiration rate in cotton at 25% RH was only double that at 90% RH, even though the vapour pressure gradient from leaf to air was about six times greater at the lower RH. This was due to reduced stomatal aperture at the lower RH. The leaf diffusion resistance was 8 sec cm^{-1} at 25% RH and 5 sec cm^{-1} at 90% RH. Similarly, Drake *et al.* (1970) found that transpiration did not increase proportionately with the increase in $\triangle e$ between 70% RH and 10% RH, which also was attributed to higher leaf diffusion resistance at the lower humidity. There are other examples in the literature that also support this conclusion. Whether the decreased turgor in the guard cells in response to lowering the atmospheric humidity is due to a water deficit incurred directly by the guard cells due to their own transpiration or is a response to a deficit incurred by the entire leaf is not clear. Lange *et al.* (1971) feel that the stomatal aperture changes quickly in response to increased transpiration by the guard cells themselves, and they consider this an important advantage because it would result in reduction of transpiration before the water potential of the other leaf cells drops. However, Raschke (1970) has demonstrated that stomatal aperture reacts extremely quickly to changes in water supply to other cells of the leaf, and it may be that all the cells of the leaf do in fact incur a water deficit regardless of where the primary site of origin may be. The range of water potentials involved may be so low, anyway, that it is not of significance. At least the changes may be so small that they are not measurable. The important point is that with increase in the evaporative demand of the air, plant control is exerted through reduction of stomatal aperture, thereby increasing the diffusion resistance of the leaf, *when* the delivery of water to the leaves becomes limiting. As long as water supply to the leaf is maintained favourably, transpiration will follow the change in vapour pressure gradient from leaf to air.

The advantage of this to the plant obviously is related to maintaining a favourable water balance. Macklon and Weatherley (1965), for example, found that even though changes in stomatal aperture led to changes in transpiration rate, the leaf water potential was unchanged. The advantage of maintaining the leaf water potential high is clear from the above discussion relating leaf expansion to leaf turgor and water potential. However, the consequence of reducing stomatal aperture to maintain leaf water potential high is an increased leaf diffusion resistance to CO_2, and photosynthesis thereby will be reduced. Thus, the major effect of low relative humidity in limiting crop yields may be through its effect on CO_2 uptake rather than through its effect on development of water stress.

Absorption of Atmospheric Moisture by Leaves

Since Biblical times, man has been interested in the possibility of absorption of atmospheric moisture by plant leaves, especially in arid areas of the world (Wallin, 1967). If the vapour pressure gradient in equation (1) above were reversed, i.e., e_{air} was greater than e_{leaf}, then it might be expected that water vapour would diffuse from the outside atmosphere into the leaf. The difficulty, however, is that the vapour pressure gradient rarely, if ever, would be in that direction. The intercellular air space within the leaf is saturated or nearly so, which means that the vapour pressure therein is the saturation vapour pressure for that temperature (i.e. the leaf temperature). Thus, even if the outside atmosphere is saturated, i.e., the RH is 100%, there would have to be a temperature gradient toward the leaf in order to have a vapour pressure gradient in that direction. This condition probably exists primarily at night in arid areas where outgoing radiation from leaves is high. Since the stomata of most crop plants typically are closed at that time, water vapour absorption by these plants does not seem too likely. However, if the leaf temperature is lower than air temperature and the humidity of the atmosphere is sufficiently high, water will condense on the leaf surface, and this liquid water then is potentially available for absorption by the leaves. Vaadia and Waisel (1963) have shown quite clearly, in fact, that atmospheric moisture is preferentially absorbed as liquid after condensation on the leaf surface rather than directly by vapour diffusion, even when the stomata were open. Furthermore, it seems clear that most water absorbed in this way is absorbed directly through the cuticle.

Condensation of moisture on leaves, or dew deposition, is a frequent occurrence in arid areas of the world, and there is an extensive literature on this subject. Most of this literature has been reviewed by Stone (1957) and Wallin (1967). In many areas of the world where rainfall is scant, there is significant dew formation. Since many arid areas of the world lie reasonably close to continental coasts or near larger bodies of water, the humidity of air blowing inland across these areas of little rainfall often is high enough to favour condensation of moisture out of the air. Wallin (1967) cites many examples of relatively high amounts of dew formation in various parts of the world. There are many different methods used to measure dewfall, however, and this makes it difficult to accurately assess the importance of these values. The agricultural significance of the condensed moisture is even more difficult to assess. It is difficult to imagine that much of the moisture which condenses on leaves ever finds its way down through the plant and even out into the soil, as some studies would suggest (Breazeale et al., 1950, 1951a, b). The time needed to completely reverse the water potential gradient in the plant probably is greater than overnight, so at sunrise when transpiration resumes, the water potential gradient is re-established from soil to atmosphere, and water movement within the plant again is in the direction from roots to leaves.

The most likely advantages to the plant from moisture condensed on leaves is through reduction of transpiration, and restoration of leaf cell turgor. Leaf growth is dependent upon a critical minimum turgor pressure (Boyer, 1968), and restoration of sufficient leaf turgor at night is dependent on the amount of stress developed during the day and the length of time it takes the plant to overcome the deficit incurred as a result of the daytime lag of absorption behind transpiration. If dew formation occurs, and moisture is absorbed by leaf cells directly through the leaf surface, restoration of leaf turgor is accelerated, and growth is thereby enhanced. Also, at sunrise when conditions for transpiration become favourable, there obviously is an advantage to the plant in having a film of water on the leaf surface to be evaporated first before cellular water is lost through transpiration. The delay in reduction of leaf cell turgor below the critical minimum each day may be of significant benefit toward total production of the crop. There is some feeling that this may not be a significant effect (Waggoner et al., 1969), but there has not been enough experimental work done yet to warrant any definitive conclusions at this time.

While investigators may disagree on the amount of benefit plants derive from dew, they agree that dew does benefit plants in the absence of other moisture sources (Wallin, 1967). In some areas, the annual dewfall may even exceed the annual rainfall. For example, in the Avdat agricultural area in the Negev desert, during the extreme drought year of 1962, the annual dewfall was 23.0 mm while the annual rainfall was only 18.1 mm (Evenari et al., 1964). There may be some decided benefit under conditions of low atmospheric humidity to light overhead sprinkling of crops prior to dawn. Research in this area would be worthwhile. For some crops, the problem of enhanced pathogen development in the free water on the leaf surface (Baier, 1966; Wallin, 1967) may outweigh the advantage of improving the water balance of the plant by artificially increasing the humidity of the atmosphere within the crop.

Humidity and Salinity

One of the major effects of excessive salinity in irrigation water is enhancement of the development of water stress in plants (O'Leary, 1970). As the salinity around plant roots increases, the plant responds by adjusting its osmotic pressure correspondingly (O'Leary, 1971). One of the consequences of this increased osmotic pressure, however, is a decrease in hydraulic conductivity or permeability of the roots to water. This means that the osmotically adjusted plant is more likely to incur a water stress because of the greater likelihood of transpiration rate exceeding the rate of water delivery to leaves. Thus, the evaporative demand of the air does not have to be as low to cause water stress in plants growing in saline conditions as it does in plants growing in non-saline conditions. It follows that more saline irrigation water can be tolerated in areas of higher humidity than in areas with relatively dry air. This conclusion is substantiated by work on bean, an extremely salt sensitive plant (Hoffman & Rawlins, 1970; Prisco & O'Leary, 1973), but with cotton, a relatively salt tolerant crop, humidity had no effect on the relationship between yield and salinity (Hoffman et al., 1971). In the halophyte, *Atriplex halimus*, high humidity did not relieve growth reductions due to increasing salinity either (Gale et al., 1970). Apparently, salt tolerance involves the ability by the plant to maintain water balance through regulation of stomatal aperture as well as tolerance to certain concentrations of various ions. In salt-sensitive plants, however, this ability is lacking, and the decreased water uptake under saline conditions (whether it be due to a decreased water potential gradient or decreased root permeability) is not mirrored by reduced transpiration, and water stress occurs. The water stress, of course, is masking the direct effects of salinity which limit the growth of all plants under saline conditions (O'Leary, 1971; Prisco & O'Leary, 1972), and humidity obviously does not affect these metabolic disruptions. Nevertheless, for use of saline irrigation water on those crops classed as salt-sensitive, high humidity is a desirable environmental condition (Gallatin et al., 1963).

High Humidity Effects

So far discussion has been concentrated on the growth-limiting and undesirable effects of atmospheric humidity being too low. However, there are some potentially harmful physiological effects of humidity being too high. One of these is heat damage. As humidity increases and transpiration thereby decreases, heat loss from leaves by conduction and convection becomes more important. The efficiency of conductive heat loss is highly dependent on the rate of air movement across the leaf surface. Thus, if high atmospheric humidity and little or no air movement through the crop occur simultaneously, the chances of leaves suffering heat damage are good. Kinbacher (1962) has clearly shown that heat damage in oats increases with increasing relative humidity, and this is because of the effect of relative humidity on transpiration rate from the plants. There apparently are varietal differences in the ability to tolerate high temperature and high humidity (Kinbacher, 1962). A close correlation between leaf temperature and atmospheric humidity also has been shown in soybeans (Carlson et al., 1972).

Another potential harmful effect of high humidity is related to damage from air pollution. Because of the greater stomatal aperture at higher humidities, plants are more severely damaged by atmospheric pollutants at high humidity. Otto and Daines (1969) found a close correlation between the ozone injury to bean plants and tobacco plants and the stomatal aperture, and both were correlated with relative humidity of the air. O'Gara (1956) also found the same relationships for SO_2 damage to several crops. In situations with harmful levels of atmospheric pollutants, a slight water stress seems to have important survival benefit (Ting & Dugger, 1971). If the atmospheric humidity is high, this could be achieved through control of the irrigation amounts and frequency. It must be remembered, however, that the price to be paid for reduced turgor and stomatal aperture is reduced growth, both from decreased cell turgor and decreased CO_2 uptake.

The reduction in transpiration at high humidities reduces the amount of mass flow of water up through the plant, and this might be expected to reduce mineral delivery to leaves. For example, Gale and Hagan (1966) said that "a very large reduction in transpiration may, under extreme circumstances, affect the plants' mineral balance". Several experiments have been conducted from which it is possible to extract some general conclusions. In general, there does not seem to be any serious reduction in total amount of salts transported to leaves, no matter how high the humidity may be (O'Leary & Knecht, 1972). However, there are suggestions that calcium transport may be reduced (Freeland, 1936; Nieman & Poulsen, 1967), and this would be important in plants such as tomato and apple in which physiological disorders of the fruit are related to reduced calcium content (Wiersum, 1966). Tromp and Oele (1972) did find less delivery of calcium to developing apple fruits at 75-100% RH than at 45-55% RH. O'Leary and Knecht (1972) did not find any significant reduction in calcium transport to bean leaves under high humidity, however, boron transport to leaves also has been found to be reduced at 95% RH (Michael *et al.*, 1969; Bowen, 1972).

In some plants, hormones such as gibberellins and cytokinins apparently are synthesized in the roots and transported to the leaves via the transpiration stream (Letham, 1967; Skene, 1967). Thus, it has been suggested that the reduced mass flow of water to leaves under high humidity might cause a decreased delivery of these hormones to the leaves (O'Leary & Knecht, 1971), and the consequences of such a decreased hormone delivery have been discussed by Itai and Vaadia (1968) and O'Leary (1971). The formation of adventitious roots on stems of plants grown at high humidity (Hughes, 1966; Jensen, 1972) and abnormal flower development at high humidity (Jensen, 1972) suggest that there may be hormonal imbalance brought about by reduced transport of hormones from roots to leaves under high atmospheric humidity. This, however, has not been demonstrated yet for any plant.

Crafts and Crisp (1971) have reviewed the literature relating the foliar absorption and translocation of exogenously applied materials to RH of the air. High RH greatly enhances the uptake and transport out of leaves of many different substances, from inorganic salts to growth regulators such as herbicides. This applies to a wide variety of plants. Rossi and Beauchamp (1971) also found more salts absorbed by soybean leaves from foliar application at 70% RH than at 25% RH. Conversely, it seems that translocation of photosynthate out of leaves is less at high RH. Ehara and Sekioka (1962) found that ^{14}C labelled sucrose applied to sweet potato leaves was translocated to roots at a much higher rate under 70% RH than at 100% RH. Nightingale and Mitchell (1934) found that more carbohydrate accumulated in leaves at high humidity, which could also indicate decreased translocation of photosynthate at high humidity. They also found that the increased carbohydrate accumulation led to formation of thicker cell walls. Sale (1970) also found greater dry weight per unit leaf area at high humidity which suggests more cell wall material also. There obviously is a lot more information needed on translocation of photosynthate at various humidities. An interesting interaction between photosynthate translocation and mineral translocation brought on by high humidity is suggested by Wiersum's (1966) observations in developing tomato and apple fruits. During the phase of most rapid growth of fruit, sugar is being translocated very rapidly to the fruit. Thus, there also is much water coming into the fruit via the phloem. If the RH of the atmosphere is high and transpirational water loss from the fruit is low, this may be more than enough water to fulfil the needs. Thus, xylem-water flow into the fruit may stop or even be reversed. Since calcium only apparently moves in the xylem, this would mean that calcium transport into the fruit is checked, and a calcium deficiency in the fruit results. This could explain why Tromp and Oele (1972) found less calcium delivery to developing apple fruits at high RH, for example, while O'Leary and Knecht (1972) found no decrease in calcium delivery to leaves at high RH.

Humidity and Water Use Efficiency

As predicted by the previous discussion, there is a close relationship between rate of transpiration or water consumption and ambient humidity as long as water supply to the leaves is non-limiting (Wallace & Stout, 1962; Slatyer & Bierhuizen, 1964; Chang, 1968). It might be expected, therefore, that the ratio of water consumed to dry matter produced (Transpiration Ratio, Relative Water Use, etc.) should decrease with increasing humidity, or the Water Use Efficiency of the crop should increase with increasing humidity. In general, that conclusion seems to hold. Bierhuizen and Slatyer (1965) found a linear relationship between the transpiration ratio for cotton and the atmospheric humidity. Furthermore, they used the data collected by Briggs and Shantz (1913) to demonstrate that the same relationship holds also for wheat, oats, barley, rye, peas, corn and potatoes, grown in different parts of the world. Under controlled environment conditions, O'Leary and Knecht (1971) found highly significant differences in the transpiration ratio for beans at different humidities, and the differences were due almost exclusively to differences in water consumption at the different humidities. In general, it can be concluded, therefore, that the efficiency of water use increases with the humidity of the air (Chang, 1968).

Conclusions and Suggestions

Considering all of the beneficial and harmful effects of high *vs* low atmospheric humidity, it seems quite clear that the desirable situation for crop growth is to have a reasonably high humidity. It is clear that leaf water status must be maintained high for maximum growth rates. Further, it is clear that the prime determinant of the leaf water status is the rate of transpiration which in turn is a function of the humidity of the air. The common practice in the past to maintain leaf water status favourable has been to provide water to the root system attempting to maintain water delivery to the leaves sufficient to keep up with the transpirational loss. It seems, however, that under conditions of low atmospheric humidity, these attempts may be insufficient regardless of the method of surface irrigation. Because of constraints at the root surface or within the plant itself, water transport to leaves may be unable to keep up with the high transpirational rate at the low ambient humidity and leaf water deficits result. Thus, it may be advantageous to try to reduce the transpiration rate by raising the ambient humidity. That is, rather than applying all of the water as surface irrigation, it may be wiser to apply some on the surface and some fraction of the total irrigation water via overhead sprinkling with the intent of reducing water loss directly from the plant. Overhead sprinkling has been used for this purpose in apple orchards (Unrath, 1972), and it raised the relative humidity from 62% to 70%. The additional cooling effect of the applied water also reduced fruit temperature by about 8 °F. This approach apparently has not been tried with field crops yet, but the justification exists for seriously considering it. As Hoffman and Rawlins (1971) found with beets, when the RH was 45% and the soil water potential was −0.4 bar, there was no way to improve yield by adding more water to the root system, but by increasing the RH to 90%, the yield was increased by 50%. Thus, it is strongly recommended that intensive research be directed toward modification of humidity within crop canopies as a means of improving yield. This will require investigation of means of adding moisture to the air, the best times to do so, on which crops, and in what particular environmental situations it will be economical to do so. This may not seem to be a profitable venture to some, I am sure, but I also am sure that the possibility of significantly increasing the CO_2 concentration in the open field seemed just as unlikely, or more so, to many people. However, this recently has been done with a cotton crop (Harper et $al.$, 1973) much to many peoples' surprise. The CO_2 concentration was maintained significantly higher than normal within and over a cotton field by releasing CO_2 into the air within the crop, and daily net photosynthesis increased by 35%. The potential benefits from adding moisture to the air within a crop seem even more promising.

REFERENCES

AUBERT, B. and J. CATSKY, 1970. The onset of photosynthetic CO_2 influx in banana leaf segments as related to stomatal diffusion resistance at different air humidities. Photosynthetica 4: 254-6.

BAIER, W. 1966. Studies on dew formation under semiarid conditions. Agric. Meteorol. 3: 103 12.

BIERHUIZEN, J. F. and R. O. SLATYER, 1965. Effect of atmospheric concentration of water vapour and CO_2 in determining transpiration—photosynthesis relationships of cotton leaves. Agric. Meteorol. 2: 259-70.

BOWEN, J. E. 1972. Effect of environmental factors on water utilization and boron accumulation and translocation in sugarcane. Plant & Cell Physiol. 13: 703-14.

BOYER, J. S. 1968. Relationship of water potential to growth of leaves. Pl. Physiol. 43: 1056-62.

BOYER, J. S. 1970. Leaf enlargement and metabolic rates in corn, soybean and sunflower at various leaf water potentials. Pl. Physiol. 46: 233-5.

BREAZEALE, E. L.; W. T. McGEORGE and J. F. BREAZEALE, 1950. Moisture absorption by plants from an atmosphere of high humidity. Pl. Physiol. 25: 413-20.

BREAZEALE, E. L.; W. T. McGEORGE and J. F. BREAZEALE, 1951a. Movement of water vapour in soils. Soil Sci. 71: 181-5.

BREAZEALE, E. L.; W. T. McGEORGE and J. F. BREAZEALE, 1951b. Water absorption and transpiration by leaves. Soil Sci. 72: 239-44.

BRIGGS, L. J. and H. L. SHANTZ, 1913. The water requirements of plants. 1. Investigations in the Great Plains. 2. A review of literature. U.S.D.A. Bureau Plant Industry Bull. 284: 1-48; 285: 1-96.

BROUWER, R. and C. T. DEWIT, 1969. A simulation model of plant growth with special attention to root growth and its consequences, pp. 224-44. In: Root Growth, Whittington, W. J. (ed), Plenum Press, New York, p. 450.

CAMPBELL, C. A.; D. S. McBEAN and D. G. GREEN, 1969. Influence of moisture stress, relative humidity and oxygen diffusion rate on seed-set and yield of wheat. Can. J. Pl. Sci. 49: 29-37.

CARLSON, R. E.; D. N. YARGER and R. H. SHAW, 1972. Environmental influences on the leaf temperatures of two soybean varieties grown under controlled irrigation. Agron. J. 64: 224-9.

CHANG, JEN-HU, 1968. Climate and Agriculture. Aldine Publishing Co. Chicago, p. 304.

CLELAND, R. 1967. A dual role of turgor pressure in auxin-induced cell elongation in Avena coleoptiles. Planta 77: 182-91.

COTTER, D. J. and J. N. WALKER, 1967. Occurrence and biological effect of humidity in green-houses. Proc. 17 Int. Hort. Cong. 3: 353-68.

CRAFTS, A. S. and C. E. CRISP, 1971. Phloem Transport in Plants. W. H. Freeman & Co., San Francisco, p. 481.

DRAKE, B. G.; K. RASCHKE and F. B. SALISBURY, 1970. Temperature and transpiration resistances of Xanthium leaves as affected by air temperature, humidity and wind speed. Pl. Physiol. 46: 324-30.

EHARA, K. and H. SEKIOKA, 1962. Effect of atmospheric humidity and soil moisture on the translocation of sucrose-^{14}C in the sweet potato plant. Proc. Crop Sci. Soc. Japan 31: 41-4.

ELFVING, D. C. and M. R. KAUFMANN, 1972. Diurnal and seasonal effects of environment on plant water relations and fruit diameter of citrus. J. Am. Soc. hort. Sci. 97: 566-70.

ELFVING, D. C.; M. R. KAUFMANN and A. E. HALL, 1972. Interpreting leaf water potential measurements with a model of the soil-plant-atmosphere continuum. Pl. Physiol. 27: 161-8.

EVANS, L. T. 1963. Environmental Control of Plant Growth. Acad. Press, New York, p. 449.

EVENARI, M.; L. SHANAN and N. H. TADMOR, 1964. Runoff-farming in the Negev Desert of Israel. Second Progress Report. Avdat and Shivta Farm Projects, 1962/63 Season. National and Univ. Inst. of Agric., Rehovat.

FORTANIER, E. J. 1957. De Beinvloeding van de Bloei By *Arachis hypogaea* L. Meded. Land. Wageningen 57: 1-116.

FREELAND, R. O. 1936. Effect of transpiration upon the absorption and distribution of mineral salts. Am. J. Bot. 23: 355-62.

GALE, J. and R. M. HAGAN, 1966. Plant antitranspirants. Ann. Rev. Pl. Physiol. 17: 269-82.

GALE, J.; R. NAAMAN and A. POLJAKOFF-MAYBER, 1970. Growth of *Atriplex halimus* L. in sodium chloride salinated culture solutions as affected by the relative humidity of the air. Aust. J. biol. Sci. 23: 947-52.

GALLATIN, M. H.; J. LUNIN and A. R. BATCHELDER, 1963. Brackish water irrigation of several vegetable crops in humid regions. Agron. J. 55: 383-6.

HANKS, R. J.; L. H. ALLEN and H. R. GARDNER, 1971. Advection and evapotranspiration of wide-row sorghum in the central Great Plains. Agron. J. 63: 520-27.

HARPER, L. A.; D. N. BAKER; J. E. BOX, JR. and J. D. HESKETH, 1973. Carbon dioxide and the photosynthesis of field crops: a metered carbon dioxide release in cotton under field conditions. Agron. J. 65: 7-11.

HOFFMAN, G. J. and S. L. RAWLINS, 1970. Design and performance of sunlit climate chambers. Trans. Am. Soc. agric. Eng. 13: 656-60.

HOFFMAN, G. J. and S. L. RAWLINS, 1971. Growth and water potential of root crips as influenced by salinity and relative humidity. Agron. J. 63: 877-80.

HOFFMAN, G. J.; S. L. RAWLINS; M. J. GARBER and E. M. CULLEN, 1971. Water relations and growth of cotton as influenced by salinity and relative humidity. Agron. J. 63: 822-6.

HUGHES, A. P. 1966. The importance of light compared with other factors affecting plant growth, pp. 121-46. *In*: Light as an Ecological Factor, Bainbridge, R.; G. C. Evans and O. Rackham (eds), Wiley, New York, p. 452.

ITAI, C. and Y. VAADIA, 1968. The role of root cytokinesis during water and salinity stress. Israel J. Bot. 17: 187-95.

JENSEN, M. H. 1972. The use of waste heat in agriculture, pp. 21-38. *In*: Waste Heat Utilization: Proceedings of the National Conference. Oak Ridge Nat. Lab.

KALDY, M. K. 1966. Fibre content of green snap beans as influenced by variety and environment. Proc. Am. Soc. hort. Sci. 89: 361-7.

KINBACHER, E. J. 1962. Effect of relative humidity on the high temperature resistance of winter oats. Crop Sci. 2: 437-40.

LANGE, O. L.; R. LOSCH; E. D. SCHULZE and L. KAPPEN, 1971. Responses of stomata to changes in humidity. Planta 100: 76-86.

LEE, T. A.; D. L. KETRING and R. D. POWELL, 1972. Flowering and growth response of peanut plants (*Arachis hypogaea* L. var. Starr) at two levels of relative humidity. Pl. Physiol. 49: 190-93.

LETHAM, D. S. 1967. Chemistry and physiology of kinetin-like compounds. Ann. Rev. Pl. Physiol. 18: 349-64.

MACKLON, A. E. S. and P. E. WEATHERLEY, 1965. Controlled environment studies of the nature and origins of water deficits in plants. New Phytol. 64: 414-27.

McINTYRE, G. I. 1973. Environmental control of apical dominance in *Phaseolus vulgaris*. Can. J. Bot. 51: 293-9.

MEIDNER, H. and T. A. MANSFIELD, 1968. Physiology of Stomata. Mc-Graw-Hill Book Co., New York, p. 179.

MICHAEL, G.; E. WILBERG and K. KOUHSIAHI-TORK, 1969. Durch hohe Luftfeuchtigkeit indrezierter Bormangel. Zeit. fur Pflanz. und Boden-kunde 122: 1-3.

MILLAR, A. A. and W. R. GARDNER, 1972. Effect of the soil and plant water potentials on the dry matter production of snap beans. Agron. J. 64: 559-62.

MILLAR, A. A.; W. R. GARDNER and S. M. GOLTZ, 1971. Internal water status and water transport in seed onion plants. Agron. J. 63: 779-84.

NIEMAN, R. H. and L. L. POULSEN, 1967. Interactive effects of salinity and atmospheric humidity on the growth of bean and cotton plants. Bot. Gaz. 128: 69-73.

NIGHTINGALE, G. T. and J. W. MITCHELL, 1934. Effects of humidity on metabolism in tomato and apple. Pl. Physiol. 9: 217-36.

O'GARA, R. 1956. Air pollution handbook. Section 9, 2, 4. McGraw-Hill Book Co., New York.

O'LEARY, J. W. 1970. The influence of ground water salinity on plant growth, pp. 57-63. *In*: Saline Water, Mattox, R. B. (ed), Texas Tech. Press.

O'LEARY, J. W. 1971. Physiological basis for plant growth inhibition due to salinity, pp. 331-6. *In*: Food, Fibre and the Arid Lands, McGinnies, W. G.; B. J. Goldman and P. Paylore (eds), Univ. of Ariz. Press, Tucson.

O'LEARY, J. W. 1973. Development and reversal of plant responses to salinity and water stress. *In*: Plant Morphogenesis as a Basis for Management of Rangeland Resources. U.S.D.A. Washington, D.C. (in press).

O'Leary, J. W. and G. N. Knecht, 1971. The effect of relative humidity on growth, yield and water consumption of bean plants. J. Am. Soc. hort. Sci. 96: 263-5.

O'Leary, J. W. and G. N. Knecht, 1972. Salt uptake in plants grown at constant high relative humidity. J. Ariz. Acad. Sci. 7: 125-8.

Otto, H. W. and R. H. Daines, 1969. Plant injury by air pollutants: influence of humidity on stomatal apertures and plant response to ozone. Science 263: 1209-10.

Pareek, O. P.; T. Sivanayagam and W. Heydecker, 1969. Relative humidity: a major factor in crop plant growth. Univ. of Nottingham School of Agriculture Report 1968-69: 92-5.

Prisco, J. T. and J. W. O'Leary, 1972. Enhancement of intact bean leaf senescence by NaCl salinity. Pl. Physiol. 27: 95-100.

Prisco, J. T. and J. W. O'Leary, 1973. The effects of humidity and cytokinin on growth and water relations of salt stressed bean plants. Plant & Soil (in press).

Rackham, O. 1966. Radiation, transpiration and growth in a woodland annual, pp. 167-185. In: Light as an Ecological Factor, Bainbridge,R.; G. C. Evans and O. Rackham (eds), Wiley, New York, p. 452.

Raschke, K. 1970. Leaf hydraulic system: rapid epidermal and stomatal responses to changes in water supply. Science 167: 189-91.

Raschke, K. and U. Kuhl, 1969. Stomatal responses to changes in atmospheric humidity and water supply. Experiments with leaf sections of Zea $mays$ in CO_2-free air. Planta 87: 36-48.

Rossi, N. and E. G. Beauchamp, 1971. Influence of relative humidity and associated anion on the absorption of Mn and Zn by soybean leaves. Agron. J. 63: 860-63.

Sale, P. J. M. 1970. Growth and flowering of cacao under controlled atmospheric relative humidities. J. hort. Sci. 45: 119-32.

Skene, K. G. M. 1967. Gibberellin-like substances in root exudate of $Vitis$ $vinifera$. Planta 74: 250-62.

Slatyer, R. O. and J. F. Bierhuizen, 1964. Transpiration from cotton leaves under a range of environmental conditions in relation to internal and external diffusive resistances. Aust. J. biol. Sci. 17: 115-30.

Stone, E. C. 1957. Dew as an ecological factor. I. A review of the literature. Ecology 38: 407-13.

Ting, I. P. and W. M. Dugger, 1971. Ozone resistance in tobacco plants: a possible relationship to water balance. Atmospheric Environ. 5: 147-50.

Tromp, J. and J. Oele, 1972. Shoot growth and mineral composition of leaves and fruits of apple as affected by relative air humidity. Pl. Physiol. 27: 253-8.

Unrath, C. R. 1972. The evaporative cooling effects of over-tree sprinkler irrigation on 'Red Delicious' apples. J. Am. Soc. hort. Sci. 97: 55-8.

VAADIA, Y. and Y. WAISEL, 1963. Water absorption by the aerial organs of plants. Pl. Physiol. 16: 43-51.

WAGGONER, P. E.; J. E. BEGG and N. C. TURNER, 1969. Evaporation of dew. Agric. Meteorol. 6: 227-30.

WALLACE, A. M. and N. B. STOUT, 1962. Transpiration rates under controlled environment: species, humidity and available water as variables. Ohio J. Sci. 62: 18-26.

WALLIN, J. R. 1967. Agrometeorological aspects of dew. Agric. Meteorol. 4: 85-102.

WATSON, D. J. 1964. Rothamsted Expt. Station Report for 1963: 78-9.

WATTS, W. R. 1972. Leaf extension in *Zea mays*. II. Leaf extension in response to independent variation of the temperature of the apical meristem, of the air around the leaves and of the root zone. J. exp. Bot. 23: 713-21.

WENT, F. W. 1944. Plant growth under controlled conditions. II. Thermoperiodicity in growth and fruiting of the tomato. Am. J. Bot. 31: 135-50.

WENT, F. W. 1957. The Experimental Control of Plant Growth. Ronald Press Co., New York, p. 342.

WIERSUM, L. K. 1966. Calcium content of fruits and storage tissues in relation to the mode of water supply. Acta. Bot. Neerl. 15: 406-18.

WILSON, C. C. 1948. The effect of some environmental factors on the movement of guard cells. Pl. Physiol. 23: 5-37.

WINNEBERGER, J. H. 1958. Transpiration as a requirement for growth of land plants. Pl. Physiol. 11: 56-61.

YANG, S. J. and E. DE JONG, 1972. Effect of aerial environment and soil water potential on the transpiration and energy status of water in wheat plants. Agron. J. 64: 574-8.

Dr. J. W. Sturrock

After obtaining B.Sc. in Agriculture at the University of Edinburgh in 1953, Dr. Sturrock obtained first class Postgraduate honours the following year, before reading for the Diploma in Agriculture at the University of Cambridge. He then returned to Edinburgh to undertake biochemical research into aspects of culinary quality in cultivars of the potato, becoming a Senior Carnegie Trust Research Scholar. After obtaining Ph.D. in 1959, Dr. Sturrock joined the Biochemistry Department of Rothamsted Experimental Station and was a member of a team engaged in the exploitation of leaf protein as a source of protein in human nutrition. In 1966, Dr. Sturrock took up his present position with the Crop Research Division of the New Zealand, DSIR. As a leader of a newly established section within the Division, he initiated studies into the effect of wind on crop plants and means of mitigating the adverse influences of wind. In 1971, he spent some weeks at the Long Ashton Research Station, University of Bristol, working on the effect of windbreaks on features of the orchard microclimate.

6. WIND EFFECTS AND THEIR AMELIORATION IN CROP PRODUCTION

J. W. STURROCK
Crop Research Division
Department of Scientific and
Industrial Research
Lincoln, New Zealand

Introduction

Wind affects plants in several ways. It affects the exchange processes between plants and the atmosphere, thereby influencing the heat and water balances; it exerts mechanical effects leading to breakage of plant parts; and it alters enzyme activities through metabolic changes arising from wind-induced water stress or from injury inflicted by wind-eroded soil particles.

These changes are at once profound and complex. Long exposure to strong winds may produce morphological and anatomical changes. Whitehead and Luti (1962) and Whitehead (1962, 1963a, b) working with several species including maize and sunflower, showed that strong wind promotes the development of xerophytic characters, with production of thicker leaves, development of more woody and vascular tissue, changes in number and size of stomata and increases in root : shoot ratios. Plants may therefore, given time, "adapt" to windy situations, but recent theoretical and experimental work—to be described—based on the energy relationships of the transpiring leaf has shown that transpiration does not necessarily increase with increasing wind speed.

Although the main benefit from reduction in wind exposure arises from improved water balance, the "shelter effect" is more complicated because the reduction in wind affects most of the parameters determining the shelter microclimate. Moreover, the shelter microclimate is subject to continual alteration depending on the prevailing weather, windbreak efficiency and changes wrought by growth of the shelter crop itself (Fig. 6.1). Hence, the terminal yield of a sheltered crop represents a complex integration of numerous interacting factors that have operated from sowing until harvest. For this reason, the interpretation of crop reaction to shelter has usually had to be inferred from the known response of plants to variation of individual environmental parameters, under carefully controlled experimental conditions.

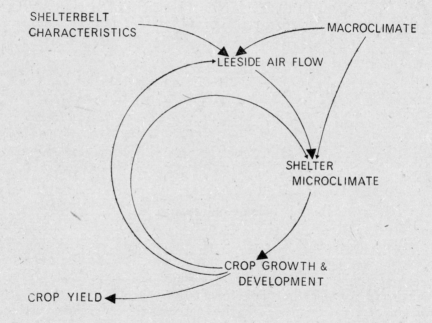

FIG. 6.1. Scheme representing the interrelationships of major factors influencing shelter responses. Detailed investigations of these relationships may quantify the effect of shelter on crop yield.

Fig. 6.1 presents the interrelations of broad groups of factors. Omitted from the diagram are insect pests and diseases whose severity may, in certain situations, be exacerbated by the microclimate formed by the shelter and thereby affect crop production. Progress towards quantifying and hence predicting the effect of shelter on crop yields consists of linking together the major factors shown in Fig. 6.1. Thus wind tunnel experiments and field tests using artificial windbreaks have begun to link the nature of the approaching wind and windbreak characteristics to the features of the lee-ward flow.   Also, more detailed work on the relation between leeward flow and the induced microclimate has commenced.   A beginning, too, has been made in the study of the complex relation between shelter microclimate and the crop itself.

In this chapter some of the recent work is described, with an outline of practical measures that can be taken to improve tolerance to wind.

Air Flow and the Nature of the Shelter-belt

The main factors affecting air flow in shelter are the height, length, shape, orientation and porosity of the barrier, and the turbulence of the approach wind, its angle of attack, and the roughness of the surface over which it blows.

Much work has been devoted to the question of barrier porosity. A dense barrier with little porosity deflects most of the approaching air over the top, to descend further out and mix turbulently with the underlying air. In extreme cases part of the flow may be reversed; a large eddy forms that flows back to the barrier because of a drop in leeside pressure. This mechanically-induced turbulence is manifestly undesirable. Further, barriers of low porosity cause speed to be more quickly restored than barriers with greater porosity, so shortening the shelter zone.   On the other hand, an open type of windbreak prevents the development of significant turbulence but in this case shelter protection is sacrificed.   The importance of porosity to leeside speed recovery is shown in Fig. 6.2.   The essential aerodynamic problem is to find the best compromise between porosity and leeside flow

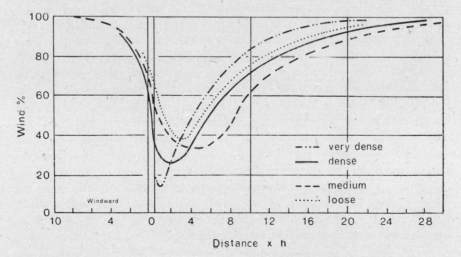

FIG. 6.2.   Wind speed reductions by belts of different porosity (after Nägeli, 1946).

in terms of minimum turbulence and maximum area of usefully reduced wind speed.

Tests of artificial barriers have shown that the best porosity is 40-50%, the gaps being evenly distributed.   In Fig. 6.2 the "medium" density conforms to this porosity.

The turbulence of the approach wind considerably modifies the leeside flow pattern.   An air layer flowing over a roughened surface becomes turbulent.   In addition, heating of the lower layers causes thermal mixing, and warmed air may be further displaced by buoyancy forces.   This mixing of air under unstable atmospheric conditions ensures quicker speed restoration of underlying layers that have been checked by an obstacle such as a windbreak than occurs in stable conditions.   In a stable layer of air the temperature gradient is negligible or inverted, and the air shows little tendency to rise and mix with faster-moving air above; hence restoration of speed is delayed and the shelter zone extended.

The extent of the differences in protection that arise from the thermal stratification of air was shown by Smalko, cited by Van Eimern (1968). Behind a dense shelter-belt of height h, 90% of open wind speed was reached at a horizontal distance of 14-15h with a superadiabatic lapse rate; at 22h in isothermal stratification; and at 44h with an inversion.   Van Eimern recommended that measurements of wind profiles in the vicinity of shelterbelts should cover representative differences in air mass thermal stratification.

For a given level of turbulence in the approach wind, the relative reduction of wind speed, $100(1-U_1/U_w)$, where U_1 is wind speed at a given leeward position and U_w is the average speed of the incident flow, measured predominantly in the horizontal plane, is independent of incident wind speed up to speeds at which significant movement of branches and leaves changes the porosity of the shelter-belt.   Nägeli (1965) and Brown and Rosenberg (1972) have, however, shown that a lower speed limit also exists; below wind speeds of about 1.2 to 1.5 metres per second, shelter becomes less effective.

Between these limits the wind-reducing ability of shelter-belts can be compared under different absolute wind speeds.   However, in view of the influence of prevailing turbulence level on leeside flow, valid comparisons can only be made by measuring or estimating atmosphere stability.   Moreover, most leeside measurements rely on conventional anemometers and since these cannot measure flow that is markedly divergent from horizontal, some ambiguity arises regarding the value of the indicated speed reductions, particularly behind the denser kinds of barrier.   Studies recently initiated, using sophisticated equipment, will yield more details of leeside flow. Knowledge of turbulence levels is required to interpret shelter-belt effects, particularly regarding microclimatic influences on crop growth.

The extent of leeward protection is directly proportional to height. A system of parallel belts, however, fails to produce a cumulative breaking of the wind because of diffusion of momentum from the deflected flow. Nägeli (1965) showed that it was possible for turbulence produced by the first barrier to increase velocity between the second and third barriers (Fig. 6.3).

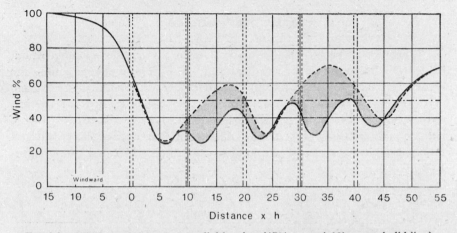

FIG. 6.3.   Wind speeds between parallel barriers (47% porous) 10h apart (solid line) and after removal of alternate barriers from the system (dashed line), with wind normal to the barriers (after Nägeli, 1965).

Under neutral conditions of stability and with wind at 90° to the barrier, a medium-porous shelter-belt effects a mean reduction in horizontal speed out to 30h of about one-third. With less porous belts the mean speed reduction is less (Fig. 6.2).

It is obviously important to orientate shelter-belts across the prevailing wind. With oblique winds the area of shelter behind medium porous belts is reduced in geometric proportion to the angle of the wind. With dense belts there is relatively greater reduction in the shelter zone with increasing obliqueness of wind direction, and correspondingly lesser reduction than geometrically predicted with very open belts (Van Eimern, 1968). These effects arise because changes in wind angle alter the effective porosity and hence the size of the protected zone (cf. Fig. 6.2). Nägeli (1965) found that average speed reductions over the lee area extending to 25h from a medium porous barrier were 46, 37, 19 and 5% with wind directions of 90°, 65°, 40° and 15° respectively in relation to the barrier. Shelter-belts of good length however, effectively reduce oblique winds provided the angles are not too great; long belts also protect more land and reduce to a minimum the effects from wind blowing around the ends.

The former tendency in the United States and Russia to use elaborate, multi-row plantings of trees and shrubs often produced shelter-belts that were excessively dense. In general, more efficient use of land and better air flow characteristics are achieved by narrow, straight sided belts. Barriers which in cross-section are an inverted "V" are aerodynamically unsound, since they deflect too much air over the barrier and prevent adequate filtering of wind through the trees.

Shelter Microclimate

Turbulence, because of its importance to the transfer of momentum, heat, water vapour and carbon dioxide, plays a dominant role among the features of microclimate. Except behind dense windbreaks, where strong vertical flow may increase exchange rates, well-designed wind barriers reduce turbulent transport. As a consequence there occurs reduced loss of heat by upward dissipation or consumption in evaporation, increased daytime temperatures and reduced night temperatures, increased vapour pres-

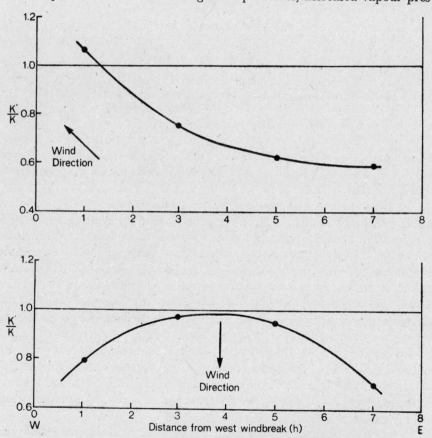

Fig. 6.4. Ratio of exchange coefficients in shelter (K') and in the open (K) as a function of wind direction and distance from two-row corn windbreaks (after Brown & Rosenberg, 1971).

sure and lower saturation deficits, and initially at least, increased soil moisture content and soil temperature.

Some attempts have been made in Russia and the United States to determine the exchange coefficient within shelter. Technically this is difficult because the surface boundary layer is reforming downwind from the

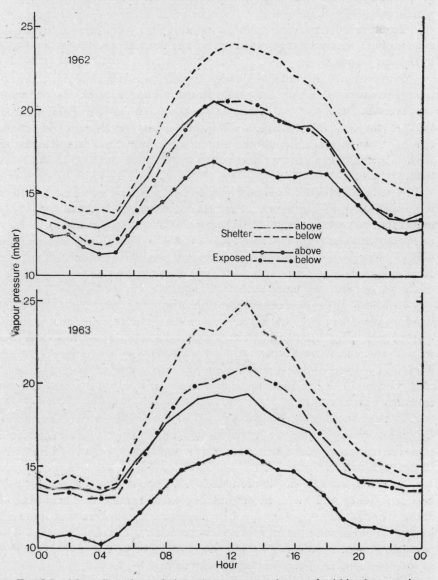

Fig. 6.5. Mean diurnal trends in vapour pressure above and within the canopies of sheltered and exposed beans (*Phaseolus vulgaris*) (after Rosenberg, 1966).

barrier and representative conditions are not easily found. However, Brown and Rosenberg (1971) found that the exchange coefficient over an irrigated sugar beet crop grown between parallel maize windbreaks was 25% lower on an average than in the open (Fig. 6.4).

In the case of water vapour, this reduction in mass transfer explains the increase in absolute humidity that is a consistent feature of well-designed windbreaks (Fig. 6.5).

Together with the reduction in wind velocity this lowers potential evaporation. Daily average vapour pressure increases of as much as 4 mb have been reported.

Suppression of upward sensible heat flux may on an occasion be countered by increased consumption of energy in transpiration, leading to cooling of the leaves and so of the air in shelter. Hagen and Skidmore (1971) showed that air temperature patterns are also influenced by the leeward eddy zone, rising air currents near the barrier increasing temperatures and descending flows further from the barrier decreasing temperatures relative to the open field.

A reduction in the exchange coefficient might be expected to affect the availability of CO_2 to shelter plants, but Brown and Rosenberg (1972) found that on average daytime CO_2 concentration was reduced by only one ppm, with a negligible effect on photosynthesis and this was substantially offset by increased CO_2 flux due to decreased stomatal resistance (Brown & Rosenberg, 1970). Air mixing in shelter thus appears to be sufficient to maintain normal concentrations of CO_2.

In warm, dry crop areas evaporation of moisture may be increased by wind transfer of energy (advection). There have been suggestions (Ripley, 1967; Carr, 1972a) that shelter-belts around tea crops grown in East Africa might be beneficial in reducing the effect of advection. Even in humid areas advection may at times contribute significantly to total energy balance, and here, as in dry regions, the effectiveness of shelter-belts has not been investigated.

The radiant energy moeity is affected by the shadow cast by the barrier but probably only slightly in the remainder of the shelter zone; it is possible that differential growth of shelter and exposed plants may lead to differences in net radiation receipt.

Similarly, rainfall distribution does not appear to differ significantly between shelter and the open ground beyond the immediate rain-shadow area. Dewfall, on the other hand, is promoted by barriers and increases in dew extend beyond the immediate barrier zone. The significance of dew to plant growth is difficult to assess, however, although it may contribute to the development of certain disease organisms.

Other features of the microclimate, including soil moisture, are more conveniently considered in the next section.

The Nature of Crop Responses

WATER RELATIONS

The reduction of potential evapotranspiration leads to an expectation that the rate of actual transpiration will be reduced in comparison to that from plants grown fully exposed to wind. Both theoretical and experimental work has shown, in humid and sub-humid climates at least, that plant water deficits usually increase less quickly and photosynthesis proceeds for longer periods in shelter, so allowing better dry matter production and increased efficiency in the use of water. The overall use of water may thus be less than or equal to that used by the crop in the open.

However, evaporation from leaves and soil depends on the energy partitioned for it from the total energy budget, and for surfaces other than those that are wet, by various resistances to diffusion of water vapour that in turn are affected by various plant and meteorological factors. The rate of transpiration (E) is given by:

$$E = \Delta e/r = [\, e_s\,(T_0)\, -e_0\,(T_a)\,]\,/(r_1 + r_a)$$

where Δe is stomatal saturation vapour pressure at leaf temperature minus vapour pressure in free air at air temperature, and r—the sum of leaf resistance and leaf boundary layer resistance. At a dry leaf surface the vapour pressure is always less than the stomatal saturation vapour pressure during transpiration, and the surface air is never saturated. The environmental factors besides radiant energy affecting E are air temperature, relative humidity and wind speed. Plant factors include stomatal structure, leaf dimensions, leaf age and the geometry of the crop canopy.

Theoretical and leaf model work by Monteith (1965) and Gates (1968) showed that an increase in wind speed may increase or decrease transpiration, or have no effect, depending on the temperature and vapour pressure differentials between leaf and air, concomitant changes in leaf boundary-layer resistance, and alteration to internal leaf resistance.

Fig. 6.6, from Gates (1968), shows relationships between transpiration and variation in wind speed, temperature and humidity for the fixed conditions given. Changes in the internal leaf resistance (effectively stomatal resistance) brought about by changes in leaf water potential in response to atmospheric evaporative demand or soil water supply modify the transpiration: wind-speed relationships.

Gates (1968) concluded that within a crop transpiration will, on the whole, be increased with increase of wind speed, and only occasionally will it be reduced. The basis for this expectation is the likely influx during morning hours of warmer drier air from outside the canopy, increasing leaf

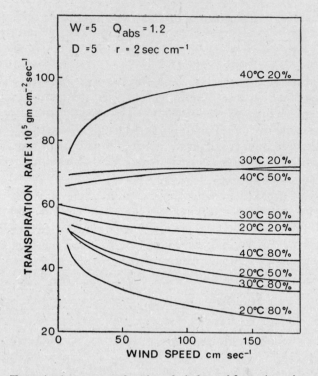

FIG. 6.6.   Transpiration rate as a function of wind speed for various air temperatures and relative humidities for a leaf of dimensions (D & W) of 5 cm × 5 cm and total resistance (r) of 2 sec cm^{-1}, with radiant energy absorption (Qabs) of 1.2 cal cm^{-1} (after Gates, 1968).

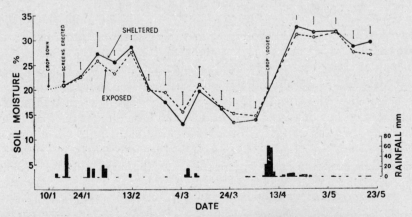

FIG. 6.7.   Changes in soil moisture content (% dry soil) in the 0-15 cm horizon under sheltered and exposed plants of soybeans.   Short vertical lines represent least significant differences ($P < 0.05$) between treatments (after Sturrock, 1970b).

temperature and hence water vapour pressure within the leaf, and thereby
increasing the driving force for transpiration, i.e. Δe.   On the other hand,
Monteith's analysis predicts, at least for temperate climates, that transpiration will usually be insensitive to changes in wind speed and when stomatal
resistance exceeds a critical value the transpiration rate will decrease
as wind speed increases.

Evidence which supports Monteith's prediction was obtained in recent
field work that showed increased use of water by sheltered plants of beans
(Rosenberg, 1966) and tea (Carr, 1972b).   Greater depletion of soil water
by sheltered crops of soybeans (Sturrock, 1970a) and peas was observed in
Canterbury, New Zealand.   After approximately four to five weeks' growth,
during which moisture remained significantly greater in the upper soil
horizon in shelter, moisture values became significantly less than corresponding values in the open crop and remained thus for the rest of the growing
season, or until the crop lodged (Figs. 6.7 & 6.8).

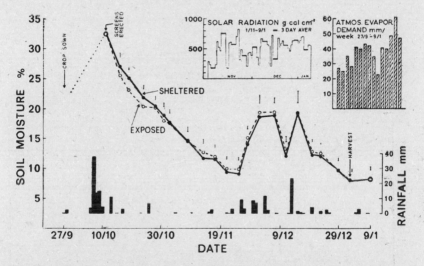

FIG. 6.8.   Changes in soil moisture content (% dry soil) in the 0-15 cm horizon
under sheltered and exposed plants of peas, together with summaries of Class A pan
evaporation and solar radiation.   Short vertical lines represent least significant
differences (P < 0.05) between treatments (after Sturrock, in press).

Earlier work in Canada (Staple & Lehane, 1955) showed that greater
use of soil water, accumulated during winter, accompanied increase in
wheat yields between shelter barriers (Fig. 6.9).

Rosenberg's investigations (Rosenberg, 1966) revealed that the stomata
on sheltered plants were open wider and for longer period during the day
(Fig. 6.10).

He observed increased water use in sheltered irrigated plants of *Phaseolus*

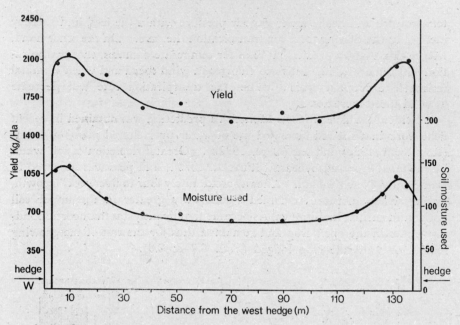

FIG. 6.9. Wheat yield and soil moisture used between hedge shelter at Aneroid, Saskatchewan (after Staple & Lehane, 1955).

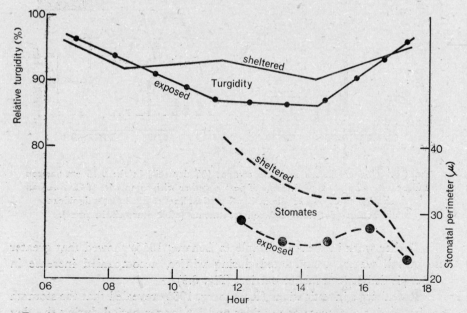

FIG. 10. Relative turgidity and stomatal aperture of leaves of beans (*Phaseolus vulgaris*) under sheltered and exposed conditions during daylight hours (stomatal aperture from 1200 hrs), August 9, 1963 at Scottsbluff, Nebraska (after Rosenberg, 1966).

vulgaris with the same leaf area as exposed plants. It could be expected also that larger leaf areas, often found in sheltered plants (see Fig. 6.15) would contribute to increased transpiration. Bigger root systems often accompany increases in leaf area, and in dry climates their greater foraging ability for water may sustain increased growth of wind-protected plants. Sheltered plants of soybeans produced more roots than exposed plants (Sturrock, 1970a). Most of the roots were found in the upper horizon. Additional moisture for enhanced growth of the sheltered plants (Fig. 6.15) and a yield increase of 30% probably came from below the main root zone, as was shown by Jordan and Ritchie (1971) for cotton growing under normally exposed, dry conditions. Such a mechanism is consistent with the contemporary view that tolerance to drought depends more on the ability of crops to obtain and conserve moisture than on their being able to maintain low rates of transpiration. The experimental results obtained by Denmead and Shaw (1962) are also relevant to the shelter situation, since they show that initial plant water deficits are reached at lower soil moisture contents when potential evapotranspiration levels are also reduced (Fig. 6.11).

Some shallow rooting species can be expected to be at a disadvantage in shelter in dry climates. After the greater initial supply of soil moisture in

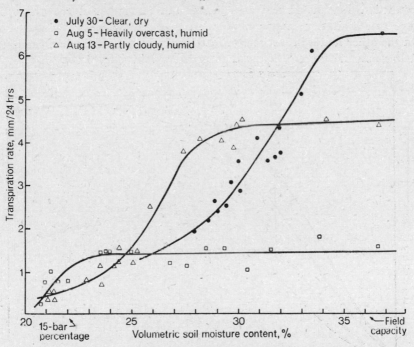

Fig. 6.11. Effect of soil moisture contents on transpiration rate in maize. Potential evapotranspiration rates, July 30, 6.5 mm day^{-1}; August 5, 1.4 mm day^{-1}; August 13, 4.5 mm day^{-1} (after Denmead & Shaw, 1962).

shelter has been exploited, the effect of shelter on final yield will be critically dependent on the amount and distribution of summer rain or on irrigation. Thus Guyot (1963) and Fougerouze (1968) found that under very dry
conditions windbreaks reduced yield in the absence of supplementary water.

In shelter the initial soil moisture advantage to germination and seedling growth obviously depends on the moisture status of the soil and the
efficiency of the shelter in minimising evaporative loss of soil moisture. This
advantage may be made more apparent by slower development of the plant
canopy in the open (Rosenberg et al., 1967).

Farrell et al. (1966) advanced a theory, since taken up by others, that
vapour transfer through soil near the surface can be expedited by wind-induced
pressure fluctuations near the surface. Such a mechanism would hasten drying of the soil in the open before a crop cover was achieved. It might also
contribute to the increased evaporation reported behind dense shelter-belts
because the increased turbulence there, would favour vapour transfer by this
means. However, a similar pressure fluctuation at the leaf surface caused
by leaf flutter did not significantly affect plant transpiration (Wooley, 1961).

Rapid plant growth after seedling emergence is important to overall
production, since until a crop forms a complete canopy of leaves, dry matter
production depends on leaf area index, and restriction of growth at this
stage can limit dry matter production over the whole growing season.
On the other hand, in wet seasons earlier production of the leaf canopy in
shelter may not necessarily lead to greater yield (Fig. 6.12).

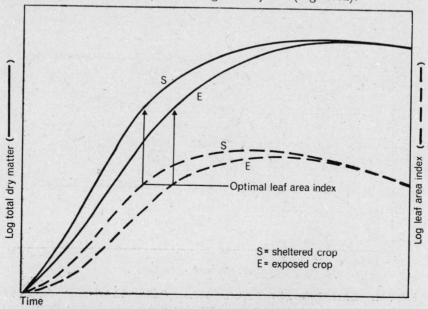

Fig. 6.12. Generalized response of crops to shelter in a wet season (after Caborn, 1971).

Recent work has shown that very small decreases in soil and plant water potentials cause large reductions in the growth and photosynthesis of some species (Figs. 6.13 & 6.14).

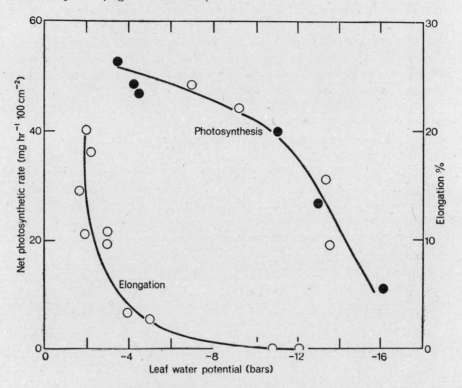

FIG. 6.13. Effect of leaf water potential on enlargement and photosynthesis in maize (after Boyer, 1970).

These results are relevant to the shelter effect because even a slight conservation of soil water under dry conditions can lead to dramatic improvement in the growth and yield of sensitive species (Fig. 6.15).

It would seem that the main advantage of windbreaks lies with improved availability of water to the leaf, leading to longer daily opening of stomata, increased flux of CO_2 and hence increased photosynthesis. Brown and Rosenberg (1970) found an average increase in CO_2 flux of 6% in sheltered sugar beet plants, and hence a 6% increase in photosynthetic rate; the maximum increase in photosynthesis was as much as 25%. The importance of stomatal width throughout their range in respect of transpiration has only been appreciated in the last decade or so (Waggoner, 1969).

In windy climates, moisture deficiencies cannot be entirely removed by irrigation. When atmospheric evaporative demand is considerable, many plant species with roots well-supplied with water suffer loss of leaf turgor

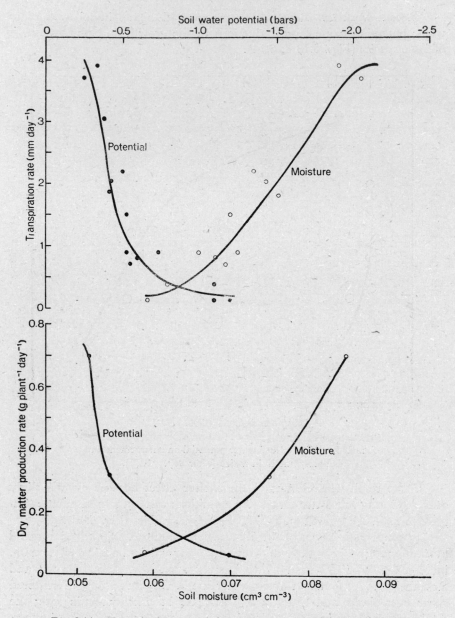

Fɪɢ. 6.14. Transpiration rate and day matter production rate of beans (*Phaseolus vulgaris*) as a function of soil moisture and soil-water potential (after Millar & Gardner, 1972).

and stomatal closure. Recent work has shown that under such conditions windbreaks increase the utilization of irrigation water and produce additive effects on crop yields.

Fig. 6.15. *Top*: Growth of non-irrigated beans (*Phaseolus vulgaris*) under various degrees of wind exposure: well sheltered (*left*), moderately sheltered (*centre*) and fully exposed (*right*). Note relative pod production.
Bottom: Growth of non-irrigated soybeans under sheltered conditions (*left*), contrasted with growth in full exposure (*right*). Plants have completed flowering and pods are beginning to form (after Sturrock, 1970a).

Temperature

Increased soil and air temperatures contribute to improved germination and early growth in shelter, but it is difficult to isolate these parameters and ascertain their precise effects. Higher temperatures promote earlier spring production and prolong growth in autumn, thus extending the growing season of perennial crops when unsheltered temperatures are below the threshold for growth (Marshall, 1967). In summer, shelter will tend to increase leaf temperature and leaf vapour pressure, so increasing transpiration, but whether this will be beneficial or otherwise to cropping will depend on ambient temperature, water supply and the species of crop.

Mechanical Damage

Mechanical wind damage to crops ranges from obvious physical damage to more subtle physiological damage. There have, however, been few reports of the effects of damage during early phases of crop growth on subsequent growth and final yield, and effects on yield are usually known only when damage occurs close to harvest. In Ireland, Gallagher (1966) showed that crop responses to fertilizers on exposed land can be masked as a result of retardation of growth by wind damage.

Experimental vibration of leaves, that produced no visible damage, resulted in increased respiration, diminished photosynthesis and transpiration, and in most cases closure of stomata and marked reductions of plant growth, even with very short periods of treatment (Caldwell, 1970; Neel & Harris, 1971; Todd et al., 1972).

Wind damage is accentuated by the abrasive action of windborne soil particles, and beyond a threshold value damage tends to be proportional to wind speed and the quantity of soil blown. Recently, Armbrust (1972) found that the nitrogen metabolism of injured plants may be affected before visual damage is apparent.

Although shelter-belts at recurring intervals appear to control foci of soil blowing, erosion can be cumulative and once started generates further centres downwind from the first (Caborn, 1971), so that other methods often supplement use of shelter-belts. In areas subject to severe erosion low wind barriers at relatively frequent intervals may be best.

Crop Yields

Many comparisons of crop yields in shelter with yields obtained under full exposure have been made, the majority of them from trials conducted with temporary windbreaks. Many results are given by Van Eimern et al. (1964) and Marshall (1967). Table 6.1 gives some recent results obtained in a diversity of climates.

Leeward yield usually attains a maximum at a point coinciding with maximum protection, yield tapering off on either side more or less in accordance with the wind profile. Biological response, however, rarely seems to be significant beyond 15h. Figure 6.16 gives an example of a "yield profile".

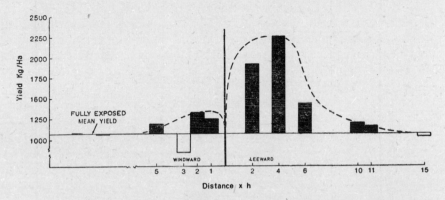

FIG. 6.16. Yield response of a soybean crop in the vicinity of a 45% porous artificial windbreak; yields were obtained from combine-harvested strips cut parallel to the windbreak (after Sturrock, 1970b).

The greatest percentage increases in yield are usually where yields are below-average, and they may then represent comparatively small additions to total production. Similarly, at a given location yield responses are generally greater in "dry" years than "wet" years.

Negative shelter responses, which are sometimes observed, may be due to prolonged drought, root competition from shelter-belts, excessive shade or disease.

Crop cultivars may respond differentially to shelter (Table 6.2) but little is known about the morphological and physiological causes of such variation.

Very large responses to shelter from crops grown in Russia have long been reported, partly the result of winter snow trapped in the vicinity of shelter-belts replenishing soil moisture in the shelter zone. The generally poorer response of American Great Plains crops, grown in a comparable continental climate, has been ascribed to breeding programmes that have improved drought tolerance and disease resistance of American crop varieties.

There is little data on grassland. In temperate areas gains in shelter are usually confined to dry years and, as already mentioned, shelter may benefit spring and autumn growth. Shelter is reported to hasten production of marketable yield of some crops but not of others. Contrasts in maturation rate of dwarf beans and soybeans are observable in Figure 6.15.

Table 6.1. Recent examples of reported yield increases from shelter protection

Country	Crop	Yield increase % gain	Yield increase Actual gain	Notes	Reference
U.S.A. (Nebraska)	Beans (*Phaseolus vulgaris*)	92	202 g/plant	Accumulated yield increase within 15 m² snowfence enclosure	Rosenberg *et al.* (1967)
United Arab Republic	Cotton	36	218 kg/ha	Increase from shelter-belt protected 16 ha field with irrigation	Hussein *et al.* (1969)
Belgium	Strawberry	215	234 g/plant	Accumulated yield increase from protected zone afforded by a plastic windbreak	Benoit (1973)
Guadaloupe, French W. Indies	Sweet potato	19 76	2, 200 kg/ha 12, 100 kg/ha	Yield increases in 2 seasons as far as approx. 10h from plastic wind-breaks	Fougerouze (1968)
U.S.A. (Nebraska)	Tomato	30	10,850 kg/ha	3-year average yield increase bet-ween 13 m parallel barriers with irrigation	Bagley (1964)
Canada	Wheat	43	416 kg/ha	Max. yield increase at 3h to lee of snowfence (snow factor excluded)	Pelton (1967)

Table 6.2. Maximum yield responses of soybean cultivars obtained to lee of 45% porous shelter at Lincoln, New Zealand

Cultivar			Yield increase (%)
Merit	..	..	11
OAC-85	..	..	21
Altona	..	..	27
Hardome	..	..	55
Hawkeye	..	..	110

There seems little doubt that shelter benefits a considerable number of crops, but it remains to be shown how economic these increases are under general farming conditions. Extrapolation of experimental results is hazardous in regions with much variation in soil type and climate. Where the region is relatively uniform, cautious extrapolation can be attempted, provided the average yield increase over the whole zone of response is used, and allowance made for the spatial limitations of the protection afforded by local shelter-belts or those planned for the area.

Crop Quality

Investigations have shown that plants protected from full exposure may undergo changes in chemical composition. Protected pastures are reported to have increased protein contents, and Miloserdov (1970) reported greater gluten content in winter wheat. The quality of other economically important crops, including tobacco, is influenced by the degree of exposure. Gupta (unpublished) observed that tobacco plants grown in a mango orchard developed larger and thinner leaves but the root growth was poor and plants became more susceptible to moisture stress. Total alkaloid content also decreased. These changes involve complex biochemical and physiological processes. The water balance of the plant may be implicated, since enzyme activity is known to be affected by drought.

Diseases and Pests

Increased humidity in sheltered zones might be expected to encourage fungal diseases prejudicial to crop production, but there has been little demonstration of such effects. Wet weather exacerbated disease problems in sheltered beans (Shah, 1961) and lettuce (Hogg, 1964).

Shelter-belts and hedges exert complex effects on the ecology of insects. Although the number of insect pests has been observed to increase in the lee of shelter, the number of beneficial predators and parasites of these pests also increases (Van Emden, 1965). Lewis (1969) concludes that present information is insufficient to decide if the effect of shelter in promoting both pests and beneficial insects is predominantly harmful or useful.

Crop Pollination

Shelter-belts are reported to increase seed yields of sunflower and sainfoin from improved pollination (Free, 1970) and it has been suggested that shelter-belts could be used to improve the pollination of many tropical crops. De Datta and Zarate (1970) reported that strong winds during pollination induce sterility in rice.

Planning Shelter

In areas with little shelter or where new lands are to be brought into cultivation, preliminary assessment of exposure is required for planning the most effective and economical shelter. Methods include wind surveys using anemometers, visual estimation of wind effects on local vegetation, and determining the rate of tatter of flags of standard material and dimensions. A method recently introduced for assessing relative exposure is based on measuring the angle of inclination of the horizon at the eight major points of the compass and adding the eight angles to give the "topex" value (Pyatt *et al.*, 1969) (Table 6.3).

Table 6.3. **Tentative scale of relative exposure based on the "topex" value (Pyatt** *et al.*, **1969)**

Range of topex values		Exposure category	Suggested cartographic colour code
0-10	..	Severely exposed	Purple
11-30	..	Very exposed	Red
31-60	..	Moderately exposed	Yellow
61-100	..	Moderately sheltered	Green
101-150	..	Very sheltered	Blue

Where damaging winds from any direction are likely, a meshwork of belts gives best control. Parallel belts are acceptable in arid zones where changes in wind directions are infrequent (Raheja, 1963). Generally, the more valuable the crop or the greater the problem of soil erosion by wind, the closer must be the distance between shelter-belts to assure adequate overlap of shelter zones. Experiments (Nägeli, 1965) with porous screens in various parallel groupings showed that removal of alternate screens in a 10h or 15h system increased mean wind strengths by 11 to 12% (Fig. 6.3).

Given information on local winds and an estimate of median shelter-belt height it should be possible to calculate the approximate area of land required for trees for a stated average degree of shelter with allowance for the inevitable variation in the efficiency of individual belts. Sturrock (1973) estimated that with numerous, well-distributed, narrow belts about 5 to 6% of land is needed to provide at least a 20% reduction in the general wind speed over the entire area. With uniformly high efficiency, 2-3% of land will suffice.

Where surveys have been made of existing shelter, they have invariably revealed many deficiencies. There may be faults in planning, maintenance, weed control, porosity and choice of species; sometimes a considerable incidence of disease, pest and livestock damage, mainly through human negligence; neglect of timber potential; and lack of an effective replacement policy. It must be concluded that in the majority of cases the value of existing shelter is considerably less than its potential worth.

Ideally a shelter tree needs to be adaptable to a range of soils and climates, cheap to propagate, upright in growth, resistant to wind, frost, pests and diseases and retentive of its foliage to ground level. Further attributes would include the production of useful by-products and, ultimately, timber of value. In parts of India, for example, the castor bean (*Ricinus communis*) is a shelter tree valued for its bean production (Misra & Jain, 1968).

Breeding, more or less specifically for shelter trees, is carried out in Russia (see, for example Albenskii, 1969). Continuing forest-tree breeding and selection programmes will result in better trees becoming available for shelter-belts, but research into the potential of species of trees other than those for production forestry is needed, particularly to find kinds suitable for difficult climatic situations.

Management

On exposed sites temporary shelter is valuable for tree establishment. In England, height growth of several conifer species was much improved by shelter (Lines, 1963), and Fourt (1968) found that the best growth of Sitka spruce resulted from a combination of shelter and irrigation (*cf.* similar effects with crops given above).

In many semiarid areas trees are difficult to establish and new techniques for irrigating shelter-belt trees are being investigated. Irrigation may also be useful for extending the habitat range of species and increasing the choice of species for use in dry climates. Again, control of weeds is usually necessary during establishment, particularly in dry climates, to avoid heavy tree mortality from excessive competition for soil moisture.

The importance of porosity to air flow pattern has been described. Dense belts are usually justified only where exposure is exceptionally severe, as a means of maintaining a low belt porosity in the face of very strong winds and ensuring a reasonable degree of speed reduction over a restricted leeside area.

The inability to judge porosity directly forces reliance, in the absence of instrument tests of air flow, on subjective assessment. According to Caborn (1965) a belt is near optimum porosity when one can just perceive from the windward side, movement, but not detail, of livestock, machinery etc., on the leeward side.

As a general rule it is better to plant slightly too thickly, since judicious pruning and even removal of odd trees carried out later can adjust porosity to near the ideal, whereas little can be done with a loose, open barrier, other than to replace it.

In areas subject to wet conditions in winter, deciduous belts have utility in permitting better drying of the soil for spring cultivation than do evergreen ones. According to Geiger (1965) the effectiveness of deciduous belts in winter is usually about 60% of what it is in summer. Figure 6.17 shows variation in flow patterns through a deciduous belt at different leaf stages.

It is desirable however, that trees come into leaf early enough to protect emerging crops.

Where possible evergreen shelter-belts are best orientated north : south, and for east : west orientation single row deciduous belts minimize shading of adjacent land. Single-row shelter-belts or a combination of a tall growing species with a shrub layer in a 2-tier system can be aerodynamically efficient, and take up little land, and the latter arrangement assures leaf cover to ground level for long periods. Shelter-belts of mixed species can be maintained indefinitely by selective filling and replacement of tree groups, and by using the ability of many hardwoods to coppice when cut, thus maintaining ground level cover.

With other belts there is a limit to their useful life and variation in protective value (Fig. 6.18). This illustrates the need for shelter-belts of differing ages and a replacement plan that maintains continuity of shelter.

An interesting recent development in some countries is the use of grazing forest and arable forest, aimed at encouraging increased investment in joint forest-farm enterprises. With widely spaced trees, animal or crop production, in the early part of the rotation increases the economic returns of the unit as a whole. The grazing forest may be particularly useful for effectively and profitably sheltering large areas of upland pasture where traditional shelter-belts are of limited value and are usually uneconomic.

Other Wind Control Measures

Apart from breeding plants for increased tolerance to wind and drought,

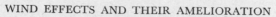

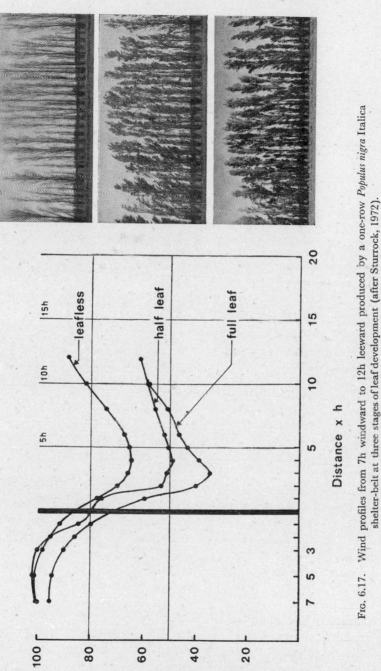

Fig. 6.17. Wind profiles from 7h windward to 12h leeward produced by a one-row *Populus nigra* Italica shelter-belt at three stages of leaf development (after Sturrock, 1972).

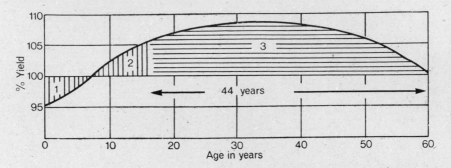

FIG. 6.18.   Estimated long term effect of a five-row shelter-belt with lifespan of 60 years on crop yield as a percentage of unprotected yield (100%):
Period 1 represents loss in crop yields due to occupation of land by establishing trees; period 2 is gain in crop yield that offsets losses in the first period; period 3 is the time of actual net gain in crop yield. The average annual gain over the 60 years would be 3 to 5% net i.e. including land lost to agriculture by the trees (from Stoeckeler, 1962, based on actual crop data in Dakota, U.S.A.).

which is essentially a long-term solution to the problem, various practical measures can be used to supplement shelter-belt control of wind. These include use of strip crop barriers, plastic windbreaks and chemicals that improve the water balance of plants.

Strip crop barriers: Wind barriers of living crops, often cereals or grasses, have long been used in both temperate and tropical lands to protect more sensitive crops and particularly to control soil erosion by wind. Severe erosion, and effective distribution of winter snow to replenish soil moisture reserves, are controlled better by strip barriers at close intervals than by taller shelter-belts more widely spaced in parts of the American Great Plains, particularly when wind direction is not perpendicular to the barrier (Siddoway, 1970).

Various erosion equations have been proposed to calculate the optimum spacing of these barriers and to ensure that any soil particles moved between barriers are trapped within the first barrier encountered. The equation derived by Hagen *et al.* (1972) shows the dependence of trapping efficiency on barrier height, width and mean wind-speed and the adjustments in barrier spacing needed to avoid excessive soil movement.

Plastic windbreaks: Windbreaks made of plastic take up the minimum of land and those that are semi-transparent cast minimum shade. Their use is confined to providing additional wind protection to high value crops in existing horticultural areas where other climatic factors favour production but wind damage must be avoided. Although the price of material is relatively small, costs are significantly increased by the labour of erection and the expense of the supporting structure.

Chemicals to control growth and transpiration: Growth retardant chemicals lessen mechanical damage from wind by reducing plant height and they may improve tolerance to drought. Treated plants acquire some of the features of xeromorphism, and the work by Mishra and Pradhan (1972) and others show that such treatments delay wilting, enabling plants to survive brief periods of drought. Unfortunately field results are still awaited, and the potential of these chemicals to pre-adapt plants to wind and drought economically remains unknown.

Antitranspirants have also been closely studied. These act either by forming a film on the leaf surface or by preventing complete stomatal opening. Although they are expected to reduce photosynthesis and growth, the latter is also a function of cell expansion which depends on the maintenance of a high water potential (see Fig. 6.13). Davenport *et al.* (1972) concluded that since antitranspirants increase plant water potential, it is possible for them to increase growth in spite of reduced photosynthesis.

Although further investigation is justified, the economic value of these supplementary measures may be limited (in parts of western Europe, however, growth retardants are used routinely as insurance against lodging of cereals). The provision of effective permanent shelter will, in general, be the most effective way of avoiding damage and growth restriction by wind.

References

ALBENSKII, A. V. 1969. Selection and seed production for protective plantings. 2nd FAO/IUFRO World Consult. For Tree Breed., Washington, FAO-FTB-69-8/18.

ARMBRUST, D. V. 1972. Recovery and nutrient content of sandblasted soybean seedlings. Agron. J. 64: 707-8.

BAGLEY, W. T. 1964. Response of tomatoes and beans to windbreak shelter. J. Soil. Wat. Conserv. 19: 71-3.

BENOIT, E. 1973. Strawberry yields greatly improved by wind screens, but growers doubtful about economics. The Grower 79: 34.

BOYER, J. S. 1970. Leaf enlargement and metabolic rates in corn, soybean and sunflower at various leaf water potentials. Pl. Physiol. 46: 233-5.

BROWN, K. W. and N. J. ROSENBERG, 1970. Effect of windbreaks and soil water potential on stomatal diffusion resistance and photosynthetic rate of sugar beets (*Beta vulgaris*). Agron. J. 62: 4-8.

BROWN, K. W. and N. J. ROSENBERG, 1971. Turbulent transport and energy balance as affected by a windbreak in an irrigated sugar beet (*Beta vulgaris*) field. Agron. J. 63: 351-5.

BROWN, K. W. and N. J. ROSENBERG, 1972. Shelter effects on microclimate, growth and water use by irrigated sugar beets in the Great Plains. Agr. Meteorol. 9: 241-63.

CABORN, J.M. 1965. Shelter-belts and Windbreaks. Faber and Faber,London.

CABORN, J. M. 1971. The agronomic and biological significance of hedgerows. Outl. Agric. 6: 279-84.

CALDWELL, M. M. 1970. Plant gas exchange at high wind speed. Pl. Physiol. 46: 535-7.

CARR, M. K. V. 1972a. The climatic requirements of the tea plant: a review. Expl. Agr. 8: 1-14.

CARR, M. K. V. 1972b. The internal water status of the tea plant (*Camellia sinensis*); some results illustrating the use of the pressure chamber technique. Agr. Meteorol. 9: 447-60.

DAVENPORT, D. C.; M. A, FISHER and R. M. HAGAN, 1972. Some counteractive effects of antitranspirants. Pl. Physiol. 49: 722-4.

DE DATTA, S. K. and P. M. ZARATE, 1970. Biometeorological problems in developing countries. *In:* Proceed. 5th Int. Biomet. Congr., Montreux, Switzerland Biometeorol. 4: 71-89.

DENMEAD, O. T. and R. H. SHAW, 1962. Availability of soil water to plants as affected by soil moisture content and meteorological conditions. Agron. J. 54: 385-90.

FARRELL, D. A.; E. L. GREACEN and C. G. GURR, 1966. Vapour transfer in soil due to air turbulence. Soil Sci. 102: 305-13.

FOUGEROUZE, J. 1968. The effect of windbreaks in a tropical trade-wind climate. Agron. Trop. 23: 1137-58 (in French).

FOURT, D. F. 1968. Sitka spruce, shelter and moisture. Res. Dev. Pap. For. Comm., London, No. 72, p. 8.

FREE, J. B. 1970. Insect Pollination of Crops. Academic Press, London, p. 544.

GALLAGHER, P. A. 1966. The importance of replication of site in field experiments on field beans. Ir. J. agric. Res. 5: 137-40.

GATES, D. M. 1968. Transpiration and leaf temperature. Ann. Rev. Pl. Physiol. 19: 211-38.

GEIGER, R. 1965. The Climate near the Ground. Harvard Univ. Press, Cambridge, Mass., p. 611.

GUPTA, U. S. (Personal communication).

GUYOT, G. 1963. Windbreaks: modification of microclimates and improvement in agricultural production. Ann. Agron. 14: 429-88 (in French).

HAGEN, L. J. and E. L. SKIDMORE, 1971. Turbulent velocity fluctuations and vertical flow as affected by windbreak porosity. Trans. Am. Soc. Agric. Engrs. 14: 634-7.

HAGEN, L. J.; E. L. SKIDMORE and J. D. DICKERSON, 1972. Designing narrow strip barrier systems to control wind erosion. J. Soil Wat. Conserv. 27: 269-72.

HOGG, W. H. 1964. Lath shelter screens for lettuce at Stockbridge House 1959-1961. Expl. Hort. 11: 23-8.

HUSSEIN, M. F.; M. S. IMAN; I. HEIKAL; G. E. EL-SHERBINI and A. A. MOHAMED, 1969. Effects of windbreaks and shelter-belts. Agric. Res. Rev. Cairo 47: 81-9.

JORDAN, W. R. and J. T. RITCHIE, 1971. Influence of soil water stress on evaporation, root absorption and internal water status of cotton. Pl. Physiol. 48: 783-8.

LEWIS, T. 1969. The diversity of the insect fauna in a hedgerow and neighbouring fields. J. appl. Ecol. 6: 453-8.

LINES, R. 1963. Experiments with artificial shelters. In: Rep. For. Res. For. Comm., London, 1961/62, pp. 40-41.

MARSHALL, J. K. 1967. The effect of shelter on the productivity of grass-lands and field crops. Field Crop Abstr. 20: 1-14.

MILLAR, A. A. and W. R. GARDNER, 1972. Effect of the soil and plant water potentials on the dry matter production of snap beans. Agron. J. 64: 559-62.

MILOSERDOV, N. M. 1970. Quality of winter wheat grain in fields protected by forest strips. Agrokhimiya 76-86 (in Russian).

MISHRA, D. and G. C. PRADHAN, 1972. Effect of transpiration-reducing chemicals on growth, flowering and stomatal opening of tomato plants. Pl. Physiol. 50: 271-4.

MISRA, D. K. and T. C. JAIN, 1968. Castor bean production in India's arid zone. World Crops 20: 44-5.

MONTEITH, J. L. 1965. Evaporation and Environment. In: "The State and Movement of Water in Living Organisms", Symp. Soc. exp. Biol. 19, Cambridge Univ. Press, pp. 205-31.

NÄGELI, W. 1946. Further investigation of wind conditions in the vicinity of shelter-belts. Mitt. schweiz. Anst. forstl. Vers Wes. 24: 659-730 (in German).

NÄGELI, W. 1965. On wind conditions in the range of staggered shelter-belts. Mitt. schweiz. Anst. forstl. Vers Wes. 41: 219-300 (in German).

NEEL, P. L. and R. W. HARRIS, 1971. Motion induced inhibition of elongation and induction of dormancy in Liquidambar. Science 173: 138-41.

PELTON, W. L. 1967. The effect of a windbreak on wind travel, evaporation and wheat yield. Can. J. Pl. Sci. 47: 209-14.

PYATT, D. G.; D. HARRISON and A. S. FORD, 1969. Guide to site types in forests of north and mid Wales. For. Comm. Rec. No. 69, HMSO, p. 35.

RAHEJA, P. C. 1963. Shelter-belts in arid climates and special techniques for tree planting. Ann. Arid Zone 2: 1-13.

RIPLEY, E. A. 1967. Effects of shade and shelter on the microclimate of tea.

E. Afr. agric. For. J. 33: 67-80.

ROSENBERG, N. J. 1966. Microclimate, air mixing and physiological regulation of transpiration as influenced by wind shelter in an irrigated bean field. Agr. Meteorol. 3: 197-224.

ROSENBERG, N. J.; D. W. LECHER and R. E. NEILD, 1967. Responses of irrigated snap beans to wind shelter. Proc. Am. Soc. hort. Sci. 90: 169-79.

SHAH, S. R. H. 1961. The influence of excessive rainfall in the protective value of windscreens with respect to crop yields. Neth. J. agric. Res. 9: 262-68.

SIDDOWAY, F. H. 1970. Barriers for wind erosion control and water conservation. J. Soil Wat. Conserv. 25: 180-84.

STAPLE, W. J. and J. J. LEHANE, 1955. The influence of field shelter-belts on wind velocity, evaporation, soil moisture and crop yield. Can. J. agric. Sci. 35: 440-53.

STOECKELER, J. H. 1962. Shelter-belt influence on Great Plains field environment and crops. USDA, Prod. Rep. No. 62, p. 26.

STURROCK, J. W. 1970a. Studies of the effects of wind reduction on soybeans 1—a preliminary assessment. N. Z. J. agric. Res. 13: 33-44.

STURROCK, J. W. 1970b. Progress in shelter research. Fm. For. Wellington 12: 62-78.

STURROCK, J. W. 1972. Aerodynamic studies of shelter-belts in New Zealand 2—medium height to tall shelter-belts in mid Canterbury. N. Z. J. Sci. 15: 113-40.

STURROCK, J. W. 1973. Surveys of tree and hedge shelter in mid Canterbury: a summary of results. N. Z. J. expl. Agr. 1: 105-7.

TODD, G. W.; D. L. CHADWICK and S. D. TSAI, 1972. Effect of wind on plant respiration. Pl. Physiol. 27: 342-6.

VAN EIMERN, J. 1968. Problems of shelter planning. In: "Agroclimatological Methods. Proceeds. Reading Symp.", UNESCO, Paris, pp. 157-66.

VAN EIMERN, J.; R. KARSHON; L. A. RAZUMOVA and G. W. ROBERTSON, 1964. "Windbreaks and Shelter-belts". WMO Tech. Note No. 59, p. 188.

VAN EMDEN, H. F. 1965. The role of uncultivated land in the biology of crop pests and beneficial insects. Sci. Hort. 17: 121-36.

WAGGONER, P. E. 1969. Environmental manipulation for higher yields. In: Physiological Aspects of Crop Yield, Eastin, J. D.; F. A. Haskins; C. Y. Sullivan and C. H. M. van Bavel (eds), Am. Soc. Agron., Madison, Wisconsin, pp. 343-73.

WHITEHEAD, F. H. 1962. Experimental studies of the effects of wind on plant growth and anatomy. II. *Helianthus annuus*. New Phytol. 61: 59-62.

WHITEHEAD, F. H. 1963a. Experimental studies of the effects of wind on plant growth and anatomy. III. Soil moisture relations. New Phytol. 62: 80-85.

WHITEHEAD, F. H. 1963b. Experimental studies of the effects of wind on plant growth and anatomy. IV. Growth substances and adaptive anatomical and morphological changes. New Phytol. 62: 86-90.

WHITEHEAD, F. H. and R. LUTI, 1962. Experimental studies of the effect of wind on plant growth. I. *Zea mays*. New Phytol. 61: 56-8.

WOOLEY, J. T. 1961. Mechanisms by which wind influences transpiration. Pl. Physiol. 36: 112-4.

Dr. David C. Davenport

Dr. Davenport was born in north India. He obtained his B.Sc. degree from the Allahabad Agricultural Institute in 1960, and M.S. from the Indian Agricultural Research Institute (Dept. Agron.), New Delhi, in 1962. He attended the University of Nottingham School of Agriculture (U.K.) from 1963-1966. During this period he carried out investigations on variations of evaporation in space and time, including studies on advection in the Sudan Gezira in 1963. He also carried out research with stomatal inhibitors, and in 1966 completed his Ph.D. thesis on "Effects of environment and antitranspirants on evaporation". He has been with the Department of Water Science & Engineering, University of California, Davis since 1967, where he has been carrying out research, in association with Prof. Robert M. Hagan, on effects and potential uses of antitranspirants.

Prof. Robert M. Hagan

Dr. Hagan is Professor of Water Science, Irrigationist in the Agricultural Experiment Station and Extension Environmentalist (Land and Water Use). He received B.S. in Chemistry in 1937 and M.S. in Soil Physics in 1940 from the University of California, Berkeley; and Ph.D. in Soil Science in 1948 from the University of California, Davis where he is serving since 1937. He was Chairman of the Department of Irrigation from 1954 to 1963. As one-half time Specialist as Extension Environmentalist (Land and Water Use), he is assisting in developing a more complete and balanced understanding of the environmental aspects of land and water use problems.

His research is particularly concerned with problems of water use in irrigation agriculture. As a specialist on water-soil-plant relationships, he has investigated crop responses to irrigation and the application of this research information to planning and managing the use of water in agriculture. He has served as a consultant for the United States Department of Agriculture, Agricultural Research Service, U.S. Agency for International Agriculture Organization of the United Nations. He has participated in numerous national and international symposia on optimising water use in agriculture. He was the irrigation specialist in the U.S. delegation to the U.N. Conference on Application of Science and Technology to the less developed areas of the world.

He is author or co-author of more than 100 technical publications. He is senior editor of the Monograph on Irrigation of Agricultural Lands and co-editor of the FAO/UNESCO International Sourcebook on Irrigation and Drainage of Arid Lands in Relation to Salinity.

Elected Fellow of the American Association for Advancement of Science in 1960 and Fellow of American Society for Agronomy in 1964.

Dr. David C. Davenport   Prof. Robert M. Hagan

7. ROLE OF ANTITRANSPIRANTS IN ARID AGRICULTURE

**DAVID C. DAVENPORT &
ROBERT M. HAGAN**
*Department of Water Science and Engineering
University of California, Davis
California* 95616 *U.S.A.*

Introduction

An antitranspirant is any material applied to transpiring plant surfaces with the aim of reducing water loss from the plant. Approximately 99% of the water taken up by plant roots is transpired to the atmosphere through stomatal pores in the leaves. Since stomata are located at a point in the water pathway where the vapour-pressure gradient is steepest, i.e., between the leaf and the atmosphere, the stomata-bearing leaf surfaces are the most strategic sites for antitranspirant application. Antitranspirants such as phenylmercuric acetate and certain alkenylsuccinic acids act by inhibiting stomatal opening (Zelitch, 1965, 1969); film-forming antitranspirants (e.g., waxy or plastic emulsions) produce an external physical barrier to retard the escape of water vapour from plants (Gale, 1961); silicones penetrate the leaf and may act directly on the wet cell walls (Haigh & Heinlein, 1973); and white reflecting materials (e.g., whitewash or kaolinite) lower leaf temperature and reduce the vapour-pressure gradient from leaf to atmosphere (Abou-Khaled *et al.*, 1970). These approaches to reducing transpiration were reviewed by Gale and Hagan (1966), Waggoner (1966) and Zelitch (1969).

Although reduced transpiration is the primary goal of applying antitranspirants, that goal may be sought for considerably different reasons: (1) conservation of water supplies, particularly where water is scarce and costly; or (2) improved plant performance via an increase in plant water potential. In discussing the role of antitranspirants in arid agriculture, our use of 'arid' is shifted from the normal geographical context to focus on conditions of plant water stress. We thus consider a situation to be 'arid' whenever a climatic or microclimatic situation results in transpiration rates high enough that: (1) groundwater is severely depleted; and/or (2) plant water potential decreases enough to retard plant performance. In some cases soil water available to roots may be adequate but the foliage can be in an 'arid' environment because of a high evaporative demand.

Before discussing the role of antitranspirants, however, we should survey current knowledge of their effects on plants and interactions with the environment.

Effects of Antitranspirants

Since the processes of transpiration and photosynthesis involve the passage of water vapour and carbon dioxide via the same apertures (stomata), both processes are affected when these apertures are narrowed by a stomatal inhibitor. A slowing of transpiration and photosynthesis after treatment with, say, phenylmercuric acetate, is well-documented in the literature (Slatyer & Bierhuizen, 1964; Zelitch, 1969). Whether photosynthesis is slowed less than transpiration, however, will depend on whether: (1) the stomata-inhibiting chemical affects the site of photosynthesis in the mesophyll (Meidner & Mansfield, 1966; Bravdo, 1972); and (2) the mesophyll resistance is large (Gaastra, 1959; Slatyer & Bierhuizen, 1964) or small (Barrs, 1968) relative to the epidermal and boundary-layer resistances in the CO_2 pathway.

On the other hand, the effect of a film-forming antitranspirant on photosynthesis relative to transpiration will depend on the relative permeabilities of the film to carbon dioxide and water vapour (Wooley, 1967; Gale & Poljakoff-Mayber, 1967). No known films inhibit the passage of carbon dioxide minimally relative to water vapour. The ultimate effect of the film on a plant, however, involves not only its physical permeability to gaseous exchange but also: (1) the extent of foliar coverage; and (2) its effect on stomatal apertures.

Although a film-forming emulsion may completely wet the leaf, the film which forms on drying is seldom, if ever, complete (Davenport & Hagan, 1970). This was demonstrated with a scanning electron microscope by Fisher and Lyon (1972) and Albrigo (1972). However, a film which effectively retards transpiration increases the turgidity of the leaves and stomatal guard cells, resulting in wider stomatal apertures not only under the film but also on areas of the treated leaf missed by the film (Davenport et al., 1972a). Thus, the combination of wider stomatal apertures and imperfect coverage of the leaf would tend to minimize the adverse effect of the film on carbon dioxide and oxygen exchange but still retard transpiration sufficiently.

Any increase in the permeability of films to carbon dioxide would be a welcome improvement, and would possibly enhance photosynthesis because of the wider stomatal apertures under the film. Film antitranspirants currently available reduce transpiration and photosynthesis by about 20-80% within 24 hour of treatment, the effect diminishing with time. Whether water use efficiency (dry weight/transpiration) is improved over that of untreated plants, however, will depend on the extent to which the controls are stressed.

This implies that antitranspirants are not equally effective under all conditions. They are most effective when water losses from leaves are not restricted by natural stomatal closure in response to leaf water deficits (caused by dry soil and/or high evaporative demand) or darkness. Thus, an antitranspirant will be of little benefit to an already wilted plant but will delay wilting onset if applied when the plant is transpiring freely. The effectiveness of an antitranspirant is also determined by plant factors: stomatal distribution on the leaves is important, and spraying only the upper surface of a hypostomatous leaf will obviously have little effect on transpiration. The surface anatomy of some leaves often hinders wetting and film formation. Antitranspirants will, of course, have minimal value when applied to plants which continually produce new leaf surface, especially if the new growth occurs at the outer extremities of the plant, where transpiration rates are generally highest. Depth of rooting often determines the duration of water supply from roots to leaves and therefore influences the duration of antitranspirant effectiveness. Further details on the interaction of antitranspirants with environmental and plant factors are given by Gale (1961), Zelitch and Waggoner (1962), Gale and Hagan (1966), Gale et al. (1966) and Davenport et al. (1969a).

While antitranspirants of the reflecting type reduce leaf temperature, the film-forming and stomata-closing types tend to increase leaf temperature by reducing evaporative cooling. Under normal conditions, however, this increase is only slight, since evaporative cooling is less important to heat dissipating than are re-radiation and convection.

By increasing the resistance to water vapour diffusing from a leaf from 0.04 (control) to 0.11 (treated) min cm^{-1}, an antitranspirant increases leaf water potential from -20 (control) to -15 (treated) atm (Davenport et al.,

1972a). Increased plant water potential after antitranspirant treatment has been shown also by Turner and Waggoner (1968), Davenport (1972) and Davenport et al. (1972b). This is an important effect because plant growth depends not only on the accumulation of raw materials via photosynthesis and mineral uptake, but also on maintaining high plant water potential to enable cell elongation.

With this background in mind, we shall consider the role of antitranspirants in 'arid' agriculture.

Role of Antitranspirants

WATER CONSERVATION

This section discusses the use of antitranspirants when the primary purpose is to conserve water otherwise lost through transpiration, with the effects on plant growth being of only secondary importance. Several studies, based on pot or leaf chamber experiments (Poljakoff-Mayber & Gale, 1967; Slatyer & Bierhuizen, 1964; Davenport, 1967; Brooks & Thorud, 1971), demonstrate reductions in transpiration following antitranspirant treatment. The value of extrapolating these data to field conditions is somewhat dubious, however, for problems of complete canopy coverage and environmental interactions are magnified there. Hence, we refer below mainly to experiments conducted under field conditions.

Watershed and Riparian Vegetation

Since efficient crop production depends on timely availability of water, any water-conservation practice which enhances this availability should be useful. Thus, since vegetation on watersheds and riparian and phreatophytic plants consume underground and surface water supplies, spraying them with antitranspirants to reduce transpiration (Waggoner & Bravdo, 1967; Hart et al., 1969; Davenport et al., 1969a, b) should conserve water for competitive agricultural, industrial and domestic uses. When Waggoner and Turner (1971) sprayed phenylmercuric acetate in a plantation of red pine (Pinus resinosa Ait) to reduce soil water extraction (measured by a neutron moisture-meter), yields of water to the groundwater system increased by 16-24 mm per year. Hart et al. (1969) used a helicopter to obtain effective coverage of aspen trees (Populus tremuloides) on a Utah watershed by phenylmercuric acetate. However, it is important to emphasize the dangers to humans and wild life of using compounds containing heavy metals such as mercury.

Vast quantities of water are also lost by plants such as salt-cedar, cottonwood and willow growing along stream beds or around lakes and reservoirs.

The potential usefulness of antitranspirants for reducing transpiration from these plants is being explored by Brooks and Thorud (1971) and by the present authors (unpublished data). Antitranspirants certainly provide a more attractive alternative for reducing transpiration from these wild species than eradicating them (along with their beauty and the shelter they provide to wildlife) by bulldozing and/or herbicide treatment.

Water Quality

Many arid agricultural areas have problems with salts and poor water quality. Malcolm (1967) attempted to reduce foliar injury to citrus leaves by spraying film antitranspirants to curtail the intake of chlorides dissolved in sprinkler water (Gale & Poljakoff-Mayber, 1962) and Davenport et al. (1972c) also attempted to make use of this 'prophylactic' effect of film antitranspirants, though for different purposes.

In some irrigated areas the dissolved salts in the irrigation water may be so high that each irrigation, though indispensable for the crop, actually degrades the soil. Reducing irrigation frequency could prove beneficial in such cases. Since transpiration is actually the transmittance of *pure water* to the atmosphere, transpiring crops concentrate salts in the soil solution. Furthermore, since water in the terrestrial part of the hydrologic cycle is usually purest in the watershed area rather than in the area of agricultural demand, the curtailment of transpiration from watershed and riparian vegetation might increase the flow of pure water to downstream users, diluting salts and improving water quality there.

Field and Horticultural Crops

At the farm level, water wastage is perhaps greatest from inefficient irrigation, e.g., applying more water than necessary to wet the rooting zone of the soil profile. Irrigation application efficiencies are often no better than 50% (Jensen et al., 1967) and few growers make the measurements required to determine and improve their application efficiencies. Improvement is therefore possible through reducing the number of (inefficient) irrigations, i.e., prolonging the interval between irrigations by slowing soil water depletion with an antitranspirant.

Gale et al. (1964), using a polyethylene-based film antitranspirant on field-grown banana plants, reduced soil water extraction by 21-44% during 7 irrigation cycles without affecting growth or fruit quality. They estimated that the antitranspirant: (1) saved an average of 87 m³ water/ha for each irrigation cycle; and (2) extended safe irrigation intervals from the normal 7 days to 9½ days.

In another field demonstration Waggoner et al. (1964) showed that a stomatal inhibitor (nonenyl succinic acid) on a crop of barley (*Hordeum vulgare*, var. Proctor) with a leaf area index of 6 reduced transpiration by 12-33%.

Davenport *et al.* (1973b) showed that a film-forming antitranspirant effectively reduced soil water depletion (measured by a neutron moisture-meter) of field-grown ornamental oleander plantings in California, so that irrigation intervals could be extended by at least 2 weeks. Costly irrigations by tanker trucks along highways would thereby be minimized, as well as reducing the traffic hazards associated with this type of irrigation.

These field experiments illustrate the potential of antitranspirants for reducing water loss from non-agricultural vegetation and from field and horticultural crops.

INCREASING PLANT WATER POTENTIAL TO IMPROVE GROWTH

In many cases the primary purpose in using an antitranspirant is not water conservation *per se*, but improvement of plant performance by increasing plant water potential. Of course, soil water is also conserved in the process, but the grower's main benefit lies in greater monetary returns from the crop because plant water stress is minimized particularly at stages where the crop is sensitive to low plant water potentials.

Transplanting

"Transplant shock" occurs when transpiration exceeds water uptake through a damaged root system. Therefore, reducing transpiration by applying antitranspirant to the foliage (by dipping or spraying) before transplanting should: (1) increase plant survival; and (2) improve crop stand uniformity. Gale and Hagan (1966) reviewed literature on the use of antitranspirants in transplanting. Most reported experiments deal with transplanted seedlings of perennials, such as pines for reforestation (Emerson & Hildreth, 1933; Gale *et al.*, 1966), or annuals such as com-mercially transplanted vegetables (Fieldhouse *et al.*, 1966). Poljakoff-Mayber and Gale (1967) showed that survival of transplanted pine seedlings was greatly enhanced if, in addition to antitranspirant treatment, the soil around the transplants was mulched to reduce evaporation of initially needed moisture near the soil surface. Davenport *et al.* (1972b) showed that spraying a film-forming antitranspirant on 7-year old citrus trees before lifting them limited the decline in leaf water potential after trans-planting to only 6 atm, compared with a 21 atm decrease in untreated trees. Antitranspirants have also been used by nurserymen as an aid in transplanting ornamentals (Herman, 1969). They may also prove useful in establishing transplants to form a windbreak to protect crops against desiccating winds in arid areas.

It must be remembered that antitranspirants should be a supplement to, rather than a substitute for, good management and prompt irrigation after transplanting. Since antitranspirants are usually used in situations where survival, rather than maximum growth, is the critical problem, any reductions in photosynthesis by the chemical are of only secondary importance. Once the transplant is established, new foliar growth should permit efficient photosynthesis.

Annual Field Crops

In general, field crops are highly dependent on current photosynthesis for growth and final yield. Therefore, it is unlikely that currently available antitranspirants would increase yields of an annual crop unless the crop became stressed from inadequate water and/or a very high evaporative demand, particularly during a moisture-sensitive stage of development, e.g., at bloom (Salter & Goode, 1967).

In a field trial, Gale (1961) showed that periodic applications of a film antitranspirant to beans (*Phaseolus vulgaris*, var. Bulgaria) increased dry matter production under conditions of both adequate and inadequate soil moisture. Also, there was only a slight difference in plant dry weights between the untreated well-irrigated plots and the antitranspirant-treated inadequately irrigated plots. It thus appears that the evaporative demand induced hydroactive closure of stomata in control plants, thereby curtailing photosynthesis, particularly when soil moisture was inadequate. The antitranspirant apparently inhibited this closure and enhanced photosynthetic activity.

On the other hand, Davenport and Hagan (1970) found in a field experiment with snap beans (*Phaseolus vulgaris* var. Tender crop) that another film antitranspirant reduced leaf expansion, plant height, and yield of green beans under conditions of adequate soil moisture and moderate evaporative demand. Thus, the conditions were such that the antitranspirant either (1) could not improve leaf hydration enough to increase photosynthesis and growth; or (2) had some undetected side effect (e.g., phytotoxicity, increased respiration) which inhibited plant performance.

In a green-house pot study Brengle (1968) sprayed phenylmercuric acetate on spring wheat (*Triticum aestivum* L. var. 'Lee') at various growth stages and at moderate (-0.3 to -1 bar) and low (to -9 bar) soil water potentials. He found that: (1) treatment at the tillering or boot stages had no significant effect; whereas (2) treatment at the heading or flowering stages reduced both water use and growth (partly because of phytotoxicity), and therefore did not increase water use efficiency. He concluded that "phenylmercuric acetate at the rates used in this study, offers very little promise of adequate transpiration retardation in wheat when high water stress can reduce yields."

On the other hand, when Fuehring (1973) sprayed stomata-inhibiting or film-forming antitranspirants on field-grown sorghum (*Sorhgum bicolour* L. Moench) under limited irrigation conditions, he found that: (1) grain yield increased 5-17%; and (2) antitranspirant applications just before the boot stage were more effective than later sprays. He emphasized the need for more information on rates and volumes of spray.

These experiments with annual crops (beans, wheat and sorghum) suggest that antitranspirants are capable of: (1) inhibiting growth because of reduced photosynthesis, phytotoxicity or other undetermined side effects; or (2) improving growth under certain conditions if the antitranspirant material, concentration, amount and timing of spray are properly chosen. Obviously, more research is required on specific crops to determine these parameters.

Perennial Crops

Since established perennial plants normally have more food reserves in storage tissues than annual plants do, perennial growth is expected to be affected less severely by photosynthetic reduction by an antitranspirant. Thus, there is some justification for expecting positive yield responses by perennials, especially if the antitranspirant is applied at a stage when the growth of a particular plant part depends more on plant water potential than on photosynthate accumulation.

Since diurnal radial changes of tree trunks depend on the tree's water status and photosynthetic accumulation (both affected by antitranspirants), dendrometer measurements (Verner, 1962) of trunk shrinkage and growth provide a good index of antitranspirant effectiveness. Various workers (Waggoner & Bravdo, 1967; Turner & Waggoner, 1968; Davenport *et al.*, 1969b, 1972d) have observed significant reductions of daytime shrinkage of trunks after antitranspirant treatment, indicating that the lag between water uptake and transpiration had been minimized and that tree water status as a whole had been improved. At the same time, radial trunk growth was reduced over a period of several weeks. Nevertheless, knowing that the water potential of the trees could be greatly improved, we sprayed film antitranspirants on fruit trees in commercial orchards one or two weeks before harvest, when carbohydrate accumulation in the fruits was essentially complete and fruit sizing depended chiefly on maintaining cell turgidity. As a result, fruit volumes were increased by 5-15% for olives (Davenport *et al.*, 1972), peaches (Davenport *et al.*, 1972a) and cherries (Langer, 1948; Davenport *et al.*, 1972e). Furthermore, fruit size was increased because of antitranspirant coverage of the stomata-bearing surfaces of the leaves rather than coverage of the fruit itself (Davenport *et al.*, 1973a). Although fruit dry weight of these crops was not reduced significantly unless the antitranspirant was sprayed too early, there must have been a decrease in photosynthetic accumulation elsewhere in the tree (e.g., in the trunk). The long-term effects of antitranspirants on trees obviously require further study.

One of the problems faced by fruit growers in hot arid environments is fruit shrinkage and even irreversible fruit shrivel. Antitranspirants curtailed daytime shrinkage of peaches (Davenport & Hagan, 1970), and reduced irreversible olive fruit shrivel from 85% per tree (controls) to only 10% (treated) (Davenport *et al.*, 1972d).

Poljakoff-Mayber and Gale (1967) found that a film antitranspirant reduced the total yield of orange fruit (over all size grades) by about 40%, though there was no reduction in yield of fruit of marketable size. On grapevines, film-forming antitranspirants increased berry size (Fleming & Alderfer, 1949), increased grape yield under conditions of water shortage (Gale *et al.*, 1964), and increased total leaf area but decreased dry-weight production of vines (Possingham *et al.*, 1969).

In ornamentals, a film antitranspirant improved the plant water status of oleanders so that internodes and leaves grew faster even though photosynthesis was inhibited (Davenport & Hagan, 1970).

Conclusions

Although antitranspirant materials presently available curtail both transpiration and photosynthesis, they can nevertheless play a useful role in agriculture by: (1) conserving (pure) water supplies, especially where water is scarce and costly; and (2) improving crop performance by maximizing plant water potential.

REFERENCES

ABOU-KHALED, A.; R. M. HAGAN and D. C. DAVENPORT, 1970. Effects of kaolinite as a reflective antitranspirant on leaf temperature, transpiration, photosynthesis and water use efficiency. Water Resour. Res. 6: 280-89.

ALBRIGO, L. G. 1972. Appearance and persistence of pinolene antitranspirant sprayed on "Valencia" orange leaves. Hort. Sci. 7: 247-8.

BARRS, H. D. 1968. Effect of cyclic variations in gas exchange under constant environmental conditions on the ratio of transpiration to net photosynthesis. Pl. Physiol. 21: 918-29.

BRAVDO, BEN-AMI, 1972. Effect of several transpiration suppressants on carbon dioxide and vapour exchange of citrus and grapevine leaves. Pl. Physiol. 26: 152-6.

BRENGLE, K. G. 1968. Effect of phenylmercuric acetate on growth and water use of spring wheat. Agron. J. 60: 246-7.

BROOKS, K. N. and D. B. THORUD, 1971. Antitranspirant effects on the transpiration and physiology of tamarisk. Water Resour. Res. 7: 499-510.

DAVENPORT, D. C. 1967. Effects of chemical antitranspirants on transpiration and growth of grass. J. exp. Bot. 18: 332-47.

DAVENPORT, D. C. 1972. Relative water content of leaves: underestimation caused by antitranspirant film. J. exp. Bot. 23: 651-4.

DAVENPORT, D. C. and R. M. HAGAN, 1970. Potential usefulness of antitranspirants for increasing water use efficiency in plants. Tech. Completion Rep. 1967-70, OWRR B-054-CAL, WRC-174. Water Resources Centre, Univ. of Calif., Los Angeles.

DAVENPORT, D. C.; R. M. HAGAN and P. E. MARTIN, 1969a. Antitranspirants research and its possible application in hydrology. Water Resour. Res. 5: 735-43.

DAVENPORT, D. C.; R. M. HAGAN and P. E. MARTIN, 1969b. Antitranspirants uses and effects on plant life. Calif. Agric. 23: 14-6.

DAVENPORT, D. C.; M. A. FISHER and R. M. HAGAN, 1972a. Some counteractive effects of antitranspirants. Pl. Physiol. 49: 722-4.

DAVENPORT, D. C.; P. E. MARTIN and R. M. HAGAN, 1972b. Antitranspirants for conservation of leaf water potential of transplanted citrus trees. Hort. Sci. 7: 511-12.

DAVENPORT, D. C.; K. URIU and R. M. HAGAN, 1972c. Antitranspirant film; curtailing intake of external water by cherry fruit to reduce cracking. Hort. Sci. 7: 507-8.

DAVENPORT, D. C.; K. URIU; P. E. MARTIN and R. M. HAGAN, 1972d. Antitranspirants increase size, reduce shrivel of olive fruits. Calif. Agric. 26: 6-8.

DAVENPORT, D. C.; K. URIU and R. M. HAGAN, 1972e. Sizing of cherry fruit with antitranspirant sprays. Calif. Agric. 26: 9-10.

DAVENPORT, D. C.; K. URIU and R. M. HAGAN, 1973a. Leaf vs fruit coverage with antitranspirants for sizing fruit. Hort. Sci. 8: 98.

DAVENPORT, D. C.; P. E. MARTIN and R. M. HAGAN, 1973b. Effects of an antitranspirant on water use by highway oleander plantings. J. Am. Soc. hort. Sci. 98: 421-5.

EMERSON, J. L. and A. C. HILDRETH, 1933. Preliminary report on reducing transpiration of transplanted evergreens. Science 77: 433-4.

FIELDHOUSE, D. J.; J. C. RYDER and E. L. RATLEDGE, 1966. A wax base transpiration suppressant for use on tomato and pepper transplants.

Trans. Peninsula hort. Soc. 56: 23-8.

FISHER, M. A. and T. L. LYON, 1972. Antitranspirant film detection by scanning electron microscopy of cathodoluminescene. Hort. Sci. 7: 24-7.

FLEMING, H. K. and R. B. ALDERFER, 1949. The effects of urea and oil wax emulsion sprays on the performance of the Concord grapevine under cultivation and in Ladiao clover sod. Am. Soc. hort. Sci. Proc. 54: 171-6.

FUEHRING, H. D. 1973. Effect of antitranspirants on yield of grain sorghum under limited irrigation. Agron. J. 65: 348-51.

GAASTRA, P. 1959. Photosynthesis of crop plants as influenced by high carbon dioxide, temperature and stomatal diffusion resistance. Meded. Landbouwhogesch., Wageningen 59: 1-68.

GALE, J. 1961. Studies on plant antitranspirants. Pl. Physiol. 14: 777-86.

GALE, J. and R. M. HAGAN, 1966. Plant antitranspirants. Ann. Rev. Pl. Physiol. 17: 269-82.

GALE, J. and A. POLJAKOFF-MAYBER, 1962. Prophylactic effect of a plant antitranspirant. Phytopathology 52: 715-7.

GALE, J. and A. POLJAKOFF-MAYBER, 1967. Plastic films on plants as anti-transpirants. Science 156: 650-52.

GALE, J.; A. POLJAKOFF-MAYBER; I. NIR and I. KAHANE, 1964. Preliminary trials of the application of antitranspirants under field conditions to vines and bananas. Aust. J. agric. Res. 15: 929-36.

GALE, J.; A. POLJAKOFF-MAYBER; I. NIR and I. KAHANE, 1966. Effect of antitranspirant treatment on the water balance of pine seedlings under different climatic and soil moisture conditions. Plant & Soil 24: 81-9.

HAIGH, W. G. and J. P. HEINLEIN, 1973. Silicone antitranspirants: a possible mechanism of action. Pl. Physiol. 51 (Suppl.): 46.

HART, G. E.; J. D. SCHULTZ and G. B. COLTHARP, 1969. Controlling trans-piration from Aspen with phenylmercuric acetate. Water Resour. Res. 5: 407-12.

HERMAN, D. 1969. The value of antidesiccasits. Turf Grass Times (May): 9.

JENSEN, M. E.; L. R. SWARNER and J. T. PHELAN, 1967. Improving irrigation efficiencies. In: Irrigation of Agricultural Lands, Hagan, R. M. et al. (eds), Am. Soc. Agron. Monograph No. 11: 1120-42.

LANGER, C. A. 1948. Effect of wax sprays on the yield of cherries, pears and apples. Am. Soc. hort. Sci. Proc. 51: 191-5.

MALCOLM, C. V. 1967. Reducing salt damage from sprinkler irrigation. Calif. Citrog. 52: 122, 124-5.

MEIDNER, H. and T. A. MANSFIELD, 1966. Rates of photosynthesis and respiration in relation to stomatal movements in leaves treated with a hydroxysulphonate and glycollate. J. exp. Bot. 17: 502-9.

POLJAKOFF-MAYBER, A. and J. GALE, 1967. Effect of plant antitranspirants on certain physiological processes of forest seedlings and other plant materials. Project Number A10FS10. Final Tech. Report, Hebrew Univ., Jerusalem, Israel, p. 107.

POSSINGHAM, J. V.; G. H. KERRIDGE and D. E. BOTTRILL, 1969. Studies with antitranspirants on grape vines. Aust. J. agric. Res. 20: 57-64.

SALTER, P. J. and J. E. GOODE, 1967. Crop responses to water at different stages of growth. Research Rev. No. 2, Commonwealth Bureau of Horticulture and Plantation Crops, East Malling, Maidstone, Kent, U.K., p. 246.

SLATYER, R. O. and J. F. BIERHUIZEN, 1964. The influence of several transpiration suppressants on transpiration, photosynthesis and water use efficiency of cotton leaves. Aust. J. biol. Sci. 17: 131-46.

TURNER, N. C. and P. E. WAGGONER, 1968. Effects of changing stomatal width in a red pine forest on soil water content, leaf water potential, mole diameter and growth. Pl. Physiol. 43: 973-8.

VERNER, L. 1962. A new kind of dendrometer. Idaho A. E. S. Bull. 389: 1-7.

WAGGONER, P. E. 1966. Decreasing transpiration and the effect upon growth. In: Plant Environment and Efficient Water Use, Pierre, W. H.; D. Kirkham; J. Pesek and R. Shaw (eds), Am. Soc. Agron., Madison, Wis., pp. 49-72.

WAGGONER, P. E. and BEN-AMI BRAVDO, 1967. Stomata and the hydrologic cycle. Proc. Nat. Acad. Sci. 57: 1096-1102.

WAGGONER, P. E.; J. L. MONTEITH and G. SZEICZ, 1964. Decreasing transpiration of field plants by chemical closure of stomata. Nature 201: 97-8.

WAGGONER, P. E. and N. C. TURNER, 1971. Transpiration and its control by stomata in a pine forest. Conn. A. E. S. Bull. 726, New Haven, p. 87.

WOOLEY, J. Y. 1967. Relative permeabilities of plastic films to water and carbon dioxide. Pl. Physiol. 42: 641-3.

ZELITCH, I. 1965. Environmental and biochemical control of stomatal movement in leaves. Biol. Rev. 40: 463-82.

ZELITCH, I. 1969. Stomatal control. Ann. Rev. Pl. Physiol. 20: 329-50.

ZELITCH, I. and P. E. WAGGONER, 1962. Effect of chemical control of stomata on transpiration of intact plants. Proc. Nat. Acad. Sci. 48: 1297-9.

Dr. Andrew Goldsworthy

Dr. Goldsworthy was born in London of British parentage just before the Second World War. After spending his earlier life in the small industrial town of Ebbw Vale, he studied at the University College of Swansea where he received a first-class honours degree in Botany. After graduating, he continued his studies at Swansea where he received a Ph.D. for his work on the carbohydrate metabolism of excised roots. He then returned to London where he took up a lecturing appointment in Plant Physiology at Imperial College. At 'Imperial' he has worked on a number of topics, ranging from Crassulacean metabolism to the transfer of organelles between species. However, his main research contribution has been in the physiology and biochemistry of photorespiration. He was, perhaps, the first person to recognize that photorespiration was a detrimental process which arose due to changes in the CO_2 concentration of the atmosphere during evolution, and he suggested a mechanism by which the rather curious metabolism of the C_4 plants could serve to inhibit this process.

8. PHOTORESPIRATION IN RELATION TO CROP YIELD

ANDREW GOLDSWORTHY
*Imperial College of Science &
Technology, London*

Introduction

There is overwhelming evidence that the bulk of present-day land plants lose a considerable amount of their photosynthate as CO_2 within a few seconds of its being fixed. This process of CO_2 release is light dependent and, because of its otherwise superficial resemblance to respiration, it has been given the name *photorespiration*. However, unlike true respiration (frequently called dark respiration) it performs no useful function in making energy available to the plant. Instead, its occurrence leads to a *loss* of energy and this is responsible for a considerable reduction in the yield of many of our crops.

Photorespiration probably arose in evolution due to the gradual loss of CO_2 from the Earth's atmosphere to a level at which most land plants cannot take it up without losing some of what has already been fixed. However, there is evidence that some of the newer arrivals on the evolutionary scene, the so-called C_4 plants, have evolved a CO_2 concentrating mechanism which generates a high CO_2 concentration for their photosynthetic enzymes, and have in this way almost eliminated photorespiration.

In this chapter, I shall attempt to summarize the present state of knowledge in the field of photorespiration and the way in which it affects crop yields.

The Measurement of Photorespiration

Photorespiration is a process by which green plants take up oxygen and release CO_2 in the light and it can be measured by measuring either of these two activities. Unfortunately, most photorespiring tissues also show an oxygen uptake and CO_2 release in the light due to true respiration. This leads to an error in measurements of photorespiration, but this error is small, the rate of photorespiration for a tissue being normally several times greater than its rate of true respiration as measured in the dark. Furthermore, there is evidence that the rate of true respiration is reduced to an even lower level in the light (Goldsworthy, 1970; Jackson & Volk, 1970). These authors have reviewed various techniques for measuring photorespiration, but there are difficulties involved with each method which make precise measurement impossible. The main problem is that, under normal circumstances, photosynthesis and photorespiration occur simultaneously in the same tissue and carry out opposite overall reactions.

$$CO_2 + H_2O \underset{\text{PHOTORESPIRATION}}{\overset{\text{PHOTOSYNTHESIS}}{\rightleftarrows}} \text{PHOTOSYNTHATE} + O_2$$

Some of the simpler ways of measuring photorespiration are to inhibit photosynthesis and to measure O_2 uptake or CO_2 output. One means of doing this is to put a plant or leaf in the light into a CO_2-free air stream, so that photosynthesis is inhibited by lack of CO_2 and photorespiration can be measured as the rate of CO_2 output. This is not an accurate measurement because some of the CO_2 released by photorespiration is refixed by photosynthesis so that the rate of photorespiration is underestimated. Although the degree of this underestimate can be minimized by using fast air flow rates to sweep as much as possible of the CO_2 away from the leaf before it is refixed, the error cannot be eliminated altogether by this means.

Another way of measuring photorespiration is to turn off the light and to measure the CO_2 released immediately afterwards. This is because photorespiration goes on for a minute or so after photosynthesis has stopped and takes the form of a sudden outburst of CO_2 at the onset of darkness which rapidly declines to the much lower level of CO_2 release due to true respiration. The peak rate of CO_2 release is taken as a measure of photorespiration (Decker, 1955). However, this too could lead to an underestimate if the cessation of photosynthesis is not as abrupt as assumed and some of the outburst is refixed.

Other more sophisticated methods of measuring photorespiration are also not without their difficulties. Because of the criticism that the above two methods measure photorespiration when photosynthesis is absent, or at least greatly reduced, and that its rate may not be normal under these circumstances, attempts have been made to measure photorespiration actually during active photosynthesis by the use of isotopic tracers. For example, photorespiration has been measured as the rate of $^{18}O_2$ uptake from an atmosphere containing this isotope, but again this leads to an underestimate of photorespiration because some of the $^{16}O_2$ released by photosynthesis is taken up by photorespiration in addition to the supplied $^{18}O_2$.

In conclusion, it may be said that, to date, all methods for measuring photorespiration are somewhat inaccurate and most lead to an underestimate of the true rate. Despite this, it has been generally found that measured rates of photorespiration are very high, commonly three or four times the rate of true respiration measured for the same tissue in the dark.

Differences between Photorespiration and True Respiration

THE EFFECT OF OXYGEN CONCENTRATION

The most obvious difference between true respiration and photo-respiration is the effect of oxygen concentration on the rates of the two processes. In most tissues true respiration is saturated at oxygen concentrations as low as two or three per cent (Beevers, 1960) and virtually no increase in rate is observed above these concentrations. Photorespiration, on the other hand, increases steadily with oxygen concentration all the way from zero to one hundred per cent (Forrester et al., 1966a, b).

THE REQUIREMENT FOR THE PHOTOSYNTHETIC APPARATUS

Although true respiration can occur in any living cell, photorespiration is intimately linked to photosynthesis and occurs only in cells which are capable of photosynthesis.

Non-photosynthetic tissues, such as non-green floral parts and the leaves of mutants which have lost the ability to photosynthesize, do not photo-respire. This was shown by Hew and Krotkov (1968) who demonstrated that although such tissues evolved CO_2 in the light, this was not due to photorespiration because it was insensitive to changes in oxygen concentration. A similar finding was noted by Downton and Tregunna (1968b) who observed that normal green tissues which had been treated with the photosynthetic inhibitor DCMU (dichlorophenyl-dimethylurea) also became incapable of photorespiration, although they were still capable of an oxygen insensitive CO_2 output, presumably due to true respiration.

THE NATURE OF THE SUBSTRATE

Goldsworthy (1966) showed that photorespiration and true respiration used different substrates. He allowed pieces of tobacco leaf to accumulate radioactive photosynthate by a period of photosynthesis in $^{14}CO_2$. A CO_2-free air stream was then passed over them and the specific radioactivity of the CO_2 released by the leaves was measured, either in the light or in the dark. It was noted that the CO_2 evolved in the light was about twice as radioactive per unit volume as that given off in darkness. This was interpreted as meaning that two different substrates with differing specific radioactivities were being oxidized, the more radioactive one being oxidized in the light. The specific radioactivity of the CO_2 given off in the light approached that of the labelled CO_2 originally fed and it was tentatively suggested that the substrate from which it arose was mainly the stored photosynthate within the chloroplasts. The CO_2 evolved in the dark, being less heavily labelled, probably arose to a greater extent from other materials, perhaps mainly outside the chloroplasts.

ENERGY RELATIONSHIPS

It is now clear that the biochemistry of photorespiration differs fundamentally from that of true respiration. True respiration brings about the oxidation of its substrates to yield CO_2 and energy, mainly in the form of ATP and reduced pyridine nucleotides. Photorespiration, however, does not lead to a net production of ATP or reduced nucleotides. Instead, its main function appears to be the oxidation of glycollate which arises as an unwanted byproduct of photosynthesis. The bulk of the carbon of glycollate, after oxidation, is converted to carbohydrate, but the remainder is converted to CO_2 which is released as the CO_2 of photorespiration. To do this, photorespiration actually *uses* energy in the form of ATP and reduced pyridine nucleotides.

The Metabolism of Photorespiration

EVIDENCE FOR GLYCOLLATE AS THE SUBSTRATE FOR PHOTORESPIRATION

Evidence that glycollate is the source of much of the CO_2 which is given off in photorespiration comes from a number of sources. Zelitch (1958) observed that green leaves produced large quantities of glycollate in the light but not in the dark. Marker and Whittingham (1967) and later,

Kisaki and Tolbert (1970) showed that leaves could oxidize artificially supplied glycollate to yield, amongst other things, CO_2. The inhibition of an enzyme which oxidizes glycollate appears to inhibit photorespiration and causes a temporary increase in the apparent rate of photosynthesis in leaves which photorespire, but not in leaves which do not (Zelitch, 1966).

THE BIOSYNTHESIS OF GLYCOLLATE

Glycollate synthesis appears to be widespread in photosynthetic organisms and has been demonstrated in many of the algae (Hellebust, 1965) and in higher plants (Zelitch, 1958). That glycollate is an unwanted metabolite is evidenced by the fact that many of the algae excrete it into the surrounding water (Tolbert & Zill, 1956; Hellebust, 1965). Higher plants cannot excrete it in this way, but oxidize it instead by the process of photorespiration. However, whatever its ultimate fate, the origin of the glycollate seems to be similar in all of these organisms. For example, environmental factors affect glycollate production in the same way in both the algae and the higher plants, in particular, glycollate production occurs only in the light and is stimulated by high oxygen and low CO_2 concentrations (Benson & Calvin, 1950; Wilson & Calvin, 1955; Zelitch & Walker, 1964; Coombs & Whittingham, 1966; Ellyard & Gibbs, 1969). In addition the pattern of labelling in glycollate when $^{14}CO_2$ is being photosynthesized is the same in both algae and higher plants.

The site of glycollate production is the chloroplast. Isolated chloroplasts are capable of synthesizing glycollate (Kearney & Tolbert, 1962; Ellyard & Gibbs, 1969). It is an early product of photosynthesis and becomes labelled within seconds when $^{14}CO_2$ is being photosynthesized (Benson & Calvin, 1950). The exact mechanism of glycollate synthesis has been a matter for argument for many years and many possible mechanisms have been postulated (see Zelitch, 1971). However, the best documented mechanism is that proposed by a group of workers in Illinois (Ogren & Bowes, 1971; Bowes *et al.*, 1971). They obtained evidence that a derivative of glycollate, namely, 2-phosphoglycollate, was produced as a result of the apparent malfunctioning of the enzyme RuDP carboxylase. The proper function of this enzyme is to fix CO_2 for the Calvin cycle. It does this by adding a molecule of CO_2 to the 5-carbon compound ribulose-1, 5-diphosphate (RuDP) to form the two 3-carbon molecules of phosphoglyceric acid (PGA) which are further metabolized into sugars etc. by the Calvin cycle. However, these workers showed that oxygen was able to function as an alternative substrate for this enzyme in place of CO_2. Using purified preparations of RuDP carboxylase they showed that when oxygen underwent the reaction in place of CO_2, *phosphoglycollate* was produced. The exact mechanism of the reaction was not investigated but it is probably an oxidative splitting of the 5-carbon RuDP into a 2-carbon and a 3-carbon unit:

Normal

RuDP (5-carbon) $+ CO_2$ $\rightarrow$ PGA (3-carbon) $+$ PGA (3-carbon)

Malfunction

RuDP (5-carbon) $+ O_2$ $\rightarrow$ Phosphoglycollate (2-carbon) $+$? (3-carbon)

Phosphoglycollate, produced by this means, can be converted within the chloroplasts to free glycollate by phosphoglycollate phosphatase. This enzyme, first demonstrated by Richardson and Tolbert (1961) and shown to be located in the chloroplasts by Thompson and Whittingham (1967) is irreversible, highly active and specific for phosphoglycollate. Its only possible function is to produce glycollate from phosphoglycollate and its very existence has been taken as evidence that glycollate arises in nature from phosphoglycollate.

The above proposition for the mechanism of glycollate biosynthesis is particularly satisfactory because it explains all of the following observations.

(1) High oxygen and low CO_2 concentrations stimulate glycollate production. If glycollate arises due to oxygen competing with CO_2 for an enzyme, then anything which increases the O_2/CO_2 ratio would be expected to increase glycollate synthesis.

(2) Glycollate is produced only in the light. The enzyme RuDP carboxylase, when in its natural state in the chloroplasts, is only active in the light (Jensen & Bassham, 1968).

(3) Glycollate becomes labelled when $^{14}CO_2$ is being photosynthesized after approximately the same time interval as RuDP.

(4) If this mechanism is correct, glycollate would arise from carbon atoms 1 and 2 of RuDP. In tracer experiments, when these two atoms of RuDP are equally labelled (as in short periods of photosynthesis in $^{14}CO_2$) both carbon atoms of glycollate are also equally labelled (Rabeson *et al.*, 1962). In other experiments, when carbon atoms 1 and 2 of RuDP would be expected to be unequally labelled (as when specifically labelled glucose is supplied in the light) the two carbon atoms of glycollate are also unequally labelled (Marker & Whittingham, 1966).

(5) The capacity to produce glycollate has been retained during evolution, even though it appears to be detrimental to the plant. Naturally, the loss of the enzyme which leads to the production of glycollate, namely RuDP carboxylase, would also lead to the loss of the plant's ability to photosynthesize.

In conclusion, we may say that there is a satisfactory explanation for the mechanism of glycollate production which is firmly backed by experimental evidence. It remains possible that there may also be other mechanisms, but these have yet to be demonstrated in quite such unequivocal terms.

The Further Metabolism of Glycollate

From the foregoing, it would seem that phosphoglycollate is produced, apparently by accident, from an essential intermediate of photosynthesis. As far as can be judged at present, the remainder of the pathway leading from phosphoglycollate is concerned with recapturing as much of this byproduct as possible and converting it to more useful materials. Experiments in which labelled glycollate was fed to leaves and leaf preparations indicate that it is oxidized and converted via a number of intermediates to carbohydrate. During the process, some of its carbon is lost as CO_2 and it is this which gives rise to CO_2 of photorespiration. This metabolism can be conveniently divided into three stages.

1. Metabolism of Glycollate by the Peroxisomes

No further metabolism of glycollate takes place within the chloroplasts. Glycollate leaves the chloroplasts and enters small cytoplasmic organelles called peroxisomes. Peroxisomes can be regarded as packets of enzymes, at least one of which generates hydrogen peroxide as a byproduct. Catalase is also present to destroy this peroxide, which might otherwise be toxic. There are many different kinds of peroxisomes and they occur in both animals and plants (De Duve, 1969). Those of green leaves contain enzymes for glycollate metabolism. They contain glycollate oxidase which oxidizes the hydroxyl group of glycollate to the corresponding aldehyde using oxygen derived from the atmosphere and, at the same time, generating hydrogen peroxide. The product of this reaction, glyoxylate, is then converted to the corresponding amino acid, glycine, still within the peroxisome, by an amino-transferase reaction. The donor of the amino group in this reaction may be one of a number of other amino acids, but glutamate seems to be the most active in this respect, becoming converted to α-oxoglutarate in the process (Kisaki & Tolbert, 1969).

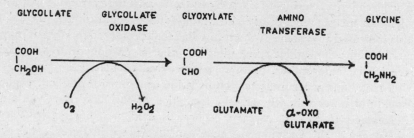

2. Metabolism of Glycine by the Mitochondria

The peroxisomes carry out no further reactions with glycine. Instead the glycine is released and enters the mitochondria for the next stage in its metabolism. This stage is complex, probably involving many enzymes, but the overall reaction is the conversion of two molecules of glycine to one of the amino acid serine, with the loss of one molecule of CO_2 and one of ammonia. This process, which involves an oxidation, appears to be coupled to the oxidative phosphorylation system of the mitochondria so that two molecules of ATP are produced for each molecule of serine formed (Bird et al., 1972).

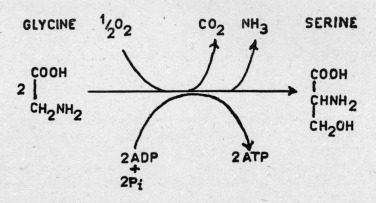

It is the CO_2 given off at this stage which is evolved in the process of photorespiration.

3. The Conversion of Serine to Carbohydrate

Ongun and Stocking (1965) reported that in tobacco leaves some of the label from photosynthesized $^{14}CO_2$ first entered glycine and serine and then became incorporated into carbohydrate. Similarly, artificially added serine-3-^{14}C also became incorporated into carbohydrate, but only in the light. This suggested that the last stage in the photorespiratory pathway, the conversion of serine to carbohydrate, is an energy requiring process which can use the energy of light. Non-aqueous separation of the chloroplasts indicated that some of the serine had in fact entered them, so it may be that this light dependent conversion of serine to carbohydrate was taking place in the chloroplasts. However, since the carbohydrate products of serine metabolism accumulated both inside and outside the chloroplasts, it could not be certain whether the formation of carbohydrate from serine was confined to the chloroplasts. There is evidence that at least some of the stages in this reaction sequence can take place in peroxisomes since these particles have been shown to contain some of the necessary enzymes (Tolbert & Yamazaki, 1969). In particular, peroxisomes derived from spinach leaves were shown to contain an aminotransferase which converts

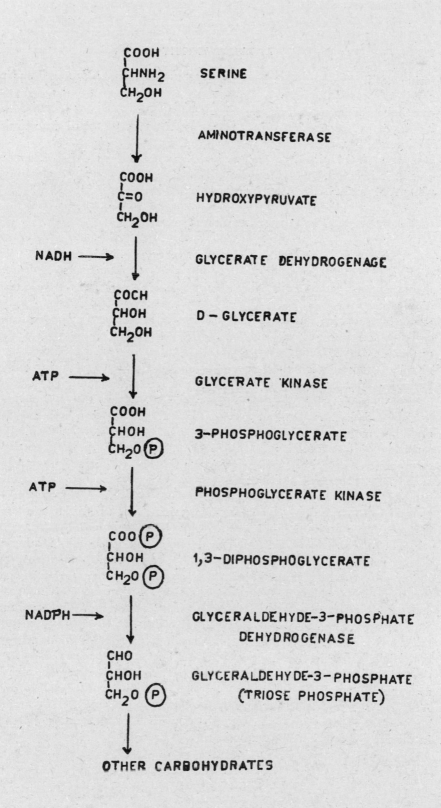

serine to hydroxypyruvate and a NAD-linked dehydrogenase which converts hydroxypyruvate to D-glycerate. The exact location of the remainder of the pathway is not clear, but a D-glycerate kinase enzyme has been demonstrated in higher plant leaves which uses ATP to convert D-glycerate into 3-phosphoglycerate (Cheung *et al.*, 1968). This compound (PGA) is, of course, an intermediate of the Calvin cycle and would, if it entered the chloroplasts, become converted to carbohydrate, using ATP and NADPH, by the normal processes of photosynthesis.

The Energetics of Photorespiration

Unlike true respiration, which makes energy available in the form of ATP and reduced pyridine nucleotides, photorespiration actually uses these substances and entails a net energy loss. To convert two molecules of glycollate to carbohydrate *generates* two molecules of ATP in the conversion of glycine to serine and CO_2, but the subsequent conversion of serine to carbohydrate *uses* two molecules of ATP and two of reduced pyridine nucleotide (NADH and NADPH). If all the carbon of the original two glycollate molecules is to be recovered, then the CO_2 released during serine formation must be refixed by normal photosynthesis and this requires two further molecules of NADPH and three of ATP. Thus, to restore to the level of carbohydrate the four carbon atoms lost in the form of a pair of glycollate molecules, the plant must use a net total of four molecules of reduced pyridine nucleotides and three of ATP. To put this in perspective, this represents nearly half the energy which was needed in the form of ATP and NADPH to fix those four carbon atoms initially from CO_2. The situation is, therefore, like that of a merchant who has to buy back, at half price, property which was stolen from him by a thief. He may not be pleased, but it is better than having to pay the full price elsewhere.

The total amount of energy lost by the plant will depend on the amount of glycollate produced. That this can be considerable was shown by Zelitch (1959) who measured the rate of glycollate synthesis by following the rate of its accumulation when its further metabolism was blocked by an enzyme inhibitor. He found that, in tobacco, about half of the carbon fixed by photosynthesis was passing into glycollate. Other measurements, based on the rate of CO_2 release by photorespiration suggest that this proportion might be even higher (see Zelitch, 1971). It can be seen, therefore, that photorespiration must represent a considerable loss of the plant's available energy. Were it not for photorespiration, more NADPH and ATP would be available for the initial CO_2 fixation reaction, thus causing an increase in the rate of photosynthesis, with a corresponding increase in the rate of dry matter accumulation and growth.

The Inhibition of Photorespiration and the Increase in Yield

Dramatic increases in growth rate of the order of 50 to 100 per cent have been obtained by growing plants under conditions where photorespiration is inhibited. This has been done by inhibiting the synthesis of phosphoglycollate. Attempts to inhibit later stages in the photorespiratory pathway are counterproductive since they prevent the proper recovery of the carbon lost as glycollate. So far, the only effective means of reducing phosphoglycollate production without producing toxic effects is to reduce the O_2/CO_2 ratio in the air surrounding the plant. This can be done either by reducing the oxygen concentration or increasing the CO_2 concentration.

INCREASING PRODUCTIVITY AT LOW OXYGEN CONCENTRATIONS

It is now well-documented that low oxygen conditions inhibit photorespiration and bring about a corresponding increase in the rate of photosynthesis of many plants. Zelitch (1971) has collected data from several authors which indicate that reducing the oxygen concentration from its normal 21% to 2% increases the rate of photosynthesis of a variety of plants by factors ranging from 35% to 100%. These include many important crop plants such as wheat, sunflower and sugar beet. That such increases in photosynthesis also result in increases in growth rate was shown by Björkman and his co-workers (1969) who observed that lowering the oxygen concentration to 4% roughly doubled the rate of dry matter production by *Mimulus*.

Despite these obviously spectacular results, it is unlikely that this technique will be exploited commercially for crop production because of practical difficulties and expense. The technique requires that the plants be grown in an air-tight enclosure in which four-fifths of the atmosphere must be replaced by nitrogen gas. Because the enclosure is air-tight, the CO_2 required for photosynthesis must also be added artificially. Apart from this, if we consider the practical difficulty of tending crops in an atmosphere which will not support human life, it is not difficult to see why it is unlikely that these methods will be used for large-scale agricultural production.

INCREASING PRODUCTIVITY AT HIGH CO_2 CONCENTRATIONS

While it is difficult and expensive to reduce the O_2/CO_2 ratio by reducing the oxygen concentration, it is relatively cheap and easy to achieve the same effect by increasing the CO_2 concentration and the concentrations required are not harmful to human life. A moderately air-tight enclosure is still required, but because the normal atmospheric CO_2 concentration is so small (0.03%) it requires very little additional CO_2 to alter the O_2/CO_2 ratio considerably so as to produce a large inhibition of photorespiration. For example, to lower the O_2/CO_2 ratio by a factor of five, by lowering the O_2 concentration requires that four-fifths of the air be swept out of the chamber by nitrogen, but the same effect can be achieved by increasing the CO_2 concentration by a factor of five. This, however, only requires the addition of an extra 0.12% of CO_2. The fact that CO_2 concentrations of this order inhibit photorespiration is evidenced by the observation of Egle and Fock (1967) that the 'dark outburst' of CO_2, occurring due to photo-respiration, was inhibited by 0.12% CO_2 in sunflowers and beans.

It has been known for a very long time that the rate of growth of green-house crops can be increased tremendously by enriching the air within the green-house to about 0.1 to 0.15% with CO_2 (Wittwer & Robb, 1964) although the inhibition of photorespiration as being a prime causal factor has only recently been postulated (Goldsworthy, 1969).

This hypothesis explains the observation that CO_2 enrichment is effective during the winter months when photosynthesis is limited by low light intensity rather than CO_2 availability. This is because the CO_2 concen-trations used are sufficient to inhibit photorespiration and so prevent the consequent drain on the plant's limited energy resources when little light is available. Other evidence indicating that photorespiration is an impor-tant factor in the CO_2 enrichment effect can be found in the work of Bishop and Whittingham (1968) who observed, using $^{14}CO_2$, that tomato plants growing under conditions of CO_2 enrichment were relatively deficient in the photorespiratory intermediates, glycine and serine.

It would perhaps be wrong of me to discuss the practicalities of CO_2 enrichment here since it has been well-documented elsewhere (see Wittwer & Robb, 1964; Wittwer, 1974). However, I might say, in summary, that CO_2 enrichment, as a means of increasing crop production in green-houses is already widely practised and produces increases in yield of the same order as those induced by low oxygen in plants which normally photorespire; increases in the region of 30 to 100% being common. However, like the low oxygen technique, it suffers from the disadvantage that a more or less air-tight enclosure is needed in which to grow the plants and it is, therefore, unsuitable for large-scale agricultural use in the open air.

INCREASING PRODUCTIVITY WITH CHEMICAL INHIBITORS

If there were an enzyme inhibitor which could be sprayed onto plants to prevent phosphoglycollate synthesis, it could be used, even in the open air, to suppress photorespiration. If it were cheap enough and non-toxic it could be used in agriculture to increase the yield of field-grown crops.

Unfortunately, as yet, no such chemical exists. A few, such as the α-hydroxy-sulphonates and the weedkiller monuron (CMU) have been reported to inhibit glycollate synthesis (Zelitch, 1971) but these are also inhibitors of photosynthesis. The problem of finding an inhibitor for phosphoglycollate synthesis which does not also inhibit photosynthesis may be considerable, for, if the enzyme responsible for both processes is RuDP carboxylase, it may not be possible to inhibit one of its activities without also inhibiting the other.

C_4 Plants—Nature's Answer to the Problem

It would seem probable that most of the evolution of the photosynthetic mechanism took place when the Earth's atmosphere was richer in CO_2 than it is now. Because of this, glycollate synthesis was inhibited and photorespiration did not occur. It would be only comparatively recently on a geological time-scale that the CO_2 level has fallen sufficiently to permit photorespiration to occur at today's high rates. Nevertheless, it is now clear that some plants have evolved so as to inhibit photorespiration. They do so by possessing a CO_2 pumping mechanism which increases the CO_2 concentration in the region of their RuDP carboxylase to such a level as to inhibit phosphoglycollate production. The operation of this pump involves the participation of certain 4-carbon acids as CO_2 carriers. Early experiments by Hatch and Slack (Hatch & Slack, 1966; Hatch et al., 1967) revealed that these 4-carbon acids appeared to be the first labelled products when $^{14}CO_2$ was being photosynthesized; such plants were consequently called C_4 plants, or sometimes 'Hatch and Slack' plants. Other plants, not possessing this pump, fix CO_2 directly into the Calvin cycle, in which the 3-carbon phosphoglyceric acid is the initial product. These are now called C_3 plants, or sometimes 'Calvin' plants. C_4 plants appear to lack photorespiration, their rates of photosynthesis are roughly double those of most C_3 plants and these rates are not further stimulated by low oxygen concentrations (Downes & Hesketh, 1968).

The C_4 plants appear to have arisen independently at several points in evolution. Examples are found in both the Monocotyledons and the Dicotyledons, although most of the economically important ones occur in the Gramineae amongst the tropical grasses. Those grasses in the chloridoideragrostoid and panicoid lines of evolution are typically C_4 plants, maize, sorghum and sugarcane being prominent examples (Downton & Tregunna, 1968a, b). Most other tropical grasses, e.g. rice, are C_3 plants and so are nearly all of the temperate grasses such as the cereals, wheat, oats and barley. Amongst the Dicotyledons a number of isolated examples of C_4 plants are found, mainly within the Centrospermeae, *Amaranthus* and *Atriplex* being examples. The genus *Atriplex* is interesting because it contains both C_3 and C_4 species which are sufficiently closely related for interbreeding to be possible. In an elegant series of breeding experiments within this genus, Björkman and his co-workers (1971) have shown that the C_4 characteristic is controlled by several genes which segregate independently. Hybrids between C_3 and C_4 plants in these experiments were less efficient photosynthetically than either of the parents.

No matter what their taxonomic group all C_4 plants have a similar anatomy in which the photosynthetic tissue is confined to two concentric layers of cells, each only one cell deep, surrounding each of the vascular bundles. The inner one is called the *bundle sheath* and the outer one the *mesophyll*. By carefully controlled grinding techniques, it has proved possible to prepare extracts from each of these layers, moderately free from contamination by the other. When this was done, it was found that the two layers contain different photosynthetic enzymes (Björkman & Gauhl, 1969; Hatch *et al.*, 1971; Berry *et al.*, 1970). In particular, nearly all of the leaf's RuDP carboxylase is in the bundle sheath, whereas the mesophyll contains another CO_2 fixing enzyme, PEP carboxylase. This fixes CO_2 by making it react with phosphoenol-pyruvate (PEP) so as to form the 4-carbon acid oxaloacetate. This, in turn, is rapidly transformed into two other 4-carbon acids, malate and aspartate by a dehydrogenase and an aminotransferase enzyme respectively, which are also active in the mesophyll. Berry *et al.* (1970) showed by autoradiographic techniques that these 4-carbon acids are rapidly translocated into the bundle sheath cells probably via the highly developed plasmadesmata which connect the two layers. Further, it was shown that the chloroplasts of the bundle sheath contain enzymes which liberate CO_2 from these C_4 acids, leaving behind the C_3 acid pyruvate. The CO_2 liberated is refixed by the RuDP carboxylase in the bundle sheath chloroplasts, where the remainder of the plant's photosynthesis occurs via a normal Calvin cycle. The pyruvate formed is translocated back to the mesophyll, where it is reconverted to PEP by the enzyme PEP synthetase, using ATP and inorganic phosphate, so as to be ready to pick up another molecule of CO_2.

It was for a while a puzzle why these plants do not appear to photorespire. That is to say, they do not release CO_2 into CO_2-free air in the light, they do not show an outburst of CO_2 at the onset of darkness and their rates of photosynthesis are not stimulated by low oxygen concentrations (Forrester *et al.*, 1966b). Despite this apparent lack of photorespiration, there is evidence that C_4 plants do, nevertheless, contain the enzymes for photorespiration. Enzymes for glycollate oxidation are found in peroxisomes in the bundle sheath cells (Kisaki & Tolbert, 1970). It was claimed by these workers that C_4 plants *do* photorespire, but they do not release their photorespiratory CO_2 into CO_2-free air, simply because it is generated in the bundle sheath and is refixed by the PEP carboxylase of the mesophyll on its way out.

While such a total refixation of photorespired CO_2 may be possible, this simple hypothesis does not explain why low oxygen levels do not stimulate photosynthesis in C_4 species.   This is because if they were to refix all their photorespired CO_2, they would need extra energy to do it, and even more energy to convert to carbohydrate the serine formed in this photorespiration.   The inhibition of photorespiration by low oxygen should, therefore, make more energy available for photosynthesis, and so stimulate photosynthetic rates in C_4 species as well as C_3 species.   This has been found not to be the case (Forrester *et al.*, 1966b; Bull, 1969; Björkman *et al.*, 1969). Furthermore, since the rate of glycollate synthesis in a C_4 plant appears to be only a small fraction of that in C_3 plants (Zelitch, 1958) it would seem more likely that the success of the C_4 plant is due to its more limited capacity to synthesize glycollate and photorespire than due to its ability to refix its photorespired CO_2.

Goldsworthy and Day (1970a) put forward a suggestion that the most likely mechanism for the inhibition of glycollate synthesis and photorespiration in C_4 species is that the C_4 pathway is acting as a pump, generating a high CO_2 concentration in the chloroplasts of the bundle sheath, and by so doing, inhibiting glycollate production.   This hypothesis was later shown to be substantially correct when Hatch (1971) measured the size of the CO_2 pool generated from the C_4 acids in these plants.   After making certain assumptions as to the volume of the pool, he concluded that its concentration must be something like one hundred times greater than that of a tissue in direct equilibrium with the atmosphere.   If this is correct, it should accomplish an almost complete inhibition of glycollate synthesis and photorespiration, with no further reduction being possible by altering the oxygen concentration of the air.

Pleasing as the above explanation is, there still remains one point to be met.   If C_4 plants do not normally produce glycollate, what need have they for peroxisomes and why was glycollate detected in them by Zelitch (1958)?   The answer might be that although under normal circumstances glycollate is not produced, it can be produced under adverse conditions. For example, if the stomata close due to dry conditions, the CO_2 concentration in the air spaces of the leaf falls due to photosynthesis.   Sooner or later a point is reached when the pump, starved of its CO_2 input, fails to maintain the CO_2 concentration in the bundle sheath chloroplasts at a level adequate to prevent glycollate synthesis.   Glycollate production and its consequent photorespiration would then occur and peroxisomes would be required, much as in a C_3 plant.   The only difference between a C_4 plant under these conditions and a C_3 plant is that a C_4 plant is able to refix all of its photorespired CO_2 using the PEP carboxylase in the mesophyll.   It is worth noting that when Zelitch (1958) detected glycollate synthesis in C_4

leaves, he did so in the presence of α-hydroxysulphonate, a substance which is known to cause stomatal closure (Zelitch & Walker, 1964).

Apart from their greater maximum rates of photosynthesis, C_4 plants have another advantage over C_3 plants. This is because they have low CO_2 compensation points which help them photosynthesize under dry conditions. The CO_2 compensation point is the lowest CO_2 concentration from which a plant can carry out net photosynthesis. A C_3 plant cannot carry out net photosynthesis from air containing less than about 50 ppm of CO_2 (the exact value depends on species and temperature (see Goldsworthy & Day, 1970b for means of measuring compensation points). This is because at this concentration photosynthesis has been slowed to a level at which it is exactly counterbalanced by photorespiration. C_4 plants, because they do not photorespire, can reduce the CO_2 concentration of the air virtually to zero and are said to have near-zero compensation points. In either case, when the stomata are almost closed under dry conditions, the CO_2 concentration within the air spaces of the leaf must fall to near the compensation point. Because for a C_4 plant, this is lower than for a C_3 plant, then the concentration gradient for CO_2 diffusing into the leaf from the atmosphere is steeper in C_4 plants. This means that diffusion of CO_2 into the leaf and hence photosynthesis will be correspondingly faster in the C_4 plant, and that for a given amount of water lost due to transpiration, the C_4 plant should capture more CO_2 than the C_3 plant. Examination of the literature on the subject suggests that this is broadly true, the general finding being that for a given water loss, C_4 plants fix about twice as much CO_2 as C_3 plants (Hesketh, 1963; Bull, 1969; Shantz & Piemeisel, 1927).

It can be seen that the C_4 plant has overcome the problem of photorespiration. This gives it the potential for a higher maximum photosynthetic rate and also the ability to photosynthesize more rapidly and with less water loss under dry conditions. It is almost certain for these reasons that C_4 species make such good crop plants. So far, their cultivation is very largely limited to the tropical and warmer regions of the world, maize, sorghum and sugarcane being typical examples. Unfortunately, most C_4 plants do not grow very well in the temperate and colder regions. The reason for this is not yet clear. It may be that there is something inherent in C_4 metabolism which makes it unsuitable for operation at cooler temperatures. Alternatively, it may be because nearly all C_4 plants arose in the drier regions of the tropics, where selection pressure for them was greatest, they arose from species which were already adapted to tropical conditions, and have merely retained that adaptation. If the latter explanation is correct we would expect C_4 species to spread to the cooler regions of the world, either naturally, or by artificial selective breeding. There is some evidence that this has already been happening, e.g. the C_4 plant *Spartina anglica* grows well in the wild state on the temperate coastline of the British Isles. If plant breeders can separate the genes for C_4 metabolism from those giving adaptation for tropical environments it may be possible to extend to all parts of the world the tremendous benefits of having crops which do not photorespire.

REFERENCES

BEEVERS, H. 1960. Respiratory Metabolism of Plants. Row Peterson, New York.

BENSON, A. A. and M. CALVIN, 1950. The path of carbon in photosynthesis. VII. Respiration and photosynthesis. J. expt. Bot. 1: 65-8.

BERRY, J. A.; W. J. S. DOWNTON and E. B. TREGUNNA, 1970. The photosynthetic carbon metabolism of *Zea mays* and *Gomphrena globosa*: the location of the CO_2 fixation and carboxyl transfer reactions. Can. J. Bot. 48: 777-86.

BIRD, I. F.; M. J. CORNELIUS; A. J. KEYS and C. P. WHITTINGHAM, 1972. Oxidation and phosphorylation associated with the conversion of glycine to serine. Phytochemistry 11: 1587-94.

BISHOP, P. M. and C. P. WHITTINGHAM, 1968. The photosynthesis of tomato plants in a carbon dioxide enriched atmosphere. Photosynthetica 2: 31-8.

BJÖRKMAN, O. and E. GAUHL, 1969. Carboxydismutase activity in plants with and without β-carboxylation photosynthesis. Planta 88: 197-203.

BJÖRKMAN, O.; E. GAUHL; W. M. HIESEY; F. NICHOLSON and M. A. NOBS, 1969. Growth of *Mimulus, Marchantia* and *Zea* under different oxygen-carbon dioxide levels. Ann. Rep. Carnegie Inst. Wash. 1967-8: 477-9.

BJÖRKMAN, O.; R. W. PEARCY and M. A. NOBS, 1971. Hybrids between *Atriplex* species with and without β-carboxylation photosynthesis. Photosynthetic characteristics. Ann. Rept. Carnegie Inst. Wash. 1969-70: 640-48.

BOWES, G.; W. L. OGREN, and R. H. HAGEMAN, 1971. Phosphoglycollate production catalyzed by ribulose diphosphate carboxylase. Biochem. Biophys. Res. Comm. 45: 716-22.

BULL, T. A. 1969. Photosynthetic efficiencies and photorespiration in Calvin cycle and C_4 dicarboxylic acid plants. Crop Sci. 9: 726-9.

CHEUNG, G. P.; I. Y. ROSENBLUM and H. J. SALLACH, 1968. Comparative studies of enzymes related to serine metabolism in higher plants. Pl. Physiol. 43: 1813-20.

COOMBS, J. and C. P. WHITTINGHAM, 1966. The effect of high partial pressures of oxygen on photosynthesis in *Chlorella*. I. The effect on end products of photosynthesis. Phytochemistry 5: 643-51.

DE DUVE, C. 1969. The peroxisome: a new cytoplasmic organelle. Proc. Roy. Soc. B 173: 71-83.

DECKER, J. P. 1955. A rapid post-illumination acceleration of respiration in green leaves. Pl. Physiol. 30: 82-4.

DOWNES, R. W. and J. D. HESKETH, 1968. Enhanced photosynthesis at low oxygen concentrations: differential response of temperate and tropical grasses. Planta 78: 79-84.

DOWNTON, W. J. S. and E. B. TREGUNNA, 1968a. Carbon dioxide compensation: its relation to photosynthetic carboxylation reactions, systematics of Gramineae and leaf anatomy. Can. J. Bot. 46: 207-15.

DOWNTON, W. J. S. and E. B. TREGUNNA, 1968b. Photorespiration and glycollate metabolism: a re-examination and correlation of some previous studies. Pl. Physiol. 43: 923-9.

EGLE, K. and H. FOCK, 1967. In: Biochemistry of Chloroplasts, Goodwin, T. W. (ed). Acad. Press, New York.

ELLYARD, P. W. and M. GIBBS, 1969. Inhibition of photosynthesis by oxygen in isolated spinach chloroplasts. Pl. Physiol. 44: 1115-21.

FORRESTER, M. L.; G. KROTKOV and C. D. NELSON, 1966a. Effect of oxygen on photosynthesis, photorespiration and respiration in detached leaves. I. Soybean. Pl. Physiol. 41: 422-7.

FORRESTER, M. L.; G. KROTKOV and C. D. NELSON, 1966b. Effect of oxygen on photosynthesis, photorespiration and respiration in detached leaves. II. Corn and other monocotyledons. Pl. Physiol. 41: 428-31.

GOLDSWORTHY, A. 1966. Experiments on the origin of CO_2 released by tobacco leaf segments in the light. Phytochemistry 5: 1013-19.

GOLDSWORTHY, A. 1969. The riddle of photorespiration. Nature (London) 224: 501-2.

GOLDSWORTHY, A. 1970. Photorespiration. Bot. Rev. 36 : 321-40.

GOLDSWORTHY, A. and P. R. DAY, 1970a. Further evidence for the reduced role of photorespiration in low compensation point species. Nature (London) 228: 687-8.

GOLDSWORTHY, A. and P. R. DAY, 1970b. A simple technique for the rapid determination of plant CO_2 compensation points. Pl. Physiol. 46: 850-51.

HATCH, M. D. 1971. The C_4 pathway of photosynthesis. Evidence for an intermediate pool of carbon dioxide and the identity of the donor C_4 dicarboxylic acid. Biochem. J. 125: 425-32.

HATCH, M. D.; C. B. OSMOND and R. O. SLATYER, 1971. Photosynthesis and Photorespiration. Wiley-Interscience, New York.

HATCH, M. D. and C. R. SLACK, 1966. Photosynthesis by sugarcane leaves: a new carboxylation reaction and the pathway of sugar formation. Biochem. J. 101: 103-11.

HATCH, M. D.; C. R. SLACK and H. S. JOHNSON, 1967.   Further studies on a new pathway of photosynthetic carbon dioxide fixation in sugarcane and its occurrence in other plant species.   Biochem. J. 102: 417-22.

HELLEBUST, J. A. 1965.   Excretion of some organic compounds by marine phytoplankton.   Limnology Oceanography 10: 192-206.

HESKETH, J. D. 1963.   Limitations to photosynthesis responsible for differences among species.   Crop Sci. 3: 493-6.

HEW, C. S. and G. KROTKOV, 1968.   Effect of oxygen on the rates of CO_2 evolution in light and in darkness by photosynthesizing and non-photosynthesizing leaves.   Pl. Physiol. 43: 464-6.

JACKSON, W. A. and R. J. VOLK, 1970.   Photorespiration. Ann. Rev. Pl. Physiol. 21 : 385-432.

JENSEN, R. G. and J. A. BASSHAM, 1968.   Photosynthesis by isolated chloroplasts.   III. Light activation of the carboxylation reaction.   Biochem. Biophys. Acta 153: 227-34.

KEARNEY, P. C. and N. E. TOLBERT, 1962.   Appearance of glycollate and related products of photosynthesis outside of chloroplasts.   Arch. Biochem. Biophys. 98: 164-71.

KISAKI, T. and N. E. TOLBERT, 1969.   Glycollate and glyoxylate metabolism in isolated peroxisomes and chloroplasts.   Pl. Physiol. 44: 242-50.

KISAKI, T. and N. E. TOLBERT, 1970.   Glycine as a substrate for photorespiration.   Pl. & Cell Physiol. 11: 247-58.

MARKER, A. F. H. and C. P. WHITTINGHAM, 1966.   The photoassimilation of glucose in *Chlorella* with reference to the role of glycolic acid.   Proc. Roy. Soc. B 165: 473-85.

MARKER, A. F. H. and C. P. WHITTINGHAM, 1967.   The site of synthesis of sucrose in plant cells.   J. expt. Bot. 18: 732-9.

OGREN, W. L. and G. BOWES, 1971.   Ribulose diphosphate carboxylase regulates soybean photorespiration.   Nature New Biology 230: 159-60.

ONGUN, A. and C. R. STOCKING, 1965.   Effect of light on the incorporation of serine into the carbohydrates of chloroplasts and non-chloroplast fractions of tobacco leaves.   Pl. Physiol. 40: 819-24.

RABESON, R.; N. E. TOLBERT and P. C. KEARNEY, 1962.   Formation of serine and glyceric acid by the glycollate pathway.   Arch. Biochem. Biophys. 98: 154-63.

RICHARDSON, K. E. and N. E. TOLBERT, 1961.   Phosphoglycolic acid phosphatase.   J. biol. Chem. 236: 1285-90.

SHANTZ, H. L. and L. N. PIEMEISEL, 1927.   The water requirements of plants at Akron. Colo. J. agric. Res. 34: 1093-1189.

SLACK, C. R.; M. D. HATCH and D. J. GOODCHILD, 1969.   Distribution of enzymes in mesophyll and parenchyma sheath chloroplasts in maize leaves in relation to the C_4 dicarboxylic acid pathway in photosynthesis.

Biochem. J. 114: 489-98.

THOMPSON, C. M. and C. P. WHITTINGHAM, 1967. Intracellular location of phosphoglycollate phosphatase and glyoxylate reductase. Biochem. Biophys. Acta 143: 642-4.

TOLBERT, N. E. and R. K. YAMAZAKI, 1969. Leaf peroxisomes and their relation to photorespiration and photosynthesis. Ann. New York Acad. Sci. 168: 325-41.

TOLBERT, N. E. and L. P. ZILL, 1956. Excretion of glycolic acid by algae during photosynthesis. J. biol. Chem. 222: 895-906.

WILSON, A. T. and M. CALVIN, 1955. The photosynthetic cycle. CO_2-dependent transients. J. Am. Chem. Soc. 77: 5948-57.

WITTWER, S. H. 1974. Carbon dioxide fertilization of crop plants. *In:* Crop Physiology, Gupta, U. S. (ed), H. A. U., Hissar, India.

WITTWER, S. H. and W. ROBB, 1964. Carbon dioxide enrichment of greenhouse atmospheres for food crop production. Econ. Bot. 18: 34-56.

ZELITCH, I. 1958. The role of glycolic acid oxidase in the respiration of leaves. J. biol. Chem. 233: 1299-1303.

ZELITCH, I. 1959. The relationship of glycolic acid to respiration and photosynthesis in tobacco leaves. J. biol. Chem. 234: 3077-81.

ZELITCH, I. 1966. Increased rate of net photosynthetic carbon dioxide uptake caused by the inhibition of glycollate oxidase. Pl. Physiol. 41: 1623-31.

ZELITCH, I. 1971. Photosyntheses, Photorespiration and Plant Productivity. Acad. Press, New York.

ZELITCH, I. and D. A. WALKER, 1964. The role of glycolic acid metabolism in opening of leaf stomata. Pl. Physiol. 39: 856-62.

Dr. Fumio Iwata

Dr. Iwata was born in 1931 at Kyoto. He did his graduation and Ph.D. in Agronomy from Hokkaido University. In 1957 he joined the agronomy staff at Shikoku National Agricultural Experiment Station and worked on water consumption by forage crops. In 1963 he was placed in charge of field crop researches, especially of management problems in the capacity of Research Agronomist, for Tohoku National Agricultural Research Station, Ministry of Agriculture and Forestry, Japan and is continuing there.

From 1965 to 1967 he joined the University of Hawaii, Hawaii Agricultural Experiment Station, and Ohio Agricultural Research and Development Centre for studying field crop agronomy on East-West Centre scholarship. He was a delegate to the Seventh Inter-Asian Corn Improvement Workshop in Philippines and spent a couple of months studying field crops in south-east Asia in 1971. He received the Japan Crop Science Award with his collaborators for distinguished research in 1971.

His researches have recently emphasized the influence of climatic factors on the growth of field crops especially on corn plant.

9. HEAT UNIT CONCEPT OF CROP MATURITY

FUMIO IWATA
Tohoku National Agricultural
Research Station
Japan

Introduction

Although many climatic factors influence plants, temperature is one of the primary factors affecting growth. Any physiological and morphological development occurring in plants are markedly influenced by temperature. An interesting agronomic application of the temperature effect on plants is the heat unit concept which is based on the idea that plants have a temperature requirement for their growth, development and maturity.

The heat unit system has been widely used as a guide in planting schedules for an orderly harvest of canning crops and as an index in making crop zonation maps for extension of undeveloped agricultural land and multiple cropping systems for effective land use. Furthermore, it has been adopted to flowering time of parent varieties in cross pollination crops for synchronizing the flowering time for breeding and seed production. Considerable effort has been devoted to the development of the heat unit system and numerous attempts have been made to develop accurate methods for estimating the times of flowering and maturity.

This review is an attempt to summarize briefly the present state of knowledge regarding the heat unit systems and to discuss the practical application of the concept for agricultural use.

Remainder Index

It was first suggested by Reaumur in 1735, as cited by Robertson (1968), that the sum of the mean daily shade temperature of air between one stage of development and another was constant for a particular species of plant. Although little attention was paid to this concept for any practical use for a century subsequent to his proposal, thereafter numerous summations of mean daily temperatures during growing period for various crops have been computed by many investigators. However, the summations found for the same variety of plant frequently have varied greatly under different conditions. For example, those with rice plants from planting to heading are 1458 and 1598 °C in hotter and cooler years (Date, 1963), and with potato, 1914 and 2756 °C in hotter and cooler sections (Kurihara *et al.*, 1963), respectively.

In summer crops, generally, the increased summations would be obtained in early plantings; cool years and northern parts showed opposite cases, probably owing to the fact that sums of ineffective temperatures below the cessation of plant growth become larger in the former cases than in the latter. To overcome the weakness in the summations of the whole degrees of daily mean temperatures, the temperatures below the cessation of plant activity should be discounted for the calculation of heat requirements. The point of temperature above which it is accumulated for the summations is called the base temperature. The base temperatures have been determined for various crops empirically and theoretically, as shown in Table 9.1.

Least variability methods for determining the base temperatures are the most common, in which the summations of degree-days from a series of planting or location are calculated on a number of base temperatures and the one showing the least variation in the standard deviation or in the coefficient of variation is found by process of elimination. However, these methods are troublesome since numerous calculations to find out a correct base temperature must be done. Arnold (1959) proposed x-intercept method. According to his explanation, the method makes use of two items of information from each planting; the mean temperature and the mean rate of growth. The latter is presented as follows:

$$\text{Rate of growth} = \frac{100}{\text{Number of days from planting to harvest}}.$$

The values from a series of plantings are then used to calculate a regression equation in which the mean temperature is x and the mean rate of growth

Table 9.1. Base temperature for various crops

Crop			Base temperature °F	Reference
Spinach	..	..	36	Boswell (1934)
Peas	..	..	36	Hope (1962)
Peas	..	..	40	Nagy (1965)
Wheat	..	..	40	Nuttonson (1955)
Barley	..	..	40	Nuttonson (1957)
Lettuce	..	..	40	Madariaga & Knott (1951)
Asparagus	..	..	40	LeCompte & Blumenfeld (1958)
Asparagus	..	..	40	Culpepper & Moon (1939)
Potato	..	..	41	Trenkle (1969)
Potato	..	..	45	Rosca (1968)
Maize	..	..	50	Andrew et al. (1956)
Snap beans	..	..	50	Gould (1950)
Lima beans	..	..	50	Bomalaski (1948)
Pumpkin	..	..	55	Holmes & Robertson (1959)
Tomato	..	..	50	Valli & Jaworski (1965, 1966)
Tomato	..	..	59	Holmes & Robertson (1959)

is y. In this equation the base temperature is obtained as the value of x and y equals 0. This method gives the same answer as the coefficient of variation method.

It is well-known that the base temperature is not so definite. It is varied by the external conditions, by the age of plants and by their previous treatments. Warnock and Isaacs (1969) stated that response to temperatures during the seedling stage of tomatoes might be different than the response during the fruit setting or fruit ripening periods. Likewise, Balvoll and Bremer (1965) described that the base temperature should be varied according to the stage of plant growth.

However, without regard to indefiniteness of the base temperature, estimating development of crops by the remainder index, which is the total summation of the degree-days above the base temperature to reach a particular stage of development, has been often successful. The degree-days during a day are calculated by subtracting the base temperature from the daily mean temperature, as presented by the following formula:

$$\text{Degree-days} = \frac{(\text{minimum} + \text{maximum})}{2} - \text{base temperature}.$$

According to Nuttonson (1955), a wide variety of synonymous terms have been used for the remainder index system to express the heat requirement of crops. Thus, the terms "day-degree", "degree-day", "heat unit", and "thermal unit" are all used to designate one degree per day, on a given scale of mean temperature above the base temperature.

Using the remainder index numerous workers—Ferwerda (1953) with
corn, Lana and Haber (1952) with sweet corn, Austin and Ries (1968) with
tomatoes, Trenkle (1969) with potatoes, LeCompte and Blumenfeld (1958)
with asparagus, and Nagy (1965) with peas, have successfully achieved the
estimation for progress of growth and development of each crop. Airy (1955)
described that the mean of the remainder indices from planting to flowering
for 50 inbreds of corn for each of three planting dates is considerably
constant. Holmes and Robertson (1959) also stated that the indices of
several pea varieties remained almost constant from year to year when the
base temperature was taken at 50 °F. Further, a nearly equal index was
obtained from the data of Andrew et al. (1956) in corn hybrids planted at
two locations, Wageningen (Netherlands) and Spooner, Wisconsin,
(U.S.A.). Similar results in planting date, year and location experiments
have been obtained by several workers as shown in Table 9.2.

Table 9.2. Remainder index for several crops

Crop	Period*	Remainder index °F	C. V. %	Base temperature °F	Season, year or location	Reference
Wheat	P~R	2024	7.5	40	20 locations	Nuttonson (1955)
Wheat	,,	1929	7.6	,.	19 years	,,
Barley	P~R	1958	7.4	40	20 locations	Nuttonson (1957)
Barley	,,	2196	7.0	,,	16 years	,,
Oats	P~R	2089	4.2	40	2 years and 16 plantings	Wiggans (1956)
Peas	P~H	1321	2.5	40	3 years	Katz (1952)
Peas	P~F	683	2.5	,,	3 plantings	Reath & Wittwer (1952)
Maize	P~S	1473	6.1	50	5 plantings	Gilmore & Rogers (1958)
Maize	,,	1505	11.4	,,	2 years and 2 locations	Gunn & Christensen (1965)
Tomato	P~H	4044	1.7	43	4 plantings	Warnock & Isaacs (1969)

*P—planting, R—ripe, H—harvest, F—flowering, and S—silking.

Madariaga and Knott (1951) reported that in 389 fields of commercially
grown lettuce, plants did not utilize the same amount as remainder index
to reach maturity when planted at varying dates. Likewise, in spinach
the remainder index between plant emergence and seed stalk appearance
varied widely with differences of years, planting dates and locations as
described by Boswell (1934). Arnold (1960) pointed out that when the
minimum temperature falls below the base temperature, the degree-day
value is no longer accurate.

Thus, out of the numerous reports published on the remainder index for various crops, some work out fairly well, while the others do not. Therefore, it must be noted that a reasonable consistency of the remainder index obtained from data of a single location, year or planting season may mislead users when the relationship is extrapolated to others.

Growth of plants is retarded when temperature increases above optimum which frequently happens even in the temperate zones. A correction for such excessive temperatures should be considered for refining the method to determining the remainder index (Gunn & Christensen, 1965; Hope, 1962).

Gilmore and Rogers (1958) compared the coefficients of variation of remainder index calculated by taking into account temperatures above and below the bases for growth of corn planted at six different dates. The base temperature here was 50 °F and corrections were made for temperature above 86 or 90 °F. Table 9.3 shows six calculation methods and their coefficients of variation. The coefficients of variation of the corrected indices calculated by the second and third methods are compared to that of the first, and those by the fifth and sixth, to that of the fourth, respectively. In the comparisons of the coefficients of variation between with and without corrections for the optimum temperatures, it was found that the corrections decreased the variations of the remainder indices.

Table 9.3. Comparison of coefficients of variation of heat units required for silking from planting of corn planted at various dates, as calculated by six methods (after Gilmore & Rogers, 1958)

Method of calculation*			Coefficient of variation
Temperature °F	Base	Optimum	%
1. x-50			6.08
2. x-50		90	4.49
3. x-50		86	2.74
4. x-50	50		3.65
5. x-50	50	90	2.05
6. x-50	50	86	1.63

$$* 1: \frac{min+max}{2} -50; \quad 2 \ \& \ 3: \frac{min+(max-degrees\ over\ optimum)}{2} -50;$$

$$4: \frac{(50+min\ above\ 50°)+max}{2} -50;$$

$$5 \ \& \ 6: \frac{(50+min\ above\ 50°)+(max-degrees\ over\ optimum)}{2} -50$$

Recently, Iwata and Okubo (1969a) have calculated the remainder index of corn planted on different dates, in which the least variability method was used for determining the extent of daily mean heat units accumulated. The method was based on the idea to minimize coefficients of variation of the remainder index for a series of plantings by eliminating temperatures above excess and below the base. The extent of a daily mean temperature to be accumulated was evaluated by the coefficient of variation for the remainder index among the planting dates. In this study the least coefficient of variation, 1.43 per cent, was obtained by discounting the temperatures above 25 °C and below 10 °C of a daily mean temperature. Iso-coefficients of variation in relation to upper and lower limit temperature to be accumulated is shown in Fig. 9.1. The mean remainder index for silking of corn and its 95 per cent confidence interval is 807±11 °C. This ± 11 °C fell in only two days. From the above results the silking times can be accurately estimated regardless of planting dates and moreover eliminated temperatures above and below the bases were determined simultaneously.

Further studies on an application of the above-mentioned remainder index to years and locations showed that reasonable small variations were found when environmental and cultural variations were considered

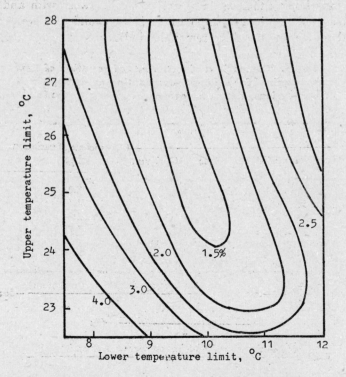

FIG. 9.1. Iso-coefficients of variation of heat unit accumulations with varying upper and lower limits of a daily mean temperature to be accumulated for maize from planting to silking.

(Iwata & Okubo, 1969b).

Exponential Index

Since the remainder index is based on a linear basis of the temperature effectiveness to a plant, a criticism is raised from the standpoint that a plant activity does not operate at equal rate at different temperatures. The exponential index is based on the principle that plant growth rates follow the rule of van't Hoff and Arrhenius. The index is the summation of the efficiency of a mean daily temperature calculated by using the following formula:

$$u = 2^{\frac{t-40}{18}}$$

or in a more workable form, $\log u = \frac{\log 2}{18} (t-40)$

where u is the daily temperature efficiency and t represents the daily mean temperature in F scale. The zero point of vital activity is taken at 40 °F. Accordingly, at 40 °F of the daily mean temperature the temperature efficiency is taken 1, and at 58 °F, doubles.

Katz (1952) computed the exponential index on two canning pea varieties for three years, in which the variations of the indices from year to year were relatively small. He also stated that the difference between the results obtained from the exponential and remainder index systems were small. In another study worked by Klages (1951) high correlation coefficients between the exponential and remainder indices in 16 cool and 16 warm-weather crops were observed.

In this index, however, there is the obvious fault that temperatures above 80 °F are given too much weightage because of the exponential nature. Boswell (1934) in a comparison of the exponential and remainder indices between plant emergence and seed stalk appearance in seven varieties of spinach grown in different regions and seasons, indicated that in every case except one the coefficients of variation of the exponential index are higher than for remainder index, and in some cases considerably higher as shown in Table 9.4. Brown (1960) working on a comparison of some heat unit indices stated that the exponential index would be least suitable for estimating stages of development in soybeans. Thus, it is generally assumed that the exponential index, in spite of its theoretical assumption, is not superior to the remainder index as a measure of heat requirement, rather inferior when temperatures become higher.

Physiological Index

Both the remainder and exponential indices increase infinitely with

Table 9.4.　Comparison of coefficients of variation of exponential and remainder indices between plant emergence and seed stalk appearance in seven varieties of spinach (after Boswell, 1934)

Variety				Coefficient of variation, %	
				Exponential index	Remainder index
Virginia Savoy	..	..	..	21.6	20.5
Bloomsdale Savoy	..	..	..	14.2	12.5
Viroflay	..	..	..	10.7	11.4
Long Standing Bloomsdale	..	..	..	24.6	12.5
Nobel or Gaudry	..	..	..	23.9	14.0
Princess Juliana	..	..	..	34.5	16.7
King of Denmark	..	..	..	21.6	13.1

increase of temperature even when plants are retarded by high temperatures. This is not true for physiological index.　The physiological index is derived from the temperature efficiency to the actual plant growth reported by Lehenbauer (1914) who measured the rates of elongation of corn seedling for a period of 12 hours at constant temperatures and developed growth rate curve.　Fig. 9.2, taken from Livingston (1916), shows the magnitude

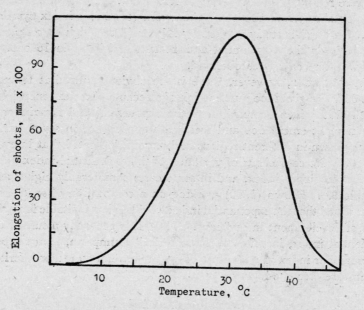

Fig. 9.2.　Relationship between temperature and rate of elongation of the shoots of maize seedlings (after Livingston, 1916).

of the physiological temperature efficiency indices for increasing temperatures. To determine the physiological index, according to Klages (1951), the ordinates of the graph are measured for each degree of temperature considered; the numbers thus obtained represent the average hourly rate of elongation, in hundredths of a millimetre.

Livingston (1916) presented the physiological index for various crops and a chart of the United States climatic zonation. However, the index has limitations since it is based upon tests of only a single plant species grown in limited environmental conditions and derived from the growth rates of seedling only, as he pointed out.

Hanyu and Uchijima (1962) devised an unique modification of the physiological index method to estimate the heading dates of rice plants in relation to their thermoreaction. The thermoreaction of the plants to air temperature was measured by effective temperature. The relationship between the effective temperature and air temperature has been illustrated in Fig. 9.3, in which the effective temperature starts at 10 °C and becomes constant above 28 °C. Using this method the estimation of the heading

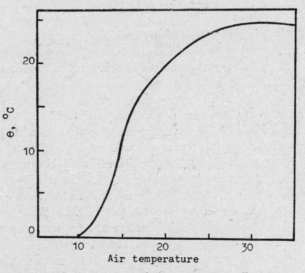

FIG. 9.3. Relation of the equivalent of air temperature effective for the heading of rice plants (θ) to the air temperature (after Hanyu & Uchijima, 1962).

dates at 12 locations for six years agreed well with the actual dates observed. The largest difference of days from transplanting to heading between the actual and estimated dates calculated by this method was only three days.

Hydrothermal Index

Precipitation is one of the factors influencing greatly the plant growth and development. Multamäki (1961) observed that total precipitation was positively related to the effective temperature sum of the total period during 32 seasons with peas. Livingston (1916) has presented the hydrothermal index (I_{mt}) envolving the index of temperature efficiency evaluated on the basis of physiological index (I_t), precipitation intensity (I_p) and atmospheric evaporating power (I_e) for growing period as follows:

$$I_{mt} = I_t \frac{I_p}{I_e}.$$

This index system is subject, since it is based in part on the physiological index, to the same criticism as the latter as pointed out by Klages (1951). Another shortcoming is that plant growth does not always follow the magnitude of precipitation intensity and atmospheric evaporating power ratio directly. In rainy zones the index has a tendency to increase its value than in dry zones.

Photothermal Units

Day and night length is one of the basic factors controlling the period of vegetative growth for photosensitive plants. In such plants, heat requirement calculated by temperature only varies widely with different photoperiodic conditions.

Although the theory of photoperiodism, the effect of the relative lengths of day and night on plants, was not known until 1920, Tisserand (1875) first reported that the ratio of development of crops could be represented by the product of the mean temperature and number of hours of daylight between sunrise and sunset. Following Garner and Allard's discovery of photoperiodism (1920), many investigators studied the relationship between daylength and heat units of crops. Attempts have been made by Nuttonson (1955) to incorporate the effect of photoperiod into "heat summation" to account for heading and maturity behaviour of wheat grown in widely varying latitudes. According to his noted works, a multiple of the average length of day and the summation of day-degrees, referred to as photothermal units, provides a less variable unit of measurement of the interval between phenological events than the use of day-degree summations alone as shown in Table 9.5. Similarly, Reath and Wittwer (1952) working with 13 varieties of peas planted successively in Michigan found that for most varieties, the photothermal summations for flowering is a less variable expression than is the "degree-days summation."

For soybeans, a short day plant, the author found that substituting night length for day length of photothermal units could be applicable for measuring development of the plants: it is calculated by multiplying the degree-day

Table 9.5. Comparison of coefficients of variation of remainder index and photothermal units for all phases of growth-development of wheat (after Nuttonson, 1955)

Growth phases			Remainder index%	Photothermal units%
Sown to headed	..	..	12.3	8.3
Emergence to headed	..	..	13.6	9.2
Headed to ripe	..	..	5.2	4.7
Sown to ripe	..	..	7.5	4.6
Emergence to ripe	..	..	8.0	5.0

by length of the dark period of a day. Table 9.6 shows the summations calculated by the author from the data of Van Schaik and Probst (1958) on Clark and Midwest varieties of soybean in a growth chamber experiment. In these calculations the base temperature is set at 40 °F and the temperatures above 77 °F are assumed to be 77 °F since optimum temperature for flower-bud formation of the plant is 77 °F (Nagata, 1956). The coefficients of variation of the summations for both varieties are relatively small.

Nuttonson (1957) worked on a comparison of photothermal units and day-degrees required by a photosensitive variety (Olli) and an insensi-

Table 9.6. Dark-thermal units required by two soybean varieties to reach flowering at various temperatures and dark lengths (calculated from Van Schaik & Probst, 1958)

Temperature °F	Dark length, hours	Planting to flowering period, days		Dark-thermal units	
		Clark	Midwest	Clark	Midwest
60	12	55	53	13,200	12,720
60	10	58	62	11,600	12,400
60	8	—	74	—	11,840
70	12	34	33	12,240	11,880
70	10	35	36	10,500	10,800
70	8	—	50	—	12,000
80	12	29	27	12,876	11,988
80	10	31	28	11,470	10,360
80	8	—	38	—	11,248
90	12	28	25	12,432	11,100
90	10	36	30	13,320	11,100
90	8	—	35	—	10,360
Coefficient of variation, %				7.9	7.7

The base temperature is 40 °F and all temperatures above 77 °F are assumed to be 77 °F.

tive variety (Trebi) of barley. According to his studies, it was shown that in Trebi variety the photothermal units, as evidenced by the coefficients of variation, do not improve the consistency of the summations compared with degree-day summations for any of the growth periods. On the other hand, in Olli variety the photothermal units yield more consistent summations than do degree-days for all phases as shown in Table 9.7. Thus, the effectiveness of an application of the photothermal unit system for plants depends upon their sensitivity to photoperiod.

Table 9.7. Comparison of coefficients of variation of remainder index and photothermal units required by Olli and Trebi barley grown at various locations in North America (after Nuttonson, 1957)

Growth phases		Olli		Trebi	
		Remainder index	Photothermal units	Remainder index	Photothermal units
Sown to headed	..	11.2	4.7	13.7	14.0
Emergence to headed	..	9.4	4.1	13.1	12.9
Headed to ripe	..	12.9	8.2	14.2	14.0
Sown to ripe	..	11.5	6.5	7.4	6.8
Emergence to ripe	..	8.5	4.4	7.3	6.7

Brown (1960) has developed another photothermal unit system for soybeans in a growth chamber experiment conducted by Van Schaik and Probst (1958). He proposed the term, "soybean development units" or SDU, as a photothermal unit which was based on the rates of development for the number of hours of darkness as a function of the mean daily temperature. From his calculations, nearly the same number of night hours were required to reach flowering for all photoperiods at any one temperature. Therefore, rate of development units (Y) at each temperature is defined as reciprocal of night hours from planting to flowering with the decimal point shifted to make whole numbers,

$$Y = \frac{10,000}{\text{night hours to flowering}} .$$

The relationship between the rate of development and temperature proved to be curvilinear and parabolic in nature as the base temperature of 50 °F as shown in Fig. 9.4 and then the SDU was obtained from the equation as follows:

$$SDU = 4.39T - 0.0256T^2 - 155.18$$

where T represents the average temperature. The number of SDU required to flowering was determined by accumulating SDU for each daily mean temperature. Following the above relationship, obtained under controlled conditions, field studies conducted by Brown and Chapman (1961) in Canada and U.S.A. indicated that the SDU could serve as a heat index required for soybean development. Likewise, Varga-Haszonits (1971) reported recently on the effect of sunshine hours and temperature on the development of winter wheat that a photothermal index for the plant was expressed by substituting day hours for night hours in Brown's method.

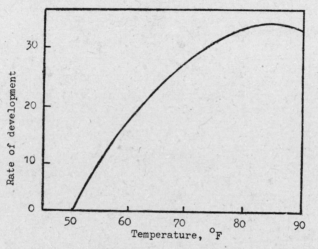

FIG. 9.4. Relationship between temperature and rate of development of soybeans (after Brown, 1960).

Interrelationship of Various Heat Units

The above-mentioned heat units are more or less interrelated. Photothermal index is the product of remainder index and day or night length. The highly theoretical exponential index is the exponential expression of temperatures. Physiological index and hydrothermal index are based on the actual response of a plant to increasing temperatures and the latter involving precipitation and evaporation factors is a modification of the former.

Klages (1951) gave the values of the correlation coefficients between the two indices taken from the general regions of intensive production of eight cool and eight warm-weather crops in U.S.A. The values of correlation coefficients are in all instances sufficiently high to be used for the purpose of prediction.

Brown (1960) illustrated the changes of several index curves with increase of temperatures as shown in Fig. 9.5. According to his comparison, SDU and physiological index systems have similar optimum temperatures which occur near 86 and 89 °F, respectively. On the contrary, remainder index and exponential index, in their nature have no optimum, and increase with increasing temperatures. Thus, they give markedly different results from those obtained with SDU and physiological index and the values in the former two indices give too much weight to the calculations when temperatures occur above 86 °F, especially in the exponential index system. However, these two indefinitely increasing series have often appeared so satisfactory in practical application in the cases that natural shade temperatures above this critical point are infrequent or that the excess temperatures are eliminated.

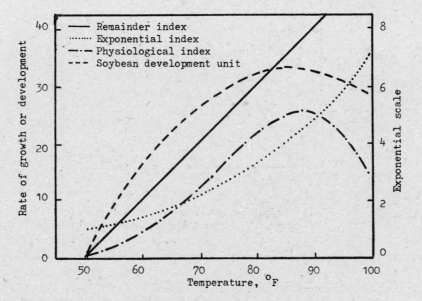

FIG. 9.5. Comparison of various heat unit index curves with increasing temperatures (after Brown, 1960).

Some Environmental Factors Fluctuating Consistency of Heat Units

Many environmental conditions may cause fluctuations in the heat units of a crop. Photoperiod is one of the primary factors and the rate of development for photosensitive plants are never estimated accurately by temperature only. Humidity conditions also influence plant growth and fluctuate consistency of heat units. Nuttonson (1957) reported that when the locations are divided into two groups of relatively inadequate and adequate moisture conditions, the coefficients of variation of the remainder index are lower for each group than for the whole.

It is commonly known that certain plants have proper temperatures to differentiate and develop the flower-buds. Some winter crops will not develop their flower-buds until they have gone through a chilling period. Certain varieties of tomatoes set fruit only when the night temperature is near 64 °F (Went, 1944). Optimum tuber set of potatoes occurs only if the night temperatures during set fall between 50 to 57 °F (Holmes & Robertson, 1959).

Other than climatic factors, soil conditions also influence the heat units greatly. Low soil fertility, generally, decreases growth rate and delays maturity. For instance, phosphorus deficiency delays flowering and maturity. On the contrary, high nitrogen also delays maturity by making the plant more vigorous. Excess or lack of soil moisture also delays plant growth. On poorly drained soils, plant growth is retarded due to lack of increase in temperature, especially in early spring and by nutrient shortage. Drought during the early growth period causes late flowering and maturity because plant growth is retarded. On the other hand, drought during the later part of growth usually hastens maturity. Using soil temperature instead of air temperature makes the heat units more accurate up to emergence since plants are influenced by soil temperature more than air temperature during that period (Sayre, 1949).

Higher plant population also delays maturity because of limitations of nutrients and water, and over mutual shading.

Some Climatic Factors Affecting Heat Unit Systems under Dryland Conditions

Since the heat unit concept is a theory based on growth response of crops to temperature and demonstrates its validity under favourable growth conditions, an application of the heat unit systems under dryland conditions is often confronted with the difficult situation of inconsistency of the heat units.

Under dryland conditions, deficient rainfall and excessively high temperature are the main climatic factors leading to a more or less marked retardation in crop growth and fluctuating the heat units. Influences of a low air humidity and soil moisture caused by an insufficient supply of water on the heat units are complicated as they vary with differences in growth and development periods. Soil drought increases heat requirement of crops when occurring at times of greatest need of water such as during germination and emergence periods, and the low humidity of air decreases it for grain crops when occurring during the ripening periods. The wheat data of the Ural Experiment Station indicated by Nuttonson (1955) show that when irrigation was applied, the sown-to-emergence phase became shorter by 1 to 5 days, the headed-to-wax ripe phase was prolonged by 3 to 6 days and consequently total length of the growing period from sowing to ripe either remained unchanged or increased.

It is assumed that in the regions having the rainy seasons, the heat units required during total growing periods of the same variety varies considerably with the season even if temperature conditions are equal: generally more heat units are required for crops sown in the dry season and ripening in the rainy season than for those grown in the opposite seasons.

The high temperature above optimum which is normal in dryland conditions depresses crop growth, but the heat units increase. This is another cause of fluctuating heat units under dryland conditions. In such conditions adjusting for the temperatures above the optimum for growth is indispensable to determining accurate heat units. The methods for eliminating excessively high temperatures, as pointed out earlier, are useful. Growth chamber experiments are also valuable to determining the optimum temperature for eliminating excessively high temperatures.

Generally, though not always, high temperatures above optimum are associated with a low humidity under dryland conditions and this combination may cause confusion in consistency of heat units. However, considerable confusion can be avoided by taking into consideration amount of rainfall and the rainfall cycle in each region. Hot winds usually accompanied by a low humidity also fluctuate the consistency of heat units as the growth of plants is slowed down by water deficits in plants. Although light alone does not greatly influence the heat units, an intense light leads to effects similar to high temperature, since light and heat are definitely associated in field conditions.

Thus, as the factors and interactions fluctuating heat units are much more complicated under dryland conditions, a wide application of the heat unit calculated at a single location and season, to different locations and seasons is hardly expected, and individual experiments at each location and season are recommended at the present state.

Conclusions

Since many environmental factors influence growth and development of plants, the heat unit concept based mainly on air temperature is not infallible. However, for estimating plant growth and development some systems and their modifications developed either in theoretical or empirical studies, give satisfactory results for a given plant at the locations where they have been developed. Besides that, an index or unit developed for a certain crop and area is often fairly applicable for other crops and areas.

Although each index has some merits and demerits either in actual calculation or in wide range application for plants and locations, the remainder index and photothermal unit systems, of all indices and their modifications mentioned above, have been most accepted, in spite of the fact that they are based on simple assumptions. Generally the former is for the insensitive crops to photoperiod and the latter is for photosensitive ones.

In the present state of the development of heat unit concept, it is not feasible to set a definite value for any one variety and expect it to be usable under all conditions. Users of them must necessarily establish their own summation values.

REFERENCES

AIRY, J. M. 1955. Production of hybrid corn seed. Corn and Corn Improvement. Agronomy, Vol. V. pp. 386-7, Academic Press Inc., New York.

ANDREW, R. H.; F. P. FERWERDA and A. M. STROMMEN, 1956. Maturation and yield of corn as influenced by climate and production technique. Agron. J. 48: 231-6.

ARNOLD, C. Y. 1959. The determination and significance of the base temperature in a linear heat unit system. Proc. Am. Soc. hort. Sci. 74: 430-45.

ARNOLD, C. Y. 1960. Maximum-minimum temperatures as a basis for computing heat units. *Ibid.* 76: 682-92.

AUSTIN, M. E. and S. K. RIES, 1968. Use of heat units to predict dates for once-over tomato harvest. Hort. Sci. 3: 41.

BALVOLL, G. and A. H. BREMER, 1965. Varmesum og planteavl i samband med vekst og utvikling au ymse grønsakvokstrar, Meld. Norg. Landbr Høgesk. 44: 1-18.

BOMALASKI, H. H. 1948. Growing degree-days; how to apply this unit to measure maturity of crops. Food Packer 29: 51-9.

BOSWELL, V. R. 1934. A study of the temperature, day length and development interrelationships of spinach varieties in the field. Proc. Am. Soc. hort. Sci. 32: 549-57.

BROWN, D. M. 1960. Soybean ecology. I. Development temperature relationships from controlled environment studies. Agron. J. 52: 493-5.

BROWN, D. M. and L. J. CHAPMAN, 1961. Soybean ecology. III. Soybean development units for zones and varieties in the Great Lakes Region. Agron. J. 53: 306-8.

CULPEPPER, C. W. and H. W. MOON, 1939. Effect of temperature on the rate of elongation of the stems of asparagus grown under field conditions. Pl. Physiol. 14: 255-70.

DATE, S. 1963. Agro-meteorological study on the determination method of the period cultivating paddy rice plants in the Tohoku, district of Japan. Bull. Tohoku Natl. agric. Exp. Sta. 28: 1-41.

FERWERDA, F. P. 1953. Methods to synchronize the flowering time of the components in crossing plots for the production of hybrid seed corn. Euphytica 2: 127-34.

GARNER, W. W. and H. A. ALLARD, 1920. Effect of the relative length of day and night and other factors of the environment on growth and reproduction in plants. J. agric. Res. 18: 553-606.

GILMORE, E. C. and J. S. ROGERS, 1958. Heat units as a method of measuring maturity in corn. Agron. J. 50: 611-5.

GOULD, W. A. 1950. Here's a unit guide for 47 varieties of snap beans. Food Packer, March.

GUNN, R. B. and R. CHRISTENSEN, 1965. Maturity relationships among early to late hybrids of corn. Crop Sci. 5: 299-302.

HANYU, J. and T. UCHIJIMA, 1962. Studies on relation of the weather conditions to the growth of crops. I. Relation of air temperature to the heading date of rice plant. J. agric. Met. 18: 109-17.

HOLMES, R. M. and G. W. ROBERTSON, 1959. Heat units and crop growth. Canada Deptt. Agric. Publ. 1042: 1-35.

HOPE, G. W. 1962. Modification of the heat unit formula for peas. Can. J. Pl. Sci. 42: 15-21.

IWATA, F. and T. OKUBO, 1969a. Physiological and ecological studies on corn growth and yield. I. On the constancy of heat unit accumulation in the effective degrees required for the growth of corn planted at various dates. Proc. Crop Sci. Soc. Japan 38: 91-4.

IWATA, F. and T. OKUBO, 1969b. Physiological and ecological studies on corn growth and yield. II. An application of the heat unit accumulation in the effective degrees to corn planted in different years and at different locations. Ibid. 38: 211-3.

KATZ, Y. H. 1952. The relationship between heat unit accumulation and the planting of canning peas. Agron. J. 44: 74-8.

KLAGES, K. H. W. 1951. Ecological Crop Geography, pp. 238-58. The Macmillan Co., New York.

KURIHARA, H.; H. NISHIKAWA; K. TABATA and T. OKUBO, 1963. Studies on the relationships between cultural conditions and growing process in potato crop. Bull. Tohoku Natl. agric. Exp. Sta. 28: 143-200.

LANA, E. P. and E. S. HABER, 1952. Seasonal variability as indicated by cumulative degree hours with sweet corn. Proc. Am. Soc. hort. Sci. 59: 389-91.

LECOMPTE, S. B. and D. BLUMENFELD, 1958. Degree-days used to predict time of asparagus heavy cut. N. J. Agric. 40: 12-13.

LEHENBAUER, P. A. 1914. Growth of maize seedling in relation to temperature. Physiol. Res. 1: 247-88.

LIVINGSTON, B. E. 1916. Physiological temperature indices for the study of plant growth in relation to climatic factors. Physiol. Res. 1: 399-420.

MADARIAGA, F. J. and J. E. KNOTT, 1951. Temperature summations in relation to lettuce growth. Proc. Am. Soc. hort. Sci. 58: 147-52.

MULTAMÄKI, K. 1961. Der Einfluss Klimatischer Faktoren auf die Entwicklung von Erbse. Maataloust. Aikakausk 33: 256-66.

NAGATA, T. 1956. Agronomy series. Soybeans, pp. 66-7. Yakendo, Tokyo.

NAGY, J. 1965. A borsó fenológiai vizsgálata a hömérséklei összegek, függvényében. Növénytrmelés 14: 337-44.

NUTTONSON, M. Y. 1955. Wheat-climate relationships and the use of phenology in ascertaining the thermal and photothermal requirements of wheat. Am. Inst. Crop Ecol., Washington, D.C.

NUTTONSON, M. Y. 1957. Barley-climate relationships and the use of phenology in ascertaining the thermal and photothermal requirements of barley. Am. Inst. Crop Ecol., Washington, D.C.

REATII, A. N. and S. H. WITTWER, 1952. The effects of temperature and photoperiod on the development of pea varieties. Proc. Am. Soc. hort. Sci. 60: 301-10.

ROBERTSON, G. W. 1968. A biometeorological time scale for a cereal crop involving day and night temperature and photoperiod. Int. J. Biometeor. 12: 191-223.

ROSCA, V. 1968. Contributions to the study of thermic factor influence upon the development of the potato vegetation stages. Hidrotchn. Gosp. Apclor Meteorol. 13: 254-7.

SAYRE, C. B. 1949. Heat unit method of forecasting maturity of peas. Ann. Rep. Now York agric. Exp. Sta.

TISSERAND, E. 1875. Mémorie sur la végétation dans les hautes latitudes. Mémoires de la Société Centrale d'Agriculture. Cited by G. W. Robertson, 1968.

TRENKLE, H. 1969. Heat sum and vegetative period of early potatoes. Kartoffelbau 20: 82-3.

VALLI, V. J. and C. A. JAWORSKI, 1965-66. Influence of biometeorological factors in tomato transplant production. Proc. Fla. St. hort. Soc. 78: 102-6.

VAN SCHAIK, P. H. and A. H. PROBST, 1958. Effects of some environmental factors on flower production and reproductive efficiency in soybeans. Agron. J. 50: 192-7.

VARGA-HASZONITS, Z. 1971. Effect of sunshine hours and temperature on the development of the winter wheat variety Bánkùti 1201. Acta

Agronomica Academiae Scientiarum Hungaricae 20: 392-7.

WARNOCK, S. J. and R. I. ISAACS, 1969. A linear heat unit system for tomatoes in California. J. Am. hort. Sci. 94: 677-8.

WENT, F. W. 1944. Plant growth under controlled conditions. XI. Thermoperiodicity in growth and fruiting of tomato. Am. J. Bot. 31: 135-50.

WIGGANS, S. C. 1956. The effects of seasonal temperatures on maturity of oats planted at different dates. Agron. J. 48: 21-5.

AUTHOR INDEX

Numbers in bold face refer to the pages on which references are listed

Aamodt, O. S., 47, 53, 58, **124**, 210, **217**
Abu-Khaled, A., 116, **124**, 315, **323**
Adams, F., 33, **124**
Adams, J. E., 123, **124**, 240, 242, 243, 248, 249, **252**
Aeshein, T. S., 122, **126**
Agarwal, M. C., 248, **253**
Airy, J. M., 354, **367**
Albasal, N., 202, **223**
Albe, E. M., 19, **124**
Albenskii, A. V., 117, 118, **124**, 305, **309**
Albrigo, L. G., 317, **323**
Alderfer, R. B., 323, **325**
Aldrich, S. A., **140**
Alexander, J. D., 194, **221**
Allard, H. A., 360, **368**
Allen, L. H., 267, **277**
Allen, R. R., 241, 251, **257**
Allessi, J., 24, **131**
Allmaras, R. R., 216, **217**, 243, 248, 249, **252**
Amemiya, M., 105, **124**
Anderson, D. T., 216, **217**, 243, 249, **252**
Andrew, R. H., 202, **217**, 353, 354, **367**
Angus, D. E., 147, **164**
Ansari, A. Q., 113, **124**
Anson, R. B., 27, **138**
Appleby, A. P., 122, **138**
Ardakani, M. S., 178, **231**
Armbrust, D. V., 246, **253**, 300, **309**
Army, T. J., 92, 108, 110, 122, **124**, **135**, **136**, **145**, 238, 239, 240, 244, 245, 246, 248, 250, **252**, **255**, **257**
Arnold, C. Y., 352, 354, **367**
Arnon, I., 19, 60, 63, 67, 90, 92, 112, **125**
Asana, R. D., 40, 43, 46, 58, 62, 65, 66, 68, 82, **125**
Ashen, C. J., 195, **227**
Asher, C. J., 203, **217**
Ashley, D. A., 191, **220**
Ashton, F. M., 28, **125**
Ashton, T., 59, **125**, 208, 211, **217**
Aspinall, D., 30, 31, 33, 37, 38, **125**, **132**, **141**
Atkinson, T. G., 191, **227**
Aubert, B., 268, **275**
Audus, L. J., **137**

Aufhammer, G., 173, 189, 213, **217**
Aurangabadkar, K. K. 106, **142**
Austin, R. B., 240, 242, 248, **252**, 354, **367**
Azizbekova, Z. S., 38, **125**

Bagga, A. K., 65, 66, **125**
Bagley, W. T., 302, **309**
Bagnold, R. A., 10, **125**
Bahl, P. N., 46, **125**
Baier, W., 271, **275**
Bailey, L. H., 103, **126**
Bainbridge, R., **277**, **279**
Baker, D. G., 15, 113, **132**
Baker, D. N., 27, 28, 36, 42, **126**, 275, **277**
Baker, H. M., 194, **234**
Baker, L. O., 122, **126**
Balaam, L. N., 65, **128**, 192, 209, **220**
Baldwin, J. P., 179, **217**
Baldy, C., 95, **126**
Balvoll, G., 353, **367**
Bansal, S. P., 240, 243, 248, **252**
Barber, S. A., 178, 179, 180, 208, **217**, **218**, **227**, **228**
Bark, L. D., 240, **253**
Barley, K. P., 184, 185, **218**
Barnett, N. M., 154, **162**
Barroccio, A., 240, 242, 248, **252**
Barrs, H. D., 316, **323**
Bartlett, B. O., 191, **222**
Bassham, J. A., 334, **347**
Batchelder, A. R., 271, **277**
Baumer, M., 240, 248, **252**
Bavel, C. H. M. van, **164**
Bay, C. E., 247, 248, **256**
Bear, R. E., 177, **218**
Beauchamp, E. D., 273, **279**
Beevers, H., 331, **345**
Begg, J. E., 270, **280**
Belcher, D. J., 202, **218**
Bell, D. T., 156, **162**, **164**
Bell, G. P. H., 212, **218**
Belyakov, I., 189, **218**
Bennett, O. L., 191, **220**
Benoit, E., 302, **309**

Benson, A. A., 333, **345**
Bergmann, W., 181, 182, 215, **218**
Berry, J. A., 342, **345**
Beyers, E. M. Jr., 156, **162**
Bhan, S., 10, 31, 74, 75, 86, 118, **126**, **136**
Bierhuizen, J. F., 274, **275**, **279**, 316, 318, **326**
Bilbro, J. D., 89, **144**
Bird, I. F., 336, **345**
Bishop, P. M., 340, **345**
Björkman, O., 339, 342, 343, **345**
Black, A. L., 241, 243, 246, 250, **252**, **253**, 216, **217**
Black, C. A., 26, **126**, 177, **218**
Black, J. N., 13, 83, **126**
Blackman, C. E., 13, 83, **126**
Bloodworth, M. E., 94, **218**
Blum, A., 63, 67, 79, **125**, **126**
Blumenfeld, D., 30, **136**, 151, **164** 353, 354, **368**
Boersma, L., 240, 242, 248, **254**
Bole, J. B., 185, 215, 217, **218**, **220**
Bomalaski, H. H., 353, **367**
Bond, J. J., 71, 110, **124**, **126**, 243, 250, **252**, **257**
Bonner, J., 14, **126**
Borthwicks, H. A., 88, **143**
Bosemark, N. O., 181, **218**
Boswell, V. R., 353, 354, 357, 358, **367**
Bottrill, D. E., 323, **326**
Bowen, G. D., 191, 202, **218**
Bowen, J. E., 273, **276**
Bowers, S. A., 240, 243, 248, **253**
Bowes, G., 333, **345**, **347**
Bowser, W. E., 216, **218**
Box, J. E. Jr., 122, **144**, 240, 246, 250, **257**, 275, **277**
Boyer, J. S., 52, **126**, 156, **162**, 266, 267, 270, **275**, 297, **309**
Brag, H., 71, 72, **126**
Brandfield, R., 60, 95, **142**
Bravdo, Ben-Ami, 316, 318, 322, **324**, **326**
Bray, R. N., 179, **218**
Breazeale, E. L., 270, **276**
Breazeale, J. F., 270, **276**
Bremer, A. H., 353, **367**
Bremner, P. M., 43, 46, 64, **140**
Brenchley, W. E., 182, **218**
Brengle, K. G., 243, **253**, 321, **324**
Brewster, J. L., 179, **218**
Briggle, L. W., 205, **218**
Briggs, L. J., 274, **276**
Brind, W. D., 237, 238, **254**

Britten, E. J., 14, **143**
Brix, H., 153, 156, **162**, 171, **225**
Broeshart, H., 177, 180, **221**
Brooks, K. N., 318, 319, **324**
Brouwer, R., 21, **126**, 176, 184, **219**, 263, **276**
Brown, B. L., 85, **127**
Brown, D. A., 70, **127**, 184, **219**
Brown, D. M., 357, 362, 363, 364, **367**
Brown, N., 33, **124**
Brown, P. L., 70, 71, **127**
Brown, W. K., 286, 288, 290, 297, **309**
Bruce, R. R., 216, **231**
Buchinger, A., 58, **127**
Bull, T. A., 343, 344, **345**
Bunger, W. C., 248, **255**
Bunting, A. H., 43, **127**
Burnett, E., 122, **145**, 172, **229**, 240, 246, 250, **257**
Burnside, O. C., 121, **127**
Burrows, W. C., 22, **140**, 243, 248, 249, **252**, **253**, **257**
Burton, G. W., 147, **164**, 171, 212, 215, **219**
Buttrose, M. S., 43, **130**

Caborn, J. M., 296, 300, 306, **310**
Cairns, R. R., 216, **218**
Calder, D. M., 13, **127**
Caldwell, M. M., 300, **310**
Callaghan, A. R., 90, **127**
Calvin, M., 333, **345**, **348**
Campbell, C. A., 12, **127**, 263, **276**
Cannell, R. Q., 207, **219**
Carlson, R. E., 272, **276**
Carlton, W. M., 182, **219**
Carly, H. E., 195, **219**
Carnelius, M. J., 336, **345**
Carr, M. K. V., 290, 293, **310**
Carter, D. L., 243, 248, 249, **253**
Carter, O. G., 117, **135**
Catsky, J., 268, **275**
Chadwick, D. L., 300, **312**
Chan, E. C. S., 191, **219**
Chang, Jen-Hu, 274, **276**
Chapman, L. J., 363, **367**
Charles, C. A., 29, **127**
Chen, D., 55, **127**
Cheung, G. P., 338, **345**
Childers, N. F., 156, **164**
Chinoy, J. J., 65, **127**, 170, 187, 208, **219**
Christensen, R., 354, 355, **368**
Ciofu, R., 240, **255**

Clapp, A. L., 92, **134**
Clark, F. E., 124, **137**
Clark, H. E., 182, **228**
Clayton, J. S. 184, 202, 214, **229**
Cleland, R., 266, **276**
Cocheme, J., 77, 78, **127**
Cochran, V. L., 216, **227**
Cohen, O. P., 243, **253**
Coile, T. S., 169, **225**
Collier, J. W., 63, **133**
Coltharp, G. B., 318, **325**
Commonwealth Agricultural Bureaux, 38, **127**
Conrad, J. O., 170, **219**
Coombs, J., 333, **345**
Cooper, C. S., 26, **141**
Cornforth, I. S., 183, **219**
Cotter, D. J., 262, **276**
Cowan, I. R., 178, **219**
Cox, M. B., 103, **131**
Crafts, A. S., 18, **127**, 156, **162**, 177, **219**, 273, **276**
Cravzov, M. N., 187, 189, **219**
Crisp, C. E., 273, **276**
Critchfield, H. J., 15, 16, **128**
Crowle, W. L., 170, 204, 205, 210, **224**
Cuddy, T. E., 88, **128**
Cullen, E. M., 262, 268, 271, **277**
Culpepper, C. W., 353, **367**
Cunningham, R. K., 186, **219**
Currier, H. B., 30, **128**
Currier, H. R., 18, **128**
Cuykendall, T. R., 202, **218**

Daines, R. H., 268, 272, **279**
Dainty, J., 168, 169, 173, **220**
Dakshinamurti, C., 107, **142**, 202, **231**
Dancer, J., 242, 243, **253**
Danielson, R. E., 181, 182, 184, **220**, **233**
Darland, R. W., 195, **233**
Darroch, J. G., 208, **228**
Dasberg, S., 20, **142**
Date, S., 352, **368**
Davenport, D. C., 116, **124**, 158, **162**, 309, **310**, 315, 316, 317, 318, 319, 320, 321, 322, 323, **323**, **324**
Davilchuk, P., 189, **220**
Davis, R. G., 238, 240, 250, **254**
Day, A. D., 217, **220**
Day, B. E., 119, 120, **128**
Day, P. R., 343, 344, **346**

Dayal, R., 96, **128**
De Datta, S. K., 304, **310**
de Duve, C., 335, **346**
de Jong, E., 185, **220**, 266, **280**
de Roo, H. C., 187, 192, 216, **220**
de Wit, C. T., 176, **219**, 263, **276**
Decker, J. P., 330, **346**
Denmead, O. T., 36, **128**, 151, 152, **162**, 295, **310**
Derera, N. F., 65, **128**, 192, 209, **220**
Dhesi, N. S., 243, 248, **253**
Dickens, L., 34, **131**
Dickerson, J. D., 308, **310**
Dinauer, R. C., **225**, **227**, **228**, **231**, **234**
Dittmer, H. J., 24, **128**, 169, 185, 187, **220**
Diwald, K., 58, **140**
Dixit, S. P., 248, **253**
Dixon, R. M., 247, 248, **256**
Dobrenz, A. K., 174, **220**
Domingo, C. E., 33, **140**
Donald, C. M., 41, 42, 70, 80, 81, 82, 83, 84, 91, **128**
Doneen, L. D., 244, **257**
Doren, C. E. van, 110, **124**
Doss, B. D., 191, **220**
Downes, R. W., 51, **128**, 341, **346**
Downton, W. J. S., 51, **128**, 331, 341, 342, **345**, **346**
Drake, B. G., 268, **276**
Dreibelbis, F. R., 239, 248, **254**
Dreier, A. F., 76, **137**
Drennan, D. S. H., 43, **127**
Drew, M. C., 185, 207, **219**, **220**
Dubetz, S., 59, **144**, 170, 217, **220**, **233**
Dugger, W. M., 272, **279**
Duley, F. L., 101, 108, **136**
Duncan, W. G., 182, **221**
Dungan, G. H., 81, 84, 85, 86, **128**, **129**, **134**, **138**, 215, **228**
Dungan, W. G., 15, 42, **135**
Dusek, D. A., 251, **255**

Eastin, J. D., 147, **163**, **164**, **165**, **312**
Eaton, F. M., 29, **129**, 155, **162**
Eavis, B. W., 188, 216, **221**, **233**
Eck, H. V., 72, **129**
Eckardt, F., 36, **129**
Edminster, T. W., **128**, **138**, **143**, **144**
Edwards, W. M., 196, **221**, 247, **254**
Egle, K., 340, **346**
Egll, D., 177, **225**

Ehara, K., 273, **276**
Ehrler, W. L., 176, **233**
Ekern, P. C., 51, **129**
Elfving, D. C., 266, **276**
El-Sharkawy, M., 17, 50, **129**
El-Sherbini, G. E., 302, **311**
Elkins, C. B., 27, **138**
Ellern, S. J., 20, **142**, 199, 201, **221**
Ellis, F. B., 202, **229**
Ellyard, P. W., 333, **346**
Emberger, L., 11, 56, **129**
Emerson, J. L., 320, **324**
Engledow, F. L., 187, 208, **221**
Ephrat, Y., 50, 66, **129, 141**
Epstein, E., 181, **221**
Ergle, D. R., 29, **129**, 155, **162**
Erickson, A. E., 88, **132**
Eshell, Y., 190, 194, **228**
Evans, A. C., 95, 96, **129**
Evans, C. E., 110, **129**
Evans, D. D., 242, 243, 244, **256**
Evans, G. C., **277, 279**
Evans, L. T., **130, 143**, 262, **277**
Evenari, M., 28, 36, 38, 39, 53, **129**, 243, **253**, 270, **277**
Evenson, P. D., 243, 248, **253**

Fanning, C. D., 87, **135**, 245, 248, 249, **253**
Farrell, D. A., 296, **310**
Feddes, R. A., 87, **129**, 168, **221**
Fehrenbacker, J. B., 194, 196, 214, **221**
Fenster, C. R., 121, **127**
Ferguson, W. S., 173, **221, 226**
Ferwerda, F. P., 353, 354, **367, 368**
Fieldhouse, D. T., 320, **324**
Fischbeck, G., 173, 189, 213, **217**
Fisher, F. L., 181, **223**
Fisher, M. A., 158, **162**, 309, **310**, 317, 322, **324, 325**
Fisher, R. A., 28, 34, **129**, 171, **221**
Fleck, S. V., 195, **228**
Fleming, H. K., 323, **325**
Flowers, T. J., 156, **163**
Fock, H., 340, **346**
Fogg, G. E., 168, **221**
Ford, A. S., 304, **311**
Forde, St. C. M., 153, **163**
Forrester, M. L., 331, 342, 343, **346**
Fortanier, E. J., 262, 263, 264, **277**
Foster, G. R., 247, **255**
Fougerouze, J., 296, 302, **310**

Fournier, D., 19, **124**
Fourt, D. E., 305, **310**
Fowler, L., 247, **253**
Fox, R. L., 31, **133**
Frank, K. D., 76, **137**
Frankel, O. H., 45, 46, **129**, 212, **221**
Franquin, P., 77, 78, **127**
Free, J. B., 304, **310**
Freeland, R. O., 272, **277**
French, R. J., 109, **129**
Frey, K. J., 193, **230**
Frey-Wyssling, A., 43, **130**
Fried, M., 177, 180, **221**
Fryrear, D. W., 241, 246, **253, 254**
Fuchs, H., 66, **130**
Fuehring, H. D., 157, 158, **163**, 322, **325**
Fujii, Y., 189, **222**
Funkhouser, E. A., 182, **228**

Gaastra, P., 16, **130**, 316, **325**
Gajri, P. R., 240, 243, 248, **252**
Gale, J., 114, 115, 116, **130, 139**, 158, **163**, 271, 272, **277**, 315, 316, 317, 318, 319, 320, 321, 323, **325, 326**
Gallagher, P. A., 300, **310**
Gallatin, M. H., 271, **277**
Garber, M. J., 262, 268, 271, **277**
Gardner, C. J., 64, **142**
Gardner, H. R., 216, **231**, 267, **277**
Gardner, L. J., **134, 141**
Gardner, W. H., 23, **130**
Gardner, W. R., 97, **130**, 168, 169, 170, 171, 172, 175, 176, **222, 230**, 266, **278**, 298, **311**
Garg, O. K., 38, **130**
Garner, W. W., 360, **368**
Gasser, J. K. R., 184, **231**
Gates, C. T., 30, 31, 32, **130**
Gates, D. M., 15, 113, 114, 116, **130, 132**, 291, 292, **310**
Gauch, H. G., 53, **136**
Gauhl, E., 339, 342, 343, **345**
Gautreau, J., 50, **130**
Geiger, R., 306, **310**
Genkel, P. A., 37, **130**
Gerechter, Z., 66, **129**
Gerge, O. K., 109, **138**
Gibbs, M., 333, **346**
Gill, K. S., 88, **141**
Gillier, P., 94, 95, **130**
Gilmore, E. C., 354, 355, **368**

Gingrich, J. R., 24, **130**
Gliemeroth, G., 170, 190, 192, **222**
Glinka, Z., 151, **163**
Glover, J., 36, **130**
Goedewaagen, M. A. J., 190, 193, 194, **222**
Goldman, B. J., **278**
Goldsworthy, A., 51, 64, **131**, 330, 332, 340, 343, 344, **346**
Goltz, S. M., 266, **278**
Gonzalez, C. L., 245, 249, **254**
Goodchild, D. J., 341, **347**
Goode, J. E., 321, **326**
Gould, W. A., 353, **368**
Grabouski, P. E., 76, **137**
Grafius, J. E., 61, 62, **131**
Grama, A., 66, **129**
Greacen, E. L., 185, **218**, 296, **310**
Greb, B. W., 241, 243, **253**
Grebner, H., 173, 189, 213, **217, 222**
Green, D. G., 12, **127**, 263, **276**
Greer, F. A., **135, 145**
Griffin, D. M., 89, **131**
Griffin, R. H. II., 239, 248, **253**
Grigsby, B. H., 109, **131**
Grimes, D. W., 34, **131**
Griveva, C. M., 191, **222**
Grundbacher, F. J., 53, **131**
Gunn, R. B., 354, 355, **368**
Gupta, M. B., 86, **141**
Gupta, U. S., 88, **126, 131, 138, 140, 142, 145, 225, 226**, 303, **310, 348**
Gurr, C. G., 296, **310**
Guyot, G., 296, **310**

Haas, H. J., 161, **163**, 182, 212, 213, **222, 223**, 239, 240, 244, 248, **258**
Haber, E. S., 354, **368**
Hackett, C., 180, 191, 193, 202, **222, 223**
Hagan, R. M., 28, 34, 114, 115, 116, **124, 128, 129, 130, 138, 143, 144**, 147, 158, **162, 163, 164**, 174, **233**, 272, **277**, 309, **310**, 315, 316, 317, 318, 319, 320, 321, 322, 323, **323, 324, 325**
Hageman, R. H., 333, **343**
Hagen, L. J., 290, 308, **310**
Haigh, W. G., 315, **325**
Haise, H. R., 24, **128, 131, 138, 143, 144**, 212, **223**
Halevy, A. H., 116, 117, **131, 139**
Hall, A. E., 50, 51, 64, **135**, 266, **276**
Halstead, E. H., 202, **223**

Hanks, R. J., 108, 123, **124**, 240, 244, 248, 250, **252, 254**, 267, **277**
Hansen, C. M., 109, **131**
Hanson, J. B., 156, **163**
Hanus, H., 117, **131**
Hanyu, J., 359, **368**
Hardman, J. A., 194, **224**
Harpaz, Y., 20, **142**
Harper, H. J., 93, **131**
Harper, J. L., 81, 82, **131**
Harper, L. A., 275, **277**
Harrington, J. B., 58, 59, **131**, 187, **227**
Harris, D. G., 27, **138**
Harris, R. W., 300, **311**
Harris, W. W., 240, **254**
Harrison, D., 304, **311**
Harrold, L. L., 239, 247, 248, **254**
Hart, G. E., 318, **325**
Hartman, T. T., 122, **126**
Hartt, C. E., 27, **131**
Haskins, F. A., **164, 312**
Hatch, M. D., 50, **131**, 341, 342, 343, **346, 347**
Hauser, V. L., 103, **131, 145**
Haynes, J. L., 84, 85, **132**
Hays, O. E., 247, 248, **256**
Heichel, G. H., 64, **132**
Heikal, I., 302, **311**
Heilman, M. D., 240, 245, 249, **254, 257**
Heinlein, J. P., 315, **325**
Heinrichs, D. H., 210, **223**
Hellebust, J. A., 333, **347**
Henckel, P. A., 33, 37, 50, **130, 132**, 151, 156, **163**
Henderson, R. C., 172, **229**
Hendricks, S. B., 88, **143**
Henerson, D. W., 147, **164**
Herbel, C. A., 88, **141**
Herman, D., 320, **325**
Herring, R. B., 72, **137**
Hesketh, J. D., 17, 42, 50, 51, **126, 128, 129**, 275, **277**, 341, 344, **346, 347**
Hew, C. S., 331, **347**
Heydecker, W., 262, **279**
Heyne, F. G., 92, **134**
Hide, J. C., 92, **124**
Hiesey, W. M., 339, 343, **345**
Hildreth, A. C., 320, **324**
Hillel, D., 87, 88, 103, **132**
Hills, E. S., **133, 145**
Hinman, W. C., 217, **233**
Hobbs, J. A., 92, **134**

Hoffman, G. J., 262, 267, 268, 271, **277**
Hogg, W. H., 303, **311**
Holliday, R., 80, **132**
Holmes, R. M., 353, 354, 365, **368**
Holt, E. C., 181, **223**
Hope, G. W., 353, 355, **368**
Hoshikawa, K., 187, **223**
Hubac, C., 37, **132**
Hubbard, V. C., 209, **223**
Hudspeth, E. B. Jr., 89, **144**, 240, **252**
Hughes, A. P., 263, 273, **277**
Humphrey, A. B., 174, **220**
Humphries, E. C., 116, 117, **132**, 189, **227**
Hunter, A. S., 31, **132**, 192, **223**
Hunter, J. R., 88, **132**
Hurd, E. A., 25, 46, 63, 65, 70, **132**, 172,
    188, 190, 192, 195, 196, 203, 204, 205,
    207, 210, 212, 213, **223**
Hurlbut, L. W., 147, **164**
Husain, I., 38, **132**
Hussein, M. F., 302, **311**
Hutcheon, W. L., 171, 201, **228, 229**
Hyder, D. N., 26, **141**
Hygen, G., 114, **132**

Idso, S. B., 15, 113, **132**
Iljin, W. C., 174, 212, **223**
Iman, M. S., 302, 311
Inamdar, S. S., 74, **135**
Ingham, F. W., 170, 212, **232**
Intalap, S., 217, **220**
Isaacs, R. I., 353, 354, **370**
Itai, C., 30, **132**, 273, **277**
Ivins, J. D., **127, 143, 219**
Iwata, F., 355, 357, **368**
Iyama, J., 50, **137**

Jacks, G. V., 237, 238, **239, 254**
Jackson, J. E., 83, **132**
Jackson, R. D., 180, **227**
Jackson, V. G., 182, **218**
Jackson, W. A., 51, **132**, 330, **347**
Jacobs, H. S., 193, **232**
Jacoby, B., 38, **132**
Jain, T. C., 305, **311**
Jarman, G. D., 240, 242, 248, **254**
Jarvis, M. S., 38, **133**
Jarvis, P. G., 38, **133**
Jaworski, C. A., 353, **369**
Jeffers, D. L., 159, **164**

Jennings, D. S., 194, **224**
Jenny, H., 179, **223**
Jensen, L. R., 24, **131**, 212, **223**
Jensen, M. E., 85, 99, **133, 139**, 319, **325**
Jensen, M. H., 264, 273, **277**
Jensen, R. D., 87, **133**
Jensen, R. G., 334, **347**
Jewitt, T. N., 70, **133**
Johnson, H. S., 50, **131**, 341, **347**
Johnson, P. E., 214, **221**
Johnson, P. R., 214, **221**
Johnson, W. A., 85, **132**
Johnson, W. C., 238, 240, 250, **254**
Johnston, W. A., 47, 53, 58, **124**
Johnston, W. H., 210, **217**
Jones, J. N. Jr., 240, 248, 249, **255**
Jones, M. B., 115, **141**
Jones, R. J., 151, **163**
Jordan, D., 243, 244, **254**
Jordan, W. R., 156, **163**, 172, **229**, 295, **311**
Jung, G. A., 153, **163**

Kafkafi, U., 202, **223**
Kahane, I., 317, 319, 320, 323, **325**
Kakri, Z., 202, **223**
Kaldy, M. K., 262, **278**
Kanemasu, E. T., 158, **164**, 193, **232**
Kappen, L., 268, **278**
Kappert, H., **130**
Karchi, Z., 66, **129**
Karshon, R., 300, **312**
Kasi Viswanath, G., 106, **133**
Kassas, M., 47, **133**
Katchaski, E., 55, **127**
Katyal, J. C., 190, 202, **224, 231**
Katz, Y. H., 354, 357, **368**
Katznelson, H., 191, **219**, 224
Kaufmann, M. R., 12, 33, **133**, 266, **276**
Kaul, R., 28, 57, **133**, 170, 174, 204, 205,
    209, 210, 211, 212, **224**
Kearney, P. C., 333, 334, **347**
Kelley, O. J., 31, **132**, 194, **224**
Kelly, D. J., 192, **223**
Kemper, A., 102, **133**
Kemper, W. D., 124, **137**, 180, **227**
Kerecki, B., 38, **138**
Kerridge, G. H., 323, **326**
Kessler, B., 29, 117, **131, 133**
Ketcheson, J. W., 215, **226**
Ketring, D. L., 263, 264, **278**
Keys, A. J., 336, **345**

Khan, R. A., 57, **133**
Killian, C., 53, **133**
Kinbacher, E. J., 158, **163**, 272, **278**
King, F. M., 123, **133**
King, J. G., 63, **133**
King, L. J., 120
Kirichenko, F. G., 193, **224**
Kirkham, D., **126**, **140**, **144**, **164**, 202, **231**, **258**, **326**
Kirton, D. J., 195, **227**
Kisaki, T., 333, 335, 342, **347**
Kissel, D. E., 172, **229**
Klages, K. H. W., 212, **224**, 357, 359, 360, 363, **368**
Klingman, G. C., 121, **133**
Kmoch, H. G., 31, **133**, 191, **224**
Knecht, G. N., 262, 263, 272, 273, 274, **279**
Kneebone, W. R., 174, **220**
Knievel, D. P., 202, **224**
Knoerr, K., 18, **134**
Knott, D. R., 215, **224**
Knott, J. E., 353, 354, **369**
Koehler, F. F., **133**, 191, **224**
Koéppe, C. E., 3, 97, **134**
Koéppe, D. E., 156, **162**, **164**
Kohnke, H., 243, **254**
Kok, B., 177, **224**
Kononova, M. M., 177, **224**
Korven, H. C., 173, **228**
Koshi, P. T., 241, **254**
Kouhsiahi-Tork, K., 263, 273, **278**
Kowsar, A., 240, 242, 248, **254**
Kozlowski, T. T., 24, **127**, **130**, **132**, **133**, **134**, **135**, **138**, **139**, **143**, **144**, **162**, **222**, **233**
Krall, J. E., 122, **126**
Kramer, P. J., 12, 15, 17, 21, 23, 25, 26, 31, 32, 52, 54, 97, 113, **134**, **136**, 147, **164**, 168, 169, 171, 174, 175, **225**
Krantz, B. A., 66, **140**
Krishnomurthy, K., 74, **135**
Krotkov, G., 331, 342, 343, **346**, **347**
Krull, E., 209, **225**
Kuhl, U., 268, **279**
Kuiper, P. J. C., 176, **225**
Kumar, B., 46, **125**
Kumar, V., 74, **140**
Kurihara, H., 352, **368**
Kurtz, E. B., 57, **134**

Laag, A. E., 111, **135**
Laetsch, W. M., 51, **134**

Lahiri, A. N., 56, 57, **134**
Laing, D. R., 26, **140**, 160, **164**
Lana, E. P., 354, **368**
Lane, D. A., 202, **230**
Lang, A., 154, **164**
Lang, A. L., 81, 84, 85, **129**, **134**, 215, **228**
Lange, O. L., 268, **278**
Langer, C. A., 322, **325**
Langer, R. H. M., 181, **225**
Larson, K. L., 147, 153, **163**, **165**, **223**
Larson, R. I., 191, **227**
Larson, W. E., 85, 109, **134**, 243, 248, 249, **252**, **253**, **257**, **258**
Laude, H. M., 57, 92, **133**, **134**
Lavee, S., 243, 249, **254**
Lavin, F., 195, **225**
Le Comple, S. B., 353, 354, **368**
Lecher, D. W., 296, 302, **312**
Lee, T. A., 263, 264, **277**
Lees, R. D., 182, **225**
Leggett, J. E., 177, **225**
Lehane, J. J., 173, 191, 217, **225**, **231**, **233**, 293, 294, **312**
Lehenbauer, P. A., 358, **369**
Lehne, I., 243, 248, **254**
Lemée, G., 11, 53, 56, **129**, **133**
Lemon, E., 19, 122, **134**
Lemon, E. R., 16, 110, 114, **129**, **137**, **163**, 176, **230**
Letham, D. S., 273, **278**
Levitt, J., 31, 37, 39, 47, 48, 49, 50, 52, 54, 55, 56, 58, **134**, **135**, 148, 149, 150, **163**, 209, **225**
Lewis, D. G., 185, **225**
Lewis, T., 303, **311**
Liebhardt, W. C., 182, **225**
Lillard, J. H., 240, 248, 249, **255**
Linden, R., 240, 242, 248, **254**
Lindsay, W. L., 178, **225**
Lindstorm, M. J., 216, **227**
Lines, R., 305, **311**
Lingcgowda, B. K., 74, **135**
Lippert, L. F., 240, 242, 248, 249, **254**, **256**
Liptay, A. M., 240, 244, **255**
Littlejohn, L., 111, **135**
Livingston, B. E., 188, **225**, 358, 359, 360, **369**
Livne, A., 30, 116, **135**
Lommasson, T., 9, **135**
Long, G. C. de, 3, 97, **134**
Long, I. F., 11, **135**
Long, O. H., 194, 203, **225**

Longeragan, J. F., 203, **217**
Loomis, R. S., 14, 15, 42, 50, 51, 64, **129, 135**
Loomis, W. E., 113, **124**
Lora, M. S., **134, 141**
Losch, R., 268, **278**
Lowe, L. B., 117, **135**
Luebs, R. E., 111, **135**
Lukeena, L. F., 193, **225**
Lundegårdh, H., 189, **225**
Lunin, J., 271, **277**
Luti, R., 283, **313**
Lyford, F. P., 242, 244, **255**
Lyles, L., 87, **135**
Lyon, T. L., 317, **325**
Lyons, J. M., 240, 242, 248, 249, **256**

Mac Key, J., 168, 187, 188, 202, **226**
Mac Millan, K. A., 243, 248, 249, **255**
Mack, A. R., 173, 189, **225, 226**
Macklon, A. E. S., 268, 269, **278**
Madariaga, F. J., 353, 354, **369**
Malcolm, C. V., 158, **163**, 319, **325**
Mallough, D., 210, 213, **223**
Manescu, B., 240, **255**
Mangelsdorf, P. C., 60, 95, 118, **135, 142**
Mani, V. S., 40, 43, **125**
Mannering, J. V., 240, 244, 247, **255**
Manohar, M. S., 38, **135**
Mansfield, T. A., 151, **163**, 268, **278**, 316, **325**
Marker, A. F. H., 332, 334, **347**
Marshall, D. R., 65, **128**, 192, 209, **220**
Marshall, J. K., 300, **311**
Martin, P. E., 317, 318, 320, 322, 323, **324**
Martin, R. E., 74, **135**
Martin, W. M., 176, **227**
Martin, W. P., **140**
Mart'yanova, K. L., 173, **226**
Massengale, M. A., 174, **220**
Mather, J. R., 113, **143**
Mathews, O. R., 110, **136**, 239, 240, **255**
Mathur, M. K., 38, **135**
Mattas, R. W., 159, **163**
Mattox, R. B., **278**
May, C. H., 31, 33, 37, **125**
May, L. H., 28, 29, 32, 33, 36, 37, 38, 64, **132, 136**, 156, **164**
Mazurak, A. P., 244, **256**
McAlister, D. F., **136**
McBean, D. S., 12, **127**, 211, 263, **276**
McCalla, I. M., 108, **136**

McCalla, T. M., 238, 240, 244, 245, 246, **255, 256**
McCartney, 215, **226**
McClaren, A. D., 177, **226**
McCurdy, E. V., 213, **231**
McDonough, W. T., 53, **136**
McElroy, W. D., 177, **226**
McGeorge, W. T., 270, **275**
McGinnies, W. G., **278**
McGuinnes, J. L., 239, 248, **254**
McIntyre, G. I., 262, **278**
McMichael, B. L., 156, **163**
McWilliam, J. R., 31, **136**
Mederski, H. J., 159, **164**
Mehta, P. C., 38, **139**
Meidner, H., 268, **278**, 316, **325**
Meige, F., 172, 216, **226**
Meyer, L. D., 240, 244, 247, **255**
Michael, G., 263, 273, **273**
Migahid, A. M., 21, **136**
Mikkelsen, S. D., 74, **135**
Millar, A. A., 266, **278**, 298, **311**
Miller, D. E., 243, 248, **255**
Miller, E. C., 191, 194, 208, **226**
Miller, R. J., 34, **131**, 156, **162, 164**
Millette, J. F. G., 243, 248, 249, **255**
Millington, A. J., 90, **127**
Miloserdov, N. M., 303, **311**
Milthorpe, F. L., 28, 29, 32, 33, 36, 37, 64, **127, 131, 136, 142**, 212, **219, 226**
Mingeau, M., 115, **136**
Minshall, W. H., 195, **226**
Mirreh, H. F., 215, **226**
Mishra, D., 309, **311**
Mishra, M. N., 100, 107, 118, **136**
Misra, B. C., 38, **130**
Misra, D. K., 10, 31, 70, 74, 75, 86, 100, 107, 118, **126, 136**, 305, **311**
Misra, R. D., 66, **140**
Mitchell, J. W., 262, 273, **278**
Mitchell, R. L., 148, **164**
Mizrahi, Y., 30, **136**, 151, **164**
Mohamed, A. A., 302, **311**
Moldenhauer, W. C., 17, **136**
Molotkovsky, U. G., 57, **138**
Molz, F. J., 176, **226**
Montcith, J. L., 11, **136**, 174, **226**, 291, **311**, 319, **326**
Moody, J. E., 240, 248, 249, **255**
Moon, H. W., 353, **367**
Moorby, J., 177, **226**
Morani, V., 240, 242, 248, **252**

Morgan, P. W., 156, **162**
Moss, D. N., 16, 50, 51, 114, **136**
Moss, P., 178, **226**
Mothes, K., 35, 44, 55, **137**
Muirhead, W., 30, **130**
Multamäki, K., 360, **369**
Murata, Y., 50, **137**, 181, **226**
Murdick, S. T., 109, **138**
Murdock, J. T., 182, **225**
Musgrave, R. B., 16, 27, 28, 36, 64, 114, **126, 132, 137**
Musick, J. T., 251, **255**
Mustafaev, Kh. M., 244, 248, **255**
Muzik, T. J., 195, **227**
Myers, L. E., 102, **137**

Naaman, R., 271, **277**
Nagata, T., 361, **369**
Nägeli, W., 285, 286, 287, 304, **311**
Nagy, J., 353, 354, **369**
Nakayama, F. S., 176, **233**
Nandpuri, K. J., 343, 348, **253**
Narasimhon, R. L., 202, **231**
Naylor, A. W., 154, **162**
Neal, J. L. Jr., 191, **227**
Neal Wright, L., 174, **220**
Neel, P. L., 300, **311**
Neild, R. E., 296, 302, **312**
Nelson, C. D., 331, 342, 343, **346**
Nelson, W. L., 77, **143**
Nerpin, S. V., 240, 242, 243, **255**
Newman, E. I., 31, **137**, 195, **227**
Newton, R., 176, **227**
Nichiporovic, A. A., 41, 42, **137**
Nicholls, P. B., 31, 33, 37, **125**, 156, **164**
Nicholson, F., 339, 343, **345**
Nielsen, K. F., 189, **220, 227**
Nieman, R. H., 262, 272, **278**
Nightingale, G. T., 262, 273, **278**
Nikitin, P. D., 117, 118, **124**
Nir, I., 317, 319, 320, 323, **325**
Nishikawa, H., 352, **368**
Nobs, M. A., 339, 342, 343, **345**
Norum, E. B., 75, **137**
Nuttonson, M. Y., 353, 354, 360, 361, 362, 364, 365, **369**
Nye, P. H., 178, 179, 185, 186, 192, **217, 220, 227**

Odell, R. T., 214, **221**

Oele, J., 263, 272, 274, **279**
O'Gara, R., 272, **278**
Ogren, W. L., 333, **345, 347**
Ohlrogge, A. J., 182, 214, **221, 234**
Okubo, T., 352, 355, 357, **368**
O'Leary, J. W., 12, 262, 263, 271, 272, 273, 274, **278, 279**
Oliver, S., 178, 180, **227**
Olsen, S. R., 180, 182, **227, 233**
Olson, R. A., 76, **137**
Olson, S. R., 124, **137**
Onchev, N. G., 243, 248, **256**
Ongun, A., 336, **347**
Oorazaleiv, R. A., 193, **224**
Opik, H., 156, **164**
Oppenheimer, H. R., 38, 53, 56, **132, 137**, 170, 174, 192, **227**
Orazem, F., 72, **137**
Osborne, D. J., 154, **164**
Osmond, C. B., 342, **346**
Ott, B. J., 239, 248, **253**
Otto, H. W., 268, 272, **279**
Overbeek, J. van, 121, **137**
Overstreet, R., 179, **223**
Oveson, M. M., 122, **138**
Owen, C. H., 210, 213, **223**
Ozanne, P. G., 195, 203, **217, 227**

Paauw, F., 76, **138**
Pakshina, S. M., 240, 242, 243, **255**
Pal, B. P., 215, **230**
Paleg, L. G., 30, **141**
Pallas, J. E. Jr., 27, **138**
Papadakis, J., 114, 116, **138**
Papendick, R. I., 216, **227**
Pareek, O. P., 262, **279**
Parker, J. J., 251, **257**
Parks, C. L., 27, **138**
Parr, J. F., 186, **227**
Pasternak, D., 17, **138**
Patterson, L. A., 210, 213, **223**
Pauli, A. W., 159, **163**
Paulsen, K., 216, **227**
Pavlychenko, T. K., 118, **138**, 187, 188, 191, 195, 202, 204, **227**
Paylore, P., **278**
Payne, D., 216, **221**
Payne, T. M. B., 191, **224**
Pearcy, R. W., 342, **345**
Pearson, R. W., 195, **228**
Pelton, W. L., 82, **138**, 195, **228**, 302, **311**

Pencic, M., 38, **138**
Pendleton, J. W., 81, 84, 85, 86, **129, 134,** **138,** 215, **228**
Penman, H. L., 114, **138**
Percival, J., 187, **228**
Perekaljskii, F. M., 86, **138**
Pesek, J., **126, 140, 164, 326**
Peters, D. B., 31, **138, 144,** 239, 248, **254, 256**
Peterson, D. R., 109, **138**
Peterson, E. A., 109, **138,** 191, **224**
Peterson, G. H., 177, **226**
Petinov, N. S., 29, 57, **138**
Pettiet, J. V., 70, **127,** 184, **219**
Phelan, J. T., 319, **325**
Phillips, W. M., 122, **139**
Philpotts, H., 38, 117, **139**
Piemeisel, L. N., 344, **347**
Pierpoint, G., 202, **228**
Pierre, W. H., **126, 140, 144, 164, 326**
Pietro, A. S., **135, 145**
Pillai, S. C., 106, **133**
Pinthus, M. J., 116, **139,** 188, 190, 194, **228**
Piper, C. S., 75, **139**
Pittman, U. J., 187, **228**
Place, G. A., 70, **127,** 184, **219**
Platt, A. W., 208, **228**
Plaut, Z., 116, 117, **139**
Pohjakallio, D., 208, **228**
Pohjakas, K., 173, **228**
Poljakoff-Mayber, A., 115, 116, **130, 139,** 271, **277,** 316, 317, 318, 319, 320, 323, **325, 326**
Polunin, N., 47, **139**
Porter, K. B., 85, **139**
Possingham, J. V., 323, **326**
Poulain, J. F., 107, **139**
Poulsen, L. L., 262, 272, **278**
Powell, R. D., 156, **163,** 263, 264, **278**
Power, J. F., 71, **126,** 240, 245, 250, **252**
Powers, W. L., 193, **232**
Pradhan, G. C., 309, **311**
Prasad, R., 118, **136**
Price, C. A., 182, **228**
Prihar, S. S., 240, 243, 248, **252, 256**
Prisco, J. T., 262, 271, **279**
Probst, A. H., 361, 362, **369**
Puckridge, D. W., 84, **139**
Puntamkar, S. S., 38, **139**
Purkas, L., 195, **228**
Pusztai, A., 240, 242, 248, **256**
Pyatt, D. G., 304, **311**

Qashu, H. K., 242, 243, 244, **255, 256**
Quirk, J. P., 185, **225**

Rabeson, R., 334, **347**
Rackham, O., **277, 279**
Racz, C. T., 201, **228**
Raheja, P. C., 304, **311**
Ramig, R. E., 31, 75, 94, **133, 139,** 191, **224,** 244, **256**
Raney, F. C., 174, **233**
Raper, C. D., 208, **228**
Raschke, K., 268, **276, 279**
Rasmussen, H. P., 51, **137**
Ratledge, E. L., 320, **324**
Ratliff, L. F., 195, 216, **228, 232**
Ravira, A. D., 191, 202, **218**
Rawitscher, F., 187, **228**
Rawitz, R., 103, **132**
Rawlins, S. L., 262, 267, 268, 271, 275, **277**
Rawson, H. M., 43, 46, 64, **140**
Ray, D., 43, **125**
Razumova, L. A., 300, **312**
Read, A. A., 202, **231**
Read, D. W. L., 173, 195, 210, **228**
Reath, A. N., 354, 360, **369**
Reed, A. J., 151, 152, 160, **164**
Reinhart, J., 187, **220**
Reinhold, L., 151, **163**
Remson, I., 176, **226**
Rennie, D. A., 171, 182, 184, 185, 201, 202, 214, **220, 223, 228, 229**
Rhoades, H. F., 75, **139**
Richards, L. A., 12, 33, **140, 257**
Richardson, K. E., 334, **347**
Richman, R. W., 216, **217**
Richmond, A. E., 30, **136,** 151, 154, **164**
Ries, S. K., 354, **367**
Rijtema, P. E., 168, **221**
Ripley, E. A., 290, **311**
Ripley, P. F., 99, **140**
Ritchie, J. T., 172, **229,** 295, **311**
Robb, W., 340, **348**
Robertson, G. W., 176, **229, 234,** 300, **312,** 352, 353, 354, 365, **368, 369**
Robertson, L. S., 109, **131**
Robins, J. S., 33, **140,** 239, 240, 244, 248, **258**
Rogers, J. S., 354, 355, **368**
Rogers, W. S., 201, **229**
Roma, A., 209, **229**
Romeike, A., 35, **137**
Rooeick, J., 202, **223**

Rosca, V., 353, **369**
Rosenberg, N. J., 117, **140**, 286, 288, 289, 290, 293, 294, 296, 297, 302, **309, 312**
Rosenblum, I. Y., 338, **345**
Rosenstiel, K., 66, **130**
Rossi, N., 273, **279**
Rouatt, J. W., 191, **219, 224**
Rudnjanjin, L. J., 38, **138**
Rudorf, W., **130**
Ruhland, W., **133, 135, 137, 142**
Ruich, J., 116, **139**
Rumbaugh, M. D., 243, 248, **253**
Runkles, J. R., 31, **138**
Russell, G. C., 216, **217**, 243, 249, **252**
Russell, J. S., 72, 73, **140**
Russell, M. B., 24, **130**, 147, **164**, 168, 174, 190, 203, 211, 212, 217, **229**
Russell, R. S., 202, **229**
Rutter, A. J., **136**
Ruwali, K. N., 65, 66, **125**
Ryder, J. C., 320, **324**

Sack, H. S., 202, **218**
Sage, G. C. M., 207, **229**
Saini, A. D., 43, **125**
Sale, P. J. M., 240, 242, 248, 249, **256**, 263, 264, 273, **279**
Salim, M. H., 39, 53, **140**, 193, **230**
Salisbury, F. B., 268, **276**
Sallach, H. J., 338, **345**
Sallans, B. J., 204, **230**
Salter, P. J., 321, **326**
Sampson, A. J., 243, 244, **254**
Sandhu, B. S., 240, **256**
Santhirasegaram, K., 86, **140**
Sarid, A., 55, **127**
Sawhney, K., 96, **140**
Sayre, C. B., 365, **369**
Sayre, J. D., 84, **132**
Schales, F. D., 240, 242, **256**
Schlehuber, A. M., 53, **140**, 193, **230**
Schmidt, H., 58, **140**
Schneider, G. W., 156, **164**
Schultz, J. D., 268, **278**, 318, **325**
Schuster, C. E., 123, **142**
Schuurman, J. J., 190, **222, 230**
Seginer, I., 116, **140**
Sekioka, H., 273, **276**
Semikina, G. G., 242, 248, 249, **258**
Sen, S., 215, **230**
Seth, S. P., 38, **139**

Shah, S. R. H., 303, **312**
Shanan, L., 243, **253**, 270, **277**
Shantz, H. L., 273, **276**, 344, **347**
Sharma, D. C., 86, **141**
Sharma, K. C., 66, 74, **140**
Sharma, P. N., 46, **125**
Sharma, R. C., 96, **128**
Sharma, Sarla, 88, **131**
Sharma, S. M., 117, **141**
Shaw, B., **140**
Shaw, R., **126, 140, 144, 164, 326**
Shaw, R. H., 26, 36, **128, 140**, 151, 152, 160, **162, 164**, 272, **276**, 295, **310**
Shawcroft, W. W., 176, **230**
Shcar, G. M., 109, **141**
Shekhawat, G. S., 86, **141**
Shields, L. M., 29, 52, 53, 54, **141**
Shimshi, D., 50, **141**
Shlifasovsky, V., 189, **220**
Shmueli, E., 116, **139**
Shrader, W. D., 85, **127**
Shrivastava, M. S., 117, **141**
Shrivastava, S. P., 76, **141**
Siddoway, F. H., 244, 245, **256, 258**, 308, **312**
Sij, J. W., 158, **164**
Sikka, S. M., 96, **140**
Simmonds, P. M., 204, **230**
Simonis, W., 53, **141**
Simpson, G. M., 43, **141**
Singh, A., 76, **141**, 243, 248, **253**
Singh, B., 240, **256**
Singh, B. P., 38, **130**
Singh, D. N., 82, **125**
Singh, G., 96, **128**
Singh, G. D., 86, **128**
Singh, K., 171, 187, **230**
Singh, O. S., 88, **141**
Singh, S., 56, 57, **134**
Singh, S. P., 74, 117, **140, 141**
Singh, T. N., 30, **141**
Sisodia, U. S., 86, **128**
Sivanayagam, T., 262, **279**
Skene, K. G. M., 273, **279**
Skerman, P. J., 16, **141**
Skidmore, E. L., 290, 308, **310**
Slack, C. R., 50, **131**, 341, **346, 347**
Slatyer, R. O., 11, 17, 24, 27, 29, 35, 36, 98, **141**, 153, 154, 155, 156, 160, **164**, 168, 169, 170, 174, 175, 176, 193, **230**, 274, 275, **279**, 316, 318, **326**, 342, **346**
Sletten, W. A., 85, **139**
Slooshnaya, N. P., 193, **225**

Slucker, R., 190, 193, **230**
Smika, D. E., 94, **139**, 241, 243, 250, **253**, **256**, **257**
Smith, F. W., 92, **134**
Smith, G. E., 75, **141**
Smith, R., 237, 238, **254**
Sneva, F. A., 26, **141**
Soper, R. J., 182, 185, 215, **229**, **231**
Sosebee, R. E, 88, **141**
Spinks, J. W. T., 202, **230**
Spratt, E. D., 25, 70, 184, 213, **230**, **231**
Squire, G. R., 115, **141**
Sreedharan, A., 96, **129**
Sreenivasan, A., 106, **142**
Stakman, E. C., 60, 95, **142**
Stalfelt, M. G., 52, **142**
Staple, W. J., 10, 106, 110, **142**, 173, 191, 217, **225**, **231**, **233**, 293, 294, **312**
Steinherdt, R., 103, **132**
Stephenson, R. E., 123, **142**
Stevenson, F. J., 178, **231**
Steward, F. C., **134**
Stewart, B. A., 72, **129**
Stewart, C. R., 155, **134**
Stewart, D. W., 176, **230**
Stewart, H. E., 193, **223**
Stocker, O., 36, 50, 58, **140**, **142**
Stocking, C. R., 18, **128**, 336, **347**
Stoeckeler, J. H., 308, **312**
Stolzy, L. H., 158, **163**
Stone, E. C., 270, **279**
Stone, J. F., 202, **231**, 239, 248, **253**
Stoughton, R. H., 12, **142**
Stout, N. B., 274, **280**
Stoy, V., 39, 44, **142**, 177, **231**
Street, H. E., 156, **164**, 193, **231**
Stringfield, C. H., 85, **132**
Strommen, A. M., 353, 354, **367**
Strong, W. M., 185, 215, **231**
Stukenholtz, K. D., 76, **137**
Sturrock, J. W., 19, 117, 118, **142**, 292, 293, 295, 299, 301, 305, 307, **312**
Stutte, C. A., 55, **142**, 170, 193, 212, **230**, **232**
Subbarami, R. D., 107, **142**
Subbaih, B. V., 190, 202, **224**, **231**
Sullivan, C. Y., **164**, 209, **225**, **312**
Swanson, W. A., 240, **257**
Swarner, L. R., 319, **325**
Swatyendruber, D., 195, **228**
Syme, J. R., 67, **142**, 209, **231**
Szeicz, G., 319, **326**

Tabata, K., 352, **368**
Tadmore, N. H., 20, **142**, 270, **277**
Takatori, F. H., 240, 242, 248, 249, **254**, **256**
Tanner, J. W., 64, **142**
Taylor, D. W., 193, 216, **231**
Taylor, H. M., 195, 216, **228**, **231**, **232**
Taylor, R. E., 247, 248, **256**
Teare, I. D., 158, **164**, 193, **232**
Teel, M. R., 195, **228**
Thompson, C. A., 76, **137**
Thompson, C. M., 334, **348**
Thorne, G. N., 34, 44, 46, 67, **142**
Thornthwaite, C. W., 8, 20, 113, 116, **143**, 238, **256**
Thorud, D. B., 318, 319, **324**
Tiessen, H., 240, 244, **255**
Ting, I. P., 272, **279**
Tinker, P. B. H., 179, **217**, **218**
Tisdale, S. L., 77, **143**
Tisserand, E., 360, **369**
Tiver, N. S., 33, **143**
Todd, G. W., 29, 30, 37, 39, 53, 55, **127**, **140**, **142**, **143**, 170, 193, 208, 212, **229**, **230**, **232**, 300, **312**
Tolbert, N. E., 333, 334, 335, 336, 342, **347**, **348**
Toole, E. H., 88, **143**
Toole, V. K., 88, **143**
Torchinsky, B. B., 202, **230**
Tourte, R., 107, **139**
Townley-Smith, T. F., 210, 211, 213, **223**
Tranquillini, W., 12, **143**
Tregunna, E. B., 51, **128**, 331, 341, 342, **345**, **346**
Trenkle, H., 353, 354, **369**
Trewartha, J. T., 12, **143**
Triplett, G. B. Jr., 247, **254**
Troll, C., 11, **143**
Tromp, J., 272, **279**
Troughton, A., 88, **143**, 181, 182, 187, 188, 190, 191, 192, 207, 208, 209, 211, 214, **232**
Tsai, S. D., 300, **312**
Turelle, J. W., 244, **256**
Turner, N. C., 270, **280**, 318, 322, **326**
Tyankova, L. A., 30, **143**

Uchijima, T., 359, **368**
Unger, P. W., 124, 139, 240, 241, 242, 244, 245, 248, 249, 251, **256**, **257**
Unrath, C. R., 275, **279**
Upchurch, R. P., 195, **233**

Uriu, K., 319, 322, 323, **324**
U. S. Salinity Lab. Staff, 245, **257**

Vaadia, Y., 30, 31, 54, 116, **132**, **135**, **143**, 147, **164**, 174, **233**, 269, 273, **277**, **280**
Valli, V. J., 353, **369**
van Bavel, C. H. M., 176, **233**, **312**
van Eimern, J., 286, 287, 300, **312**
van Emden, H. F., 170, 303, **312**
van Schaik, P. H., 361, 362, **369**
van Wijk, W. R., 248, 249, **257**
Vanra, J. P., 196, **221**
Varga-Haszonits, Z., 363, **369**
Vasey, E. H., 179, 180, **218**
Vasiliev, J., 173, **233**
Vegis, A., 56, **143**
Veihmeyer, F. J., 33, **124**, 170, **219**
Verhagen, A. M. W., 14, **143**
Verner, L., 322, **326**
Viets, F. G. Jr., 77, **144**, 159, 160, **165**, 171, **233**
Vijayalakshmi, K., 202, 209, **233**
Vogel, O. A., 205, **218**
Voigt, J. W., 195, **233**
Volk, R. J., 51, **132**, 330, **347**
Vries, M. P. C. de, 75, **139**

Wadleigh, C. H., 12, 33, **140**
Waggoner, P. E., 115, **144**, 158, **165**, 270, **280**, 297, **312**, 316, 317, 318, 319, 322, **326**
Waisel, Y., 11, 31, 38, 54, **143**, **144**, 269, **280**
Walker, D. A., 333, 344, **348**
Walker, J. M., 179, 180, **218**
Walker, J. N., 262, **276**
Wallace, A. M., 274, **280**
Wallin, J. R., 269, 270, 271, **280**
Wang, J. Y., 14, 15, **144**
Wanjura, E. F., 89, **144**
Wann, S. S., 243, 244, 248, **257**
Warder, F. G., 217, **233**
Wardlaw, I. F., 27, 33, **144**, 170, **233**
Wardlaw, S., 187, 208, **221**
Warnaar, B. C., 188, **233**
Warnock, S. J., 353, 354, **370**
Wassermann, V. D., 84, **144**
Wassinck, E. C., 13, **144**
Watanabe, F. S., 124, **137**, 184, **233**
Watson, D. J., 40, 41, 42, **144**, 176, 180, 212, **233**, 262, 263, **280**
Watson, R. D., 195, **219**

Watts, W. R., 263, **280**
Weatherley, P. E., 268, 269, **278**
Weaver, J. E., 187, 190, 191, 194, 195, 203, 204, **233**
Weaver, R. E. C., 42, **126**
Webster, D. L., 37, **143**, 208, **232**
Weiser, V., 77, **144**
Wells, S. A., 59, **144**, 170, **233**
Wendt, C. W., 240, **257**
Went, F. W., 48, **144**, 262, 263, **280**, 365, **370**
Werkhoven, C. H., 243, **254**
Westin, F. C., 17, **136**
White, G. F., 9, **143**, **144**
Whitefield, C. L., 107, **145**
Whitehead, F. H., **136**, 283, **312**, **313**
Whiteman, P. C., 36, **45**
Whiteside, A. G. O., 173, **234**
Whitfield, C. J., 238, 240, 243, 246, 249, 250, **253**, **258**
Whiting, F. L., 240, 242, **254**, **256**
Whittingham, C. P., 332, 333, 334, 336, 340, **345**, **347**, **348**
Whittington, W. J., 190, 191, 207, 208, 209, 211, 214, **218**, **219**, **220**, **221**, **222**, **229**, **231**, **232**, **233**, **234**, **276**
Whitworth, J. W., 195, **227**
Wicks, G. A., 121, **127**, 241, 250, **256**, **257**
Wiegand, C. L., 240, 245, 249, **254**, **257**
Wiersma, D., 147, **164**
Wiersum, L. K., 179, 181, 183, 185, 192, **220**, **234**, 272, 273, **280**
Wiese, A. F., 108, 122, **124**, **145**, 240, 241, 244, 245, 246, 248, 250, 251, **252**, **255**, **257**
Wiggans, S. C., 354, **370**
Wilberg, E., 263, 273, **278**
Wilkins, M. B., **220**, **224**, **235**
Wilkinson, H. F., 180, 186, **234**
Wilkinson, S. R., 214, **234**
Williams, C. H., 91, **128**
Williams, G. D. V., 176, **234**
Williams, M. S., **145**
Williams, R. F., 33, **143**, 193, **234**
Williams, T. F., 194, **234**
Williams, W. A., 14, 15, 42, 50, 51, 64, **129**, **135**, 244, **257**
Williamson, R. E., 157, **165**
Willis, W. O., 71, 85, **126**, **134**, 161, **163**, 239, 240, 242, 243, 244, 248, **252**, **257**, **258**
Wilson, A. T., 333, **348**
Wilson, C. C., 15, **145**, 268, **280**

Wilson, G. L., 17, 36, **138**, **145**
Wilson, J. H., 14, **143**
Wilson, J. W., 42, **145**
Winneberger, J. H., 263, **280**
Wischmeier, W. H., 247, **255**
Wit, C. T. de, 14, 116, **145**
Wittwer, S. H., 63, 117, **131**, **145**, 340, **348**,
    354, 360, **369**
Woodruff, N. P., 38, 39, **145**, 240, 245, **254**,
    258
Wooley, J. T., 296, **313**, 316, **326**
Wort, D. J., 172, **235**
Worzella, W. W., 192, 215, **235**
Wright, B. C., 66, **140**
Wright, S. T. C., 30, **145**

Yalsenko, G., 189, **220**

Yamazaki, R. K., 336, **348**
Yang, S. J., 266, **280**
Yarger, D. N., 272, **276**
Youker, R. E., 247, **254**

Zahnley, J. W., 92, **134**
Zakharov, N. G., 242, 248, 249, **258**
Zarate, P. M., 304, **310**
Zeevaart, J. A. D., 151, **165**
Zelitch, I., 158, **165**, 315, 316, 317,
    326, 332, 333, 338, 339, 341, 343,
    344, **348**
Zill, L. P., 333, **348**
Zimmerman, M., 177, **235**
Zingg, A. W., 103, 107, **145**, 238, 240,
    246, 249, 250, **258**

SUBJECT INDEX

Abscisic acid, 30, 151
Abscission, 155-6
Adaptation, 47-8, 51, 55, 58, 60-1, 67, 79, 216, 283, 344
Adapted varieties, 59-61
Adventitious roots, 187, 190, 264, 273
Aeration, 87-8, 108, 149, 172, 175, 188, 215-6
Agave, 51
Agriculture, defined, 238
Agronomic practices, 67
Air pollution, 15, 148
Air pollution damage, 272
Alkaline soil, 70
Alkaloid content, 303
Anatomical changes, 28
Anthesis, 33, 43, 67, 151, 156-7, 160, 170
Antitranspirants, 114-6, 309, 320-3
   alkenyl succinic acid, 315
   film forming type, 158, 315-7, 319, 322
   nonenyl succinic acid, 320
   phenyl mercuric acetate, 315-6, 318, 321
   effects of, 158, 318
   role of, 157, 316-8, 320
   side effects of, 321-2
   types of, 158
   white reflecting materials, 315, 317
Architecture, 42, 291
Aridity, 11, 23, 68
ATP, 332, 336, 338, 342
Auxin, 38, 156, 189, 193, 214
Available moisture (water), 69, 71, 75, 83, 98, 107, 112, 148, 170

Barley, 38, 42-3, 52-3, 57, 59, 64, 67, 78, 90-1, 93, 151, 156, 173, 187, 189, 208, 212, 274, 320, 341, 362
Biological yield, 42, 66-7, 80-1
Bound water, 30, 176, 209
Brassica napus (rape), 181, 185, 213
Breeding, 44, 46-7, 58-63, 66-8, 189, 207-8, 210, 212-3, 305, 344, 351
   genetic approach, 62-3
   objectives, 64-5
   physiological approach, 63-5

Calcarious soils, 70
Calvin cycle, 51, 64, 333, 341-2
Calvin plants, see C₃ plants
Canopy, 14, 19, 40-2, 64, 83-4, 176, 291, 296, 318
Carbohydrate metabolism, 155-6
Castor beans, 96, 305
Cell collapse, 54, 150
   division, 35, 152, 174
   enlargement (expansion), 35, 152, 157-8, 174, 266, 309
Chemical fallow, 250
Chemical potential, 169
Chick peas, 91, 93, 96
Chilling, 88, 149-50
Chloroplast, 167, 332-6, 342-3
Choice of crops, 4
Choice of parents, see also selection of parents, 63-4, 213
Climate, effect on:
   evapotranspiration, 6, 8
   yield, 6, 8
Climatic factors, 25
Cold injury/tolerance, see chilling
Community, 42, 83
Compensation point, 56
Components of yield, 33, 44, 67-8, 71, 76, 81
Consumptive use, 25, 97
Corn, see maize
Cotton, 27, 29, 33-4, 61, 76, 80-1, 87, 89, 96, 98, 100, 123, 156, 184, 262, 271, 274, 295
Crassulacian acid metabolism (CAM), 51
Crop (grain) production, 3, 46, 85, 89-90, 92-5, 99, 106, 110-1, 117, 159-62, 168, 176, 267, 306, 308, 318
Crop rotation, see also rotation, 77, 89-95, 100, 104, 108, 113, 213, 216
Crop zonation, 351
Crossing programmes, 63
Crusting, 87, 244
Cucurbits, 76, 95-6, 99
Cultivation, 105-9
Cultural practices, 160, 213
Cytokinins, see also kinetin, 30, 154, 193, 273
Cytoplasm, see protoplasm
C₃ plants (Calvin plants), 52, 341-4

C_4 acids, 50, 342-3
  location of, 342
  synthesis of, 342
C_4 cycle, 50-2
C_4 plants, 51, 329, 341-4
  characteristics of, 342
  drought tolerance, 51, 344
  refixation of photorespired CO_2, 343
  various species, 341

Dark respiration, *see* respiration
Dehydration/desiccation, 54-6, 79, 98, 148,
  150-2, 155, 157, 160, 168, 205
  of pollen, 12, 15
Desiccation, *see* dehydration
Development, 34, 69, 149, 156-7, 273, 353-4,
  360
Developmental changes, 33
Diffusion, 179-80
Diffusion pressure deficit (DPD), 25, 170-2,
  174
Disease resistance, 62, 301
Diseases, 19, 60, 82, 84-5, 89, 95-6, 147,
  160, 209-10, 284, 301-3, 305
DNA, 35
Drought, 38-9, 50-4, 56, 58, 67, 72, 74-5,
  89-90, 110, 117, 148, 151-3, 156-7, 160,
  174, 188, 204, 301, 306
  avoidance of, 48, 148-9, 193, 209
  conserving water, 48, 50
  defined, 148
  effects of, 147-57
  metabolic strain, 55
  response to:
    fallowing, 161
    microclimate, 160-1
    soil fertility, 160
  stage of growth, 151-2
  types of, 148
Drought hardening, 36, 38-9, 159
  changes induced, 159
  presowing treatment, 37-9
Drought resistance/tolerance, 4, 36-8, 47-8,
  53-5, 57-8, 62-5, 68, 75-6, 148-9, 170,
  176, 187, 189-90, 192, 204, 208-9, 211,
  212, 295, 309
  mechanism, 148-50
  polygenic, 47
  role of awns, 53
Drought resistant, 29, 55, 59, 64, 111, 174
Drought susceptibility, 32, 115, 193

age as a factor, 32
Dry matter production, 39-44, 67, 70-1,
  74, 80-1, 118, 171, 296, 321, 323, 338-9
Dryland, defined, 238
Dryland farming:
  dew, 11
    effect on plant growth, 11
    disease development, 290
  rainfall, 9
    effective rainfall, 10
    frequency and intensity, 9
    relation with yield, 10
Dwarfs, 57, 66, 71, 88, 301

Ear/shoot ratio, 44
Economic yield, 33, 40, 42-3, 66, 77, 80-1
Environmental factors, 364-5
Environmental stresses, 149-50
  drought resistance compared with, 150
  various types of, 149
    chilling, 149
    flooding, 149
    freezing (frost), 149
    heat (temperature), 149
    radiation, 149
    salt, 150
Enzymes, 29, 50, 56-7, 87, 283, 334-6, 338,
  340, 342
Erosion, 100, 103-4, 107-8, 161, 246-7, 300,
  304, 308
Ethylene, 156
Evaporation, 6, 10, 18, 20, 73, 85-6, 96-8,
  105-7, 110, 122-4, 159-60, 171-2, 175,
  216-7, 290-1, 296-7
Evaporative demand, 268, 291, 316, 321
Evapotranspiration (ET), 5-6, 8-12, 17, 20,
  47, 56, 68, 70-2, 74, 79, 96-8, 173-4
Exponential index, 357

Fallow, *see also* chemical fallow, 75-6, 90-5,
  107-11, 113, 122, 161, 215
Fertilization, 12, 16, 151, 156-7
Fertilizer use, 68-9
  dynamics in dry regions, 69-70
  timing and balance, 74-6
Field capacity (FC), 21-2, 79, 106, 169,
  172-3, 175
Flag leaf, 43
Flax, 31, 33, 185-6, 215
Flower development, 273

Fog, 11
Foliage pattern, 83
Foliar absorption, 273
  application, 117
Forage crops, 69, 76
Forage legumes, 76, 92-3, 111-3
Free energy, 169
Freezing, 149-50
Frost, 17-8, 149, 173, 305

Genes, 62-3, 207-8, 212, 345
Genetic analysis, 62, 191
Genetic characteristics, 62, 187
Genetic control, 209
Genotype, 45, 63, 67-8, 83, 204, 213
Geometry, see architecture
Germination, 11-2, 38, 57, 78-9, 87-9, 92,
  120, 193, 211, 216, 248, 296, 300
Gibberellins, 116, 193, 273
Gluten content, 303
Glycine metabolism, 335
Glycolate, 332-5, 338, 340-1, 343
Grain filling, 43, 156-7, 160, 181, 190-1, 204
Green manuring, 92-3, 95
Groundnuts (peanuts), 31, 50, 64, 74-5,
  85-6, 94-6, 262-3
Growth:
  effect of turgidity, 148
  relative humidity, 262-3, 266-7, 270
  role of shelter, 299
  role of water, 147-8
Growth retardants, 36, 38, 114, 116-7, 309

Harvest index, 42
Hatch and Slack plants, see also C₄ plants,
  51, 329, 341, 344
Heat damage, 272
  resistance, 56-7
  stress, 57
Heat unit concept, 351
  calculation methods, 355-6
  dryland conditions affecting, 365-6
  practical application, 351
  various heat units, relationships, 363-4
Hereditary, 210
Heretability, 62, 209, 211
Heterosis, 63
High humidity, 264, 271-3
  air pollutant damage, 272
  boron transport, 273

  calcium transport, 272-3
  heat damage, 272
  pathogen development, 271
Hormones, 30, 115, 186, 273
Humidity, 262-4, 266-72, 290, 364, 366
Hybrid vigour, 63
Hybrids, 60, 63, 67, 74, 79, 85, 193, 354
Hydrothermal index, 359-60

Infiltration, 99-102, 104-5, 107, 109-10, 161
Inheritance, 193, 207, 212
Insect pest, 82, 89, 95-6, 147, 160, 209,
  284, 304-5
Inter-cropping, 95
Introduction, 61

Kinetin, see also cytokinins, 44, 88

Leaf angle, 42, 64
  area (assimilating area), 39-40, 52, 118,
    175, 212, 295, 323
  area index (LAI), 40-2, 76, 84, 296
  growth, 263, 266
  reflectance (albedo), 52, 79, 114, 116, 269
  stem ratio, 148
  surface, 52, 57, 317
Leaf (plant) water potential, 266-7, 269,
  317-8, 320, 322,
Light, 12-5
  foliage pattern, 83-4
  intensity, 22, 25, 41, 51, 116, 366
  plant density, 84
Lodging, 84, 116-7, 182, 309

Maize (corn), 16-7, 22, 27, 29, 33, 36, 38,
  50-2, 61, 63-4, 80-1, 84, 86-7, 92-3,
  95-6, 100, 109, 115, 118, 123, 149, 151,
  159, 161-2, 182-3, 185, 191, 208, 266,
  274, 283, 290, 341, 344, 354-6
Male sterility, 63
Management practices, 68-84, 99, 107,
  113, 121, 159, 176, 305-6
  population distribution, 80
  relation with rainfall, 72-3
Mass flow, 180, 273
Maturity, 47-8, 65-6, 76, 85, 351
Membrane, 151, 156, 169
Microclimate, 19, 284-6, 288-90, 316

at plant level, 19
at soil level, 20-1
Micronutrients, 70, 91, 178, 181, 186
Microwater sheds, 101-3
Millets, 48, 52, 94, 107
Mineral nutrition, 180, 182, 188
Minimum tillage, 109
Mitochondria, 156, 335-6
Mixed cropping, 95-6
Moisture conservation, 100, 106, 110, 118, 123, 161
Moisture regime, 11, 28, 33, 40, 45, 50, 67-9, 83, 92, 96, 99, 113, 117, 191
Moisture stress, see water stress
Moisture supply, 21, 38, 42, 63, 67, 72-3, 76, 82, 85-6
  establishing stand, 86-7
  plant factors, 22-3
  rooting characters, 23-5
  soil factors, 21-2
Moisture tension, 87, 170, 183, 215
Monoculture, 93-4
Morphological changes, 31-2
Mulch, defined, 238
Mulches, 6, 100, 107-8, 122-3, 316, 161
  help in emergence, 248
  germination, 248
  seedling growth, 248
  increase water storage, 241
  yield, 241-2, 248-9
  miscellaneous types, 243
  moderate soil salinity, 245
  plastic film, 240
Multiple cropping, 351

Net assimilation rate (NAR), 43, 64, 212
Nutrient absorption, 75-6, 113, 152, 177
  absorption mechanism, 179
  availability, 177-8
  supply, 75
Nutrient (mineral) uptake, 70, 83, 153, 168, 177, 179, 184-6, 318
  deficiency, 183
Nutrients, 40, 82-3, 149, 176, 178, 214, 216, 272-3
  immobile, 179
  mobile, 179, 183

Oats, 48, 86, 93, 274, 341
Osmotic potential, 54, 72, 170

Osmotic pressure (OP), 29, 58, 70, 271

Pasture, 92, 96
Pearl millet, 70
Peas, 71-2, 188, 274, 293, 354
Pegion pea, 213-4
PEP carboxylase, 342-3
Permanent wilting point (PWP), 21, 26, 148, 193
Peroxisomes, 335-6, 342-3
Pest resistance, 62
Phenyl mercuric acetate, 115
Photoperiodism, 360, 362, 364
Photorespiration, 51, 64, 329-33, 335, 338-43
  energy relations, 332, 338
  glycolate metabolism, 335
    site of, 333
    synthesis of, 333-4
  inhibition of, 339
    by chemicals, 340-1
    by high CO_2, 339-40
    by low O_2, 339
  location of, 331
  measurement of, 330
    in CO_2 free air, 330
    in dark, 330
    in $^{18}O_2$, 331
  substrate, 332-3
  vs. true respiration, 331
Photosensitive plants, 360-1
Photosynthesis, 13-6, 18-9, 26-8, 35-7, 39-40, 43, 46, 50-1, 55-6, 64, 76, 84, 113-6, 118, 121, 148, 153, 157-60, 175, 177, 193, 197, 208, 269, 297, 308-9, 316, 331-4, 338-44
Photosynthetic efficiency, 36, 41-2, 50-1
Photothermal units, 360-3
Physiological effects, 26
Physiological index, 357-60
Physiology of yield, 39-42, 64
Pine apple, 51
Plant density (population), 45, 67, 80-5, 160
  disease incidence, 84
  lodging, 84
  plant height, 84
Plant modelling, 175-7
Planting dates, 77
  humid period, 79
  post-humid period, 79
  precipitation pattern, 77
  pre-humid period, 77-9

Planting patterns, 85-6
Plastic materials, 308
Pollen grains, 149
Pollen viability, 17, 33
Pollination, 11, 33, 65, 67, 304, 351
Potatoes, 176, 274, 352, 354
Potential evaporation, 290
Potential evapotranspiration (PET), 8, 77-9, 97, 99, 160, 291, 295
Precipitation, 8-10, 71-4, 77-9, 86, 89-90, 92, 97, 99, 101-2, 105, 110-11, 113, 161, 360
Presoaking, 38
Primary minerals, 177
Productivity, 14, 18, 22, 25, 39, 42-3, 57-9, 62-4, 92, 111, 147, 153, 205, 267, 339, 340
Progeny, 63
Proline, 29-30, 55, 154
Protein, 29-30, 35, 57, 74, 108, 150-4, 156, 160, 303
Protoplasm (cytoplasm), 29-31, 35, 37, 150-1, 159, 174-5
Pyridine, nucleotides, 338

Radiant energy, 267, 290
Radiation, 15, 17-8, 20, 51, 56, 83, 86, 93, 97, 113-4, 116, 149-50
Rainfed, 8, 10, 13, 46, 68-70, 74, 76, 86, 89, 96, 121, 186
Relative humidity, 12, 19, 22, 25, 122, 148, 158, 174, 261-5, 268-9, 291
  effect on:
    crop morphology, 263
    flowering, 264
    growth, 262 3
    vapour pressure gradient, 12
Remainder index, 252-7, 362-3
Respiration (dark or true respiration), 13-4, 16, 26, 28, 35, 37, 40, 56-7, 88, 114, 155-6, 159-60, 175, 321, 329-32, 338
Rhizosphere, 185, 191
Ribulose diphosphate (RuDP), 334
RNA, 29, 35, 55, 88, 154, 193
Role of awns, 53
Root absorbing efficiency, 185
  anchorage, 185
  characters, 23-5, 84, 244
  crown (nodal), 187, 203
  environment, 185
  growth, 21, 65, 75, 105, 107, 117, 152-3,

172, 182, 184-5, 188-9, 191, 193, 215-6
  hairs, 35-6, 169, 185-6, 188
  methods of study, 194-203
  models, 186
  pattern, 84-5, 179, 186-8, 190-3, 195-6, 199, 202-3, 207-8, 210-11, 215
  penetration, 69, 71, 88, 105, 107, 171, 182, 185, 216-7
  pressure, 185
  primary, 53, 187, 189
  proliferation (ramification), 23, 170, 172, 179, 183, 186, 203
  respiration, 186
  seminal, 37, 187, 192-3, 203
  shoot ratio, 37, 53-4, 74, 159, 175, 190, 192, 283
  systems, 6, 23-4, 53, 65, 83-4, 95, 98, 107, 148, 168, 170-1, 175, 187, 190, 207-8, 210, 212, 214-5, 320
  zone, 23-4, 31, 79, 99, 105, 109, 123, 148, 170, 176, 186, 295
Rotation, see also crop rotation, 6, 69, 89-90, 107, 110-11, 306
Row direction, 86
RuDP carboxylase, 333, 341-2
Run off, 9-10, 79, 100-3, 105, 107-10, 161
  control, 99, 246-7

Secondary minerals, 178
Segregation, 63, 191, 211-2
Selection, 58, 60, 63, 65, 68, 159, 170, 189, 203, 208, 210, 212
Selection of parents, 63-4, 213
Semiarid climate (regions), 3, 10, 13, 25, 35, 52, 61, 67, 72, 77, 91-4, 103, 105, 111, 117, 121-2, 168, 190, 213, 305
  choice of crops, 4-5
  conditions, 42, 57-8, 61, 67, 90
Semidwarfs, 50, 60, 66, 205, 207, 209
Senescence, 28, 117
Sesame, 76, 93, 96, 99, 122
Shelter belt, see also wind break, 117, 160, 284-6, 290, 300, 303-6, 308
  effects, 284-5
    on growth, 299
    on microclimate, 286, 288-9
  management, 305
    direction, 306
    planning, 304-5
  porosity, 285-7, 305-6
  wind angle, 287

radiation receipt, 290
zone, 285-7, 290, 301, 303-4, 319
Sheltered crops, 293-6
    fungal diseases, 303
    insect pests, 303-4
Shoot/root ratio, 31, 117, 148, 191-2
Sink, 33, 46
Soil aggregation, 246
    conservation, 100
    moisture (water), 5, 25, 68, 70-2, 74,
        76-7, 85, 108, 111, 216, 289, 292-3
    salinity, 53, 150, 216, 245, 319
    structure, 100, 106-7, 170, 243-4
        crusting, 105, 244
        root proliferation, 244
    temperature, 242
        organic mulches, 243
        plastic mulches, coloured, 242
Solar radiation, see also radiation, light, 12-5,
    290
Sorghum, 16, 27, 36, 38, 52-3, 61, 63-4, 67,
    69, 72, 74, 76, 80, 84-5, 87, 92-3, 95-6,
    99-100, 107, 149, 158, 161, 183, 191,
    208, 214, 239, 322, 341, 344
Soybeans, 52, 87, 96, 121, 123, 159, 180,
    184, 208, 214, 266, 272-3, 293, 295,
    301, 357, 360, 363
Sterility, 304
Stomata, 28, 35-6, 48, 50-3, 55, 58, 64,
    71-2, 114-6, 148, 153, 155, 157-9, 173-5,
    205, 268-9, 271-2, 283, 291, 293, 297,
    309, 315-7, 321, 344
Sugar beets, 42, 61, 88, 212, 262-3, 297, 339
Sugarcane, 50-1, 341, 344
Sunflower, 93, 161, 267, 283, 304, 339-40

Temperature, 15, 21, 149, 351-3, 356, 359-60
    crop production, 16-7
    efficiency, 360
Tillage, 6, 78-9, 91, 99, 103-6, 108, 119-20,
    122, 215, 217
    clean, 107-8
Tillering, 37, 45-6, 67, 71, 172, 188-90,
    207, 211
    ear bearing tillers, 45-6
Tomatoes, 262, 264, 272-3, 340, 353-4
Translocation, 27, 33-4, 51-2, 55, 103-5,
    114, 147, 157, 177, 181, 209, 261, 264,
    273, 320
Transpiration, 6, 12, 15, 18, 25-7, 35, 38,
    48, 50, 52, 54-6, 71-2, 97, 99, 105, 113-6,

    148, 153, 157-60, 170-1, 173-6, 178-9,
    209, 212, 261, 264, 266-7, 269-70, 272, 274,
    284, 290-3, 295-7, 300, 316, 318, 322, 344
    effect on leaf growth, 266
    ratio, 274
True respiration, see respiration
Turgor/turgidity, 11, 26-8, 32, 35, 54, 148,
    150, 153, 159, 175, 208, 266-7, 269-70,
    272, 297, 317, 322
    effect on:
        cell enlargement, 266
        growth, 266-7
    restored at night, 270

Vapour diffusion, 269
    pressure, 175, 264-5, 288, 290-1, 293, 300
    pressure deficit, 265-6
    pressure gradient, 265, 269, 315

Water absorption (uptake), 24, 26-7, 54,
    71-2, 113, 148, 152, 171-2, 174, 185,
    187-8, 190, 202, 209, 322
    availability, 23, 97, 170, 172, 176, 188, 248
    conservation, 48, 105, 161-2, 318
    deficiency, 26, 29, 34-6, 148, 173
    harvesting, 100-3
    holding capacity, 170
    movement, 168, 170, 173, 175-6
    physiological effects, 26-35
    potential, 31, 54, 58, 97, 158, 169-70,
        172, 175, 193, 204-5, 268-71, 297, 309,
        316-7, 320-2
    renewed water supply, 35-6
    requirement, 12, 74, 95, 212
    role of, 175
    stress (moisture stress), 5, 11, 21-3, 25-30,
        32-5, 39, 46-8, 50, 52, 59, 64, 68, 80, 82,
        98, 105, 116-7, 147, 151, 155, 159,
        168, 171-3, 175, 201-4, 208, 269, 271,
        283
    supply, 57, 95, 100, 159, 177, 190, 300
    use, 5-6, 26, 239
    use efficiency, 5-6, 10, 12, 22, 47, 52,
        61, 63, 68, 71, 76-7, 79, 85-6, 99, 118,
        159-60, 171, 192-3, 214-5, 274, 298,
        317
    utilization, 174
Weed control, 6, 77, 82, 94, 96, 106, 108-11,
    118-23, 160, 215
Wheat, 17, 24, 28-9, 31-3, 37-9, 43, 47, 50,

53, 55, 57-8, 60-1, 64-72, 74-5, 77-8, 82, 84, 86, 88, 90-4, 96, 99, 108, 110-11, 117-8, 122, 162, 170, 172-3, 176, 181, 185-91, 193, 208-9, 212, 215, 263, 266, 274, 293, 321-2, 339, 360, 363

Wilting point (WP), 22-4, 33, 35, 117, 183

Wind, 18-9, 305, 308, 366
  control, 306-7
  damage, 102
    aberasive soil particles, 300
  effects, 47, 283, 300
  erosion, 94, 104, 108, 118, 122, 246-7
  strip cropping, 118, 308
  velocity (speed), 22, 25, 97, 107, 148, 286, 290-1, 293, 300

Wind break, *see also* shelter belt, 284-6, 290, 296-7, 308, 320

Yield, 5-6, 14, 16-7, 19, 21, 26, 34-6, 38-40, 43-4, 53, 58-64, 66, 68, 70, 72, 74-5, 79-82, 84, 89, 92-6, 99-100, 104-5, 108, 110-2, 116, 157, 159-60, 170, 173, 176, 181, 184, 189-91, 207, 210-2, 214-7, 248-50, 284, 293, 295-8, 300-3, 322-3, 340
  biological and economic, 35, 42-4
  components, 33, 44-5, 62, 67-8, 71, 76, 81
  potential (production potential), 59, 61-2, 65-6, 80, 83, 156, 177, 203, 209, 213

ERRATA

Page	Line	Read	In place of
169	7, after potential gradient. *Add*	The terminology for describing the energy status of water in the soil-plant-atmosphere has changed over the years, hence water potential, diffusion pressure deficit (DPD) and suction force have been used interchangeably in the text. It must be noted that water potential is algebraically negative and the others are positive.	
169	20	very low suction force (i bar*)	very low water potential (-1 bar*)
169	23	suction force	water potential
174	29-30	24 bars	$-$ 24 bars
174	31	40 bars.	$-$ 40 bars.

DATE DUE

DEMCO 38-297